To show that the system is not only for engineers, we created this "Hall of Mirrors." It represents a reflective cylinder adjacent to a colored dodecahedron. In front and behind are mirrors. The observer stands between the mirrors but is invisible. The background light outside the mirrors is blue and there is a source of white light just far enough outside the picture frame not to appear. In the far mirror, a "hall" of images of the two objects can be seen. A distorted reflection of the hall appears in the cylinder and therefore in all its images. For details, see an article by Geoff Wyvill and Tosiyasu L. Kunii, entitled "A Functional Model for Constructive Solid Geometry," in the July 1985 issue of "The Visual Computer: An International Journal of Computer Graphics."

# Computer Graphics

## Visual Technology and Art

Proceedings of
Computer Graphics Tokyo '85

Edited by Tosiyasu L. Kunii

With 179 Figures
50 of them in Color

Springer-Verlag
Tokyo Berlin Heidelberg New York

Dr. Tosiyasu L. Kunii
Professor and Director
Kunii Laboratory of Computer Science
Department of Information Science
Faculty of Science
The University of Tokyo

Library of Congress Cataloging-in-Publication Data
Computer graphics.
Includes bibliographies and index.
1. Computer graphics — Addresses, essays, lectures.
I. Kunii, Tosiyasu.
T385.C5995 1985 006.6 85-17392

ISBN 978-4-431-68032-1        ISBN 978-4-431-68030-7 (eBook)
DOI 10.1007/978-4-431-68030-7

Softcover reprint of the hardcover 1st edition 1985

# Preface

In the design of any visual objects, the work becomes much easier if previous designs are utilized. Computer graphics is becoming increasingly important simply because it greatly helps in utilizing such previous designs. Here, "previous designs" signifies both design results and design procedures. The objects designed are diverse. For engineers, these objects could be machines or electronic circuits, as discussed in Chap. 3, "CAD/CAM." Physicians often design models of a patient's organs from computed tomography images prior to surgery or to assist in diagnosis. This is the subject of Chap. 8, "Medical Graphics." Chapter 7, "Computer Art," deals with the way in which artists use computer graphics in creating beautiful visual images. In Chap. 1, "Computational Geometry," a firm basis is provided for the definition of shapes in designed objects; this is a typical technical area in which computer graphics is constantly making worldwide progress. Thus, the present volume, reflecting international advances in these and other areas of computer graphics, provides every potential or actual graphics user with the essential up-to-date information.

There are, typically, two ways of gathering this current information. One way is to invite international authorities to write on their areas of specialization. Usually this works very well if the areas are sufficiently established that it is possible to judge exactly who knows what. Since computer graphics, however, is still in its developmental stage, this method cannot be applied. We have to depend on a different approach, which consists of the following two procedures. The first is publishing a call for papers to obtain original works, describing new findings, ideas, and experiments submitted in the traditional paper format. The second is to organize a program committee for peer review of the submitted papers. The peer reviewers, three for each paper, are judges, and the review results are available to the authors such that, if necessary, they are able to defend their papers. After screening out unsuitable contributions, the remaining papers present creative thinking, impressive research results, and innovatory ideas, sometimes so innovatory that it is difficult to assess whether they represent great errors or truly epoch-making approaches. Novel findings from many new groups of workers in different parts of the world are thus included. The presentation of such papers at international conferences and publishing the proceedings promotes rapid advances. After having organized four international conferences on computer graphics, the first in Los Angeles in 1975 and the following three in Tokyo every year since 1983, I am constantly finding new interesting, developing areas. Such areas this year are Computer Animation, presented in Chap. 6, Visual Communications and Interfaces, presented in Chap. 5, and Graphics Standardization and Packaging, presented in Chap. 2. Graphics Networks are also starting to emerge, as discussed in Chap. 4. Those workers who were rising figures at the first conference are now well established with many awards and international fame to their credit.

However, I realize that computer graphics is still in its infancy. There are many difficult and essential areas that remain undeveloped, such as graphic data-base management, texture graphics, graphic communications, engineering animation, and manufacturing process design. They need to be tackled by future research. It is to be hoped that the present volume assists in stimulating such research.

Tosiyasu L. Kunii, Editor

Cover Design: This simulation of assembling a copier is drawn by ANIMENGINE, an engineering animation system designed for computer integrated manufacturing (CIM). The details of ANIMENGINE are described in: Tsukasa Noma and Tosiyasu L. Kunii, "ANIMENGINE: An Engineering Animation System," Proceedings of Graphics Interface '85, Montreal, May 1985, pp. 83-90.
© Kunii Laboratory of Computer Science & Software Research Center of Ricoh Co., Ltd.

# Table of Contents

# List of Contributors

The page numbers given below refer to the page on which contribution begins.

# Chapter 1
# Computational Geometry

# Invertible Set Operations for Solid Modeling

Hiroshi Toriya, Toshiaki Satoh, Kenji Ueda and Hiroaki Chiyokura

Software Research Center, Ricoh Co., Ltd., 1-17, Koishikawa 1-chome, Bunkyo-ku, Tokyo, 112 Japan

ABSTRACT

The paper describes a method of representing the solid design process using a tree data structure. Previous stages in the development of a design can be quickly regenerated by specifying nodes of this tree. A detailed description of the implementation of invertible set operations is also presented.

## 1. INTRODUCTION

Effective interactive solid modeling systems are critical to the development of practical CAD/CAM. Since the solid modeling process is one of trial and error, a user must often regenerate a previous stage in the development of a design. However, this is often difficult in conventional solid modeling systems because most of the operations employed do not have corresponding inverses. In the worst case, a design may be inadvertently destroyed in the process of trying to recreate an earlier phase of the work.

We therefore propose a technique whereby the history of the design process is represented in the system as a tree data structure. Using this representation, any previous stage in the development of a solid design can be quickly regenerated. We also describe the implementation of set operations in the context of such a history mechanism. All facilities and operations discussed in this paper have been implemented in DESIGN-BASE, a solid modeling system that inherits all the characteristics of MODIF [3]. The system was written in C and runs under UNIX*.

## 2. REPRESENTATION OF THE SOLID DESIGN PROCESS

2.1 Primitive Operations Supporting UNDO and REDO Commands

In our system, boundary representations (B-reps) are used to represent solid shapes. Local operations and set operations are applied to generate and modify the B-reps of solids. Operations

---

* UNIX is a trademark of Bell Laboratories.

for generating and modifying solids always manipulate B-reps by means of primitive operations[4]. These primitive operations consist of Euler operations[1,2], geometric operations and global operations. Geometric operations modify the geometric information associated with solids, as for example, when a straight edge is changed to a curved edge. Translation and rotation of solids are global operations. In DESIGN-BASE, there are about twenty primitive operations, each of which has a corresponding inverse operation.

Mantyla and Sulonen [5,6] have proposed a solid modeling system, in which set operations are partially implemented using Euler operations. In DESIGN-BASE on the other hand, all high-level operations are implemented using primitive operations. All primitive operations used in a design are stored in a tree representing the history of the solid design process. By invoking sequences of these stored primitive operations, the system can quickly regenerate any previous stage in the development of a design. Such a previous stage is referred to as an "ancestor solid" in this paper. This method of representing the design process as a hierarchical tree structure naturally supports UNDO and REDO operations. The user simply specifies a path moving up the tree to UNDO a sequence of operations, or down the tree to REDO a previously specified sequence. The following section presents a more detailed description of the UNDO and REDO operations.

## 2.2 Procedure for Constructing a Single Solid

The operations for modifying solids can be divided into two types. One includes operations for modifying individual solids. Edge-rounding and face-sweeping operations are included in this type. Such operations are referred to as single-solid operations in this paper. The other type includes compound-solid operations in which a new solid is generated from two existing solids, for example, set operations and glue operations. The procedure for constructing a solid using single-solid operations is presented below. However, to clarify this procedure, we first show how a representation of the solid design process is produced for single-solid operations. The representation of compound-solid operations will be described in the next section.

A user constructs a solid by specifying commands that invoke primitive operations. The first command generates an initial solid; subsequent commands modify the solid. At the same time, a tree is constructed to represent the design process itself. Each node of the tree represents the state of the solid at a specific stage of design development. Arcs represent the specification of single-solid commands and the primitive operations used to execute these commands. The system assigns an internal identifier to each node. Such an ID can later be used to invoke the sequence of primitive operations specified by the original command it represents. Such an arrangement supports UNDO and REDO operations, which make use of these ID's to allow users to recover from errors and to recall any stage of the design process.

Figure 1 shows the procedure for constructing a solid, A, and a tree structure representing the design process.

(1) The root node A0 of the design representation tree is first generated. This node represents a null solid. Another node is then generated to represent the initial solid. This node's identifier, A1,1, shows it to be the the first solid created in the first stage of the design process.
(2) An edge is created in face F1 of solid A, thereby dividing F1 into two faces, F1 and F2. The node ID of the resulting solid is A1,2. Then, by sweeping face F1, solid A1,3 is generated. Finally, edge E1 is rounded.
(3) UNDO is specified twice to regenerate solid A1,2. Then, face F2 is swept. When a solid is modified after an UNDO operation, the stage number is incremented. Therefore, the ID

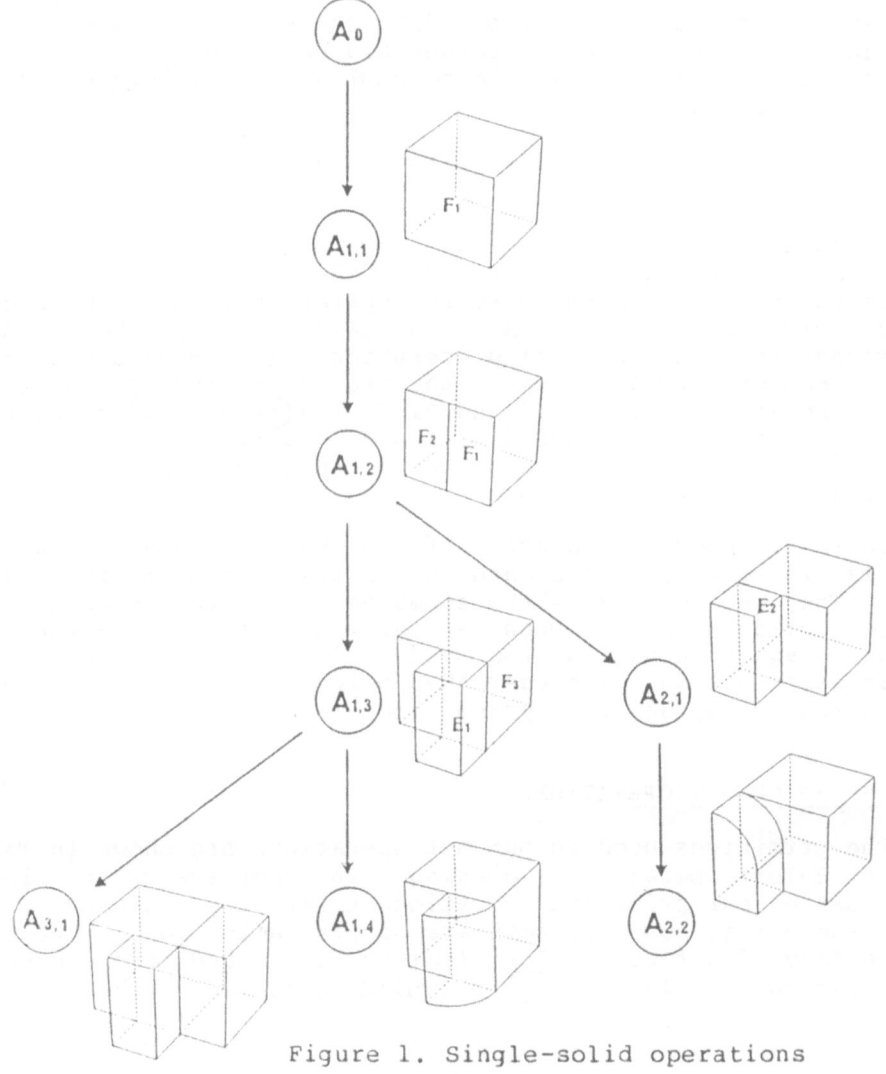

Figure 1. Single-solid operations

of the new solid is labeled A2,1.  Edge E2 is then rounded, and
solid A2,2 is generated.
(4) By specifying UNDO twice and REDO once, solid A1,3 is generated.  Face  F3  is  then  swept.  This new solid is labeled
A3,1.

Since the system represents the solid generation process  in
this  way,  it  can  quickly  regenerate  the  B-reps of ancestor
solids.  To regenerate an  ancestor  solid,  the  user  specifies
UNDO,  REDO  or some combination of the two.  When UNDO is specified, a solid higher up in the tree hierarchy is regenerated from
the current solid by applying the inverse of the primitive operations.  When REDO is specified, a solid lower down  in  the  tree
hierarchy  is  generated.  By  specifying the state (that is, the
ID) of a solid, any ancestor solid can be regenerated.  The  computation time for  UNDO and REDO operations is far less than that
required by their conventional equivalents,  because  the  latter
contain  many  procedures  other than primitive operations, e.g.,
intersection detection and  input data checks.   The  speed  with
which ancestor solids can be regenerated using our design process
representation makes it feasible to employ this technique  in  an
interactive design environment.

## 2.3 Representation of Compound-solid Operations

After a solid has been constructed using single-solid operations,  compound-solid  operations  such as  set  and glue operations, can be applied to it.  Figure 2 shows the  design  process
representation  for  compound-solid  operations.  Solid C is generated from  solids  A  and  B.   In  this  Figure,  the $\oplus$ node
corresponds to a compound-solid operation.  The upper arc of this
node is connected to solid C1,1; the two lower arcs are connected
to  the  nodes of solids A2,2 and B1,3. The $\oplus$ node indicates that
the two solids are now treated as a single solid.  The  primitive
operations  invoked  in compound-solid operations are represented
by arcs connected to the $\oplus$ node.

End-users need not be aware of how the solid generation process  is  internally  represented using trees of primitive operations.  They need only know the commands  used  to  generate  the
desired  solid  shapes.   When  a user requests regeneration of a
previous stage of a design, the system first displays the IDs  of
all  ancestor solids.  The user then selects and enters the ID of
the desired solid, and the system regenerates it.

## 3. OVERVIEW OF SET OPERATIONS

The primitives used in our set operations are shown in Table
1.   In  Euler  operations,  openings  in faces are called rings.
Since most of our primitive operations treat  the  boundaries  of
faces  and  rings equally, both are simply called loops.  We call
the boundary of a face a P-loop (parent loop), and  the  boundary
of an opening in a face a C-loop (child loop).

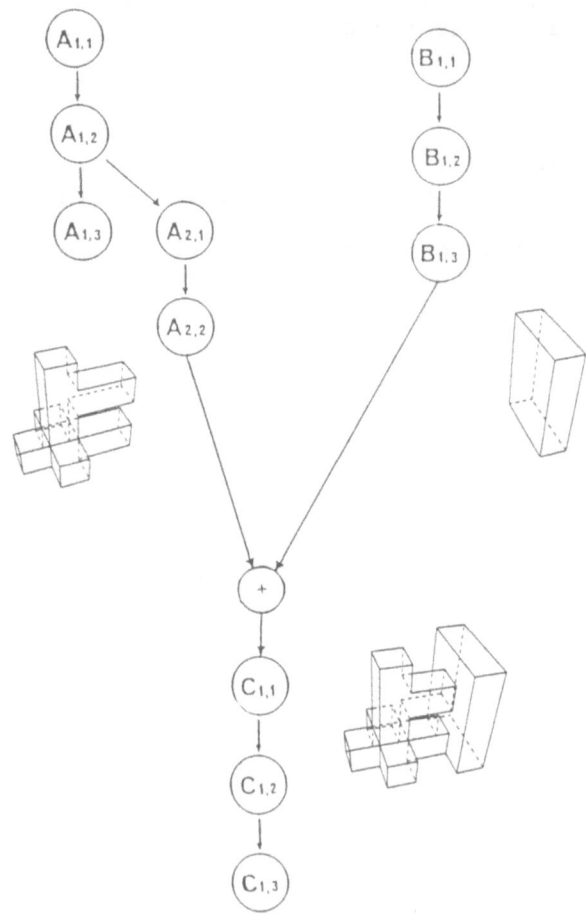

Figure 2. Compound-solid operations

Table 1. Primitive operations used in set operations

| Name | Definition |
|---|---|
| MEL | Make an Edge and a Loop |
| KEL | Kill an Edge and a Loop |
| MVE | Make a Vertex and an Edge |
| KVE | Kill a Vertex and an Edge |
| KPLMCL | Kill a P-Loop and Make a C-Loop |
| KCLMPL | Kill a C-Loop and Make a P-Loop |
| MEV | Make an Edge and a Vertex |
| KEV | Kill an Edge and a Vertex |
| MEKL | Make an Edge and Kill a Loop |
| KEML | Kill an Edge and Make a Loop |
| MEVVL | Make an Edge and a Vertex, and a Vertex and a Loop |
| KEVVL | Kill an Edge and and a Vertex, and a Vertex and a Loop |
| NS | Negate a Solid |
| AS | Add two Solids |
| DS | Decompose a Solid |

There are three kinds of set operations: union, difference and intersection. As indicated below, both difference and inter-section operations on two solids, A and B, are accomplished by a combination of the union operation and the "negate solid" (NS) primitive operation.

difference(A, B)   = NS(union (NS(A), B))
intersection(A, B) = NS(union (NS(A), NS(B)))

Because it is used to implement the other two set operations, the union operation is the major focus of this paper.

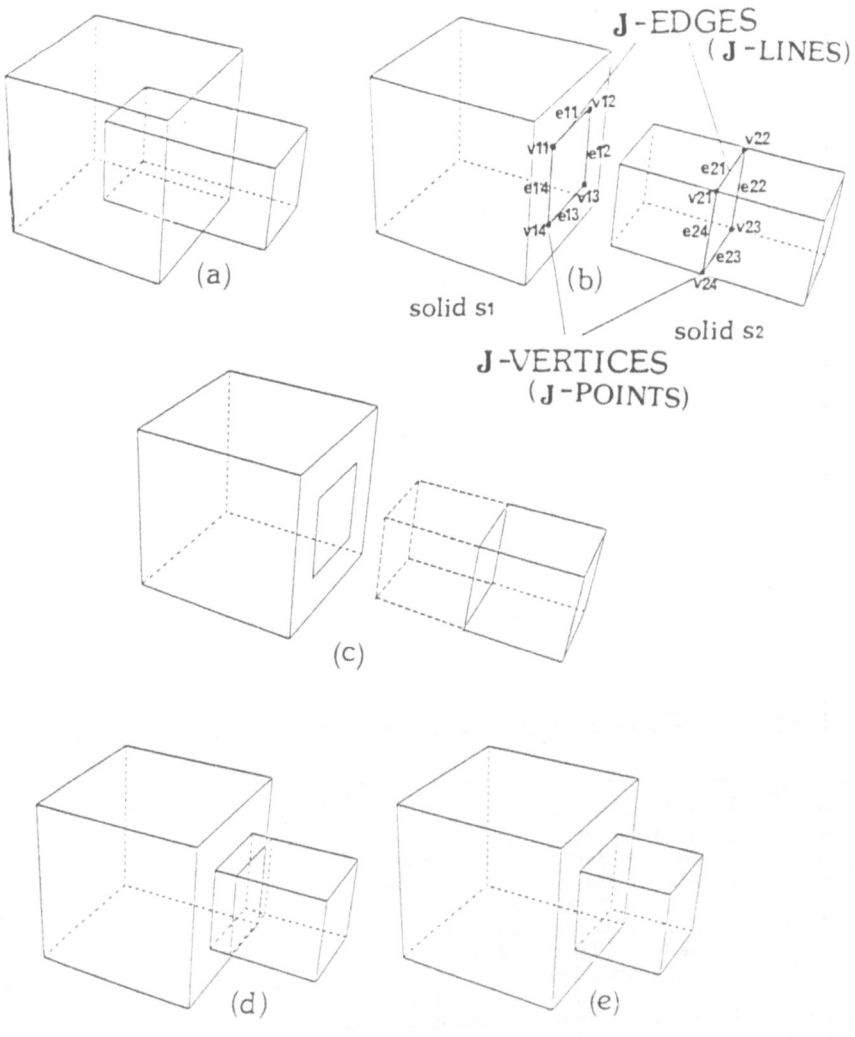

Figure 3. Procedures for union operation

With reference to Figure 3 , note that two corresponding loops, one on each solid, represent the location at which the two solids are to be joined. Such lines are therefore called <u>junction lines</u> (J-lines), and their end points are called <u>junction points</u> (J-points). After performing the necessary calculations, the system generates <u>J-vertices</u> on J-points, and <u>J-edges</u> on J-lines. For instance, vertices V21, V22, V23 and V24 are created on solid S2 (Figure 3(b)). The system then generates edges connecting these points using primitive operations. Edges E21, E22, E23 and E24 are created on solid S2. Next, J-edges E11, E12, E13 and E14, and J-vertices V11, V12, V13 and V14 are created on solid S1. J-edges delimit the interface between the two solids. The boundary of the portion of solid S2 that penetrates solid S1 is now removed using a combination of primitive operations (Figure 3(c)).

To join the two solids, zero-length edges are generated between their corresponding J-vertices (Figure 3(d)). The set operation is complete when all unnecessary edges and vertices have been removed (Figure 3(e)).

## 4. DETAILED DESCRIPTION OF THE UNION OPERATION ALGORITHM

This section provides a closer look at the union operation outlined in the previous section. The four major procedures involved are covered as follows:

| | |
|---|---|
| Calculation of J-points and J-lines | Section 4.1 |
| Generation of J-edges and J-vertices | Section 4.2 |
| Removal of included part | Section 4.3 |
| Joining the two solids | Section 4.4 |

### 4.1 Calculation of J-points and J-lines

This section includes a description of the method for determining J-points and J-lines. This procedure consists of four steps, as follows:

<Step 1> Rough intersection check
To find pairs of intersecting faces, the smallest three dimensional box that can contain a face is created for all faces of both solids. The intersection between faces of each solid can be roughly checked using these boxes.

<Step 2> Calculation of points at which face planes intersect face edges
In Figure 4 , Fa indicates a face on a solid A, and Fb indicates a face on a solid B. The system first computes the location of all points at which the plane of Fa intersects edges of face Fb. It then computes the location of all points at which the plane of Fb intersects edges of face Fa. Each point can be in one of three possible relationships to its parent solid:
   a) on a vertex
   b) on an edge (exclusive of vertices)
   c) enclosed in a loop (exclusive of edges).
These relationships are calculated in this step.

<Step 3> Determination of J-points

In this step, J-points are selected from among the points obtained in the previous step. These points lie on a straight line that represents the intersection of the planes of faces Fa and Fb (Figure 4). After such points are sorted by their coordinate values, any two that are adjacent specify a line segment. This line segment is a J-line if and only if its end points are contained in both faces. Conversely, the end points of a line segment contained in both faces are J-points; these points are determined by the algorithm for point enclosure:

- The algorithm is well known: it sums the number of intersections between a loop and a half line starting from a given target point. If the result is odd, the point lies inside the loop; if it is even, the point lies outside the loop.

- Note that all points of intersection between face planes and face edges calculated in <Step 2> lie in a straight line. Since this line is analogous to the half-line described above, we can avoid geometric calculation by simply counting the number of points of intersection calculated in <Step 2>.

<Step 4> Data collection

The system stores topological and geometrical data about the intersecting solids in two tables: one for J-points and one for J-lines.

4.2 Generation of J-edges and J-vertices

The system now generates J-vertices and J-edges using information from the J-point and J-line tables.

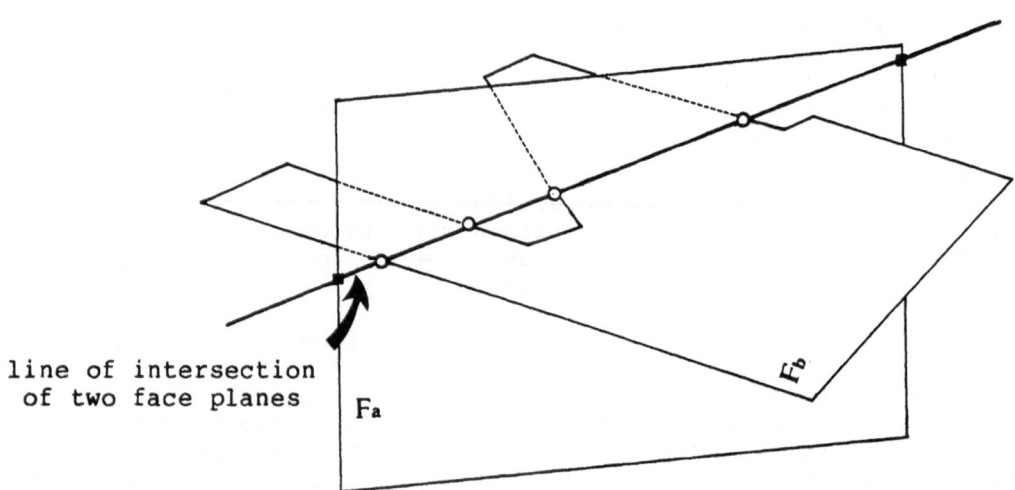

line of intersection
of two face planes

Fa

Fb

■: points at which the plane of Fb intersects face Fa
o: J-points

Figure 4. Calculation of J-points

## 4.2.1 Generation of J-vertices

The topological relationship of a J-point to its parent solid is determined by reference to the J-point table. As noted in Section 4.1, there are three such possible relationships: the J-point can be on a vertex, an edge or enclosed in a loop. If a J-point corresponds to an existing vertex of one of the solids to be joined, the system regards that vertex as a J-vertex. Primitive operation MVE is used to generate J-vertices on J-points lying on a solid's edge. All remaining J-points are on a loop; the corresponding J-vertices are created when an edge is produced starting from this point.

The creation of J-vertices makes it easier to determine which primitive operation should be applied to produce a J-edge.

## 4.2.2 Generation of J-edges

Using information from the J-line table, the system generates J-edges on J-lines by primitive operations ( Figure 5 ).

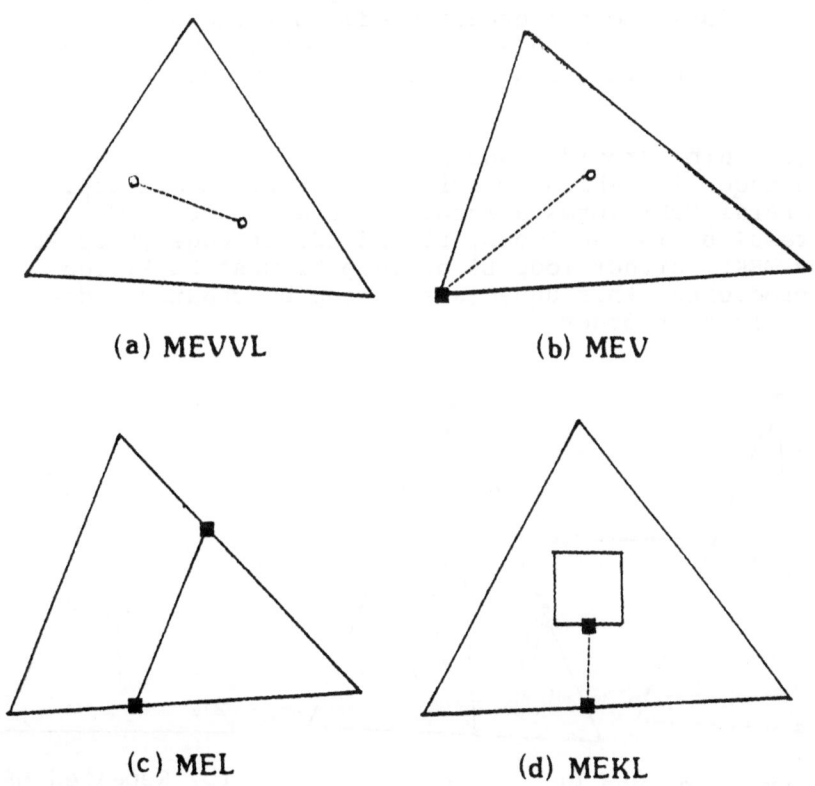

(a) MEVVL          (b) MEV

(c) MEL          (d) MEKL

o : J-points
■ : J-points on which J-vertices have been generated

Figure 5. Edge generation

A J-line falls into one of three categories depending on its stage of development:

> i) Neither of its J-vertices (end points) has yet been generated. In this case, MEVVL is used to generate a J-edge, both J-vertices and a loop (Figure 5(a)).

> ii) Only one of its J-vertices has been generated. In this case, MEV is used to generate a J-edge and a J-vertex (Figure 5(b)).

> iii) Both its J-vertices have been generated. In this case, if both J-vertices lie on the same loop and the same face (as in Figure 5(c)), MEL is used to generate a J-edge and a loop; if the J-vertices lie on the same face, but in different loops (as in Figure 5(d)), MEKL is used.

Applying primitive operations in logical sequence avoids unnecessary calculation. For example, Figure 6 shows the creation of two edges, E1 and E2, in loop L. If E2 is created by MEL before E1 is created, E1 will belong to new loop L1 rather than to L. Therefore, before creating edge E1, the system must determine the loop to which this edge will belong. This calculation is unnecessary if E1 is produced using the MEV operation before E2 is created.

Figure 6(b) provides another example of the importance of the sequence in which primitive operations are applied. Here, quadrilateral PQRS forms a loop. Creating edges PQ and RS by MEVVL results in two loops, L1 and L2. If edge QR or PS is produced by MEKL, either loop L1 or loop L2 must be killed. We can avoid producing this unnecessary loop by creating edges PQ, QR, RS and SP in that order.

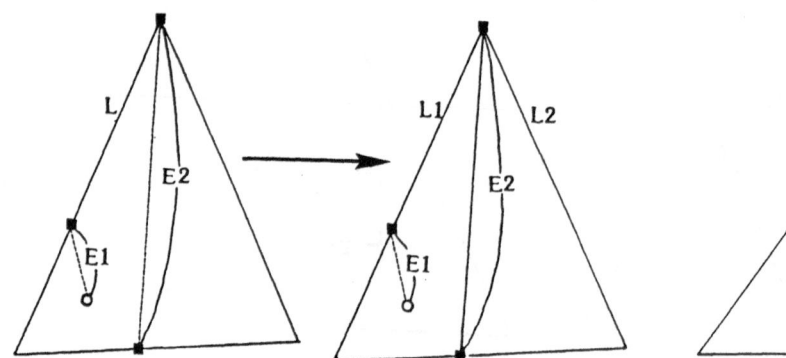
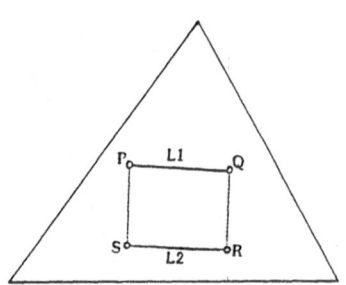

(a) MEV operation and MEL operation

(b) Repeated MEVVL operations

Figure 6. Sequence of edge generation

Figure 7 gives the algorithm used to create J-edges.

```
Make_J-Edge()
{
        do {
                make all J-edges that can be
                        created by MEV;
                make an edge that can be
                        created by MEVVL;
        } while (edge that can be
                        created by MEV or MEVVL exists);

        make all remaining edges using MEL or MEKL;
}
```

Figure 7. Algorithm for creating J-edges

Information about edges produced for solids A and B is stored in the J-edge table. This table is used in the next stage of the union operation to remove the boundaries of included portions.

4.3  Removal of included part

In our union operation, we refer to any part of a solid that penetrates the boundary of another solid as an "included part." The following briefly describes the removal of such parts.

4.3.1 Detection of faces in the included part

If a face attached to a J-edge of one solid is not included in the other solid, the system internally assigns the face a "+" label, indicating that it is to be retained. If the face of one solid is included in the other solid, the system labels it "-", indicating that this face is to be removed. Contiguous faces are labeled "0". Such faces are later marked either "+" or "-".

Figure 8 shows a cross section of two solids A and B meeting at J-edges. In this Figure, the hatched portions indicate the interiors of the solids; A1, A2 and A3 are the angles of intersection of the four faces connected to the two congruent J-edges. The labels "+", "-" and "0" can be determined by computing the angles using inverse trigonometric functions. However, because these functions are computationally costly, we use instead a quantity corresponding to the angle given by the inner-product of the normal vectors of each face. This computation is much faster than that for computing the angles.

For simplicity, we can regard angles A1, A2 and A3 as having the following values:

```
0 < A1 < 360
0 <= A2, A3 < 360
A2 ≠ A3.
```

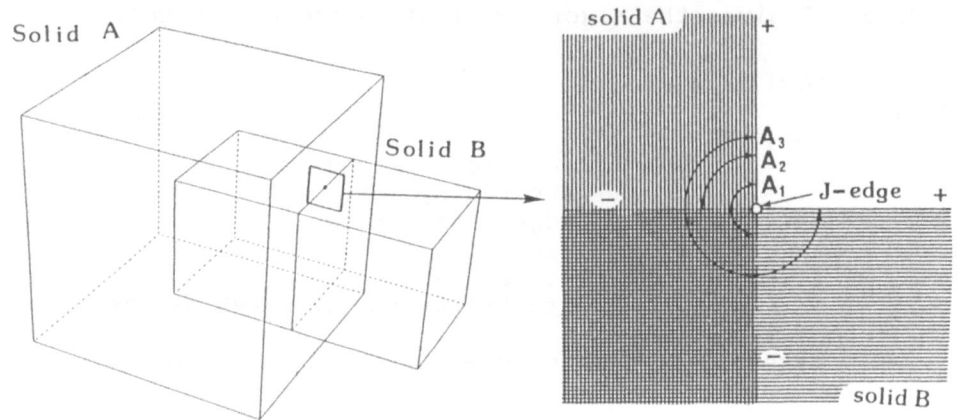

Figure 8. Cross section at junction
between two intersecting solids

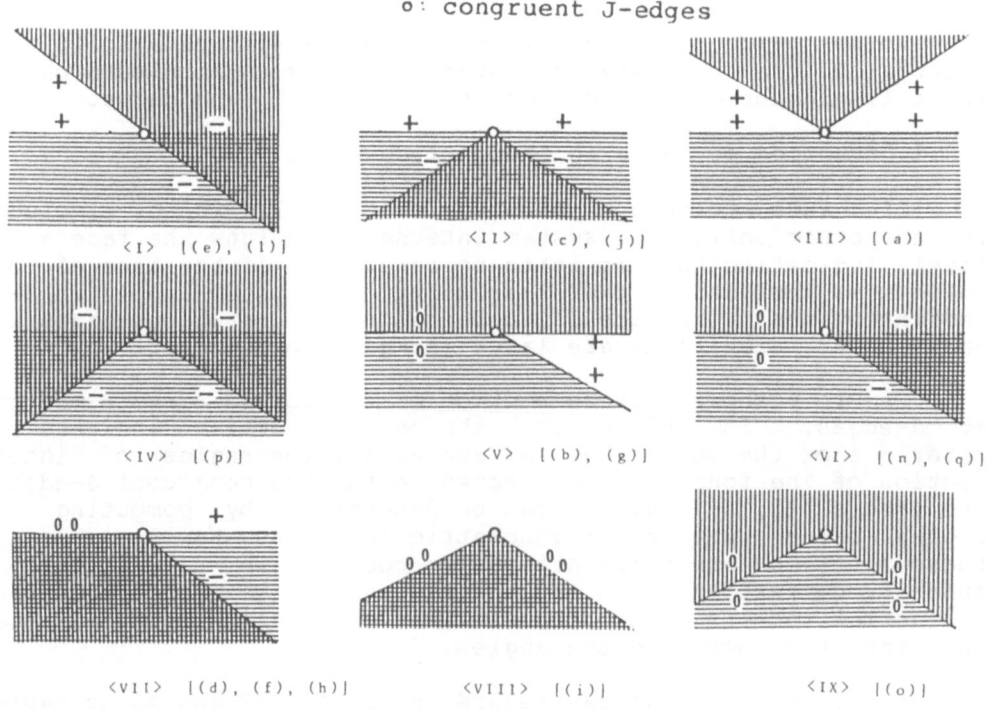

o: congruent J-edges

Figure 9. Typical relationships between intersecting solids
(Letters in brackets refer to Table 2)

## Table 2. Labels determined by angles A1, A2 and A3

| | | solid A | | solid B | | | solid A | | solid B | |
|---|---|---|---|---|---|---|---|---|---|---|
| (a) | A1 < A2 < A3 | + | + | + | + | | | | | |
| (b) | A1 = A2 < A3 | + | 0 | + | 0 | → | + | - | + | - |
| (c) | A1 < A3 < A2 | - | - | + | + | | | | | |
| (d) | A1 = A3 < A2 | - | 0 | + | 0 | → | - | - | + | + |
| (e) 0 < A2 < A1 < A3 | | + | - | + | - | | | | | |
| (f) 0 = A2 < A1 < A3 | | - | 0 | + | 0 | → | - | - | + | + |
| (g) | A2 = A1 < A3 | + | 0 | + | 0 | → | + | - | + | - |
| (h) 0 < A2 < A1 = A3 | | + | 0 | - | 0 | → | + | + | - | - |
| (i) 0 = A2 < A1 = A3 | | 0 | 0 | 0 | 0 | | + | + | - | - |
| (j) 0 < A2 < A3 < A1 | | + | + | - | - | | | | | |
| (k) 0 = A2 < A3 < A1 | | + | 0 | - | 0 | → | + | + | - | - |
| (l) 0 < A3 < A1 < A2 | | + | - | + | - | | | | | |
| (m) 0 = A3 < A1 < A2 | | + | 0 | + | 0 | → | + | - | + | - |
| (n) 0 < A3 < A1 = A2 | | - | 0 | - | 0 | → | - | - | - | - |
| (o) 0 = A3 < A1 = A2 | | 0 | 0 | 0 | 0 | → | - | - | - | - |
| (p) 0 < A3 < A2 < A1 | | - | - | - | - | | | | | |
| (q) 0 = A3 < A2 < A1 | | - | 0 | - | 0 | → | - | - | - | - |

## Table 3. Labels assigned to solid A and B
### (Roman numerals refer to Figure 9)

| | Solid A | | Solid B | | |
|---|---|---|---|---|---|
| case 1 | + | - | + | - | [<I>, <II>] |
| case 2 | + | + | - | - | [<II>, <VII>, <VIII>] |
| case 3 | + | + | + | + | [<III>] |
| case 4 | - | - | - | - | [<IV>, <VI>, <IX>] |

Each J-edge has two attached faces. Figure 9 consists of cross sections of the nine typical conditions that can occur when four of these faces meet at two congruent J-edges in a union operation. Table 2 gives "+", "-" and "0" labels as well as angle data corresponding to the examples in Figure 9. "0" is replaced with either "+" or "-", as shown in Table 2. This reduces the number of "+" and "-" combinations to four, as shown in Table 3. The system removes all J-edges involved in cases 2, 3 and 4 in Table 3 from the J-edge table. R-flags (indicating "remove") are now given to faces labeled "-", and K-flags (indicating "keep") are given to faces labeled "+".

4.3.2 Removal of edges in the included part

The boundary of the included part consists of faces to which R-flags have been assigned. The system uses these flags to determine the edges of the included part. We call such edges "included edges". In this procedure, all included edges are removed by primitive operations.

We are interested in the efficient regeneration of solids using inverse operations. Our algorithm aims to avoid geometric calculation because such calculation decreases the performance of solid regeneration. However, it is possible for an inverse procedure to require such calculation. For example, when a loop including a C-loop is split by a new edge as shown in Figure 10 , C-loop Lc is included in loop L1. However, after edge E is created, it is necessary to determine whether C-loop Lc is included in loop L1 or L2. This situation can be avoided by changing any C-loop in the included part into a P-loop. Then included edges are removed using KEV, KEVVL, KEL or KEML primitive operations.

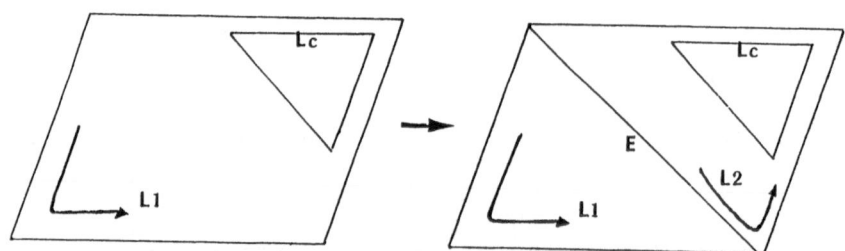

Figure 10. Splitting a loop including a C-loop
by generating an edge

4.4 Joining the two solids

As a result of removing the included part, the two solids now meet at J-edges. These J-edges form two loops, one on each solid (as previously shown in Figure 3). These loops are referred to as J-loops. The system joins the two solids using the MEKL or MEL operation to generate zero-length edges between corresponding J-vertices on the two J-loops.

4.4.1 Constricted loops

Our method of joining the solids requires that all J-vertices connected in the J-loop of one solid be in one-to-one correspondence with the J-vertices in the J-loop of the other. However, when included edges are removed, a "constricted loop" can sometimes result. As shown in Figure 11 , a constricted loop is one that is "pinched" between two or more vertices. The J-vertices of such a loop do not directly correspond to those of the intersecting solid.

A constricted loop is formally defined as follows. The sequence of vertices in a loop is represented by V0, V1, ..., Vn. Here, Vi lies between Vi-1 and Vi+1 (i = 1, 2, ..., n-1). (Note that V0 is adjacent to Vn and V1, and Vn is adjacent to Vn-1 and V0.) A constricted loop must have a vertex Vi that satisfies the following conditions:

(1) Vi = Vj for some j (i ≠ j).
(2) Vi-1 and Vi+1 must not satisfy condition (1).

We call such vertices C-vertices.

If a constricted loop occurs, our method of joining the two solids cannot be applied. Figure 11(a) illustrates such a case. The constricted loop in solid X (Figure 11(b)) corresponds to two non-constricted loops in solid Y (Figure 11(c)). It is therefore necessary to separate the constricted loop at the C-vertex. This separation is accomplished in two steps. First, the C-vertex is doubled. Then, two separate solids are generated, each of which includes one of the resulting vertices. The constricted loop is thereby separated into two non-constricted loops whose J-vertices directly correspond to those of the other solid.

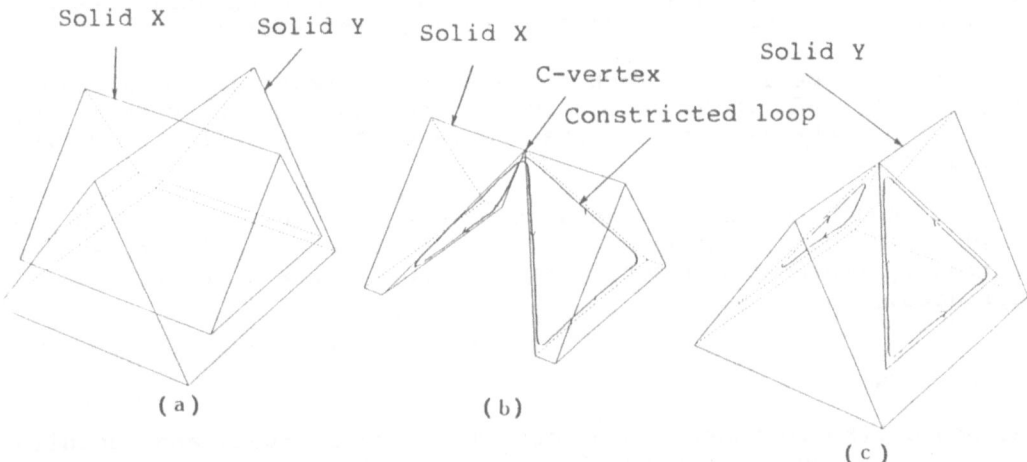

Figure 11. Constricted loop

## 4.4.2 Removing redundant loops

The two solids are now joined at duplicate J-loops. The following procedure removes one of these loops. For convenience, we assume that the two solids are labeled A and B.

(1) All J-vertices and J-edges of solid A are removed using a combination of KEL, KEV and KVE operations.

(2) Now, only the J-edges of solid B remain. If the direction of the normal vectors of both faces attached to such a J-edge is the same, the edge is not necessary to represent the solid. It is removed using the KEL or KVE operation.

The union operation is now complete.

## 5. EXAMPLE

Figure 12 shows the primitive operations used in a union operation. The original solids A and B can be regenerated using the inverses of these operations. Figure 13 shows another example of a set operation. Figure 13(a) and (b) is a line drawing of the two solids; Figure 13(c) is the result of their intersection. All examples were generated using DESIGN-BASE.

## 6. CONCLUSION

This paper has proposed a method of representing the solid design process so that previous stages can be quickly regenerated. A method of implementing invertible set operations was also described. In this method, solids are generated and modified exclusively by primitive operations. All such operations are stored in a tree structure representing the solid design process. A set operation can be undone by applying the inverses of the stored operations in reverse order. These capabilities are implemented in the DESIGN-BASE solid modeling system.

In set operations, much computation is required to calculate the points of intersection between solids. On the other hand, inverse operations are very fast because they use only primitive operations.

Although the present version of our set operations can be used only on solids whose intersecting faces are planar, we are currently implementing set operations for solids with non-planar surfaces.

## Acknowledgments

We would like to thank Professors, Tosiyasu L. Kunii and Fumihiko Kimura, of the University of Tokyo for valuable suggestions; Dr. Hideko S. Kunii, General Manager of Ricoh's Software Research Center (SRC), for valuable comments and discussion; and Christpher Locke, SRC Technical Editor, for assistance with the text.

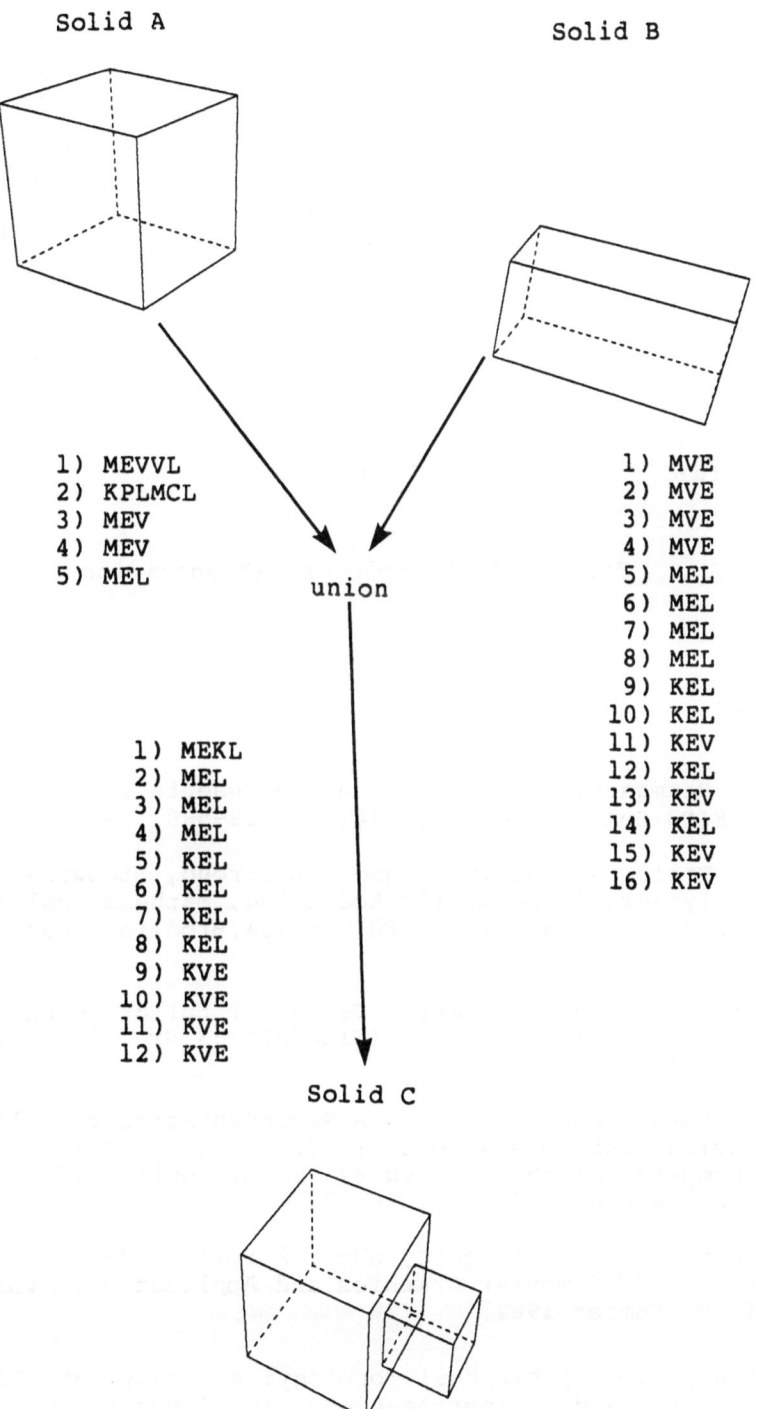

Figure 12. Primitive operations used in a union operation

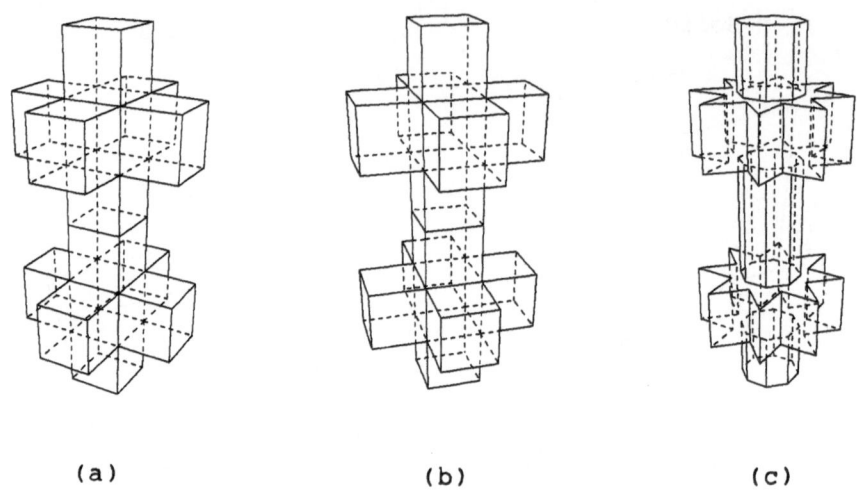

(a)                    (b)                    (c)

Figure 13. Example of set operation

REFERENCES

[1] B. G. Baumgart, A Polyhedron Representation for Computer
Vision, AFIPS Conf. Proc., Vol.44, pp.589-596, May 1975.

[2] I. C. Braid, R.C.Hillyard and I.A.Stroud, Stepwise Construction of Polyhedra in Geometric Modelling, Mathematical Methods in
Computer Graphics and Design (Ed. by K.W.Brodlie) Academic Press,
pp.123-141, 1980.

[3] H. Chiyokura and F. Kimura, Design of Solids with Free-form
Surfaces, Computer Graphics (SIGGRAPH'83 Proc.), Vol.17, No.3,
pp.289-298, 1983.

[4] H. Chiyokura and F. Kimura, A Representation of Solid Design
Process using Basic Operations, in Frontiers in Computer Graphics
- Proc. Computer Graphics Tokyo 84, T. L. Kunii, ed., Springer-
Verlag, Heidelberg, 1985, pp. 26-43.

[5] M. Mantyla and R. Sulonen, GWB : A Solid Modeler with Euler
Operators, IEEE Computer Graphics and Applications, Vol.2, No.7,
pp.17-31, September 1982.

[6] M. Mantyla, Computational Topology: A Study of Topological
Manipulations and Interrogations in Computer Graphics and
Geometric Modeling, Acta Polytechnica Scandinavica, Mathematics
and Computer Science Series No.37, Helsinki 1983.

# A Hierarchical Space Indexing Method

Kikuo Fujimura and Tosiyasu L. Kunii

Department of Information Science, Faculty of Science, The University of Tokyo, 3-1, Hongo 7-chome, Bunkyo-ku, Tokyo, 113 Japan

Abstract

Indexing methods are very important for rapid processing of a large amount of data. In this paper we discuss a spatial index, that is, a method for indexing a three dimensional space. We use a regular decomposition of the space, leading to a tree structure. The advantage of a space decomposition method over storing data in the form of a table is the quick access to a point in question by using a leaf node as an index. A set of basic algorithms is presented for generation and modification of objects. This set makes it easy to detect intersections of 3D objects, which is a useful property in such applications as interactive design of three dimensional shapes.

## 1. Background

Generally, indexing methods have been studied in the context of searching problems. In cases where a large amount of data is involved, quick access to the data to be selected is quite important. Especially in database management, efficient access and retrieval of stored data have been widely studied.

A strategy which is often used for dealing with a large amount of data is to divide the search-space into subspaces recursively, thereby skipping large blocks which cannot contain the items of interest. A binary tree data structure is well known for this type of searching method [1].

The main idea of our index system is to use this strategy for indexing a three dimensional space to facilitate processing of three dimensional data such as mechanical or civil engineering objects.

An example is taken from a designing process. In an interactive environment using a CAD system, a designer wants to test out various trial shapes one after another to see if they are what he really intends. What is very important from the engineering point of view is to ensure that these intermediate shapes do not collide. That is to make sure that one object does not occupy the same space as another, also that part of an object does not occupy the same space as another part. To find such errors in a later stage of the design process causes reworking from the beginning and might result in a considerable loss. One possible solution is to display the intermediate shape to see if there is any interference.

However, sometimes it is difficult to detect collisions using graphical output when an object is very complicated. To test for possible interference at each change requires a search through the list of edges and surfaces, which is sometimes slow.

By using a spatial decomposition as an index, searching along a given line, for example, involves only the parts which are along the line, and the other parts need not be searched. This is the essence of our spatial index for solving geometrical problems and the subject we will discuss in this paper.


2. Definitions

Any object can be described in terms of four geometric entities in B-Reps: a vertex, an edge, a surface and a body [12]. Body is the part inside an object, which is surrounded by surfaces. A surface, which is plane in our case, has edges as its boundary and an edge has two vertices as its two end points.

One restriction we impose on an object is that no object should be self-intersected and inconsistency should be detected. The following conditions must hold.

1)  Any two surfaces are either disjoint or meet at a common vertex or along a common edge.
2)  Any two edges are either disjoint or meet at one of their end vertices.
3)  Any edge and surface are either disjoint, meet at a common vertex, or the edge is part of the surface boundary.

Next, the tree structure for the index tree is introduced. At first, a cube called the entire universe U is defined. Any object to be represented must be in the entire universe U, which corresponds to the root of the tree. This entire universe is divided into eight subspaces called octants, which correspond to eight children in the tree. Each octant is recursively divided into eight octants, thus forming a octal tree structure (every non-terminal node has eight children), usually referred to as an octree (or oct-tree) [4, 5, 7, 10, 12]. As opposed to pure octree where division recurs until either an octant becomes completely inside the object or completely outside the object within the given resolution, we stop subdivision when an octant becomes simple enough. The definitions of the index tree are as follows :

There are two types of octants.

(Type 1) boundary
    An octant contains the boundary of the object. This is formally denoted as P (partial).
(Type 2) non-boundary
    An octant does not contain the boundary. It is either completely inside the object (full, denoted as 1), or completely outside the object (empty, denoted as 0). In this case, no more division is needed.

Boundary octants are further classified into two sub-classes :

(Type 1-1) dividing
> The space in the octant is still complex and need to be
> subdivided. The octant is expressed as T, which
> represents an oct-tuple (o, o, o, o, o, o, o, o), where
> the order of o indicates the position of the octant.

(Type 1-2) non-dividing
> The space is simple enough to describe the cubical
> subset of the world and no more subdivision is
> necessary. This octant is denoted as L. Three cases
> for non-dividing space are as follows :

(1) In this case, an octant contains one vertex, and it contains
neither edge that does not have the vertex as its endpoint nor
face that does not have the vertex as its boundary point. Such
an octant is called a vertex cell (denoted as V), and the
corresponding node in the tree is called a vertex node.

(2) In this case, an octant contains no vertex, and one edge
fraction, which is a part of an edge, and it contains no face
that does not have the edge as its boundary. This type of
octant is called an edge cell (denoted as E), and the
corresponding node in the tree is called an edge node.

(3) In this case, an octant contains neither vertex nor edge, and it
contains one surface fraction. This type of cell is called a
surface cell (denoted as S), and the corresponding node in the
tree is called a surface node. (See Figure 1.)

Using BNF notation, we can define the index tree o as follows :

```
U    ::= o
o    ::= 0 ¶ 1 ¶ P
P    ::= T ¶ L
T    ::= (o, o, o, o, o, o, o, o)
L    ::= V ¶ E ¶ S
```

The tree is quite sensitive to the location of the entities to be
represented. Considering the cases where two vertices are very close
each other, the tree depths are not quite the same depending on where
these two vertices lie. The first division may already separate these
two vertices into two octants, while these two may be separated very deep
in the tree. In the process of generating a tree, a cell whose type has
not been decided is called 'undecided'. (The entire universe is labeled
as undecided, before generation.)


3. Algorithms

In the following discussion, the term "boundary" is used to indicate
either a vertex, an edge or a surface, where distinction is unnecessary.
The four classes of entities we discuss here are :

```
(Class 1)  vertex
(Class 2)  edge
(Class 3)  surface
(Class 4)  body (and empty)
```

Throughout this chapter, our algorithms are based on the strategy that when a (Class i) entity is discussed, there is no entity whose class is greater than i. For example, at an edge insertion, the object may consists of vertices and edges but not any surfaces nor body. Consequently, when we make a tree for an object, we will make at first vertex nodes, then edge nodes, then surface nodes, and finally full nodes and empty nodes. As we will see in the last section of this chapter, this is not a too strong restriction to modification of the object. A different approach for generating the tree from B-Reps is given in [2, 6]. Their method is based on a divide-and-conquer strategy.

Characteristics of our approach compared to theirs are

(1) Objects can be constructed by series of small actions.
(2) Modification of objects is presented.

These dynamic properties enable us to use the tree as an interactive index system. And they fit in with some applications such as design processes. We will mention this later.

3.1 Vertex

To add a new vertex to an object, a new vertex node must be put into the tree. In this process, the tree is extended enough to provide an undecided node for a new vertex. The procedure is sketched as follows :

### Vertex Insertion Algorithm

```
input    : a vertex, an index tree
function : create a new vertex cell in the index tree
```

1. Find the leaf node in the current tree that contains the given vertex, by a simple top down tree search.

2. When the cell type is undecided, it is replaced by a vertex cell and exit the procedure.

3. When the cell type is not undecided, that is, the cell is preempted by another vertex, split the cell into eight sub-octants. (When splitting a cell, one sub-octant contains the old vertex and becomes a vertex cell, while the others become undecided cells.)

4.a) If a new vertex falls in a cell which is undecided, then it is replaced by a vertex cell and exit the procedure.

   b) If the vertex falls again in a cell which is not undecided, split the cell into eight sub-octants. Go to step 4.a).

## 3.2 Edge

After insertion of vertex nodes, the tree is organized so that every node has at most one vertex. In this section, given the vertex nodes of the two end points, edge nodes are planted in the tree. The idea here is to determine the edge cells in the course of tracing an edge from a vertex cell that contains one end point to another vertex cell that contains the other end point of the edge. (See Figure 2.)

### Edge Insertion Algorithm

input    : two end points of the specified edge, an index tree
function : create edge cells in the index tree

1.  Let n1 and n2 be the cells containing the end points of the specified edge.

2.  Find a boundary vertex A in a vertex cell n1. (A boundary vertex means an intersection between an edge and a face of the octant here.)

3.  Using A, find an adjacent cell along the edge and rename it as n1.

4.  a) When n1 is n2, exit the procedure.

    b) When n1 is undecided, replace it by an edge cell and find the other boundary vertex A in a vertex cell n1. Go to step 3.

    c) When n1 is not undecided, that is, it is preempted by another vertex or edge, split the cell until it provides an undecided cell having A as its boundary point. Replace the undecided cell by an edge cell and rename it n1 and find the other boundary vertex A in a vertex cell n1. Then go to step 3.

## 3.3 Surface

Next, in this section, surface cells are put into the tree. In determining surface nodes, a propagation algorithm similar to edge tracing in the previous algorithm is used. A surface is defined by its boundary edges. They are given in clockwise order to specify surface normal. Given a boundary cell, we search every direction in which a surface cell may exist. Searching is done in depth-first. Figure 3 illustrates how to find adjacent cells along boundary edges.

### Surface Insertion Algorithm

input    : boundary edges specifying the surface, an index tree
function : create surface cells in the index tree

1.  Mark the current cell as visited. (At first, the current cell is the cell containing a boundary entity of the given surface, that is, it is either a vertex cell or an edge cell.)

2. Find intersection between the surface fraction and six faces of the current cell (line segment L's). Using L's, do the following process for all the adjacent cells.

3.a) When a cell is undecided, replace it by a surface cell and recursively call the surface insertion algorithm. (The cell becomes the current cell.)

   b) When an adjacent cell is not undecided and it is marked as visited, do nothing.

   c) When an adjacent cell is either a vertex cell or an edge cell that is part of the boundary of the given surface. Mark the cell as visited and recursively call the surface insertion algorithm. (The cell becomes the current cell.)

   d) When an adjacent cell is not undecided (and it does not contain either vertex or edge that is part of the boundary of the given surface), split the cell until it provides an undecided cell for a given edge. Replace the adjacent splitted cell by a surface cell and recursively call the surface insertion algorithm. (The new cell becomes the current cell.)

3.4 Body cells and Empty cells

This section briefly describes how the undecided cells in the universe are identified as either body cells or empty cells. If their is a undecided leaf node, its parent node is a boundary octant. Therefore there is at least one boundary cell contained in its siblings. An undecided cell can be identified by looking at the nearest boundary cell and its location.

3.5 Modification

After an initial modeling, modification of objects is also possible. Modification consists of two processes : insertion and deletion of entities. In the case of insertion, we regard the octant involved as the universe and locally repeat the generation process within the octant. As to deletion, the process is performed in the reverse order of insertion. After deletion, we may merge the nodes to keep the tree compact.
When the union of eight siblings satisfies the non-dividing condition, merge takes place to make them one.

4. Uses of the Indexing Method

In the previous section, the outline of index manipulation algorithms which consist of insertion and deletion are shown. In this section, we consider how these operations can be used to cope with actual situations.

Many boundary representation systems are based on a set of Euler operations [9], where each modification is done by one of these operation and large changes in shape can be broken down to a sequence of these operations. However, designers may make many errors in designing process. Although some of these errors can be detected by displaying the shape, some are not detected until a much later stage of the design processes, which may cause a great loss in time and expenses. One of these errors is making a self-intersecting object. One approach is to be able to reverse each operation to restore the previous scene [3]. Here, by using our space index tree, we try to detect interference between each shape and the new entity created by an operation. This prevents possible errors and will help raise reliability of the design system. Searching along a new edge, for example, requires only voxels along the edge. Figure 4 is an example of a simple shape, with its boundary cells.

Dealing with civil engineering data, we may want to ask a question like "find all the gas pipes and water pipes whose locations are within 5 meters of a subway tunnel in the 3D space." When geometrical data for subway, the gas pipes and the water pipes are organized in the form of a table, you will find that there is no easy way to find the answer without searching throughout the list of the items.

This method also solves the problems above as follows: When searching the region within 5 meters of the subway tunnel, we only need to look for the voxels along and near the subway tunnel. We do not look at any voxels more than 5 meters away from the tunnel at all. This reduces the search-space.


## 5. Conclusions

An index method for three dimensional space using hierarchical structure has been discussed. Generation and modification of objects have been presented. The possible uses of this dynamic index tree include interactive geometric shape design and civil engineering.


## 6. Acknowledgements

We are grateful to Prof. Geoff Wyvill and Mr. Tsukasa Noma for their criticism and technical suggestions. The authors wish to express our gratitude to Dr. Hideko S. Kunii for her technical aids and also to the Software Research Laboratory of Ricoh Co., Ltd. for financial support.


## 7. References

1.  Bentley, J. L.
    "Multi-dimensional binary search tree used for associative searching,"
    CACM 18,9 1975, pp.509-517.

2.  Carlbom, I., Chakravarty, I., and Vanderschel, D.
    "A Hierarchical Data Structure for Representing the Spatial Decomposition of 3D Objects,"
    IEEE CG&A, 1985, to appear.

3.  Chiyokura, H. and Kimura, F.
    "A Representation of Solid Design Process Using Basic Operations,"
    IEEE CG&A, 1985, to appear.

4.  Doctor, L. J. and Torborg, J. D.
    "Display Techniques for Octree encoded object,"
    IEEE CG & A, Vol 1, No. 3, July 1981, pp 29-38.

5.  Fujimura, K., Toriya, H., Yamaguchi, K.,and Kunii, T. L.
    "An Enhanced Oct-tree Data Structure and Operations for Solid
    Modeling,"
    Proceedings of NASA Computer-Aided Geometry Modeling, Hampton,
    Virginia, April 20-22, 1983, pp 279-287.

6.  Hunter, G. M.
    "Geometrees for Interactive Visualization of Geology: An Evaluation,"
    Research Note, Schlumberger-Doll Research, Ridgefield,
    CT, April 1984.

7.  Jackins, C. L. and Tanimoto, S. L.
    "Oct-trees and their Use in Representing Three-Dimensional Objects,"
    Computer Grahics and Image Processing, Vol. 14,No.3,1980, pp.249-270.

8.  Kunii, T. L., Satoh, T., and Yamaguchi, K.
    "Generation of Topological Boundary Representations from Octree
    Encoding,"
    IEEE CG&A, 1985, Vol. 5, March, pp.27-31.

9.  Mantyla, M. and Sulonen, R.
    "GWB - A Solid Modeler With Euler Operators,"
    IEEE CG & A, Vol.2, No.7,1982, pp.17-31.

10. Meagher, D.
    "Geometric Modeling Using Octree Encoding,"
    Computer Graphics and Image Processing, Vol.19, No.2, 1982, pp.129-
    147.

11. Requicha, A. A. G. and Voelcker, H. B.
    "Solid Modeling:Current Status and Research Directions",
    IEEE CG&A vol.3, No.7, Oct. 1983, pp.25-37.

12. Yamaguchi, K., Kunii T. L., Fujimura, K., and Toriya, H.
    "Octree related data structure and algorithms,"
    IEEE CG & A, Vol.3, 1983.

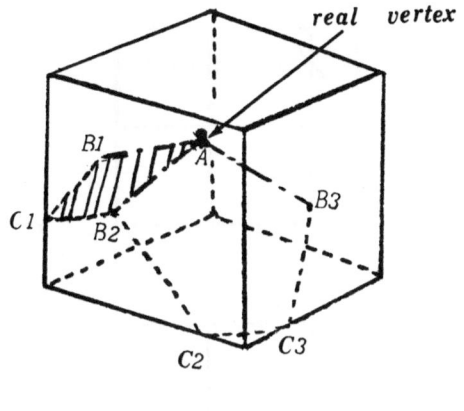

$(a)$

edge fraction

facet

facet

$(b)$ $(c)$

(a) a vertex cell

(b) an edge cell

(c) a surface cell

A real edge is expressed by A.

Figure 1.

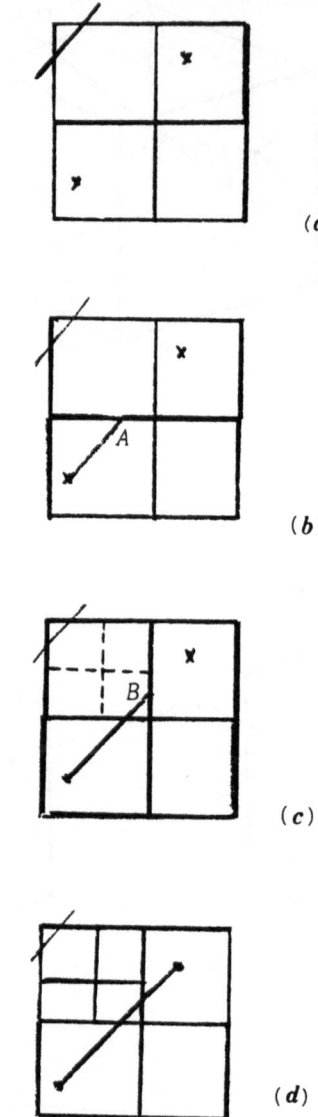

(a) Two vertex cells n1 and n2 are given.

(b) Boundary vertex A and then the adjacent cell are found.

(c) The adjacent cell is divided, because it is preempted by another edge.

(d) Finally, cell n2 is found.

Figure 2. Edge insertion. This illustration is two dimensional.

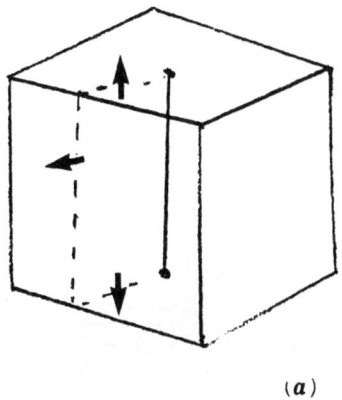

(a)

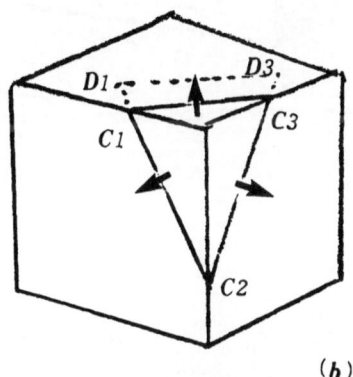

(b)

Searching directions are shown by arrows in an edge cell (a)
and a surface cell (b).

Figure 3.   Surface insertion.

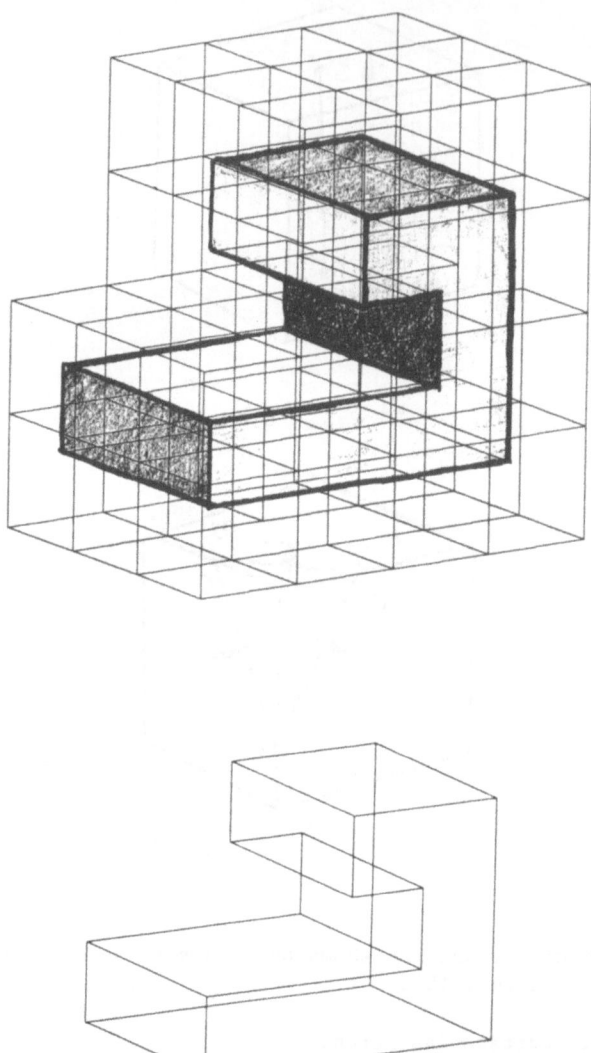

Figure 4.  A simple shape with its boundary cells.

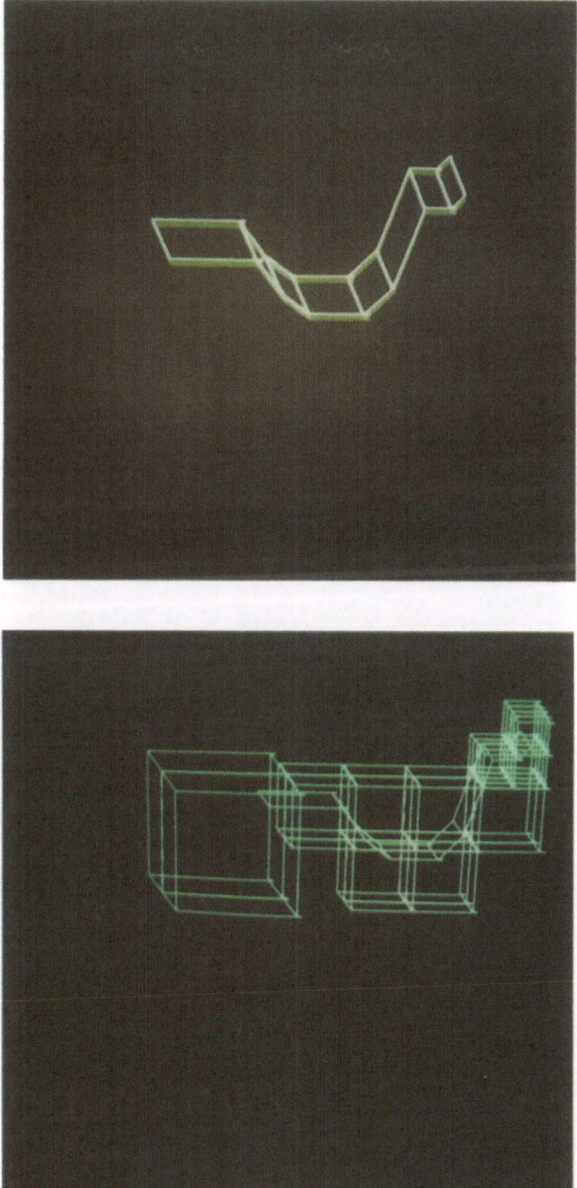

Figure 5. Boundary entities and their voxels.

# Clustering Geometric Objects
# and Applications to Layout Problems*

F. Dehne and H. Noltemeier

Lehrstuhl fuer Informatik I, Universitaet Wuerzburg, Am Hubland, D-8700 Wuerzburg,
Federal Republic of Germany

ABSTRACT

This paper deals with the relationship between cluster analysis and
computational geometry describing clustering strategies using a Voronoi
diagram approach in general and a line separation approach to improve
the efficiency in a special case. We state the following theorems:
1. The set of all centralized 2-clusterings $(S_1, S_2)$ of a planar point
   set S with $|S_1| = a$ and $|S_2| = b$ is exactly the set of all pairs of
   labels of opposite Voronoi polygons $\overline{v_a(S_1, S)}$ and $v_b(S_2, S)$ of $V_a(S)$
   and $V_b(S)$ respectively.
2. An optimal centralized 2-clustering [centralized divisive hierarchical
   2-clustering] can be constructed in $O(n\sqrt{n}\, \log^2 n + U_F(n) \cdot n\sqrt{n} + P_F(n))$
   $[O(n\sqrt{n} \cdot \log^3 n + U_F(n) \cdot n\sqrt{n} + P_F(n))$ respectively] steps with $P_F(n)$
   and $U_F(n)$ being the time complexity to compute and update a given
   clustering measure f.
Applications to layout problems (design of assembly lines; VLSI-placement
problems and board design) as well as image understanding problems
(clustering of sets of geometric objects as points, edges, polygons etc.)
will be given in the talk.

Keywords: Cluster analysis, computational geometry, image understanding,
          layout problem, line separation, Voronoi diagram

## 1. INTRODUCTION

Given a set S of n points $x_1, \ldots, x_n \in R^d$ (this paper will deal only with
planar point sets - d = 2 - and Euclidian metric), a partition of S into
C disjoint "natural groupings" $S_1, \ldots, S_C$ is called a "C-clustering" of S.
There are several ways to specify "natural groupings". You can ask for
minimization (maximization) of some "clustering measure" $f:(S_1, \ldots, S_C)$
$\to r \in R$ (e.g. minimize the maximum diameter) or you give an algorithmic
specification.
Most of the proposed strategies in clustering literature can be classified
according to fig. 1.

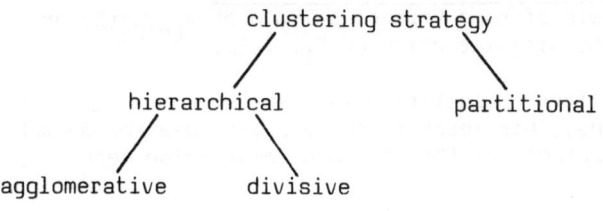

fig. 1

* This work is partially supported by the STIFTUNG VOLKSWAGENWERK.

Agglomerative hierarchical (divisive hierarchical) algorithms produce a
sequence of nested partitions with decreasing (increasing) number of
clusters hoping to approach the given goal. Partitional strategies divide
S into C clusters at one trying mostly to improve this partitioning in
some postprocessing steps (keeping the number of clusters constant) -
refer to [DE], [DJ], [M], [P], [R].
This paper will deal with the relationships between cluster analysis and
computational geometry describing two divisive hierarchical clustering
strategies using computational geometry methods.

## 2. CLUSTER CENTERS AND VORONOI DIAGRAMS

### 2.1 Basic definitions and properties

Several clustering methodologies (e.g. FORGY/ISODATA, see [DJ]) select C
cluster centers from S assigning the remaining n-C points to their nearest
cluster center (consult [DJ] for more details).
We extend this to the following

Definition 1:

(a) A cluster $S_i \subseteq S$ is called "centralized", if there exists a center
    center $x \in R^2$ with $S_i$ being the set of $s_i$ nearest neighbors of $x$
    with respect to S. (Let $s_i := |S_i|$ for the remaining of this paper.)

(b) A C-clustering $(S_1,...,S_C)$ of S is called centralized, if all $S_i (1 \le i \le C)$
    are centralized.

(c) A C-clustering $(S_1,...,S_C)$ of S is called "balanced", if for all
    $1 \le i < j \le C : |s_i - s_j| \le 1$ (This is the most interesting case in practice).

Let $v_k(S_i,S)$ be the order k Voronoi polygon of some $S_i \subseteq S (k=s_i)$ and
$V_k(S)$ be the order k Voronoi diagram of S (see [SH] and [L]). We shall
call $S_i$ the "label" of the Voronoi polygon $v_k(S_i,S)$.

Using the notations of [SH], [L] and [D] it is easy to prove the following

Lemma 1:

1.1 $S_i \subseteq S$ is a centralized cluster if and only if $S_i$ is the label of some
    Voronoi polygon $v_k(S_i,S) \ne \{\}$.

1.2 $(S_1,...,S_C)$ is a centralized C-clustering if and only if all $S_i (1 \le i \le C)$
    are labels of some Voronoi polygon of some Voronoi diagram $V_k(S)$ and
    S is the disjoint union of $S_1,...,S_k$.

1.3 $(S_1,...,S_C)$ is a balanced centralized C-clustering of S if and only if
    all $S_i (1 \le i \le C)$ are labels of some Voronoi polygon of $V_{\lfloor n/C \rfloor}(S)$ or
    $V_{\lceil n/C \rceil}(S)$ and S is the disjoint union of $S_1,..,S_C$.

It states, that a centralized C-clustering is a selection of disjoint
labels of Voronoi polygons. This leads to the idea, to use the geometric
properties of Voronoi diagrams for the design of clustering methodologies.

## 2.2 Applications to divisive hierarchical clustering

Using our above definitions a (C-nested) <u>divisive hierarchical clustering</u> is a nested sequence of C-clusterings (which we will call clustering steps) successively decomposing S into smaller subsets as demonstrated in fig. 2.

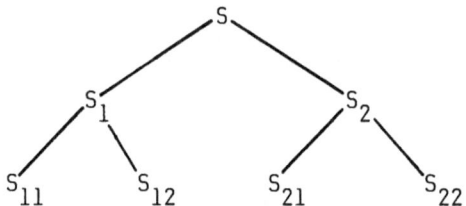

$(S_1,S_2)$, $(S_{11},S_{12})$, $(S_{21},S_{22})$ is a 2-clustering of S, $S_1$, $S_2$ respectively

fig. 2

We shall call a divisive hierarchical clustering centralized (balanced), if all clustering steps are centralized (balanced).

This chapter will demonstrate the relationship between order k Voronoi diagrams and 2-nested centralized divisive hierarchical clustering.

### Definition 2:

Two disjoint Voronoi polygons $vp_1$ and $vp_2$ are "<u>opposite</u>" to each other, if there are two nonparallel straight lines g and g' each containing two disjoint rays $r_1,r_2$ and $r_1',r_2'$ respectively with $r_1,r_1' \underline{c} vp_1$ and $r_2,r_2' \underline{c} vp_2$. (Note, that opposite Voronoi polygons are always open.)

With this definition we can prove the following lemmata:

### Lemma 2:

Let a,b be two positive integers with $a+b \leq n$, $a = |S_1|$, $b = |S_2|$ and $v_a(S_1,S)$, $v_b(S_2,S)$ two nonempty Voronoi polygons which are opposite, then $S_1$ and $S_2$ are disjoint.

and

### Lemma 3:

Let a,b be two positive integers with $a+b=n$, $a = |S_1|$, $b = |S_2|$ and $v_a(S_1,S)$, $v_b(S_2,S)$ two Voronoi polygons with S being the disjoint union of $S_1$ and $S_2$, then $v_a(S_1,S)$ and $v_b(S_2,S)$ are open and opposite.

Summarizing this, we have

Theorem 1:

The set of all centralized 2-clusterings $(S_1, S_2)$ of S with $|S_1| = a$ and $|S_2| = b$ is exactly the set of all pairs of labels of opposite Voronoi polygons $v_a(S_1, S)$ and $v_b(S_2, S)$ of $V_a(S)$ and $V_b(S)$ respectively.

Because every $S_1 \subseteq S$ has exactly one complement $S_2 = S - S_1$, it follows immediately, that every open order k Voronoi polygon $v_k(S_1, S)$ has exactly one opposite order n-k Voronoi polygon, thus the four bounding rays of these polygons having pairwise exactly opposite direction.

This is an interesting property of order k Voronoi diagrams, which appears to be new.

Consider the problem of constructing an <u>optimal</u> centralized 2-clustering $(S_1, S_2)$ of S with respect to some <u>clustering measure</u> $f(S_1, S_2) \in R$ and $|S_1| \overset{!}{=} k$, $|S_2| = n-k$. We assume a given algorithm F, which is able to compute $f(S_1, S_2)$ in time $P_F(n)$ and exchange exactly one element of $S_1$ and $S_2$ respectively in $U_F(n)$ steps (eventually using heraditary properties). The following steps are appropriate to solve the problem:

(1) Compute all open order k (and n-k) Voronoi polygons sorted by the angle of their bounding rays (respectively). (There are $O(n\sqrt{k})$ such polygons: see Theorem 1, Lemma 4 and [EW 1])

(2) Following exactly one revolution of a rotating line pointing at the current pair of opposite Voronoi polygons and select the optimal one with respect to f computing $O(n\sqrt{k})$ updates using F.

From the aspect of computational complexity step (1) is the most expensive one. Lee [L] has proposed an algorithm to construct an order k diagram in $O(k^2 n \log n)$ steps. With k being of order n in most cases of 2-clustering this would normally lead to an $O(n^3 \log n)$ algorithm, but [ERS] describe some methods to construct <u>all</u> Voronoi diagrams in $O(n^3)$. So current state of the art (as known by the authors) in constructing Voronoi diagrams leads to an $O(n^3 + n\sqrt{n}\, U_F(n) + P_F(n))$ algorithm to compute an optimal centralized 2-clustering.

A centralized divisive hierarchical clustering will be obtained by a successive application of this algorithm to the current partition of S. This leads to the same asymptotic time complexity.

Note, that we compute much more information than we actually need, leaving us with the problem to look for some better algorithm to construct an order k Voronoi diagram or all of its open polygons respectively. This will significantly improve the complexity of our algorithm.
For the special case of 2-clustering we will give a more efficient solution in the following chapter.

3. AN $O(n\sqrt{n}\, \log^2 n + U_F(n)\, n\sqrt{n} + P_F(n))$ ALGORITHM TO CONSTRUCT AN OPTIMAL CENTRALIZED 2-CLUSTERING

To construct an optimal centralized 2-clustering $(S_1, S_2)$ of S with $|S_1| = k$ and $|S_2| = n-k$ we state the following

Lemma 4:

$(S_1,S_2)$ is a centralized 2-clustering of S if and only if $S_1$ and $S_2$ are separable and S is the disjoint union of $S_1$ and $S_2$.

After constructing the k-belt of T(S) (see [EW 2]) in $O(n\sqrt{k}\,\log^2 n)$ steps we search along its upper and lower border, respectively, update the clustering value $f(S_1,S_2)$ and select an optimal partition. From [EW 1] and [EW 2] we know, that our dynamic updating procedure F will be executed $O(n\sqrt{k})$ times, leading to an $O(n\sqrt{n}\,\log^2 n + U_F(n)\, n\sqrt{n} + P_F(n))$ algorithm.

By a successive application of this procedure as described in 2.2 we obtain a centralized divisive hierarchical clustering in $O(n\sqrt{n}\,\log^3 n + U_F(n)\, n\sqrt{n} + P_F(n))$ steps.

So we have

Theorem 2:

An optimal centralized 2-clustering [centralized divisive hierarchical 2-clustering] can be constructed in $O(n\sqrt{n}\,\log^2 n + U_F(n)\, n\sqrt{n} + P_F(n))$ [$O(n\sqrt{n}\,\log^3 n + U_F(n)\, n\sqrt{n} + P_F(n))$ respectively] steps.

## 4. REMARKS

Allowing cluster centers to be points of $R^2$ gives us the possibility to apply the geometric structure of order k Voronoi diagrams as an interesting tool for solving clustering problems. The described Voronoi diagram approach has the additional advantage of apparently being extendible to centralized C-clustering (in contrast to chapter 3).

Clustering of sets of geometric objects as edges, polygons etc. can be reduced to the partitioning of sets of points in more general spaces respectively of sets of labelled points. Details are given in the forthcoming paper [DNZ 1], applications of these methods to image understanding are analysed in [DNZ 2].
Applications to layout problems in a wide range are obvious: VLSI-placement problems in chip design as well as placement of VLSI-components on boards.
By additionally use of Voronoi-trees [N] the design of assembly lines (in the case of poor precedence structure) can be done most efficiently.

## REFERENCES

[D] Dehne: AN $O(N^4)$ ALGORITHM TO CONSTRUCT ALL VORONOI DIAGRAMS FOR K NEAREST NEIGHBOR SEARCHING, Proc. 10th Colloquium on Automata, Languages and Programming, 1983.

[DE] Day, Edelsbrunner: EFFICIENT ALGORITHMS FOR AGGLOMERATIVE HIERARCHICAL CLUSTERING METHODS, Report F122, Institut für Informationsverarbeitung, TU Graz, Graz, Austria.

[DJ] Dubes, Jain: CLUSTERING METHODOLOGIES IN EXPLORATORY DATA ANALYSIS, in M.C. Yovits (Ed.): Advances in Computers, Vol.19, 1980.

[DNZ 1]     Dehne, Noltemeier, Zynderman: AGGREGATION AND PARTITION OF
            SETS OF POLYGONS, in preparation.

[DNZ 2]     Dehne, Noltemeier, Zynderman: IMAGE UNDERSTANDING BY
            PARTITIONING SETS OF POLYGONS, in preparation.

[ERS]       Edelsbrunner, O'Rourke, Seidel: CONSTRUCTING ARRANGEMENTS OF
            LINES AND HYPERPLANES WITH APPLICATIONS, Report F123
            (see  DE ), 1983.

[EW 1]      Edelsbrunner, Welzl: ON THE NUMBER OF LINE-SEPARATIONS OF A
            FINITE SET IN THE PLANE, Report F97 (see  DE ), 1982.

[EW 2]      Edelsbrunner, Welzl: HALFPLANAR RANGE ESTIMATION, Report F98
            (see  DE ), 1982.

[EW 3]      Edelsbrunner, Welzl: HALFPLANAR RANGE SEARCH IN LINEAR SPACE
            AND $O(n^{0.695})$ QUERY TIME, Report F111 (see  DE ), 1983.

[L]         D.T. Lee: AN APPROACH TO FINDING THE K-NEAREST NEIGHBORS IN
            EUCLIDEAN PLANE, Report, Department of Electrical Engineering
            and Computer Science, Northwestern Univ., Evanston, Ill. 60201
            USA, 1981.

[M]         Murtagh: EXPECTED-TIME COMPLEXITY RESULTS FOR HIERARCHIC
            CLUSTERING ALGORITHMS WHICH USE CLUSTER CENTERS, Information
            Processing Letters 16, 1983.

[N]         Noltemeier: VORONOI-TREES AND LAYOUT PROBLEMS, Technical
            Report, Würzburg, 1984.

[OL]        Overmars, Van Leeuwen: MAINTENANCE OF CONFIGURATIONS IN THE
            PLANE, Journal of Computer and System Science, Vol. 23, No. 2,
            1981.

[P]         Page: A MINIMUM SPANNING TREE CLUSTERING METHOD, Communications
            of the ACM, Vol. 17, No. 16, 1974.

[R]         Rohlf: HIERARCHICAL CLUSTERING USING THE MINIMUM SPANNING TREE,
            The Computer Journal, Vol. 16, No. 1, 1973.

[S]         Schrader: APPROXIMATIONS OF CLUSTERING AND SUBGRAPH PROBLEMS
            ON TREES, Discrete Applied Math. 6., 1983.

[SH]        Shamos, Hoey: CLOSEST POINT PROBLEMS, Proc. 16th Ann. IEEE
            Symp. on Foundations of Computer Science, 1975.

[W]         Willard: POLYGON RETRIEVAL, SIAM J. Comput., Vol. 11, No. 1,
            1982

[Y]         F.F. Yao: A 3-SPACE PARTITION AND ITS APPLICATION  (Extended
            Abstract), Proc. 15th ACM Symp. on Theory of Comp., 1983.

# Accelerated Ray Tracing

Akira Fujimoto and Kansei Iwata

Graphica Computer Corporation, 21-6, Nagayama 6-chome, Tama, Tokyo, 206 Japan

ABSTRACT

This paper proposes algorithms for dealing with two essential problems encountered in generating continuous-tone images by the ray tracing method: speed and aliasing. These two factors are considered an Achilles' heel of the method and have been the main cause preventing the method from being widely used. The paper examines previous approaches to the problem and finally proposes a scheme based on the coherency of an auxiliary data structure imposed on the original object domain. Both simple spatial enumeration and a hybrid octree approach were investigated. 3DDDA (3D line generator) was developed for efficient traversing of both structures. It constitutes the essential factor providing a dramatic improvement (order of magnitude) in processing speed in comparison to other known ray tracing methods. In particular, processing time is found to be virtually independent of the number of objects involved in the scene. For a larger number of objects (around 1500), this method actually becomes faster than scan-line methods. In order to remove jags from edges, a scheme for identifying the edge orientation and the distance from a pixel center to the true edge has been implemented. The additional time required for antialiasing depends on the total length of the edges encountered in the scene, but is normally only a fractional addition to the time required to produce such a scene without antialiasing.

INTRODUCTION

Although ray tracing (RT) is believed to have been first suggested by Appel as early as 1967 (4,6), this method of producing continuous tone images became better known following the publication of Whitted's now classic paper in 1980 (2). This paper is still strongly recommended as a very comprehensive reference to RT. RT is currently well known for providing the highest quality image synthesis. The superior image quality achieved by RT, which uses a global illumination model, is perhaps most evident when corresponding images produced by the different algorithms are compared (21).

Despite the impressive images, however, many improvements can still be made to further upgrade the image quality. These improvements include, among others, more realistic illumination models (4), antialiasing (4,7), fuzzy shadows and dull reflections (15), diffuse reflection from distributed light sources (23) etc. Hence, much of the research effort in RT is devoted to these problems.

In a cost-performance comparison with traditional, mostly scan-line methods, however, RT is seriously handicapped. The efficiency of scan-line methods is achieved by well established methods such as incremental calculation of geometry based on object and/or image coherency (see for example 29, 30, 31, 32, 33, 22, 18). On the other hand, RT is in general slow because intersection calculation is basically computation intensive, and object and image coherency is far more difficult to exploit. Nevertheless, the calculation speed of the RT method is undoubtedly one of the basic problems which must be dealt with. Without solving this problem, we cannot expect RT to achieve the widespread use which the scan-line methods enjoy, even though the latter produce far inferior images.

Results of several investigations into reducing the computational expense of RT have recently been published. In RT, most of the calculation time is known to be spent on finding intersections. According to Whitted (2), for simple scenes, 75% of the total calculation time is spent on intersections. For more complex scenes, the proportion reaches 95% . These figures were obtained in spite of the fact that so called bounding volumes or extents were used. In order to reduce the number of surfaces that must be checked against a given ray, the ray is first checked against gross volumes that bound the objects. This has been done typically by circumscribing a sphere around each object(35). It is a relatively quick procedure to determine if a ray totally misses a sphere. In addition to extents, hierarchical description of the environment has been introduced to speed up the calculations (1). The environment was subdivided into hierarchical, orthogonal subspaces, except for the lower level primitives, which were bounded by arbitrarily oriented, rectangular parallelepipeds. During picture generation, each ray was transformed in order to align it with the axes of the parallelepipeds, so that the intersection tests were reduced to simple comparisons against the limits of the bounding boxes. This method, initiated by Rubin and Whitted (1), has now become quite common practise in ray tracing, so the main lines of attack seem to be concentrated along both bounding volumes and hierarchical description of the environment. Weghorst et. al. (6) have gone further in this direction and have proposed selection of bounding volumes. They point out that the simplicity of the intersection test should not be the only consideration. In the selection of the bounding volume, other factors, such as the projected void area, should be taken into account. Minimizing these void areas results in the selection of the optimal bounding volume for the particular geometry.

They introduce three candidates for the shape of the bounding volume, namely a sphere, a rectangular parallelepiped and a cylinder. Further hierarchical structure is implemented by clustering groups of items which are in proximity to each other within a single bounding volume. Higher level clusters can be created by grouping clusters and/or items together. Topological information about the environment thus defined reduces computational time further. Also, by utilizing image-space coherence for those rays originating at the eye, a reduction in the size of the intersection list is realized. Typical visible surface algorithms (see for example 29, 30, 31, 32, 33, 22, 18) are invoked to reduce this list to a single entry for a particular pixel pierced by the ray. The relative improvement in calculation time is significant.

A very interesting approach to RT has been proposed by Heckbert and Hanrahan (7). Although beam tracing is currently limited to polygonal environments it combines features of both image and object space hidden surface s. Instead of tracing infinitesimally thin rays of light, larger areas are swept by beams. The beam tracer builds an intermediate data structure, the beam tree, which is very similar to the ray tree introduced by Whitted (2). Each branch of the beam tree, however, contains information about finite areas covered by the fragmented beams defined in its links. The beam tree is computed in object space and then passed to a polygon renderer for scan conversion to form the final shaded image. Beam tracing proves to be extremely efficient computationally for images with a limited number of objects. In general, however, it is more complicated than ray tracing and heavily dependent on the number of objects which affect the intrinsic image coherence. Low image coherence results in more fragmented beams. The higher the coherence, the higher the number of rays clustered in the beam which can be traced in parallel. This is essential for the method to be faster than RT.

All the above-mentioned methods, in spite of providing significant improvement in calculation time, do not represent the kind of breakthrough which reduces this time to the order of other classical image synthesis methods. In order to produce scenes involving significant number of objects, some "brute force" attempts were reported. Faster computers, specifically supercomputers, represent one of the approaches (see 34 for example). Another one is to devise special purpose hardware. In computer animation, where many images must be produced and image generation time must be kept to a minimum, ray tracing is still prohibitively expensive. The only extensive ray tracing animation made to date was done by parallelism in special purpose hardware (19). Both of these approaches, however, are without doubt rather expensive and generally not affordable for the majority of users. The authors are convinced that there is still much room to investigate improved software algorithms before developing expensive special purpose hardware.

In some of the papers cited above (1 and 7 for example), the notion of cell decomposition of the object space is mentioned. For each cell its relationship to the objects is recorded as a cell status. A HOMOgeneous cell corresponds to a cell which is completely outside of all objects in the scene or is completely inside one or more objects. A HETEROgeneous cell corresponds to one which contains the boundary of one or more elements. Now, if we can provide a fast means for traversing this cellular structure in any direction, then it will be possible to identify and consequently check for intersection in only those cells which are pierced by the particular ray. Irregular cell decomposition for speeding up the hidden line removal has been used by Jones (10). His approach relies on 3D objects being described in terms of a series of interconnected spatial cells. Avenues of sight through the openings between cells are explored in the process of generating display information for a perspective picture from a given point. More recently: Atherton has (3) introduced the concept of a voxel, i.e. 3D volume element, as a fundamental member of a 3D grid orthogonal to the image space coordinate system. The proposed solution, being aimed mainly at CAD applications, does not provide reflected and refracted light modeling. Also, perspective views are not feasible. At the same time, much research has been done in investigating memory-efficient ways of encoding volumes of homogeneous information, in particular the so-called octree (11, 12, 13 14, 15).

According to the authors' knowledge, the first approach to speed up ray tracing calculations by the use of auxiliary data structure imposed on the original model data, specifically octree encoding, was advocated by Matsumoto and Murakami (27). Also, Glassner (25) proposed using an octree structure similar to that of Matsumoto and Murakami i.e., by the combined use of a certain kind of clipping algorithm applied to each cell and a simple hash function. Their approach brings RT closer to practical applications because the improvement in the calculation time was of an order of magnitude.

The approach advocated in this paper (developments presented in this paper were accomplished before the authors became acquainted with the works of Murakami and Glassner) is similar to theirs in the sense that auxiliary data structures were adopted to speed up the calculations. A substantial difference, however, lies in the way in which the data structure is organized and traversed. In Murakami's and Glassner's "divide and conquer" approach to traversing, a considerable overhead time is introduced because the computational cost of moving from one cell to another is significant. On the other hand, "generative" algorithms are proposed in this paper i.e., all cells pierced by the ray are identified by its direct generation. 3DDDA has been developed for this purpose. This "generation" approach was found to be essential in obtaining improvement of another order of magnitude in the calculation time, compared with the results presented by Glassner. The total time for producing one frame in found to be virtually independent of the number of objects in the scene.

## 3DDDA

The purpose of this section is to describe the basic tool for traversing a 3D grid of equidimensional cells. This tool is the Three Dimensional Digital Differential Analyser (3DDDA). The extension of 3DDDA which enables it to traverse the octree will be discussed after the octree structure is introduced. For the time being, we make the following assumptions:
The domain of the scene is spatially enumerated i.e. it is divided into a limited number of regular cuboid subdomains (cells);
Each cuboid is orthogonal with respect to the coordinate axes. Before explaining 3DDDA, let us first recall the basic characteristics of a standard (2D) DDA. The DDA is undoubtedly one of the most essential and common algorithms applied in raster graphics. Its purpose is to generate pixel coordinates approximating the straight line on a raster grid. The DDA may be implemented in many ways (Foley or Sproull and 17), but it works basically as follows:

During the process of generating each consecutive pixel's coordinates, the coordinate corresponding to the driving axis (DA) is unconditionally incremented by one unit. (A unit corresponding to the distance between pixels, which equals one because it is common to use the screen coordinate system). The DA, (or 'axis of greatest movement') is determined by the slope of the line and is one of the coordinate axes (Fig.1). At the same time, a control term, an 'error term' which is traditionally measured perpendicular to the DA, is updated by subtracting from it the slope value and checking whether it is still smaller than half of the pixel size. When this test fails, a unit increment (or decrement) of the coordinate perpendicular to the DA is performed. The control term is corrected by adding the value corresponding to one unit whenever underflow occurs.

The process described above generates the center coordinates of those pixels which are in closest proximity on the left or right side of the mathematical line. The objective of a DDA used for line generating purposes is to enumerate those pixels that lie close to the true line. While a line may be displayed using many different pixel configurations, the configuration corresponding to the optimal line depends on several criteria including uniform line intensity or brightness(17). In general, the pixels representing the optimal line, in addition to being close to the true line,; satisfy also a condition that only one pixel is generated in each vertical column (Fig.1).
On the other hand, the objective of DDA used for cell identification purposes is to enumerate all those cells that

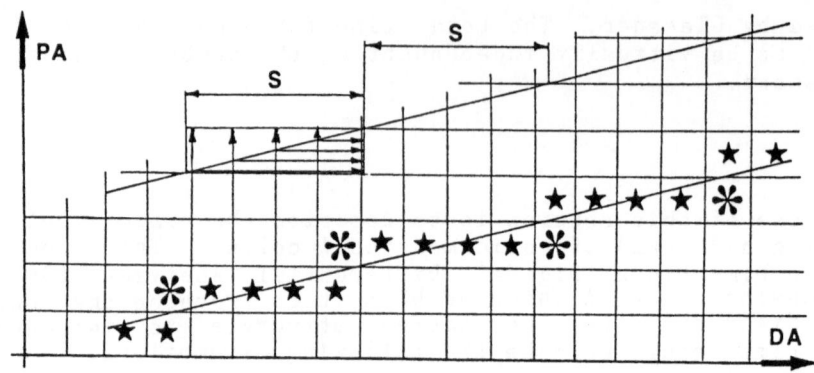

DA—driving axis, PA—passive axis, $S: \dfrac{dy}{dy}$

★ —cells identified by DDA in line generation

✳ —additional cells pierced by a straight line

Fig.1. DDA

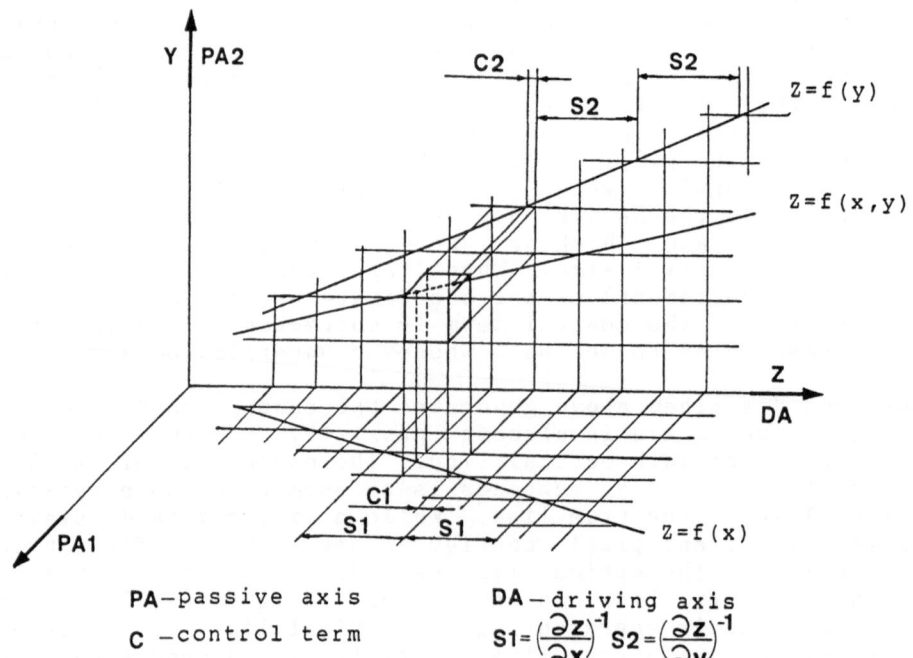

PA—passive axis

C —control term

DA—driving axis

$S1 = \left(\dfrac{\partial z}{\partial x}\right)^{-1}$ $S2 = \left(\dfrac{\partial z}{\partial y}\right)^{-1}$

Fig.2. 3DDDA

are pierced by the straight line (Fig.1). Two rather simple
modifications are necessary to convert the above scheme into
one which can identify the pixels through which the line
passes. First, movement perpendicular to the DA, which in the
standard DDA is coupled with that of the DA, must be separated
from it in order to ensure that the DDA goes always from one
pixel to an adjacent one without skipping any on its way.
Second, the threshold value against which the control term is
checked must be set to zero, instead of half of the pixel size.
With these modifications, the DDA, instead of generating pixel
coordinates closest to the center line, will generate the
coordinates of all the pixels through which the line passes.

The above scheme, however, will work only if the origin of the
traced ray and its end point correspond to the cell centers.
This, in general, obviously is not the case. Here we cannot
overemphasize the proper initialization of DDA. We reported in
(17), that such initialization was necessary to provide higher
addressability going beyond that of raster memory resolution;
it is essential for proper cell identification. Notice that
the control term can also be measured in the direction parallel
to the DA (Fig.1). Its units will then correspond to pixel
units. The range of the control term will now correspond to
the inverse value of the slope. Actually, we adopted this
approach (17) when generating smooth vectors. In that case, a
control term measured along the DA directly in gray-scale units
was used for generating the pixel's coordinates and its
intensity (for antialiasing). In the present application,
however, measuring the control term along the DA is vital
because it corresponds to the cell entry in the case of the 3D
cuboidal grid. Before explaining that, let us first extend the
notion of the DDA to three dimensions.

One way to realize 3DDDA is to use two synchronized DDA's
working in mutually perpendicular planes which intersect along
the DA (Fig.2). In each plane, the modified DDA explained
above pursues the projection of a 3D line onto that plane.
After an unconditional step in the DA direction is excuted,
control terms in both planes are processed and movement to the
neighboring cell is performed if necessary. A special
situation arises when such movement is necessary in both planes
simultaneously (Fig.3). This means that on a particular step,
both passive indices of a cell must be updated. If this
operation is performed in the wrong order, an erroneous cell
will be identified. Now, since both control terms are measured
along the same DA in units of the cuboid size, it is clear that
it is possible to provide proper identification of the string
of cells pierced by 3DDDA, simply by processing first the plane
on which the smaller control term is generated. Later we shall
see that expressing the control term in cell size units is also
essential in efficient 3DDDA traversal of the octree. 3DDDA
works very much like the (2D) DDA. The code for initialization
and for the main part of the algorithm for pursuing projection
of a ray is very similar to the one presented in our previous

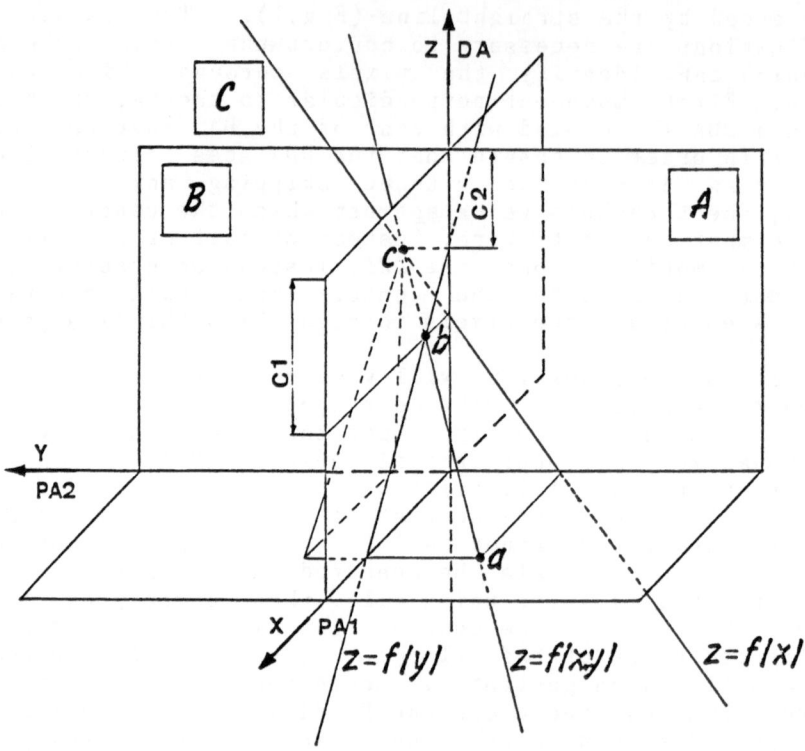

Note: After executing unconditional step along DA (driving axis), 3DDDA enters cell A through intersection point a. Both control terms (C1 and C2) measured from the front wall of the cell will overflow. This means that movements along both possive axes (PA1 and PA2) must be executed before the next unconditional step along DA is performed. Here, in order to provide proper cell entry (A→B→C), the most overflown control term (C1) must be processed first.

Fig.3. Proper cell generation in 3DDDA

work (17). The only difference is that the control term is initialized and calculated not in gray-scale units but in cell-size units.

3DDDA is applied along the ray direction and it directly identifies all three indices of the cell. (Calculation of coordinates of the intersection with the cell mesh could easily be added, but it is not necessary for cell identification.) Because incremental logic is inherent to 3DDDA, with the exception of initialization all calculations involved with cell identification are processed without any multiplication or division.

Each time the 3DDDA hits any of the planes, the next cuboid representing a mesh element is identified and checked for being in the HETERO state. If this is the case, then all of the segments which it contains are checked for possible intersection with the ray. If an intersection is found, then either ray spawning is performed, or the particular branch of the shade tree is terminated depending on the control parameters and/or model attributes. Otherwise (HOMO or ray does not intersect any of the segments within the cuboid), 3DDDA continues pursuing the ray in the same direction until some object is intersected or until it leaves the mesh domain.

In conventional RT programs, increasing the complexity of the model or the number of objects usually results in a situation where a single ray pierces a considerable number of objects. This, in turn, requires searching for the surface nearest to the observer, or possibly to a spawned ray's origin. This is one of the factors contributing to the well known phenomenon of RT: calculation time exhibits exponential growth with respect to the complexity and the number of objects in the scene. Here, it is worth noting that 3DDDA traces only the relevant extents (cuboids) in the appropriate consecutive order. No global sorting for hidden points is necessary. Local sorting, for a rather limited number of cells containing more than one element, can sometimes occur.

OCTREE

The octree encoding scheme is similar to the cell decomposition (spatial enumeration) method explained above. The information contained in the octree encoded representation of a scene is identical to that available in the cell decomposition. From the storage point of view, however, the data are stored in a hierarchical tree structure with nodes representing disjoint cubes of geometrically decreasing size. Each node of the tree corresponds to a region of the scene and has one or more values which define the region. If the value of the node completely describes the region, it is a terminal or a leaf. If not, an ambiguity exists and the node points to the eight children that represent eight subregions or octants of the parent node

(Fig.4,6). In general, the octree representation can be expected to take advantage of the spatial coherence found in most objects (13).

In this context let us analyze more closely the situation presented in Fig.4, which actually is a two-dimensional quadtree. In this particular case it is evident that the total number of nodes in the quadtree encoding and the number of cells in simple spatial enumeration happen to be equal up to level 3. This observation is important because, in general, it is more time-consuming to retrieve information or to traverse the octree than the cell-decomposed structure. In this particular case it is evident that the difference between the total numbers of nodes and cells is expected to become more and more significant as the resolution is increased. However, even if it is assumed that this is generally the case, it will be difficult to predict the resolution at which the octree encoded structure becomes superior to that of simple cell decomposition.

What resolution can we reasonably afford? Meagher (13), advocating usage of the pure octree, points out that the main disadvantage of the encoding technique is the large memory requirement. Proof has been presented that the quantity of memory required to store a quadtree 2D object is of the order of the perimeter of the object. Also the memory and processing computation for a 3D object is on the order of the surface area of the object. Depending on the object and the resolution, this can still represent a large storage requirement. Several million bytes of node storage may be necessary to represent realistic situations (13). Such memory size will not always be justified or even feasible. The seriousness of this problem was also recognized by Kunii et.al. (16). The octree is an approximation of a smooth-surfaced object by small cuboids. So it is inevitable that the encoded object entails some notched surfaces. In order to avoid displaying a jagged surface, the object must be represented by a very deep octree. A complex object with reasonably high resolution then requires enormous data storage and a high speed processor. This means the most important advantages of the octree, namely processing speed and memory economy, are lost (16). The solution proposed by Kunii et.al. is basically hybrid. Instead of using a pure octree structure, they proposed combining the octree representation with the surface model. Another example of a hybrid approach to tree encoding, applied to FEM mesh generation, is presented by Yerry and Shephard (15). In the present paper also, the hybrid approach: CSG vs OCTREE (and cell decomposition) is adopted. The hybrid approach appears at least for the time being to be more realistic than pure octree encoding or simple cell decompositioon. However, still the question remains of how much resolution can be justified. A general representation which depicts a solid body as a 3D array typically occupies 1000*1000*1000 cells (11). The maximum level value used by Kunii et.al. (16) was 10. This results in a similar

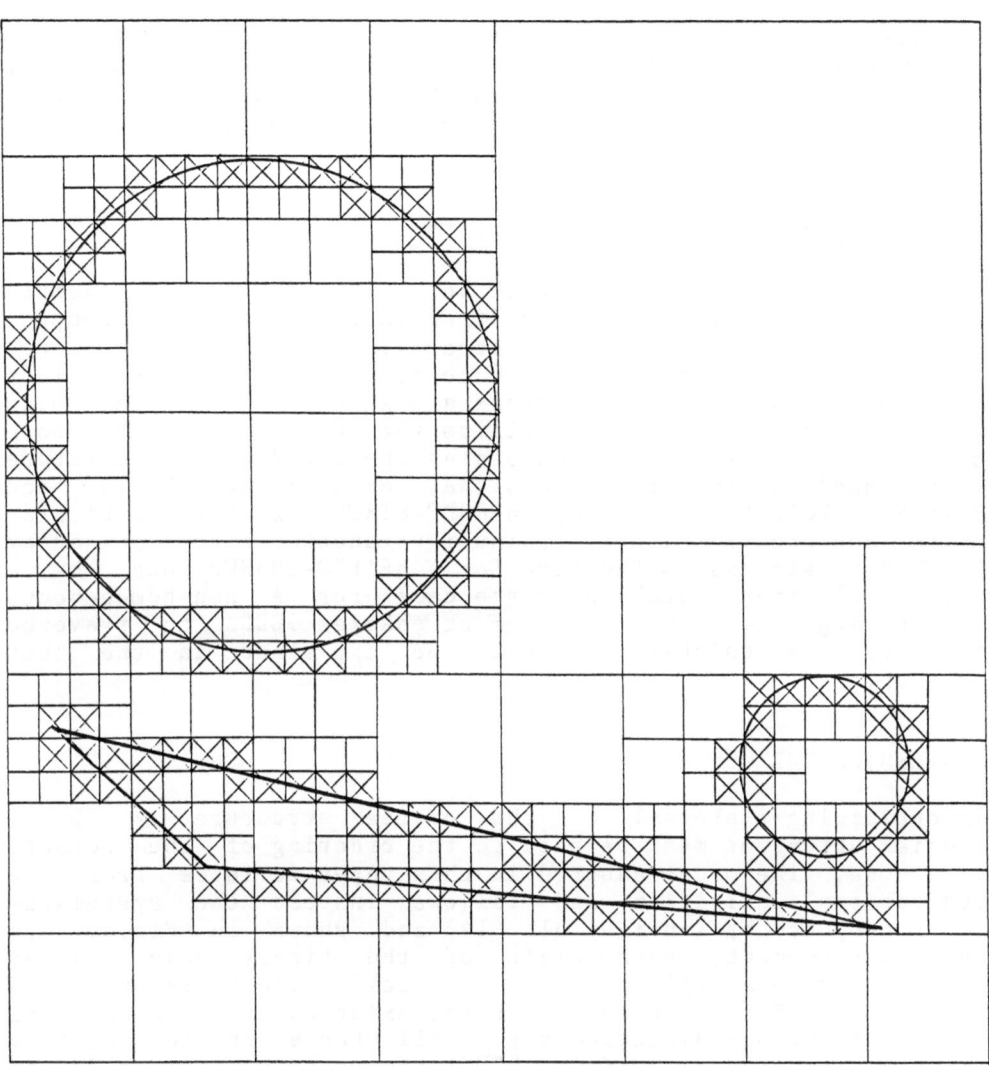

| QUADTREE LEVEL | NO. OF NODES | TOTAL NO. OF NODES | RESOLUTION | NO. OF CELLS IN SPATIAL ENUMERATION |
|---|---|---|---|---|
| 1 | 4 | 4 | 2 | 4 |
| 2 | 12 | 16 | 4 | 16 |
| 3 | 48 | 64 | 8 | 64 |
| 4 | 100 | 164 | 16 | 256 |
| 5 | 260 | 424 | 32 | 1024 |

Fig.4. Quadtree division for a cluster of objects

resolution (2**10=1024). Superiority of the octree over simple
cell decomposition will be decided by experiment. However,
even at high resolution it is possible to envisage a scene with
many objects and low homogeneity for which the octree structure
will not necessarily be justified.


## OCTREE ENCODING

The tree structure encoding will be explained by an example
(Fig.5). For simplicity, a quadtree is used in the example.
Extension to the case of a 3D octree is trivial. The scene
consists of 6 objects numbered 0 to 5. The node arrangement
and the corresponding tree levels are shown on the right side
of the figure. The legend explains the meaning of the node
status code. Information concerning the encoded tree structure
is arranged in two one-dimensional arrays: NODE-STATUS and
POINTER. POINTER, depending on NODE-STATUS of the particular
entry, can contain either a pointer to another entry in array
POINTER itself, as is the case for a HETERO-BRANCH node, or a
pointer to array OBJECT as is the case for a non-homogeneous
terminating node. This arrangement enables 3DDDA to traverse
the structure quickly, as will be explained in the next
section.


## TRAVERSING THE OCTREE

In optimizing traversal of the octree structure by 3DDDA,
special attention must be paid to the ordering of the octants
of a node. The order adopted in this paper deviates from the
conventional definition and follows instead the systematic
order proposed by Kunii et.al. (14) and shown in Fig.6. In
this arrangement, each digit of the binary node number
corresponds to a cell index in the cell decomposition of a
node. Since for a single node there exist exactly two octants
in each principal direction x,y,z, all three indices satisfy
the condition: 0<=i, j,k<=1. 3DDDA traverses a single node in
exactly the same way as it traverses the cell-decomposed
structure. When moving from one cell to an adjacent cell, it
updates one of the three indices. Changing an index results
directly in producing the number of the adjacent octant entered
by 3DDDA. The above description concludes the explanation of
how the 3DDDA traverses octants in a node. This traversing
takes place on a single level, so let us call it a horizontal
traversal. Horizontal traversal will be terminated when any of
the three indices over- or underflows. This corresponds to the
situation when the ray leaves a node. In order to identify the
adjacent node, it is necessary to ascend the tree. This will
be termed vertical traversing of the octree. Vertical
traversing can also take place in the form of descending the
tree. Descending the tree is necessary each time 3DDDA
identifies a HETERO-BRANCH node. 3DDDA execution is suspended
during vertical traversal. The octree must be traversed

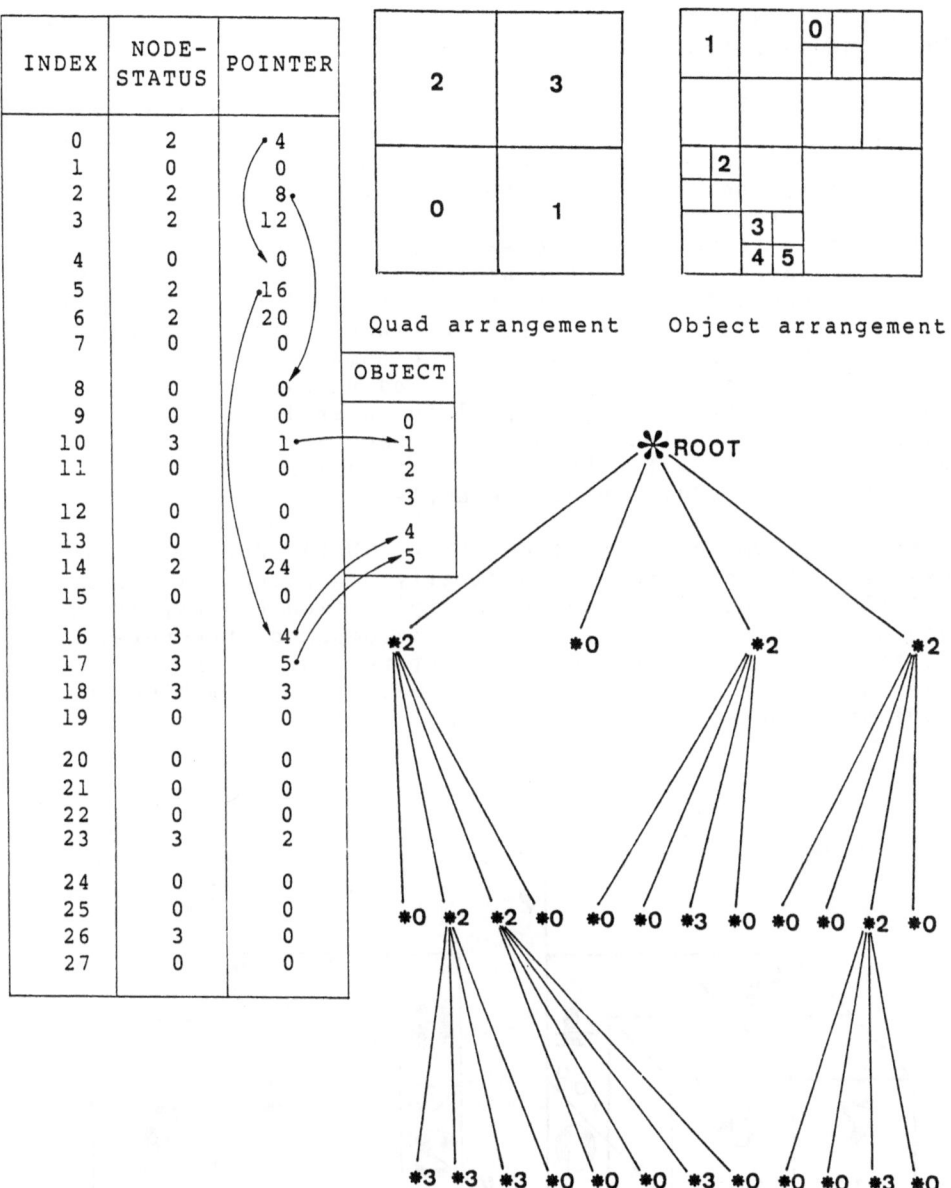

| INDEX | NODE-STATUS | POINTER |
|-------|-------------|---------|
| 0 | 2 | 4 |
| 1 | 0 | 0 |
| 2 | 2 | 8 |
| 3 | 2 | 12 |
| 4 | 0 | 0 |
| 5 | 2 | 16 |
| 6 | 2 | 20 |
| 7 | 0 | 0 |
| 8 | 0 | 0 |
| 9 | 0 | 0 |
| 10 | 3 | 1 |
| 11 | 0 | 0 |
| 12 | 0 | 0 |
| 13 | 0 | 0 |
| 14 | 2 | 24 |
| 15 | 0 | 0 |
| 16 | 3 | 4 |
| 17 | 3 | 5 |
| 18 | 3 | 3 |
| 19 | 0 | 0 |
| 20 | 0 | 0 |
| 21 | 0 | 0 |
| 22 | 0 | 0 |
| 23 | 3 | 2 |
| 24 | 0 | 0 |
| 25 | 0 | 0 |
| 26 | 3 | 0 |
| 27 | 0 | 0 |

| OBJECT |
|--------|
| 0 |
| 1 |
| 2 |
| 3 |
| 4 |
| 5 |

Quad arrangement    Object arrangement

Legend:

| NODE STATUS | POINTER (meaning depends on NODE STATUS) |
|-------------|------------------------------------------|
| 0 HOMO OUT | undefined |
| 1 HOMO IN | undefined |
| 2 HETERO BRANCH | pointer to a child node |
| 3 HETERO LEAF | pointer to OBJECT |

Fig.5. Quadtree representation

downwards (sometimes for several levels) until a HETERO-LEAF or
HOMO node is reached.

It is impossible to explain here all details concerned with
vertical traversing of the octree, because of lack of space.
The important fact is that vertical traversing of the octree is
performed by the use of the 3DDDA by products. During descent
of the tree the current values of its variables, specifically
both control terms, the inverse slopes and the octant size,
determine which child of the node has to be entered. As the
tree is descended, corresponding pointers from array POINTER
(Fig.5) are recorded in a separate, short working array. The
length of this array is equal to the number of levels in the
tree. The pointer array is not linked backwards (upwards) and
the above feature is very helpful in ascending the tree. These
values must be doubled or halved on each vertical movement from
one level to the next, but this operation is, in general,
simpler than an addition, for example.

In summary, we can conclude that 3DDDA during horizontal
traversal of the octree automatically generates all necessary
variables without division or multiplication exactly as in the
case of traversing the simply cell decomposed structure, so no
modifications in 3DDDA are necessary the for octree. On the
other hand, vertical traversal is realized by making use of
3DDDA byproducts.

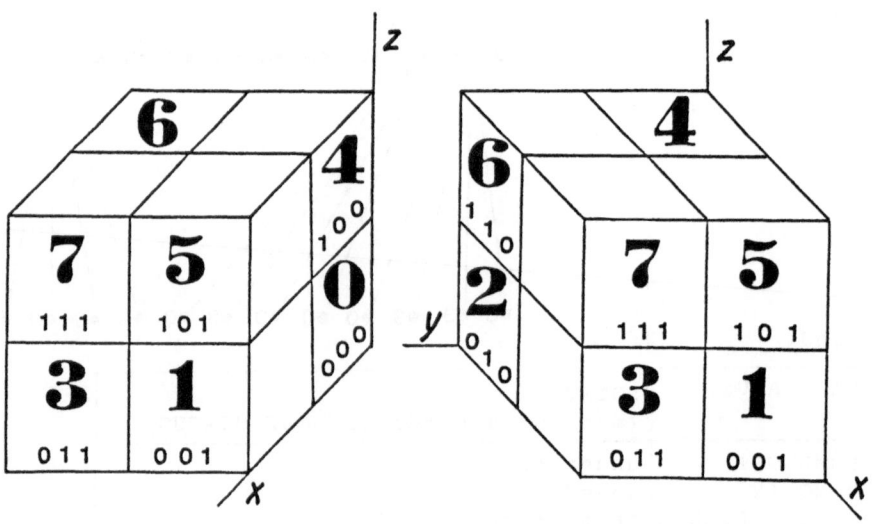

Fig.6. Systematic order of octants

ANTIALIASING

The main problem with antialiasing for ray tracing is that not enough information is associated with a single ray (5). Rays allow us to sample at the one point in the center of the pixel. Without firing additional rays there is no way of knowing or calculating what else is visible in the neighborhood surrounding the sample point.

In classical ray tracing, antialiasing is usually done by adaptive subdivision of pixels near large intensity changes or small objects (2,7). This method is now almost universally used. The method attempts to use heuristic criteria to probe the image frequently enough that small details will not be overlooked. Depending on the criteria, it will sometimes subdivided too little, resulting in aliasing, or too much, in which case processing time will be wasted. Heckbert and Hanrahan have proposed a different approach (7) in which a polygon scan converter with a pixel integrator is adopted. This method of antialiasing is sometimes used in scan line algorithms for continuous tone images. However, it was possible to adopt it in that paper because the beam tracing approach presented uses a polygon renderer for scan conversion to form the final image. Polygon edges are determined during scan conversion so that information can be used directly for antialiasing.

It is sometimes argued that the only way to antialiasing within standard ray tracing is to go to higher resolution (5). The approach presented in this paper shows that this is not exactly the case. The Adjustable Fourier Window Technique reported previously showed that high quality antialiasing can be performed with a very low computational cost (17). More recently it has been shown that it can be successfully used also for antialiasing with subpixel resolution (18). Objects having smaller size than the pixel can be properly rendered. It was also shown in that in this method, full information about the antialiased edge (position and slope) was not necessary for its antialiasing. What is essentially needed is the distance to the edge from a neighbouring pixel measured perpendicular to the DA (the notion of Driving Axis was introduced in section 2). Whether th DA is the X axis or the Y axis can be determined in 75% of cases by simple comparison of the difference of generated pixel intensities both vertically and horizontally. In the remaining 25% of cases an additional ray must be fired to resolve the ambiguity. After the DA is determined the position of the edge intersection measured perpendicular to the DA can be determined with sufficient precision (1/8 of pixel size) after firing only three rays. In general not more that four additional rays have to be fired to antialias an edge (17, 18).

RESULTS

All algorithms explained in the previous section have been implemented in a FORTRAN 77 program and tested on a Digital Equipment Corporation VAX-11/750 (4 MB CPU) under the VMS operating system.

The computational cost for 3DDDA of moving from one cell to another was initially 72.3 microseconds. After further optimization, which involved removal of all subroutine calls, substitution of one-dimensional arrays for multi-dimentional arrays, and introduction on integer logic into the main part of the algorithm, this cost was further decreased to 20.6 microseconds. This means that our current 3DDDA is able to generate the cell index an order of magnitude faster (more than 13 times) than the traversal algorithm proposed by Glassner (25) can find coordinates to the next cell. (We implemented Glassner's algorithm for simple spatial enumeration, in order to make a comparison. It requires 276.2 microseconds for that operation, also in Fortran on the VAX-11/750.)

3DDDA introduced here has to be initialized. The initialization process requires 591 microseconds. For 512x512 resolution, it will take less that 3 minutes to initialize 3DDDA for all pixels in the screen. (See starting point of line (A) in Fig.7.) The total overhead time varies with the number of cells and is shown in Fig.7 by line (A). Clearly, this time is independent from number of objects, shape of objects and degree of coherency of the scene.

On the other hand overhead time for octree encoding is quite heavily dependent on all these factors. In order to compare the overhead time for octree encoding and spatial enumeration, the total number of cells generated by the octree encoding program was recalculated to find the average number of cells along one axis. The overhead times correspond to the situation where all rays are traced throughout encoded domain without termination on pierced objects. Line (C) in Fig.7 represents overhead time for the original object (see Fig.8). Line (G) corresponds to the scene where all 7011 atoms of the original model were dispersed uniformly by the use of random numbers.

It is clear from the above results that the octree structure is very sensitive to lack of coherency and is put at a further disadvantage in comparison to spatial enumeration. It was expected that traversal of the octree structure would be more expensive than that of spatial enumeration. On the other hand, however, it was also expected that octree encoding would have an advantage for cases where high scene coherency results in a large percentage of empty areas. (The object in Fig.8. occupies less than 9% of the hexahedron domain in which it is embodied. In spatial enumeration in general it is possible to tailor overall domain dimensions to fit the shape of the scene.

This will result in a smaller number of cells. However, for comparison purposes the same hexahedron domain is used for spatial enumeration and octree encoding). In octree encoding smaller cells converge to the object surface (13) and empty areas are encoded in bigger cells. This means that in comparison to spatial enumeration a ray can reach the surface of an object by traversing fewer cells and the probability of hitting an object within the HETERO cell is bigger. Experimental results, however, suggest that all this was outpaced by the cost of vertical traversing of the octree. As was noted in previous section, vertical traversing must be performed after at most four cells are identified through 3DDDA during horizontal traversing. The average necessity of vertical traversing is, however, much higher since it may be needed as soon as one horizontal step is performed. Depending on the depth of the octree it may be quite often necessary to perform several steps of ascending and descending the octree.

From the above discussion it should be clear that the very high overhead time precludes any speed advantage of octree over spatial enumeration. This was confirmed by experiment. (Compare lines (B) and (E) with (D) and (H) in Fig.7.) Experiments show that there exists a clear optimum number of cells in spatial enumeration and an optimum number of levels for octree encoding for which the calculation time reaches its minimum. This minimum turns out to correspond to a relatively limited number of cells which can be easily handled by most contemporary minicomputers or workstations. We performed a considerable number of experiments in order to find how this optimum number of cells is affected by such factors as scene coherency, object size and number of objects. It is impossible to present all timing data, here, but the results presented in Fig.7. were found to be fairly representative also for all other cases. In particular we have found that although scene coherency influences to some extent, the overall calculation time, as does the object size, it does, however, not influence the optimum number of cells. This optimum is slightly influenced by the number of objects and moves towards a smaller number of cells with decreasing number of objects.

The above experiments provide important hints to those who advocate pure octree with a considerable number of levels. Unless the octree encoded structure can be traversed quickly, pure octree encoding will not necessaryly speed up the calculation. At least in the present application the hybrid approach proved to be essential for obtaining a considerable speed improvement. Obviously traversing speed is not only influenced by the efficiency of the algorithm. It can be assumed that the same program run on a supercomputer, for example, or special purpose hardware would yield more than propotional improvement in speed because the overhead time decrease will move the optimum number of cells upwards resulting in better performance.

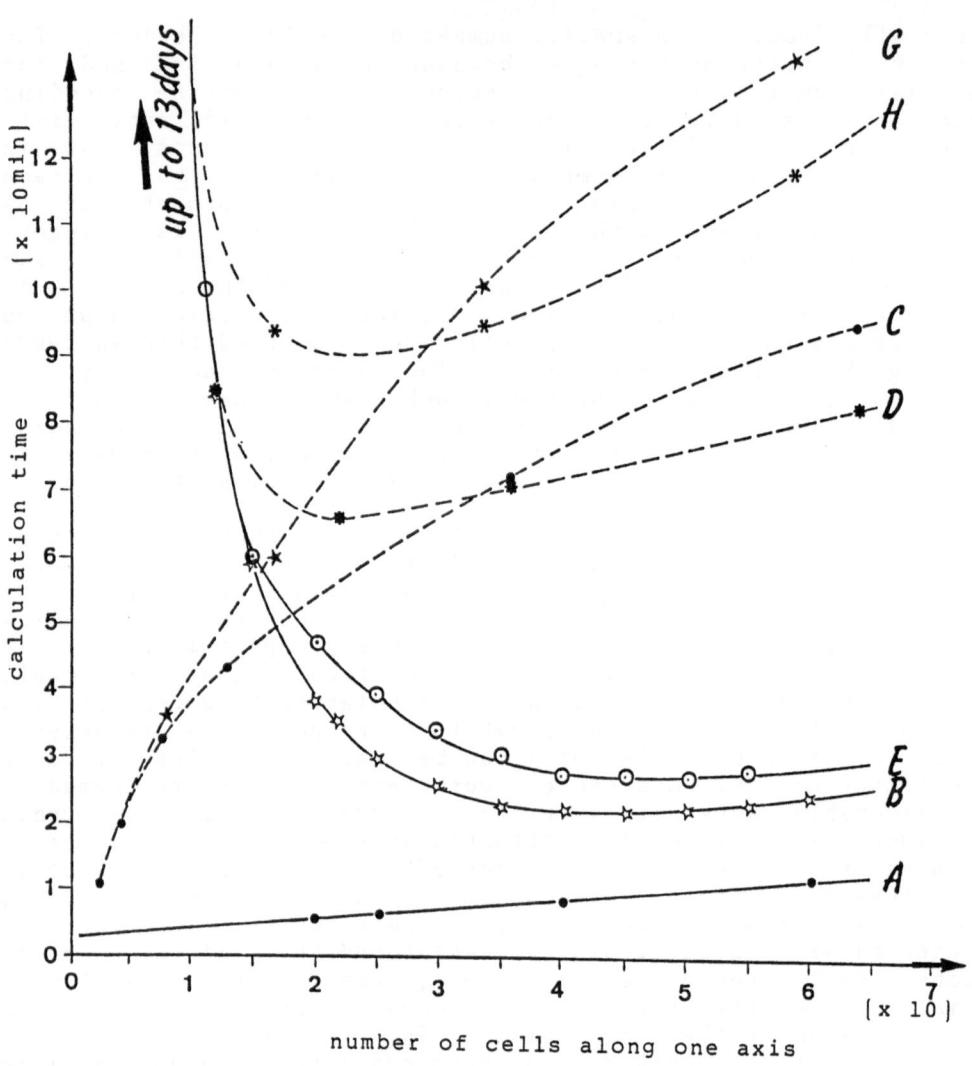

Fig.7. Calculation times for image in Fig.8

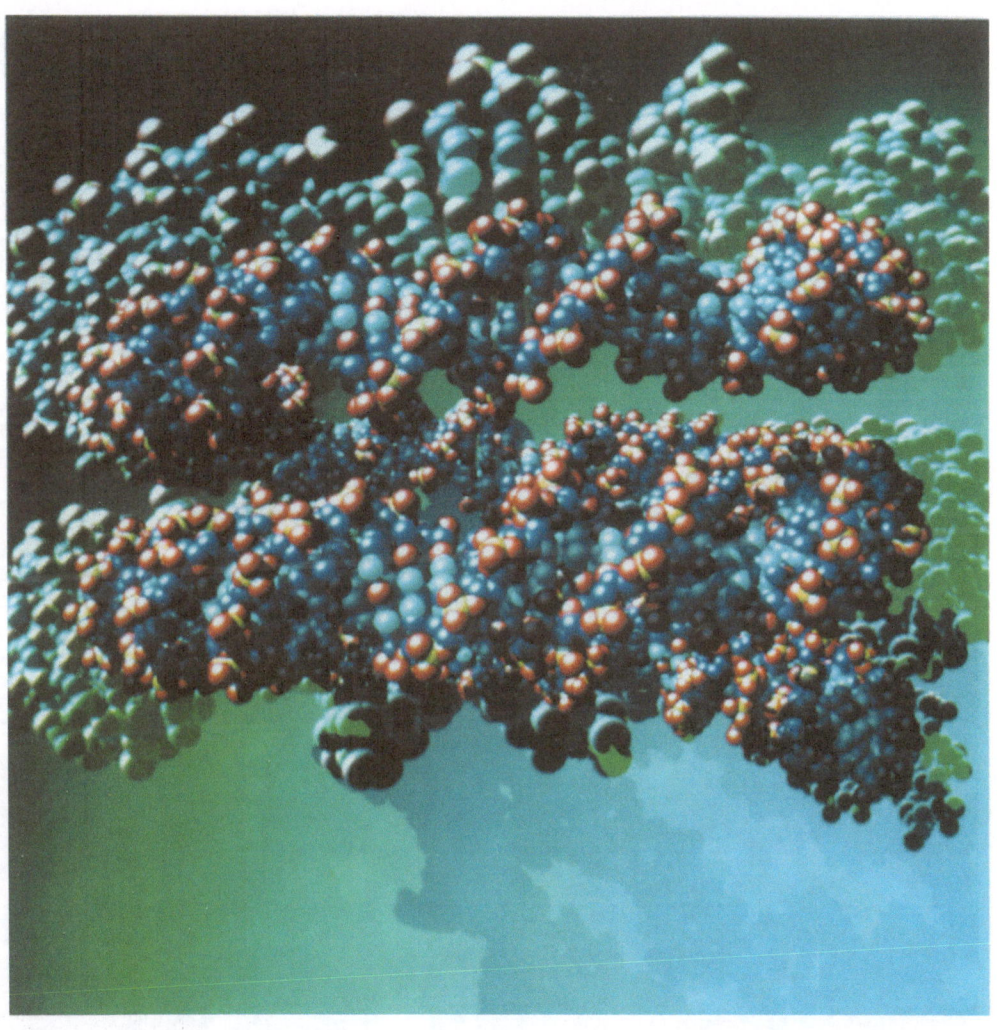

This DNA model contains 7011 atoms of various kinds (Coordinates were generated by Sussman and Trifonow). Behind the model a concave spherical surface is magnifying some of the atoms - almost all ray were spawned. The shadow of the molecule is cast on the spherical surface. The picture is antialiased. It took two hours to produce this image on VAX 11/750 using ARTS. Estimated calculation time by classical RT is one months. Timing data for depicting the model without ray spawning and shadow casting is presented in Fig.7.

Fig.8. Spherical DNA

This model was inspired by the structure depicted on the poster
advertising the present conference and exhibition. It is one
of the many models used for timing experiments in the
development of the algorithms presented in the current paper.
It contains 10584 objects. Including ray spawning and shadows
it took 2 hours and 15 minutes to generate this image on the
VAX 11/750. Estimated calculation time by classical RT is more
than a month (40 days).


Fig.9. "CG Tokyo '85"

Further experiments show that the calculation time is only very slightly influenced by the number of objects in the scene (actually this was the purpose of the present research). As a next step in evaluating the proposed algorithm are data structure, a comparison with a scan-line method was performed. The popular general purpose computer graphics package MOVIE.BYU was used. Objects were changed from spheres to hexahedrons. (MOVIE.BYU works with the boundary representation scheme, so approximateing the sphere by a number of polygons would put it at a disadvantage.) Results are presented in Fig.10. Unfortunately, because of the internal limitations of MOVIE.BYU it cannot handle more that 8192 polygons unless the number of bits in certain data structures is increased; this corresponds to 1365 hexahedrons. From simple extrapolation, however, it can be deducted that the presented Accelerated Ray Tracing Technique (ART) is as fast as MOVIE.BYU when the number of objects in the scene approaches 1600. Beyond that limit, ART actually becomes faster. For example, 16000 hexahedrons are calculated within 17 minutes by ART, whereas it would take about two hours to calculate the same scene using MOVIE.BYU. The authours aware of the obvious fact that the above cited timing sata will be influenced when calculation is performed for higher resolution. Our results of antialiasing, however, suggest that there is hardly any need to go to higher resolution than the current one (512x512). See Fig.8 and Fig.9.

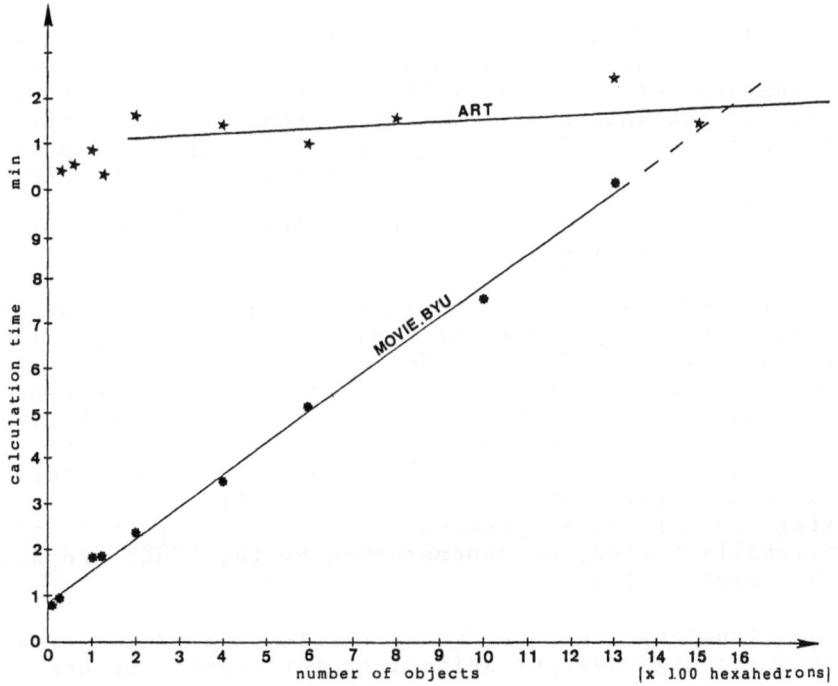

Fig.10. Calculation time: ART vs. MOVIE.BYU

CONCLUSION

This paper introduces a general method significantly improving the computational speed of a ray tracing program. This is achieved essentially due to the following two factors. First, the number of objects which have to be checked for possible intersection with the ray is practically limited to those objects which lie on the trajectory of the ray. Second, the first object intersected by the ray is the 'visible' one (the one closest to the ray's origin) so the ray can be terminated on that object and processing of other objects lying on the ray's trajectory is naturally skipped. The above scheme is realized by imposing on the object auxiliary structures (spatial enumeration or octree). In order to provide fast tracing of the ray trajectory within these structures a traversing tool in the form of 3DDDA has been developed. Experimental results show that the processing time is practically constant, i.e. independent of the number of objects in the scene. This constitutes a most significant improvement of a method which previously, because of its extraordinary processing time, was practically barred from processing complex scenes involving large numbers of objects. Also a computationally efficient antialiasing method based on the authors' Adjustable Fourier Window (17) has been introduced and tested.


FUTURE DEVELOPMENT

A fast rendering system for CSG (constructive solid geometry, see ref. 36, 37, 38, 39, 40) is under development. It is based on extensions of the algorithm presented in this paper. Encoding for spatial enumeration is already fast. However, by further exploration of the 'generative' approach presented here, we expect to achieve an order of magnitude improvement in speed. In particular, to speed up volumetric Boolean operations during encoding, the notion of 3DDDA will be extended for generating 3D surfaces.

The graphics display system described in an earlier paper by the present authors and Perrott (18) is now being modified to support ray tracing. The TMS 32010 digital signal processors will be arranged in a parallel processing configuration and each processor will have a private memory of 256 kilobytes, in which to store the segment and spatial enumeration data. The speed of a single TMS 32010 in this application is expected to be roughly comparable with that of the VAX 750. A system employing 32 or more processors can be expected to be proportionally faster, as demonstrated by the LINKS project of Osaka University (19).

These developments are expected to result in a system suitable for producing high quality animations for complex scenes at a relatively low cost.

ACKNOWLEDGMENT

The authors would like to express their gratitude to Mr. Christopher G. Perrott, chief engineer at Graphica Computer Corporation for his advice and fruitful critical remarks concerning the content of this paper, help in optimizing the code, and finally for the proofreading of the paper. Authors are also thankful to Mr. T. Tanaka for testing and interfacing the algorithms presented here and incorporating them into a ray tracing and solid modeling program. Dr. Nelson Max of Lawrence Livermore Laboratory provided us with various DNA models which were very helpful in testing our algorithms. We extend our thanks to Dr. David A. Field for carefully reviewing our paper.

REFERENCES

1. Steven M. Rubin, Turner Whitted,
   A 3-Dimensional Representation for Fast Rendering of Complex Scenes
   1980 ACM 0-89791-021-4/80/0700-0110
2. Turner Whitted,
   An Improved Illumination Model for Shaded Display,
   Communications of the ACM, June 1980, Vol.23, No.6
3. Peter R. Atherton,
   A Method of Interactive Visualization of CAD Surface Models on a Color Video Display,
   Computer Graphics, Vol.15, No.3, August 1981
4. Roy A. Hall and Donald P. Greenberg,
   A Testbed for Realistic Image Synthesis,
   IEEE CG&A, Nov, 1983
5. John Amanatides,
   Ray Tracing with Cones,
   Computer Graphics, Vol.18, No.3, July 1983
6. Hank Weghorst, Gary Hooper, and Donald P. Greenberg,
   Improved Computational Methods for Ray Tracing,
   ACM Transactions on Graphics, Vol.3, No.1, January 1984
7. Paul S. Heckbert, Pat Hanrahan,
   Beam Tracing Polygonal Objects,
   Computer Graphics Vol.18, No.3, July 1984
8. Robert L. Cook, Thomas Porte, Loren Carpenter,
   Distributed Ray Tracing
   Computer Graphics Vol.18, No.3, July 1984
9. Mark Dippe, John Swensen,
   An Adaptive Subdivision Algorithm and Parallel Architecture for Realistic Image Synthesis,
   Computer Graphics Vol.18, No.3, July 1984
10. C.B. Jones
    A New Approach to the 'Hidden Line' Problem,
    The Computer Journal Vol.14, No.3
11. Louis J. Doctor, John G. Torborg,
    Display Techniques for Octree-Encoded Objects,
    IEEE CG&A, July 1981

12. Chris L. Jackins and Steven L. Tanimoto,
    Oct-Trees and Their Use in Representing Three-dimensional
    Objects,
    Computer Graphics and Image Processing 14, 249-270 (1980)
13. Donald Meagher,
    Geometric Modelling Using Octree Encoding,
    Computer Graphics and Image Processing 19, 129-147 (1982)
14. K. Yamaguchi, T.L. Kunii, K. Fujimura, H. Toriya
    Octree-Related Data Structures and Algorythms
    IEEE CG&A, January 1984
15. Mark A. Yerry and Mark S. Shephard,
    A Modified Quadtree Approach to Finite Element Mesh
    Generation,
    IEEE CG&A, January/February 1983
16. K. Fujimura, H. Toriya, K. Yamaguchi, and T. L. Kunii,
    An Enhanced Oct-tree Data Structure and Operations for
    Solid Modelling,
    Technical Report 83-01, Dept. of Information Science,
    University of Tokyo
17. Akira Fujimoto and Kansei Iwata,
    Jag-Free Images on Raster Displays,
    IEEE CG&A, December 1983
18. Akira Fujimoto, Christopher G. Perrott and Kansei Iwata,
    A 3-D Graphics Display System with Depth Buffer and
    Pipeline Processor,
    IEEE CG&A, Vol.4, No.6, June 1984
19. Osaka University CG Group,
    LINKS-1,
    PIXEL '83 5-6 No.12, page 73-92 (in Japanese)
20. Tsuyoshi Yamamoto
    Personal Computer Graphics (in Japanese)
    CQ Publishing Corporation 1983
21. Naoki Hashimoto, Edward Lau,
    TIPS-1 '77 Version SYSTEM MANUAL,
    Computer Aided Manufacturing - International, Inc.
22. Paolo Sabella and Michael J. Wozny,
    Toward Fast Color-Shaded Images of CAD/CAM Geometry,
    IEEE CG&A, November 1983, page 65
23. Tomoyuki Nishita, Eihachiro Nakamae,
    Half-tone Representation of 3-D Objects Illuminated by
    Area Sources or Polyhedron Sources
    Proceedings of the IEEE Computer Society's
    International Computer Software and Application Conference
    (Compsac),
    November 7-11, 1983
24. You-Dong Liang and Brian A. Barsky,
    A New Concept and Method for Line Clipping,
    ACM Transactions on Graphics, Vol.3, No.1, January 1984,
    page 1-22
25. Andrew S. Glassner,
    Space Subdivision for Fast Ray Tracing,
    IEEE CG&A, October 1984
26. Nelson L. Max,
    Computer Representation of Molecular Surfaces
    IEEE CG&A, August, 1983

27. Hitoshi Matsumoto, Kouichi Murakami,
    Ray-Tracing with Octree Data Structure (in Japanese)
    Proceedings of 28th Information Processing Conference 1983
28. David F. Rogers and Linda M. Ryback
    On an Efficient Line-Clipping Algorythm
    CG IEEE, January 1985
29. G. Hamlin, Jr., and C.W. Gear,
    Raster Scan Hidden Surface Algorythm Techniques
    Computer Graphics (Proc. Siggraph '77), Vol.11, No.2
    pp. 206-213
30. I.E. Sutherland, R.F. Sproull, and R.A. Schumacker,
    A Characterization of Ten Hidden Surface Algorythms",
    Computing Surveys, Vol.6, No.1, Mar. 1974, pp.1-55
31. W. Jack Bouknight,
    A Procedure for Generation of Three-dimensional  Half-toned
    Computer Graphics Representations,
    Communications of the ACM, September 1970
32. Henri Gouraud,
    Continous Shading of Curved Surfaces,
    IEEE Transactions on Computers, June 1971.
33. Bui Tuong Phong,
    Illumination for Computer Generated Pictures,
    Communications od the ACM, Vol.18, No.6, June 1975,
    pp. 311-317
34. Kenetsu Hanabusa,
    Animation with CRAY-1 (Japanese)
    PIXEL 1983 7-8, No. 13
35. Jon Davis, Michael J. Bailey, David C. Anderson,
    Projecting Realistic Images of Geometric Solids,
    Computers in Mechanical Engineering /August 1982/
36. Peter R. Atherton,
    A  Scan-line  Hidden  Surface  Removal  Procedure  for
    Constructive Solid Geometry,
    ACM Computer Graphics, Vol.17, No.3, July 1983, pp. 73-83
37. Ken H. Sears and Alan E. Middleditch,
    Set-Theoretic Volume Model Evaluation and Picture-Plane
    Coherence,
    IEEE CG&A March 1984, pp. 41-46
38. TIPS Working Group
    TIPS-1 (Technical  Information  Processing  System  for
    CAD/CAM) Program for Continuous Tone Image Generation (scan
    section shifting method) (in Japanese),
    Hokkaido University, Faculty of Mechanical Engineering,
    Precision Machinery Dpt., 17 January 1985
39. Roth, S.D.,
    Ray Casting for Modelling Solids,
    Computer Graphics and Image Processing, No.18, 1982,
    pp. 109-104
40. Kouchi Murakami and Hitoshi Matsumoto,
    Method for Rendering CSG (Japanese),
    Proceedings of 27th Information Processing Conference 1983

Chapter 2
# Graphics Standardization and Packaging

# A Formalization for the Specification and Systematic Generation of Computer Graphics Systems

Tamiya Onodera and Satoru Kawai

Department of Information Science, Faculty of Science, The University of Tokyo, 3-1, Hongo 7-chome, Bunkyo-ku, Tokyo, 113 Japan

*ABSTRACT*

A formalization of graphical processes in computer graphics systems is presented in terms of functions and their system of axioms. The concept of the viewing pipeline is formalized as operation sequence which is a sequential composition of graphical elementary operations. The formalization includes two kinds of operation sequences which are used as the formal specifications of graphics systems and display devices. In order to generate a graphics system using a display device, we introduced the concept of functionality-preserving transformation of operation sequences in terms of various types of commutation among primitive operations. A type of transformation, what is called extraction, plays a central role in the generation algorithm.

## 1. Introduction

The Graphical Kernel System (GKS)[1] [4] which is an international standard presents an integrated system model for the world of computer graphics. Various concepts used in graphics such as geometric transformation, clipping, attribute, dynamism of displayed pictures, are systematically combined and reorganized in GKS. Among others, much efforts have been devoted to virtualize the physical graphic devices whose capabilities were so widely spread out that the conventional simple treatment using the concept of logical devices did not work. The solution adopted in GKS was to raise the level of the logical devices very high to the point where they are supposed to have almost all the capabilities required as a single graphic terminal. This type of logical devices, named *workstations* in GKS, has therefore the inevitable central importance both in defining and implementing GKS. For example, only 5 out of 110 GKS functions are workstation independent (level 2c, excluding inquiries).

As usual with the case of converting physical devices into logical ones, it is required to implement some interfacing software in order for a set of physical devices to be used collectively as a single workstation of an implementation of GKS. This software, called a *workstation driver* in this paper, tends to be very large and complicated if the capabilities of the target physical devices are either very low or different from what is required by GKS. This is the reason why much efforts have to be concentrated on the implementation of workstation drivers when a GKS is to be developed.

In this paper, we set a target on scheme in which a workstation driver is automatically generated by the use of various information such as the required characteristics of the workstation and the static and dynamic capabilities of physical devices. In order to realize the target, much formalization of the behavior of the workstation, or even of GKS itself, will be required[2] . The formalizations. of *operations* on graphical objects, such as polylines and texts, and *operation sequence* introduced in this paper are believed to be some of them. The concept of extraction which plays an important role in our formalization will be the key to realize the automatic generation of workstation drivers.

## 2. Realization of Workstation Drivers

Workstation drivers are the programs which realize the GKS workstation interface by the use of the functions of actual graphics devices (c.f. Figure 1). From the viewpoint of graphical data flow, workstation drivers can also be considered as the implementation of the logical viewing pipeline defined in GKS.

In our research, we set a requirement that the workstation drivers are to be implemented in a systematic way in which the capabilities of the physical device are utilized as much as possible.

For this purpose, we carried out a functional treatment of the concept of a viewing pipeline[3] which is modeled as a sequential composition of elementary graphical operations. Each operation in a viewing pipeline has a set of parameters which corresponds to its operating environment. For example, the operation of workstation transformation has two parameters which specify the window and the viewport limits.

A set of operation sequences thus defined is expected to be a formal specification of the output function of the graphics system in question. Our scheme of systematic implementation of GKS systems begins with the formalization of the capabilities of the GKS workstation as logical operation sequences (LOSes). In the next step, the capabilities of the physical devices used for the implementation of the workstation are formalized as physical operation sequences (POSes).

If the LOS for an output primitive happened to be the same as the corresponding POS, the implementation problem becomes trivial. The problem arises when the two operation sequences differ. The functional differences between them are classified as follows.

(1) The difference in the capabilities of an elementary operation. The operation in POS, corresponding to the one in LOS, may be missing, or inferior to the latter regarding to the range of parameters or the range of the properties of the input graphical objects. For example, there are devices that have no line width or fewer line types than required for the workstation implementation. Another example is the situation in which the target device can handle only the convex polygons for filling, while GKS workstations are required to process arbitrary closed polygonal areas.

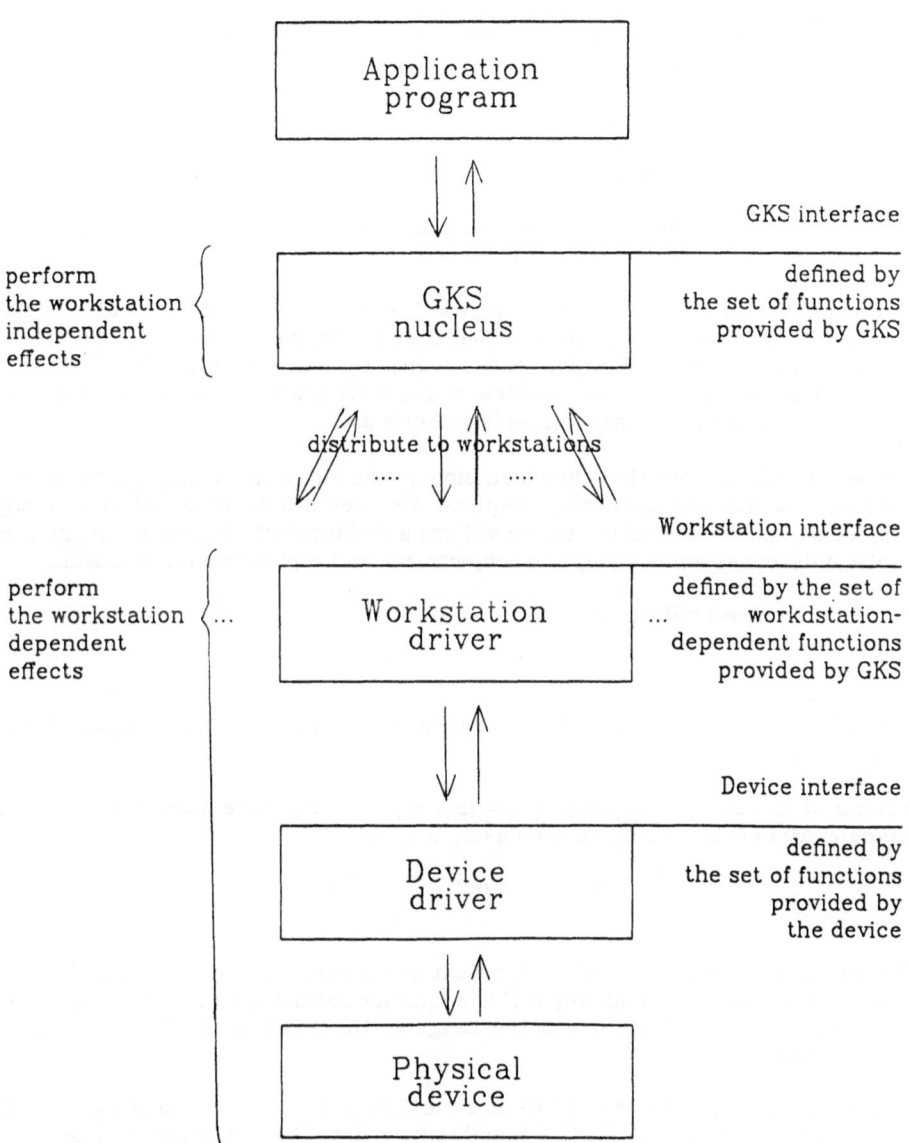

Figure 1   The layer model of a GKS system

(2)   The difference in the order of the composition of the elementary operations.

(3)   The difference in the way of value assignment for the parameters of elementary operations. The dependencies among the parameter values may be different in LOS and in POS.

(4)   The difference in the arrangement of temporary data storage (segment storage) within the operation sequence.

In the implementation algorithm proposed here, the original LOS which is not compatible with the POS is so modified that it can be divided into two subsequences the tail part of which can be directly realized with the POS. The modification is based on the scheme of stepwise transformation in which the function of the operation sequences is preserved.

It is worthwhile to note that the discussion on the equivalence of the functions of operation sequences inevitably requires the definitions of equalities among graphical objects. In this paper, we will use a definition of equality which ignores subtle differences among graphical objects, without any detailed discussion.

## 3.  Definitions and notations

### 3.1.  Pipeline function

Definition: Let $X$ be a set. $X^{*}$ denotes the set of all the *ordered-tuples* of elements of $X$.

When $x_1 = (x_{11}, x_{12}, \ldots, x_{1n})$ and $x_2 = (x_{21}, x_{22}, \ldots, x_{2m})$ are elements of $X^{*}$, the *concatenation* of $x_1$ and $x_2$, written as $x_1 \oplus x_2$, is

$$(x_{11}, \ldots, x_{1n}, x_{21}, \ldots, x_{2m}) .$$

■

Definition: $P$ is called a *pipeline function* whose range and domain are the sets $X$ and $Y$ respectively if and only if $P$ is a function from $X$ into $Y^{*}$. It is written as $P : X \to Y$ when the domain and the range of the pipeline function $P$ is to be shown explicitly. ■

Definition: The *composition* of two pipeline functions $P_1 : X \to Y$ and $P_2 : Y \to Z$, written as $P_1 \bigcirc P_2$, is the pipeline function from $X$ to $Z$ which maps $x \in X$ to

$$P_2(y_1) \oplus , \ldots , \oplus P_2(y_n)$$

where

$$P_1(x) = (y_1, \ldots, y_n) \in Y^{*}.$$

■

It is worthwhile to note that the composition is left-associative, and the component pipeline functions are applied left to right.

## 3.2. Operation, generic operation and operation sequence

Graphical objects fall into several groups. Each group is called a *graphical set* . LINE (polylines), MARK (polymarkers), TEXT (texts), FILL (fillareas) and DISPLINE (displayed lines) are examples of graphical sets we treat in this paper.

**Definition:** An *operation* is a pipeline function whose range and domain are graphical sets. An operation has some *parameters* corresponding to the environment under which the operations work. An operation $A$ with a set of parameters $\alpha$ is written as $A_\alpha$. ∎

In case there is no ambiguity, we will simply write $A$, instead of $A_\alpha$. Also, a set of parameters of an operation will be simply said a parameter of an operation, collectively. When the domain and the range of $A_\alpha$ are the same and when the function $A_\alpha$ is equal to the identity function, we will write $A_\alpha$ as $A_{\alpha_{unity}}$.

**Definition:** Let

$$G = \{g_1, \ldots, g_n\}$$

be a set of graphical sets and

$$P = \{p_1 : g_1 \to g_1, \cdots, p_n : g_n \to g_n\}$$

be a set of operations. A function $K_\kappa : G \to P$ is called a *generic operation* with a set of parameters $\kappa$ if $K_\kappa(g_i) = p_i$ for $i = 1..n$. The domain of a generic operation G is called its *operating set*. An operation $K_\kappa(g)$ is called the *g-instance* of $K_\kappa$. ∎

**Example:** The workstation transformation $\omega$ for the set LINE is an operation with two parameters window and viewport. In this case, it is written as

$$\omega_{[window,viewport]} : LINE \to LINE .$$

This operation $\omega$ is the LINE-instance of a generic operation $\Omega$ with two parameters window and viewport, i.e.,

$$\omega_{[window,viewport]} = \Omega_{[window,viewport]}(LINE)$$

The operating set of $\Omega$ includes LINE, MARK, FILL and TEXT. ∎

**Definition:** An *operation sequence* is a cascade of operations. From the functional viewport, an operation sequence is equivalent to the composition of the corresponding pipeline functions. ∎

An operation sequence is said *simple* if there is no duplication in the component operations. The operation sequences considered in this paper are all assumed to be simple.

Let $C$ be an operation and $S$ be an operation sequence.

**Definition:** If $C$ is included in $S$, $C$ is called a *component* of $S$. The set of the components of $S$ is written as $Comp(S)$.
When $C$ is a component of $S$, we will simply write $C \in S$ instead of $C \in Comp(S)$. ∎

**Definition:** A particular instance of $C$ included in $S$ is denoted as $C[S]$. ∎

This notation is used when more than one instance of the same operation is to be discussed simultaneously.

**Definition:** The *position* of $C$ in $S$, $Pos(C[S])$, is the ordinal number of $C$ in $S$, counted from the top (the leftmost) component. ∎

## 3.3. Transformation of operation sequences

**Definition:** Two operations $A_\alpha : X \to X$ and $B_\beta : X \to X$ are said *commutative* if the relation

$$A_\alpha \bigcirc B_\beta = B_\beta \bigcirc A_\alpha$$

holds, and are said *pseudo-commutative* if the relation

$$A_\alpha \bigcirc B_\beta = B_{f(\beta)} \bigcirc A_\alpha$$

holds, where $f$ is called a compensation function that "adjusts" the parameter $\beta$ of the operation $B_\beta$ to compensate the effect of the changing of the order of composition of $A_\alpha$ and $B_\beta$. ∎

**Definition:** The operation $B_\beta : X \to Y$ is called a *commutator* of the operations $A_\alpha : X \to X$ and $C_\gamma : Y \to Y$ if the relation

$$A_\alpha \bigcirc B_\beta = B_\beta \bigcirc C_\gamma$$

holds, and is called a *pseudo-commutator* of the operations $A$ and $C$ if the relation

$$A_\alpha \bigcirc B_\beta = B_{f(\beta)} \bigcirc C_\gamma$$

holds, where $f$ is a compensation function. ∎

Note that $f$ is dependent on $A_\alpha$ and $C_\gamma$.

Typical commutators are those of instances of generic operations, whose relations are of the form

$$P_\pi(X) \bigcirc B_\beta = B_{f(\beta)} \bigcirc P_\pi(Y)$$

where $B_\beta : X \to Y$ is an operation, $P_\pi$ is a generic operation whose operating set contains $X$ and $Y$, and $f$ is some compensation function. In this case, we can say $f$ is a function dependent on $P_\pi$ rather than $P_\pi(X)$ or $P_\pi(Y)$.

The commutativities defined above are naturally extended to those for operation sequences. For example, an operation $A_\alpha$ is called a pseudo-commutator of operation sequences $S$ and $T$ if the relation

$$S \bigcirc A_\alpha = A_{f(\alpha)} \bigcirc T$$

holds, where $f$ is dependent on $T$. Note that no compensation function is introduced into the parameters of operations in $T$.

**Definition:** Let $S_{i,j}$ be an operation sequence

$$S_i \bigcirc S_{i+1} \bigcirc \cdots \bigcirc S_j$$

embedded in a larger operation sequence

$$S = S_1 \bigcirc S_2 \bigcirc \cdots \bigcirc S_n \quad (1 \leq i \leq j \leq n)$$

The operation $S_k$ in $S$ is said **m-extractable in the strict sense** if $S_k$ and $S_{m,k-1}$ are either commutative or pseudo-commutative, and is said **m-extractable in wider sense** if $S_k$ is a commutator or pseudo-commutator of $S_{m,k-1}$ and some operation sequence $T$. If $S_k$ is m-extractable in the strict sense, we can transform

$$S = S_{1,k-1} \bigcirc S_k \bigcirc S_{k+1,n}$$

into

$$S' = S_{1,m-1} \bigcirc S_k' \bigcirc S_{m,k-1} \bigcirc S_{k+1,n}$$

where the compensation function in $S_k'$ is dependent on $S_m, \ldots, S_{k-1}$ ,if any. If $S_k$ is m-extractable in wider sense, we can transform

$$S = S_{1,k-1} \bigcirc S_k \bigcirc S_{k+1,n}$$

into

$$S' = S_{1,m-1} \bigcirc S_k' \bigcirc T \bigcirc S_{k+1,n}$$

where the compensation function in $S_k'$ is dependent on $T$, if any. These types of transformations are called **extraction**. •

Before we conclude this section, we present the definitions of several terms and notations concerning the operation sequence transformations.

**Definition:** Let $S$ and $T$ be operation sequences. The predicate $Perm(S,T)$ asserts that $S$ can be transformed into $T$ with only the (pseudo-)commutative relations. •

**Definition:** Let $S = C_1 \bigcirc, \ldots, \bigcirc C_n$ be an operation sequence. When the operation sequence, which is generated by the removal of $C_i$ from $S$ ($1 \leq i \leq n$), is well-defined, it is written as $Rmv(S,C_i)$. •

**Example:** When $op \in S$ is 1-extractable in the strict sense in the operation sequence $S$, we can transform $S$ into $op \bigcirc Rmv(S,op)$ without any change in their functionality. •

## 4. Logical operation sequences

### 4.1. Three generic operations

First, we show below three generic operations, whose instances are used to compose LOSes. All the operating sets of them are {LINE, MARK, TEXT, FILL}.

**(G1)** $T_{[mat]}^g$ transforms the input graphical objects by the segment transformation, the transformation matrix of which is specified by the parameter mat. •

**(G2)** $T_{[wind,view]}^{\omega}$ transforms the input graphical objects by the workstaion transformation, whose window and viewport limits are specified by the parameters wind and view, respectively. •

**(G3)** $C_{[rect]}$ clips the input graphical objects against the clipping rectangle which is specified by the parameter rect. It is not always assumed that the rectangle is parallel to an axis. The range of the possible values of a parameter is taken into consideration in Section 6.1. •

## 4.2. Operation sequence schema

We treat only the line-oriented devices in this paper. The line-oriented devices are that type of graphical devices in which the visualization of any primitive is achieved by converting it into lines at some point of the viewing pipeline. All of the LOSes and the POSes, which we build up here, follow the following schema, on which the above restriction reflects. Assume that an element in a graphical set $X$ is to be processed.

$$S = G(S) \bigcirc V(S) \bigcirc L(S) \bigcirc L^{frame}$$

where

i) $G(S) : X \to X$ is an operation sequence consisting of X-instances of the generic operations, $T^\sigma$, $T^\omega$ and $C$, defined in section 4.1. It is called an *X-sequence*,

ii) $V(S) = V^X : X \to LINE$ is an operation which converts the primitive X into lines. It is called a *v-operation*. All of the LOSes and the POSes, which we treat in this paper, have only one v-operation. For the operation sequence of LINE (polyline), $V^X$ is the identity function,

iii) $L(S) : LINE \to LINE$ is called an *L-sequence*. It is composed of several operations whose range and domain are LINE. Note that an L-sequence is not a LINE-sequence because the latter is composed of only the LINE-instances of the generic operations and, on the other hand, the former can be composed of the arbitrary operations from LINE to LINE,

iv) $L^{frame} : LINE \to DISPLINE$ is the special operation of visualization of the primitive LINE, which is defined as follows.

(DL1) $L^{frame}_{[color]} : LINE \to DISPLINE$ takes one parameter color ,which specifies the color value of the input lines, to generate the visible representations of the input lines. ∎

For any LOS, the X-sequence is further decomposed into

$$T^\sigma(X) \bigcirc T^\omega(X) \bigcirc C(X) .$$

Note that the line-oriented devices do not always mean the vector devices. Almost all graphics devices have some line-oriented interfaces, irrespective of their physical functions.

## 4.3. Logical operation sequences

We present the LOSes for all the primitives, although the other ways of constructing them might be possible.

**(PL) Polyline operation sequence**

$$T^\sigma(LINE) \bigcirc T^\omega(LINE) \bigcirc C(LINE) \bigcirc V^{LINE} \bigcirc L^{type} \bigcirc L^{wdth} \bigcirc L^{frame}$$

(PL1) $V^{LINE} : LINE \to LINE$ is the identity function. ∎

(PL2) $L^{type}_{[refp,lpat,psiz]} : LINE \to LINE$ generates line segments for each of the input lines by the following rules.

(a)  The line pattern specified by the parameter lpat is scaled until its size is equal to psiz.

(b)  The scaled line pattern is replicated from the reference point refp along the input line. If the reference point is not on the input line, then the pedal of the perpendicular from the reference point to the input line is used instead.

(c)  All of the line segments between the two edge points of the input line are output, after clipping if necessary.

(PL3) $L^{wdth}_{[lwsf,nmlw]}$ : $LINE \rightarrow LINE$ generates the lines for each of the input lines by the following rules.

(a)  repeat (b) and (c) linewidth scale factor times. The number of times is specified as the parameter lwsf.

(b)  output the input line.

(c)  shift the input line by nominal linewidth specified as nmlw in the direction of its normal vector of the line.

∎

## (PM) Polymarker operation sequence

$$T^\sigma(MARK) \circ T^\omega(MARK) \circ C(MARK) \circ V^{MARK} \circ L^{frame}$$

(PM1) $V^{MARK}_{[mtyp,mssf,nmms]}$ : $MARK \rightarrow LINE$ generates the line segments simulating the marker mtyp for each of the input points by the following rules.

(a)  The marker specified by the parameter mtyp is mapped on the coordinates system whose unit length is nmms (nominal marker size).

(b)  The mapped maker is scaled by marker size scale factor times, specified by the parameter mssf. Then it is placed at the input points.

(c)  generate all the strokes simulating the markers.

∎

## (TX) Text operation sequence

$$T^\sigma(TEXT) \circ T^\omega(TEXT) \circ C(TEXT) \circ V^{TEXT} \circ C(LINE) \circ L^{frame}$$

Note that the operation sequence is intended to process and generate the stroke precision TEXT and that $C(TEXT)$ is only used as the identity operation and the actual clipping is performed by $C(LINE)$. The data of TEXT, which flow into the operation sequence defined above, is composed of text position, character height, character up vector and character right vector.

(TX1) $V^{TEXT}_{[str,font,chsz,chsp,txal,txpa]}$ : $TEXT \rightarrow LINE$ generates the strokes, which represent the character string str on the text font font, by using the character expansion factor chsz, the character spacing chsp, the text alignment txal and the text path txpa in the manner described in the GKS standard document. ∎

(FA) Fillarea operation sequence

$$T^{\sigma}(FILL) \bigcirc T^{\omega}(FILL) \bigcirc C(FILL) \bigcirc V^{FILL} \bigcirc L^{type} \bigcirc L^{frame}$$

(FA1) $V^{FILL}_{[isty,refp,fpat,psiz]}$ : $FILL \rightarrow LINE$ generates the typed-lines simulating the fillarea. The parameter refp, fpat and psiz are used in the similar way in the operation $L^{type}$. Note that the HOLLOW fillarea, the SOLID fillarea and the HATCHed fillarea are regarded as being included in the PATTERNed fillarea. ∎

## 5. Relations among primitive operations as a system of axioms

In this section, we show the relations among the *primitive* operations, which appear in the LOSes we have constructed. In any relation we present below, $f^{\sigma}$, $f^{\omega}$ and $f^{C}$ denote some functions dependent on $T^{\sigma}$, $T^{\omega}$ and $C$.

First, the (pseudo-) commutativities hold among the X-instances of the generic operations.

(RG1) $T^{\sigma}_{[mat]}(X) \bigcirc T^{\omega}_{[wind,view]}(X) = T^{\omega}_{[wind,view]}(X) \bigcirc T^{\sigma}_{[mat]}(X)$

(RG2) $T^{\sigma}_{[mat]}(X) \bigcirc C_{[rect]}(X) = C_{[f^{\sigma}(rect)]}(X) \bigcirc T^{\sigma}_{[mat]}(X)$

(RG3) $T^{\omega}_{[wind,view]}(X) \bigcirc C_{[rect]}(X) = C_{[f^{\omega}(rect)]} \bigcirc T^{\omega}_{[wind,view]}(X)$

Note that the relation RG2 shows the fact the segment transformation do not transform the clipping rectangle in GKS (c.f. Figure 2).

Second, a v-operation is a pseudo-commutator of an X-instance and a LINE-instance of any of three generic operation.

(RV1) $T^{\sigma}_{[mat]}(X) \bigcirc V^{X}_{a} = V^{X}_{f^{\sigma}(a)} \bigcirc T^{\sigma}_{[mat]}(LINE)$

(RV2) $T^{\omega}_{[wind,view]}(X) \bigcirc V^{X}_{a} = V^{X}_{f^{\omega}(a)} \bigcirc T^{\omega}_{[wind,view]}(LINE)$

(RV3) $C_{[rect]}(X) \bigcirc V^{X}_{a} = V^{X}_{f^{C}(a)} \bigcirc C_{[rect]}(LINE)$

For example, when $X = MARK$, the $f^{\omega}$ of the relation RV2 maps the parameter list [mtyp, mssf, nmms] to [mtyp, mssf, $f^{\omega}_{3}$(nmms)], where, $f^{\omega}_{3}$ is the inverse function of the operation $T^{\omega}(MARK)$. This is illustrated in Figure 3.

The third relation RV3 supposes some non-strict (or approximate) equalities mentioned in section 2, as illustrated in Figure 4.

Last, we proceed to relations about operations in the L-sequences. For any primitive X, the (pseudo-) commutativities hold between any two of all the

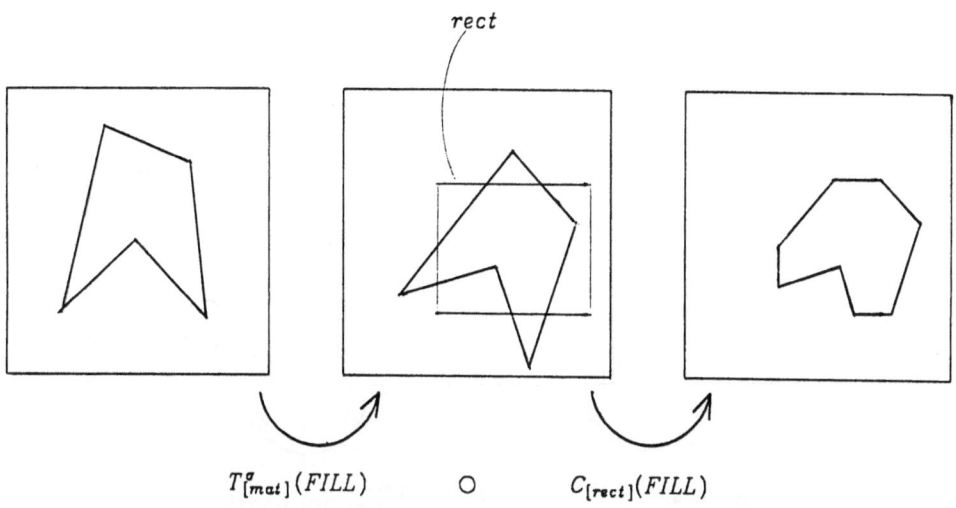

$$T^\sigma_{[mat]}(FILL) \quad \circ \quad C_{[rect]}(FILL)$$

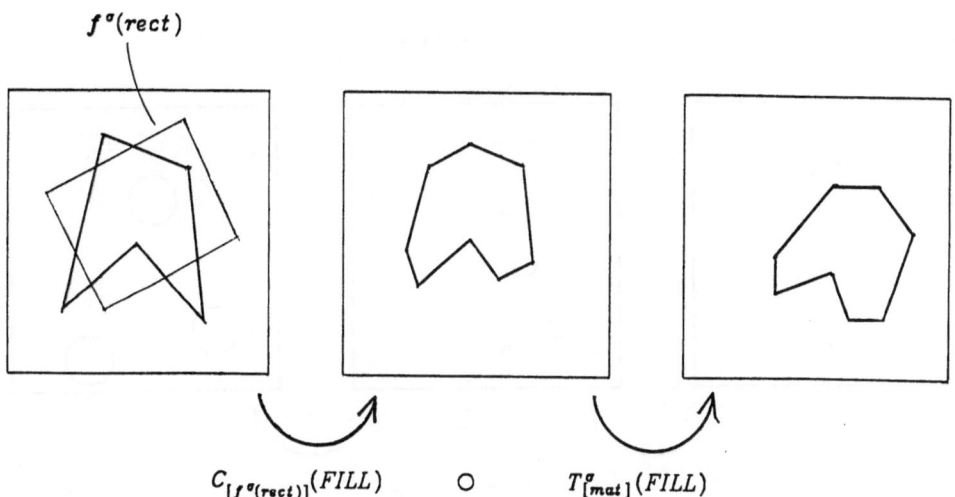

$$C_{[f^\sigma(rect)]}(FILL) \quad \circ \quad T^\sigma_{[mat]}(FILL)$$

Figure 2   The relation (RG2) (X = FILL)

generated on

the unit $nmms$

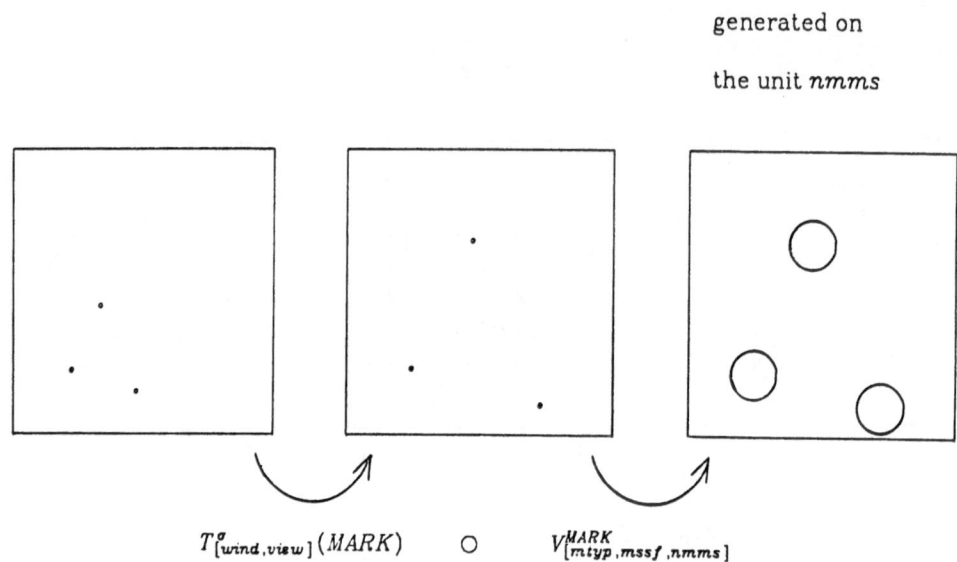

$T^{\sigma}_{[wind,view]}(MARK)$    O    $V^{MARK}_{[mtyp,mssf,nmms]}$

generated on

the unit $f^{\omega}(nmms)$

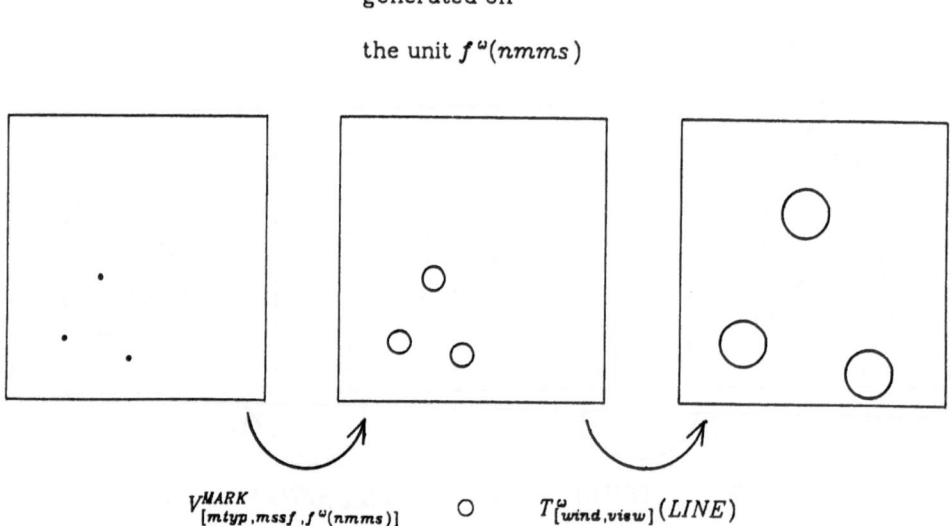

$V^{MARK}_{[mtyp,mssf,f^{\omega}(nmms)]}$    O    $T^{\omega}_{[wind,view]}(LINE)$

Figure 3    The relation (RV2) (X = MARK)

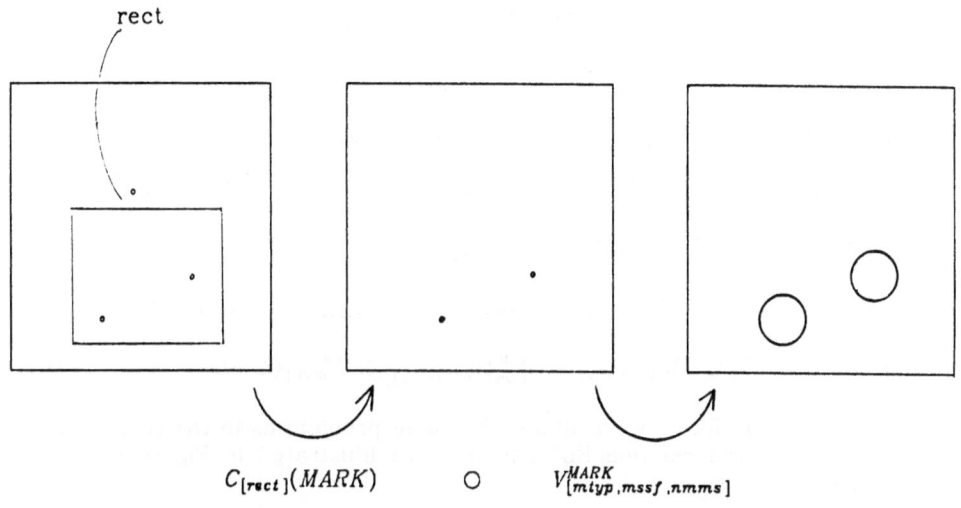

$$C_{[rect]}(MARK) \qquad \bigcirc \qquad V^{MARK}_{[mtyp,mssf,nmms]}$$

More precise picture

has been generated.

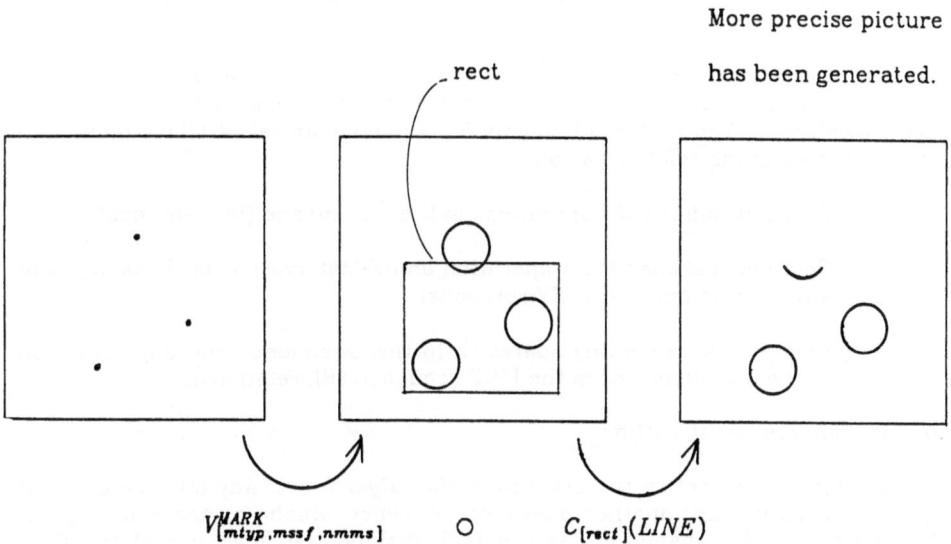

$$V^{MARK}_{[mtyp,mssf,nmms]} \qquad \bigcirc \qquad C_{[rect]}(LINE)$$

Figure 4   The relation (RV3) (X = MARK)

component operations in the L-sequence of X or the LINE-sequence.

(RL1) $L^{type}_{[refp,lpat,psiz]} \bigcirc L^{wdth}_{[lwsf,nmlw]} = L^{wdth}_{[lwsf,nmlw]} \bigcirc L^{type}_{[refp,lpat,psiz]}$

(RL2) $C_{[rect]}(LINE) \bigcirc L^{type}_{[refp,lpat,psiz]} = L^{type}_{[refp,lpat,psiz]} \bigcirc C_{[rect]}(LINE)$

(RL3) $C_{[rect]}(LINE) \bigcirc L^{wdth}_{[lwsf,nmlw]} = L^{wdth}_{[lwsf,nmlw]} \bigcirc C_{[rect]}(LINE)$

(RL4) $T^{\omega}_{[wind,view]}(LINE) \bigcirc L^{type}_{[refp,lpat,psiz]} = L^{type}_{[f^{\omega}(refp),lpat,f^{\omega}(psiz)]} \bigcirc T^{\omega}_{[wind,view]}(LINE)$

(RL5) $T^{\omega}_{[wind,view]}(LINE) \bigcirc L^{wdth}_{[lwsf,nmlw]} = L^{wdth}_{[lwsf,f^{\omega}(nmlw)]} \bigcirc T^{\omega}_{[wind,view]}(LINE)$

(RL6) $T^{\sigma}_{[mat]}(LINE) \bigcirc L^{type}_{[refp,lpat,psiz]} = L^{type}_{[f^{\sigma}(refp),lpat,f^{\sigma}(psiz)]} \bigcirc T^{\sigma}_{[mat]}(LINE)$

(RL7) $T^{\sigma}_{[mat]}(LINE) \bigcirc L^{wdth}_{[lwsf,nmlw]} = L^{wdth}_{[lwsf,f^{\sigma}(nmlw)]} \bigcirc T^{\sigma}_{[mat]}(LINE)$

As for the relation RL3, we encounter the same problem as in the relation RV3 (see Figure 5). The relation RL2 and RL7 are illustrated in Figure 6 and 7, respectively.

Note that the relations RL1-RL7 are all we need because $L^{type}$ and $L^{wdth}$ are the only two operations that appear in the L-sequences of any primitives in the LOSes defined in section 4. If more operations are in the L-sequence, the more relations must be provided.

The set of relations shown above can be regarded as a *system of axioms* for the composition operator $\bigcirc$ and primitive operations with respect to the LOSes we are considering. The system of axioms for a particular set of LOSes must contain all the following relations as ours.

* Relations among the operations in the X-sequence (RG-relations).

* Relations between the v-operation and X-instances or LINE-instances of any generic operation (RV-relations).

* Relations between any operation in the L-sequence and any operation in the L-sequence or in the LINE-sequence (RL-relations).

## 6. LOS conversion algorithm

We present in this section the *LOS conversion algorithm* . Any LOS is converted by the algorithm into another operation sequence which has the same operational effect and 'capabilities' as the LOS, making the most use of the POS. Some definitions precede the description of the algorithm.

### 6.1. Performances of operations and operation sequences

**Definition:** The *performance* of the operation $A_{\alpha}$, *Prf* $(A_{\alpha})$, is the set of possible values of $\alpha$. For the operation sequence $S = S_1 \bigcirc S_2 \bigcirc \ldots , \bigcirc S_n$, its performance is the list of performances of all the component operations of S - i.e., { Prf($S_1$), Prf($S_2$) , . . . , Prf($S_n$) }. The order of them is irrelevant because $S$ is assumed to be simple. ∎

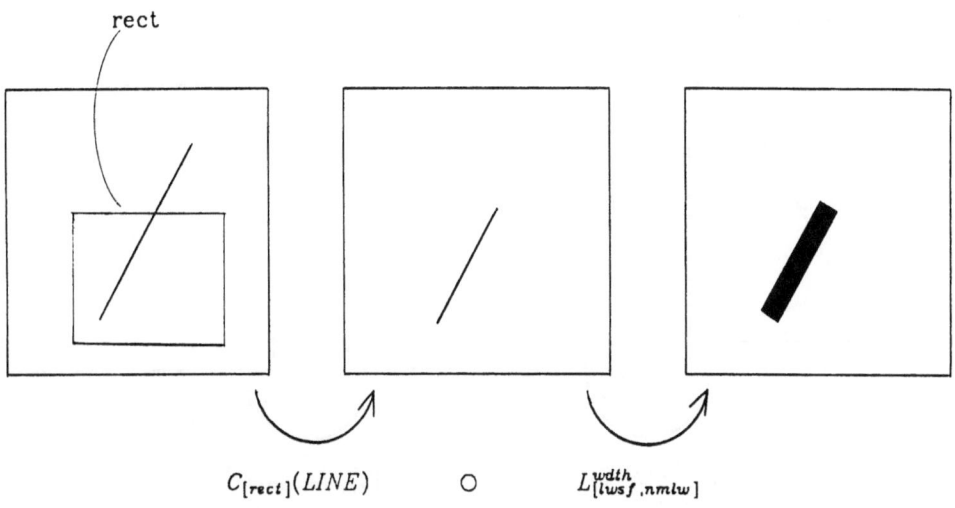

$$C_{[rect]}(LINE) \qquad \bigcirc \qquad L^{wdth}_{[lwsf,nmlw]}$$

More precise picture

has been generated.

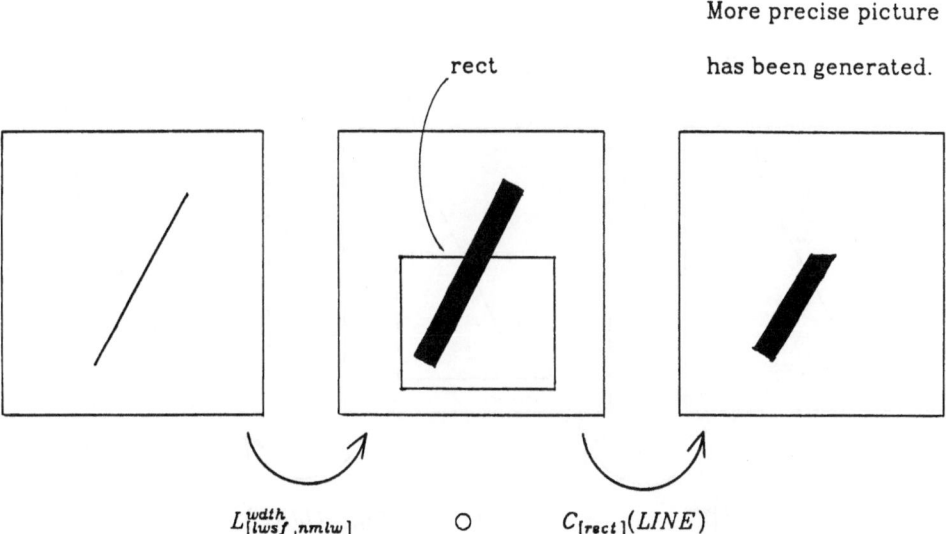

$$L^{wdth}_{[lwsf,nmlw]} \qquad \bigcirc \qquad C_{[rect]}(LINE)$$

Figure 5    The relation (RL3)

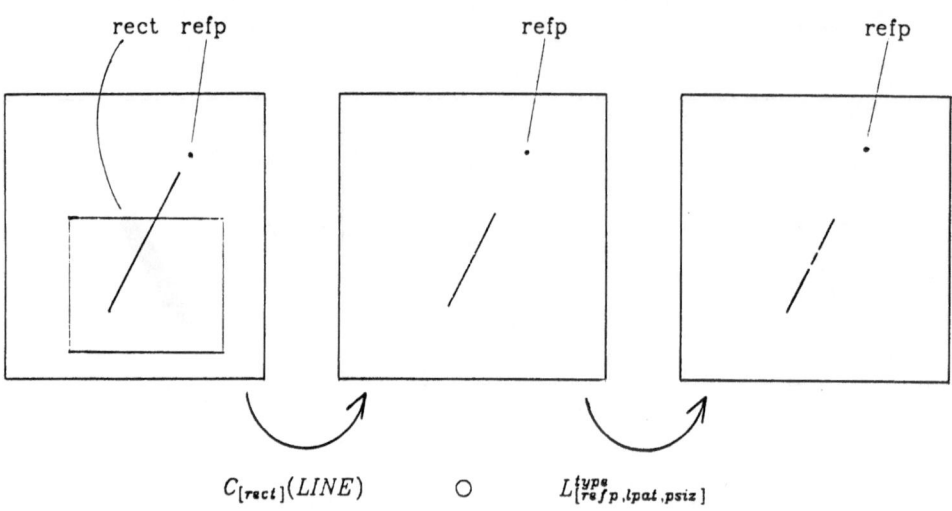

$$C_{[rect]}(LINE) \qquad \circ \qquad L_{[refp,lpat,psiz]}^{type}$$

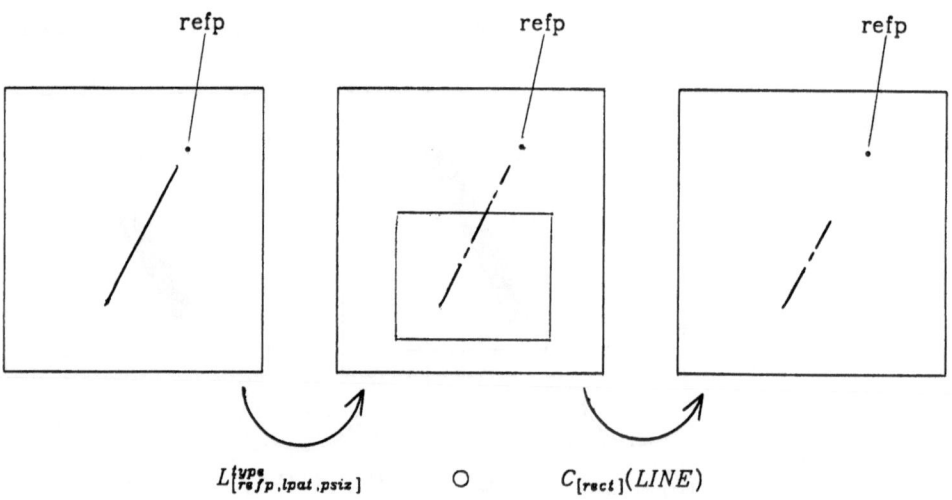

$$L_{[refp,lpat,psiz]}^{type} \qquad \circ \qquad C_{[rect]}(LINE)$$

Figure 6 The relation (RL2)

85

The line is made

wider on unit $nmlw$

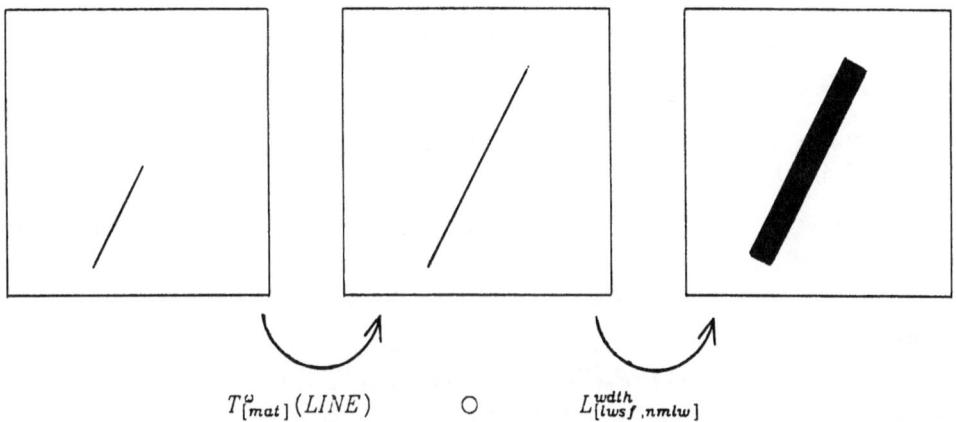

$$T_{[mat]}^{\sigma}(LINE) \qquad \circ \qquad L_{[lwsf,nmlw]}^{wdth}$$

The line is made

wider on unit $f^{\sigma}(nmlw)$

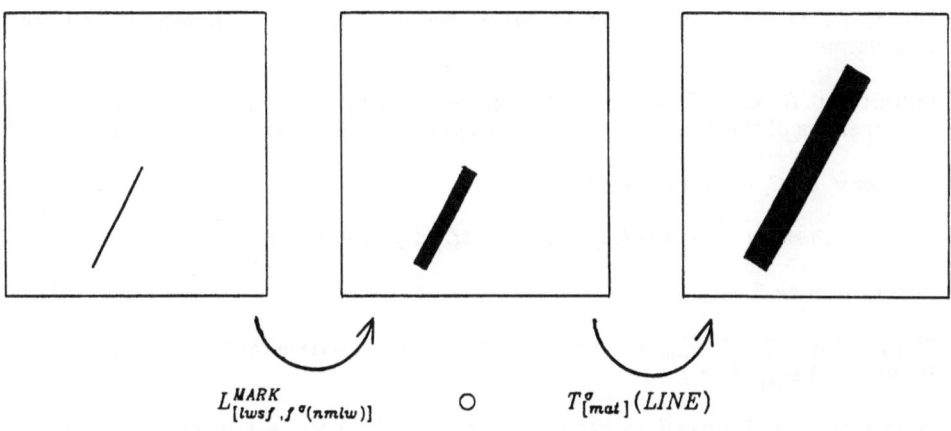

$$L_{[lwsf,f^{\sigma}(nmlw)]}^{MARK} \qquad \circ \qquad T_{[mat]}^{\sigma}(LINE)$$

Figure 7   The relation (RL7)

The performance of any primitive operation $A_\alpha : X \rightarrow X$ is assumed to contain such a value $\alpha_0$ that $A_{\alpha_0}$ is the identity operation. This assumption is not applied for v-operations.

Let $S$ and $T$ be operation sequences and $A_\alpha$ an operation. The relation between the performance and the commutativities of operations is as follows.

If $S \bigcirc A_\alpha = A_\alpha \bigcirc S$, then $Prf(S \bigcirc A_\alpha) = Prf(A_\alpha \bigcirc S)$.

If $S \bigcirc A_\alpha = A_{f(\alpha)} \bigcirc S$ with $f$ being a compensation function, then $Prf(S \bigcirc A_{f(\alpha)}) = \{f(Prf(A_\alpha)), Prf(S)\}$.

If the operation $A_\alpha : X \rightarrow Y$ is a commutator of the two generic instances $P_\pi(X)$ and $P_\pi(Y)$, i.e., if

$$P_\pi(X) \bigcirc A_\alpha = A_\alpha \bigcirc P_\pi(Y),$$

then

$$Prf(P_\pi(X) \bigcirc A_\alpha) = Prf(A_\alpha \bigcirc P_\pi(Y)),$$

which implies $Prf(P_\pi(X)) = Prf(P_\pi(Y))$. Similar relation holds for the case when $A_\alpha$ is a pseudo-commutator.

**Claim(6.1):** Let $S$ be an operation sequence. When $op \in S$ is 1-extractable and $S$ is transformed into $op \bigcirc Rmv(S, op)$, the performances of any operations in $Rmv(S, op)$ are not changed by the extraction transformation. ∎

### 6.2. Order-adaptiveness, exceeding-set and realizability

Let $S$, $S_1$, $S_2$, $T$, $T_1$ and $T_2$ be operation sequences, in the following definitions and claims.

**Definition:** $S$ and $T$ are *order-adaptive* if and only if the order of the occurrences of the common component operations in $S$ is the same as in $T$, i.e.,

for$\forall$ $C_1, C_2 \in Comp(S) \cap Comp(T)$,

$$Pos(C_1[S]) \leq Pos(C_2[S]) \leftrightarrow Pos(C_1[T]) \leq Pos(C_2[T]).$$

It is written as $S \simeq_{adp} T$. ∎

**Claim(6.2):** If $S \simeq_{adp} T$ and $op \in S$ is 1-extractable in $S$, then $Rmv(S, op) \simeq_{adp} T$. ∎

**Definition:** The *T-exceeding set* of $S$, $Exc(S/T)$, is the set of operations in $S$ which are not contained in $T$ or their performances in $S$ are not included in those in $T$. I.e.,

$$Exc(S/T) = \{op \in S \mid op \notin T \vee (op \in T \wedge Prf(op[S]) \not\subseteq Prf(op[T]))\}$$

A member of $Exc(S/T)$ is called a *T-defective (operation) in $S$*. ∎

**Definition:** $S$ is *T-realizable* if and only if the predicate

$$S \simeq_{adp} T \wedge Exc(S/T) = \varphi$$

holds. ∎

**Remark:** Note that, if $S$ is $T$-realizable and if the arbitrary operation $op$ such as $op \in T \land op \not\in S$ can be set to be the identity operation, then $S$ is able to be really implemented with $T$. ▪

## 6.3. LOS conversion algorithm

The LOSes, the POSes and the system of axioms must be provided in advance for the generation algorithm.

The LOSes are prepared in section 4. As for POSes, the following conditions must be satisfied. A POS for the primitive X

(a) follows the operation sequence schema,

(b) has the same v-operation as the LOS for X,

and

(c) has an L-sequence which is composed of operations in the L-sequence of the LOS for X.

The restriction represented by these conditions is necessary for the validity of the conversion algorithm.

We give here only an informal description of the LOS conversion algorithm. For the detail of the algorithm, see the appendix. Consider the $LOS^X$ and the $POS^X$ for the primitive X. The algorithm consists of two major parts.

The first part adapts the order of composition of operations in the $LOS^X$ to the one in the $POS^X$. As both the $LOS^X$ and the $POS^X$ follow the same operation sequence schema, the difference of order can be located within either the X-sequences or the L-sequences or both. Because the system of axioms contains the (pseudo-) commutative relations among the components of the X-sequence or the L-sequence, the order adaptation of the $LOS^X$ to the $POS^X$ can easily be performed.

In the second part, the $POS^X$-defective operations in the $LOS^X$ are extracted. The following three cases must be considered.

(case1)  If the defective operation is in $G(LOS^X)$, it can be extracted by the use of the RG relations - i.e., the (pseudo-) commutativities between the X-instances of the generic operations.

(case2)  If the defective operation is $V(LOS^X)$, it can be extracted by the use of the RV relations. Note that each time the v-operation is extracted by one operation to the left, an X-instance turns into an L-instance of the generic operation.

(case3)  If the defective operation is in $L(LOS^X)$, it can be extracted after the v-operation is extracted. At the time when the v-operation have been extracted, the transformed operation sequence consists of the extracted v-operation, a LINE-sequence, an L-sequence and $L^{frame}$. As the (pseudo-) commutative relations holds between any two of operations in the LINE-sequence and the L-sequence (the RL relations), the defective operation is 2-extractable in the strict sense in the transformed operation sequence. The extraction in this case is illustrated in Figure 8.

Note that the v-operation needs to be extracted in the case (3), too, and the extraction of it turns the X-sequence of the $LOS^X$ into the LINE-sequence.

We repeat the extraction until all the defective operations are collected to the left. Then we get the operation sequence of the form

$$E \bigcirc R$$

where $E$ is the operation sequence composed of all the extracted and defective operations, $R$ is the operation sequence composed of the non-defective operations, and $E \bigcirc R$ has the same effects and performances as the $LOS^X$. It is worthwhile to note that the extraction is an equivalent transformation of an operation sequence about the functional effects and preserves the performance of the operation sequence by mapping the performance by some compensation function, if any, too.

The operation sequence $E$ can be realized by some software simulators in the workstation driver and the operation sequence $R$ can be realized by the direct use of the device capabilities.

This is an original form of the LOS

$$X_1 \bigcirc X_2 \bigcirc X_3 \bigcirc V^X \bigcirc L_1 \bigcirc L_2 \bigcirc L_3 \bigcirc L^{frame}$$

First, extract the v-operation with RV relations.

$$V^X \bigcirc LINE_1 \bigcirc LINE_2 \bigcirc LINE_3 \bigcirc L_1 \bigcirc L_2 \bigcirc L_3 \bigcirc L^{frame}$$

Then, extract the $L_3$ operation with RL relations.

$$V^X \bigcirc L_3 \bigcirc LINE_1 \bigcirc LINE_2 \bigcirc LINE_3 \bigcirc L_1 \bigcirc L_2 \bigcirc L^{frame}$$
$$\underbrace{\phantom{V^X \bigcirc L_3}}$$
extracted operation sequence

Figure 8    The extraction of an operation in an L-sequence
($L_3$ will be extracted)

## 6.4. Examples of the LOS conversion algorithm

Two examples of the LOS conversion algorithm are shown.

**Example(1):**

Let $POS^{LINE}$ be

$$T^{\sigma}(LINE) \bigcirc T^{\omega}(LINE) \bigcirc C(LINE) \bigcirc V^{LINE} \bigcirc L^{type} \bigcirc L^{frame} .$$

and suppose the performance of the operation $L^{type}$ in $POS^{LINE}$ does not include the one in $LOS^{LINE}$. The effects of the execution of the LOS conversion algorithm for the $LOS^{LINE}$ and the $POS^{LINE}$ are as follows.

(Step1)    Nothing is performed except for the assignment $R = LOS^{LINE}$ because the $LOS^{LINE}$ and the $POS^{LINE}$ are already order-adaptive.

(Step2)    $\mathrm{Exc}(R/POS^{LINE}) = \{ L^{wdth}, L^{type} \}$, then goto (Step3).

(Step3)    $V^{LINE}$, which is the identity operation, is extracted. Again, the order-adaptation need not be performed.

$E = V^{LINE}$ ,

$R = T^{\sigma}(LINE) \bigcirc T^{\omega}(LINE) \bigcirc C(LINE) \bigcirc L^{type} \bigcirc L^{wdth} \bigcirc L^{frame}$

(Step4)    $L^{wdth}$ and $L^{type}$ are extracted. Final result is

$E = V^{LINE} \bigcirc L^{wdth} \bigcirc L^{type}$

and

$R = T^{\sigma}(LINE) \bigcirc T^{\omega}(LINE) \bigcirc C(LINE) \bigcirc L^{frame}$

■

**Example(2):**

Let the $POS^{MARK}$ be

$$T^{\omega}(MARK) \bigcirc C(MARK) \bigcirc T^{\sigma}(MARK) \bigcirc V^{MARK} \bigcirc L^{frame} .$$

and suppose the operation $V^{MARK}$ in this $POS^{MARK}$ can treat only the marker types 1 and 2 while 5 marker types are required in the corresponding $LOS^{MARK}$. Let the $POS^{LINE}$ be the same as in Example(1). The effects of the execution of the LOS conversion algorithm for the $LOS^{MARK}$ and the $POS^{MARK}$ are as follows.

(Step1)    $R$ (initially $LOS^{mark}$) is transformed into

$$T^{\omega}(MARK) \bigcirc C(MARK) \bigcirc T^{\sigma}(MARK) \bigcirc V^{MARK} \bigcirc L^{frame} .$$

(Step2)    $\mathrm{Exc}(R/POS^{MARK}) = \{ C(MARK), V^{MARK} \}$, then goto (Step3). $C(MARK)$ is included in $\mathrm{Exc}(R/POS^{MARK})$ because $\mathrm{Prf}(C(MARK)[R])$ consists of non-upright rectangles in general.

(Step3)   $R$ is reset to $LOS^{MARK}$. Then $V^{MARK}$ is extracted. The result is

$$E = V^{MARK}$$

$$R = T^{\sigma}(LINE) \bigcirc T^{\omega}(LINE) \bigcirc C(LINE) \bigcirc L^{frame}$$

Now, the target POS is $POS^{LINE}$ and then order-adaptation need not be performed.

(Step4)   $exc(R / POS^{LINE}) = \varphi$ because the performance of $C(LINE)$ in $R$ of (Step3) is also the set of rectangles parallel to the coordinate axes. No extraction occurs.  ▪

## 6.5. Selector

The LOS conversion algorithm transforms the LOS into the operation sequence of the form $E \bigcirc R$, where $E \bigcirc R = LOS$ and $R$ is POS-realizable. However, it is not an efficient way that the primitives are processed with the final form of $E \bigcirc R$ in all the cases.

For example, suppose that $LOS^{MARK}$ is the same as $POS^{MARK}$ except that the set of the parameter mtype of $V^{MARK}[LOS^{MARK}]$ is {1, 2, 3, 4, 5} and, on the other hand, the one of $V^{MARK}[POS^{MARK}]$ is {1, 2, 3, 4}. Even in this case, $LOS^{MARK}$ will be transformed by the conversion algorithm into the operation sequence of the form $E \bigcirc R$ where $V^{MARK} \in E$, $E \bigcirc R = LOS^{MARK}$ and $R$ is $POS^{LINE}$-realizable, discarding the device capability of generating markers of types 1 through 4. The way of improving this inefficiency is briefly described.

When defining the exceeding set in 6.2, members of the performance of operations are treated not individually but collectively. This is the reason of the inefficiency mentioned above. Then, in order to suppress unnecessary extractions as much as possible, some finer treatments of performance are required. An example of such treatment is to preserve all the intermediate results in the conversion algorithm, besides the final one, to implement all of the corresponding viewing pipelines, and to prepare a runtime mechanism which determines the most appropriate viewing pipeline for a (set of) parameter value(s).

This runtime mechanism, called *selector*, will be the key for the generation of adaptive graphics systems which use the device capabilities to the maximum extent.

## 7. Concluding remarks

A formal approach to the specifications and generations of computer graphics systems is presented in this paper. Though the system specified here is GKS, any kind of graphics systems can be handled by this method. Note that we have shown not only the way of the specifications of computer graphics systems but also the method of generations of them on the bases of the specifications and the system of axioms.

The concept of viewing pipeline established in the course of standardizing GKS is so universal that both the software and hardware of graphics systems can be modeled as pipelines. The formalization presented in this paper is based on the concept of operation sequence which is an abstraction of viewing pipeline. It is then highly expected that the discussion in this paper is helpful and applicable to the study of the architecture of pipeline-based graphics display device.

**Acknowledgement**

The authors thank Kunii Laboratory of Department of Information Science, University of Tokyo and Software Research Center of Ricoh Company, Ltd. for giving an opportunity to implement a workstation driver of Seillac 3 graphic display

**References**

1. International Organization for Standardization, "Information Processing - Graphical Kernel System(GKS) - Functional Description," *ISO DIS*, (7942)(1982).

2. W. R. Mallgenn, *Formal Specification of Interactive Graphics Programming Language*, MIT Press (1982).

3. J. D. FOLEY and A. VAN DAM, *Fundamentals of Interactive Computer Graphics*, ADDISON WESLEY (1983).

4. G. Enderle, K. Kansy, and G. Pfaff, *Computer Graphics Programming*, Springer-Verlag (1984).

**Appendix**   LOS conversion algorithm

The extraction algorithm, which is an important submodule in the LOS conversion algorithm, is presented first.

**Extraction Algorithm**

{ Input: $E$, $R$, $P$ }
{ Output: $E$, $R$ }
{ Precondition:
    $S = E \bigcirc R \wedge$
    $R \simeq_{adp} P \wedge$
    for $\forall\, op \in \mathrm{Exc}(R/P)$,   $op$ is 1-extractable in the strict sense in $R$.
}
{ Postcondition:   $S = E \bigcirc R \wedge R$ is $P$-realizable }
{ Invariant:   $S = E \bigcirc R \wedge R \simeq_{adp} P$ }

        **while** $(\mathrm{Exc}(R/P) \neq \varphi)$
        **do**
            **pop** $op$ **from** $\mathrm{Exc}(R/P)$;
            **extract** $op$ **from** $R$;
            $E = E \bigcirc op$;
            $R = \mathrm{Rmv}(R, op)$;
        **od**

The parameter of the operation $op$ might be applied by some compensation function.

Note that $P$ is not varied during the execution of this algorithm, and the extraction, which is done once in the loop, does not change the performance of the remaining operations in $R$ (see Claim(6.1)). Then, each iteration decreases the number of elements of $\mathrm{Exc}(R/P)$ by exactly 1. The Claim(6.2) shows that $R \simeq_{adp} P$ can be contained in the loop-invariant. The exiting condition of the while loop $Exc(R/P) = \varphi$, together with the invariant, implies the postcondition.

### $LOS^X$ conversion algorithm

The main flows of the algorithm is illustrated in Figure A.

{ Precondition:   $E = \varphi \wedge R = LOS^X$ }
{ Postcondition:
    $LOS^X = E \bigcirc R \wedge (R$ is $POS^X-realizable \vee R$ is $POS^{LINE}-realizable)$
}

### (Step1) order-adaptation

It is possible to transform $G(R)$ by the use of RG relations into $T_1$ where
$$Perm\,(G(R), T_1) \wedge T_1 \simeq_{adp} G(POS^X)$$
Similarly, with the RL relations, it is possible to transform $L(R)$ into $T_2$ where
$$Perm\,(L(R), T_2) \wedge T_2 \simeq_{adp} L(POS^X).$$

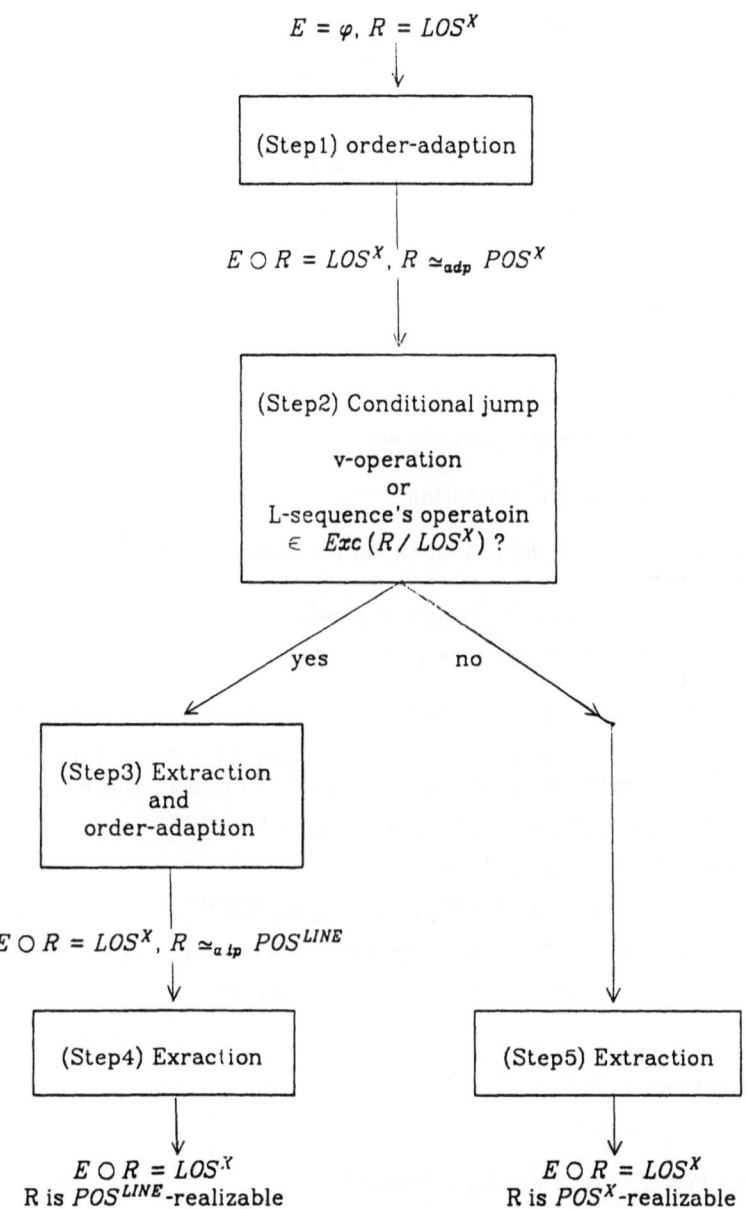

$E = \varphi, R = LOS^X$

(Step1) order-adaption

$E \bigcirc R = LOS^X, R \simeq_{adp} POS^X$

(Step2) Conditional jump

v-operation
or
L-sequence's operatoin
$\in$ $Exc(R/LOS^X)$ ?

yes          no

(Step3) Extraction
and
order-adaption

$E \bigcirc R = LOS^X, R \simeq_{a\,lp} POS^{LINE}$

(Step4) Exraction

(Step5) Extraction

$E \bigcirc R = LOS^X$
R is $POS^{LINE}$-realizable

$E \bigcirc R = LOS^X$
R is $POS^X$-realizable

Figure A  The LOS conversion algorithm

Then the condition

$$T_1 \bigcirc V(R) \bigcirc T_2 \bigcirc L^{frame} \simeq_{adp} POS^X$$

holds from the definition of order-adaptiveness.

Let $R$ newly be $T_1 \bigcirc V(R) \bigcirc T_2 \bigcirc L^{frame}$. At this point, the predicate

$$LOS^X = E \bigcirc R \ \wedge \ R \simeq_{adp} POS^X$$

holds.

### (Step2) Conditional jump

If the condition

$$Exc\,(R/\,POS^X) \cap Comp\,(V(R) \bigcirc L(R)) \neq \varphi$$

holds, goto (Step3). Otherwise, goto (Step5).

### (Step3) Extraction and order adaptation

Now we reset $R$ to $LOS^X$. $V(R)$ is 1-extractable in the strict sense in $R$ from the RV relations . Then,

$$R = G(LOS^X) \bigcirc V(LOS^X) \bigcirc L(LOS^X) \bigcirc L^{frame}$$
$$= V(LOS^X) \bigcirc G(LOS^{LINE}) \bigcirc L(LOS^X) \bigcirc L^{frame}$$

The parameter of $V(LOS^X)$ might be applied by some compensation function.

Let $E$ be $E \bigcirc V(LOS^X)$ and $R$ be $G(LOS^{LINE}) \bigcirc L(LOS^X) \bigcirc L^{frame}$. With the similar discussion as (Step1), we can transform $G(LOS^{LINE})$ into $T_3$ where

$$Perm\,(G(LOS_{LINE}),T_3) \wedge T_3 \simeq_{adp} G(POS^{LINE})$$

and transform $L(LOS^X)$ into $T_4$ where

$$Perm\,(L(LOS^X),T_4) \wedge T_4 \simeq_{adp} L(POS^{LINE})$$

Let $R$ newly be $T_3 \bigcirc T_4 \bigcirc L^{frame}$. At this point, the predicate

$$LOS^X = E \bigcirc R \ \wedge \ R \simeq_{adp} POS^{LINE}$$

holds.

### (Step4) Extraction

Note that

$$Exc\,(R/\,POS^{LINE}) \subset Comp\,(T_3) \cup Comp\,(T_4)$$
$$= Comp\,(G(LOS^{LINE})) \cup Comp\,(L(LOS^X)).$$

Therefore, by the RL relations, the predicate

for $\forall \ op \in Exc\,(R/\,POS^{LINE})$,

$$op \ is \ 1-extractable \ in \ the \ strict \ sense \ in \ R$$

holds. Then, we can apply the *extraction algorithm* with $E$, $R$ and $POS^{LINE}$ as $E$, $R$ and $P$, respectively. On the return from the algorithm, the predicate

$$E \bigcirc R = LOS^X \ \wedge \ R \ is \ POS^{LINE}-realizable$$

holds. The LOS conversion algorithm terminates.

## (Step5) Extraction

Note that, when the step is reached, the relation

$$Exc\,(R\,/\,POS^X) \subset Comp\,(T_1)(\,= Comp\,(G(LOS^X)))\,.$$

is satisfied. Therefore, by the RG relations, the predicate

for $\forall$ $op$ $\in$ $Exc\,(R\,/\,POS^X)$,

$op$ *is* $1-extractable$ *in the strict sense in* $R$

holds. Then, we can apply the *extraction algorithm* with $E$, $R$ and $POS^X$ as $E$, $R$ and $P$, respectively. On returning from the algorithm , the predicate

$$E \bigcirc R = LOS^X \wedge R\ is\ POS^X-realizable$$

holds. The LOS conversion algorithm terminates.

# Considerations in Developing High-Performance Systems with Standard Graphics Software

James R. Warner

Precision Visuals, Inc., 6260 Lookout Road, Boulder, CO 80301, USA

## Abstract

The formally sanctioned graphics standards inevitably lag behind both hardware technology and the demands of graphics users. As a result, standards-based software cannot meet all of the needs of the developers of high-performance graphics systems. Nonetheless, developers can realize considerable benefits by building their systems software with available tools that adhere to the standards, but that implement those standards in a forward-looking, flexible manner. In selecting and using graphics software tools, two important criteria are a versatile structure that promotes efficient operation in diverse environments, and device-intelligent device drivers that allow maximal access to the capabilities of advanced graphics devices.

## Introduction

As we entered the decade of the 1980's, large numbers of new, high-performance graphics devices were being introduced. Graphics technology was advancing rapidly on a broad front, driven by improvements in semiconductors, advancements in display technology, and refinements of new output concepts. Now, at the midpoint of the decade, the evolution is continuing, and perhaps even accelerating. The performance of both interactive devices and hardcopy output devices continues to rise, and the cost of obtaining this performance is falling almost as dramatically.

For systems integrators and application designers, however, the recent advancements in graphics hardware have made the design of high-performance interactive graphics systems an increasingly complex task. The engineers who are working on tomorrow's systems have more hardware choices to make, and they face more difficult decisions in designing a system architecture that lends itself to fast, efficient development, while also meeting the needs of the systems' users, both now and in the future. Concurrently, the risks of making a mistake in selecting hardware have increased, because any hardware selected is almost certain to be made obsolete by new device technology in a matter of a few years, if not months. By the same token, a new system will have a longer life if it can be completed quickly.

What is needed more than ever is an application development methodology that meets all these criteria. From my perspective as an independent supplier of graphics software, with no allegiances to a particular hardware manufacturer, I feel that the answer lies in the choice of machine-independent and device-independent software tools, based on the formally sanctioned graphics standards. The advantages of this approach to system development are many, and I will enumerate them as I continue, but standards-based tools packages are no panacea. They must be evaluated critically and then implemented intelligently, because there are pitfalls to be avoided in this approach too.

Potential value of the standards to system developers
One of the reasons for graphics standards has been to define a set of common procedures for developing graphics applications. These standard operations are implemented in the form of subroutines that can be called by application programs to generate graphic images and to obtain graphics input from interactive display devices. In order to make the standards as universally applicable as possible, the standards-making organizations have attempted to design the specifications in a machine- and device-independent fashion.

At present, we are seeing the recently-adopted ISO Graphical Kernel System (GKS) begin to achieve better acceptance outside Western Europe, where it was already widely adopted. The Core System, which was conceived during the late 1970's, remains the basis for most of the graphics systems and applications now in use. Core-like concepts are embodied in the firmware of many graphics devices currently in use. Another standard now being considered within ANSI is the Programmer's Hierarchical Interactive Graphics System (PHIGS). It addresses dynamic object modelling, nested segmentation, segment editing, and other high-performance functions that are not included in Core or GKS.

Immediate benefits provided by the standards
The major reason for using standards-based software tools is to improve productivity. Because tools are readily available that have been well tested and proven, they can get an application into production much faster than if new code had to be written to perform every graphics operation needed in the system. Also, developers who choose widely used software tools can begin development faster by drawing from the increasingly large pool of programmers who are skilled in using standards-based graphics software.

Another reason for using standards-based software is its portability. An application built with software components that adhere to the graphics standards should be portable across CPU's, compilers and peripheral devices.

The machine independence and device independence of applications built on standards may seem to be of no benefit to system designers who intend to optimize the system for a particular set of hardware. However, there are risks associated with that strategy, because new hardware products could quickly make the original equipment obsolete.

Some graphics systems have the advantage of being built from whole cloth, perhaps constrained only by an existing CPU and operating system. In this case, the designer is free to choose from among a wide selection of graphics devices. In most cases, however, some of the graphics devices for a new system will already be in place, and some means must be found to accommodate them along with the new hardware that is to be purchased. In both of these situations, device independence will probably be crucial to the design.

Device-independent tools packages can save considerable development time, by allowing a prototype system to be engineered and tested on one set of devices, and later ported to another. If some compromises have to be made for the sake of portability, it may very well be possible to refine the application code later to improve performance on the devices chosen for production.

**Realities of selecting and using standard software**
The first decision to make in using standard software, and perhaps most important, is to evaluate how well the functionality of a specific standard fits the system's requirements. The most obvious criteria will center on the availability of such basic functions as 2D or 3D transformations. These choices may be more difficult for the average designer than one might think, because the standards themselves offer many levels of functionality. Core and GKS, for example, each have more than ten possible configurations.

At some level, Core and GKS share the same functional model, with similar or identical capabilities for primitive attributes, text attributes, graphics input, segment operations, segment attributes, 2D viewing, and control functions. The Core standard adds 3D capabilities, the current position concept, and temporary segments. GKS offers a few key refinements that Core does not, including individual workstation window/viewport control, attribute bundling, segment-to-device association, and pixel arrays.

Having made this analysis and determined the desired level of standards functionality, designers must then acquire the appropriate tools to begin the application programming task. By far the easiest choice at this point is a commercial tools package, which serves as a bridge between the "pure" standard and the real world of practical applications. Commercial implementations of the standards differ largely in how successfully they meet the needs of the market without seriously compromising their compliance with the standards. These software tools products therefore should be evaluated in terms of the importance of standards compliance to the user, as well as by comparing the enhancements and extensions added by the vendor.

By adhering rigidly to a standard, software vendors may sacrifice their ability to support advanced graphics devices. On the other hand, features added to make the package more usable than the mandated minimum functionality of the standard may be very valuable, but they must not compromise portability. The tradeoff is one of usability versus total standards conformance.

Value is added to the original standard by anything that the vendor provides to help the user. For example, the quality of reference documentation and tutorial material such as sample program modules can make a great difference in how soon a programmer can begin using a tools package productively. Functional extensions that go beyond the basic standards can be quite useful, and might even be considered indispensible for certain applications. For instance, GKS includes no error processing and debugging facility, but most programmers would find this to be an invaluable aid, so they would prefer a GKS-based package that has this added capability. An intangible, but very significant, criterion is the quality of the technical support provided to users, especially during the early stages of application development. For example, training, telephone assistance, and on-site consultations could save new users weeks of programming time.

If the system developer selects a standard only on the basis of how well it initially satisfies the needs of the system, consideration should perhaps also be given to how well the tools package is designed to accomodate future changes in the standards. A possible example is the addition of 3D performance to GKS. The 3D extensions are being studied by the standards-making bodies, but are not likely to be agreed upon for some time. Users who have 2D applications now and want to be able to add 3D capability later should try to ensure that their GKS implementations will be able to accomodate the 3D extensions economically and efficiently when they do become available.

The most distinguishing qualities of a standards implementation are the intelligence with which it supports sophisticated graphics devices, and the number of different devices supported. A very robust implementation of a standard should support a large number of devices by including highly intelligent device drivers that give the user maximal access to the features of each device. For the tools vendor, a high degree of device support is by far the most costly and difficult task in implementing a standard. Building, testing, documenting and maintaining the drivers is, in fact, a more costly and time-consuming undertaking than writing the subroutines that incorporate the graphics functions specified by the standards.

If device intelligence were not an important criterion in designing a standards-based tools package, the package could employ a simple architecture, like the one illustrated in Figure 1A. The device-independent routines could be optimized to map images onto an idealized, virtual device without regard for the characteristics of the devices that might actually be used. Software simulations would perform many of the graphics functions. Very simple device drivers could then be used to control each device. The advantage of this method is that many device drivers can be added quickly and at low cost. The disadvantages, however, are that the application will use host resources inefficiently and the advanced features residing in the hardware or firmware of a high-performance device cannot be utilized. This architecture may seriously compromise the overall performance of the application.

Figure 1B represents a software architecture that is much more advantageous for high-performance applications. The device-

## Device Independence and Device Intelligence

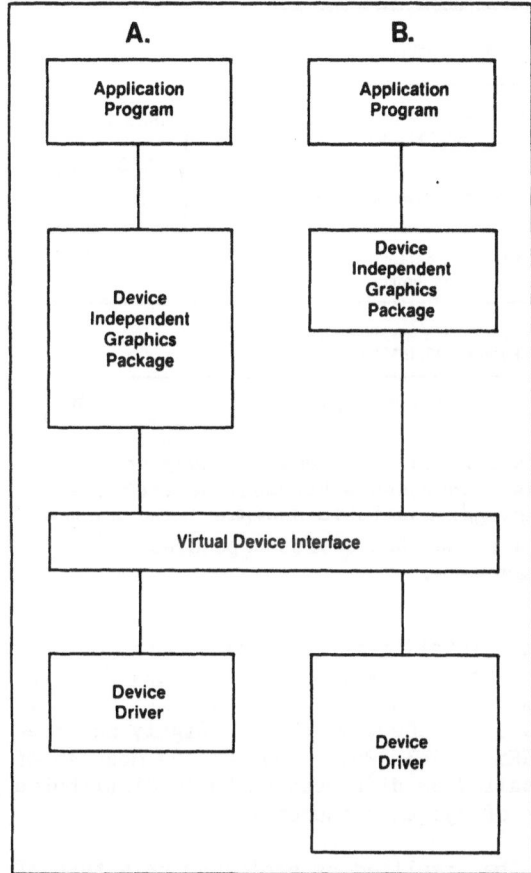

Figure 1.  Two architectural approaches to device independence are compared: Example A carries out most graphics operations in device-independent software. Example B uses more sophisticated device-intelligent drivers for better utilization of device performance.

independent subroutines are more streamlined, and more sophisticated device drivers are used to take advantage of the capabilities of each target device. Device features such as hardware text, local image manipulation, polygon fill, and 2D or 3D viewing transformations can be utilized without sacrificing the device independence of the application. If the program calls for a function that is not available on a particular device, the device driver will attempt to simulate it in software, and if the function is not applicable to the device, the driver will ignore the call and continue executing the program. If a device can perform an operation that is not provided by the subroutine package, then an escape function provides an alternate path to the device.

### Other architectural considerations
Because of the broad functionality and complexity required by the standards, applications software that is built on top of standards-based packages tends to be large and slow in some high-performance systems. But, if the package has a modular, layered structure, the user will have the option to install applications optimally in a distributed processing environment, where much of the application

## Device-Independent Graphics Tools System

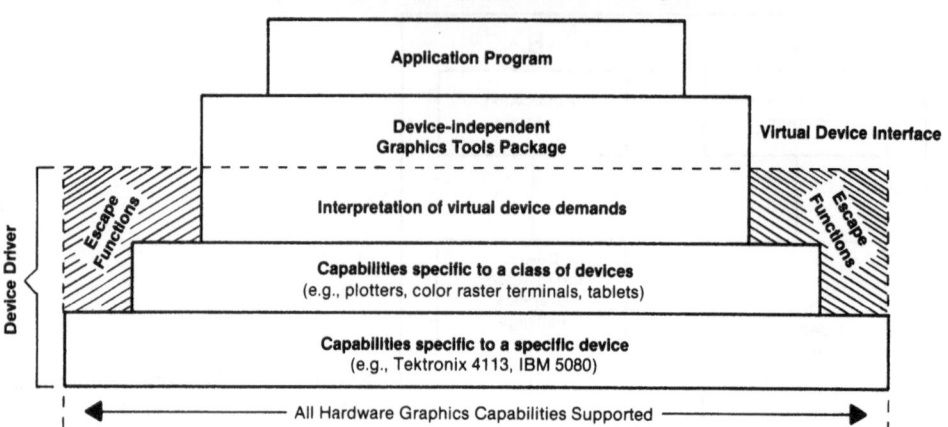

Figure 2. Device drivers are critical to a device-independent tools system. The programmer addresses a "virtual device" that incorporates the features of most available devices. The driver then translates these requests into the device-dependent sequences required by the hardware.

program can be executed on intelligent devices. Processing, communications and memory requirements will be offloaded from the host, improving total system performance. An example of this architecture is Precision Visuals' GK-2000, which is a highly machine-independent implementation of GKS level 2b. The various modules of GK-2000 are designed to be installed as different tasks in distributed systems, for optimum allocation of system resources.

The performance gains that can be realized by employing this type of structure can offset the penalties imposed by the complex viewing pipelines incorporated in the graphics standards. This software architecture is also more efficient to develop, test, and maintain, which translates into further benefits to the user.

In designing an application that will be built on a graphics tools system, it is important to plan carefully for the handling of data structures. If the application is highly specialized, the application database can store information in "world" coordinates that are appropriate to the application, such as meters, lumens, dollars, or ohms. If the system is intended for broader application, however, the designer should make a clear distinction between the application database and the graphics database. The graphics database consists of moves, draws, polygons, and segments within a virtual device coordinate system (Figure 3), rather than the coordinates of the application. The system design, therefore, must allow for keeping the application database up to date as changes are made on the virtual level.

## Summary
Finally, when all the shortcomings of the graphics standards are weighed against their benefits, the conclusion must be reached that

they can indeed be highly useful aids to the development of high-performance graphics systems, as well as those requiring less speed and operator interaction. If graphics tools packages are evaluated carefully and used wisely, they can help to minimize the time and costs of delivering versatile graphics systems, and the device independence that they provide is valuable insurance against hardware obsolescence.

## Data Structure Handling

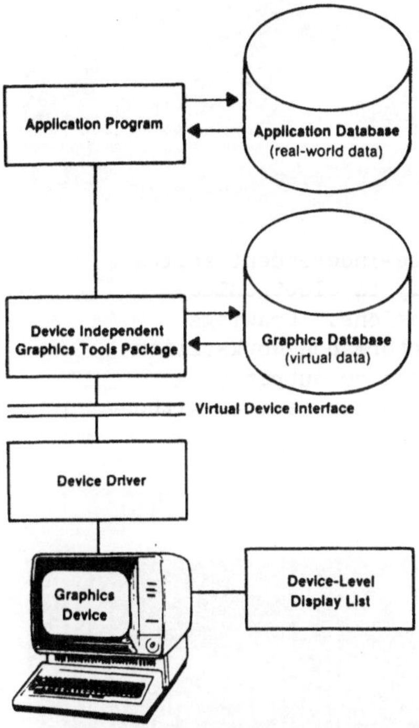

Figure 3. In an application-independent system, the application data is partitioned from the graphics database. The application developer must ensure that real-world data is kept current as graphics data changes.

## Typical Intelligent Device Drivers

| Graphics Device | Functions performed in graphics software | Functions performed in device hardware or firmware |
|---|---|---|
| Tektronix 4115 | Publication quality text | Local 2D transformations<br>Segment operations<br>Color table manipulation<br>Picking<br>Text generation |
| IBM 5080 | World-to-virtual viewing pipeline<br>Hardware display list management<br>Publication quality text | Text generation<br>Linestyle control<br>Segment operations<br>Color table manipulation<br>Picking |
| Megatek 7200 | Polygon fill<br>Software text<br>Hardware display list management<br>Publication quality text | Local 3D transformations<br>Text generation<br>Segment operations |
| Apollo 600 | Segment operations<br>Inquiry functions<br>Publication quality text | Polygon fill<br>Text generation |

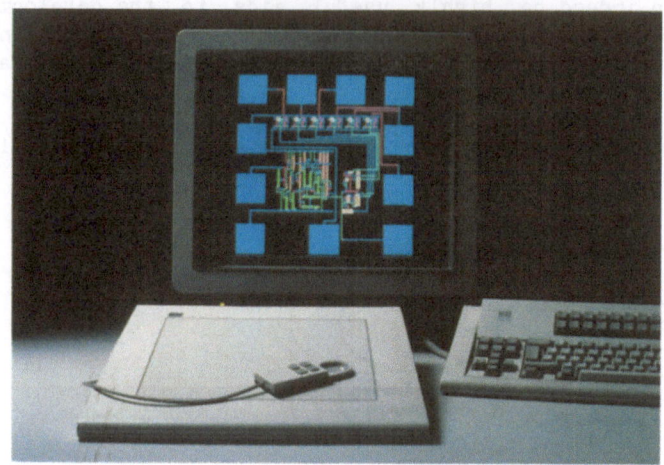

Standards-based, device-independent software
can be used effectively in electronics
circuit design applications.  Drawings
produced on a high-performance workstation
such as the IBM 5080 can be output to a
variety of plotters or other devices without
modification.

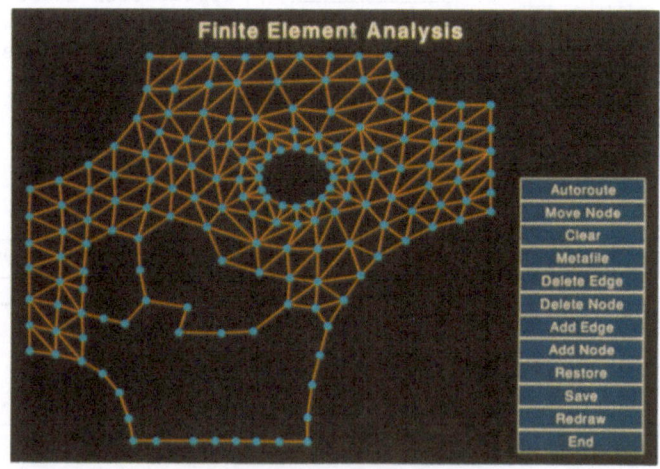

The segmentation capabilities of device-
independent graphics software are
advantageous for building applications such
as this one for finite element analysis.
The operator interacts with both the menu
and the model through various input devices.

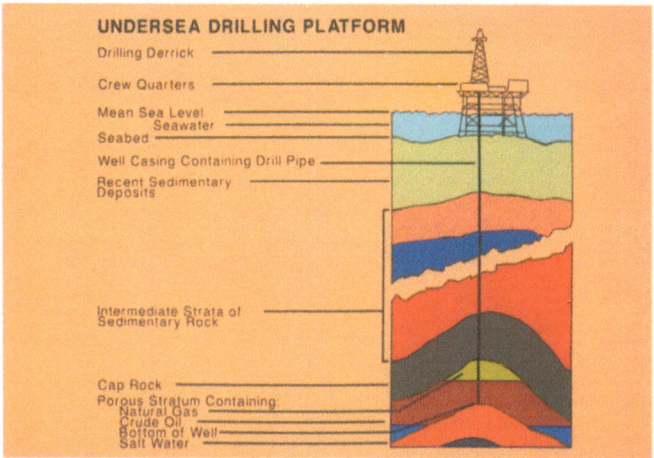

This geophysical cross-section was created
on a raster display terminal with a GKS
tools package.  The image can be directed to
output devices ranging from electrostatic
color plotters to film recorders.  The
attribute bundling feature of GKS ensures
that different hardware capabilities are
simple to access.

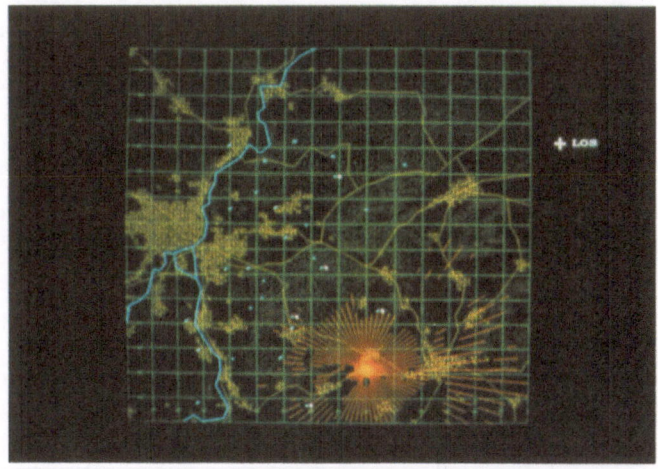

Real-time simulation applications like this
one use device-independent graphics software
to combine several types of graphical
elements on one display.  The terrain map
and grid can be stored as metafiles and
combined with the line-of-sight plot.

# Developing a Cartographic Geo-Code System (CAGES)

Robert T. Bannon

AT&T Communications, Bedminster, NJ 07921, USA

## Abstract

The purpose of this paper is to explain the development of an interactive geographic and demographic information mapping and management system to support the Engineering, Marketing and Business Research Departments.

The Cartographic Geo-coding System (CAGES) will be based on U.S. Census Bureau GBF/DIME files, as well as Photogrammy, Geodetic and Theodolite input. By using facetization of the continuous U.S. map, polygonal areas, such as cities and counties, can be downloaded on to a local processor for planning and modeling purposes. This technique also allows for rapid searches and identification of graphics attributes. CAGES will also utilize a report writer to allow for non-graphics quantitative analysis.

## Introduction

As a result of the divestiture of the Bell System, AT&T Communications is faced with creating and maintaining various geographic maps that would be used by organizations ranging from Planning and Design Engineering through Business Research and Marketing. Many of these applications were previously supported by the Bell Operating Companies or contracted to outside vendors.

Some of the traditional applications requiring mapped information are distribution service mapping for utility access in metropolitan areas (right-of-way), terrain mapping for determining radio route interference and tax block data. As the new AT&T Communications evolved, it became apparent that mapping support would also be impacted by the Modification of Final Judgement (MFJ) and the Plan of Reorganziation (POR). For example, maps are required to provide Local Access Transport Area (LATA) boundary information. These LATA boundaries quite often do not conform to municipal and county orders, therefore they represent another information layer.

To allow detailed office locations to be plotted for applications, such as facility planning, and the determination of specific "interchange point" connections the computer generated maps require a high degree of accuracy. To achieve this, location points must be plotted on the map using x,y coordinates derived from specific latitude and longitudes or from Vertical and Horizontal (V and H) coordinates, which in turn are derived from latitude and longitude. The same geo-coding capabilities are required for mapping customer locations.

Various organizations which were formerly served by the Bell Operating Companies started contracting with numerous vendors to meet their specific needs. This meant that there was a large amount of overlapping cartographic data that was being paid for by these various organizations. Since our corporate requirements are not the only demand on the cartographic vendors and service bureaus, delays are often encountered. This condition exists whether the vendor uses computer generated maps, manual drafting methods or acetate overlays on large scale public domain maps.

Based on the increasing demand from the various AT&T Communications organizations, System Engineering has undertaken a feasibility study to determine the most economical means of providing computer graphics support for the various user communities. The central part of this feasibility study will be based on a proposed interactive geographic and demographic information mapping and management system, the Cartographic Geo-Code System (CAGES).

## Post Divestiture Environment

As stated in the introduction, prior to divestiture many of the mapping applications for AT&T were handled by the Bell Operating Companies or contracted to a vendor that the Operating Companies were using for plotting shared planning data. However, as a result of the Bell System break up, AT&T Communications and the Bell Operating Companies were limited in the amount of data that could be shared. This resulted in the various departments entering into direct contracts with vendors and service bureaus to provide cartographic output.

Since there were so many separate organizations requesting maps, duplicate efforts were being performed by different vendors and service bureaus. In fact, because of time frame requirements and parochial control issues, identical requests from several groups within the same AT&T department were forwarded to a single cartography house.

In another case, information that AT&T had supplied to a Bell Operating Company could no longer be mapped for AT&T-C by a vendor because this would have been considered sharing of company proprietary data and a violation of the MFJ.

To really appreciate the diversity of the mapping requests being generated, a few applications are described below under functional headings.

Radio Route Planning

The radio engineer uses Landsat/Geodetic information to design a radio relay signal path between two towers. To accomplish this he must know of any obstruction that would interfere with signal propagation. To properly plan the route, the engineer must calculate interference along the path based on shadow mapping and elevation adjustments because of earth curvature and possible structural impairment. The radio engineer currently uses a scattergram interference output generated by DISPLAA® and overlays this on geodetic maps. Incorporation of support algorithms would result in the ability to map the route directly on the screen, and the radio route could be kept in data file with other facility maps for use in the future.

Cable Route Maintenance and Icon Tracking

Our Operations Department currently has various locations throughout the country that deal with construction contractors who will be digging in areas adjacent to our underground plant. In the current environment, a contractor calls a local office, whose telephone number is posted on a cable marker to report where he is digging. The Operations Department representative determines from the manual record drawing if it is okay to proceed with an excavation or whether an outside plant representative should be dispatched to the site. Today, two or more centers exist for each state.

Efforts are currently underway to develop a detailed facility mapping system to support this function, however this application should be incorporated into CAGES. As a result of this cartographic development, the number of reporting sites could be reduced from fifty-seven to seven or ten sites. Along with the site reduction, there would also be a corresponding personnel reduction. To achieve the user objective, the system would require an accurate detailed cartographic system that could pinpoint the exact construction location within 10 seconds. In addition, this same mapping system could be used to track construction gangs or repair trucks via the use of icons.

Customer Location Mapping

In the current environment, when an organization needs to see graphically the location of customers, they have contracted with a service bureau to plot customer record files on a map of a specific area, e.g., Anaheim, California. Their current "hit" ratio in plotting the customer location is approximately 70% accuracy for addresses fed into the service bureau computer. The remaining 30% which was originally unplottable, is resolved by manually entering additional address data into the computer or extending streets, or manually entering in new areas.

By developing or purchasing a cartography system for AT&T-C, we do not expect to increase the location matching accuracy initially. The seventy percent is considered to be an acceptable matching ratio; this is due to address inaccuracies, (street, city and zip-code), regional growth and plain old human error. However, as we build the customer data base and populate the fields for the associated latitude and longitude or Vertical and Horizontal Coordinates (V and H Coordinates), we expect approximately a ten percent increase in matches. These additional attributes can be used for various engineering criteria, therefore they are not being added just to increase the initial load ratio.

Local Area Transport Area (LATA) and Point-of-Presence (POP) Mapping

As a result of divestiture, the establishment of service boundaries or zones were established to define areas served by the various telephone entities. Both the divested Operating Companies and AT&T-C have contracted with various service bureaus to create these maps, however they must be kept up-to-date. New offices must be plotted for both the AT&T-C Point-of-Presence (POP) and the Bell Operating Company and Independent Local Serving Offices (LSO). This should also include feature group (type of service provided) information.

It does not make sense to have another company maintain our installed location information and our company proprietary planning data. This is especially true if their internal company and computer security standards do not conform to ours.

Indigenous Customer Studies

Our Business Research Department conducts studies for various organizations, such as Marketing, that identify customer grouping in a particular area.

For example, if you looked at the pharmaceutical industry around the Philadelphia, Pennsylvania area you would get one type of scattergram to overlay on an area map. However, if you expand the scope to include other chemical producing customers, you get a different perspective. And if you expand the scope to include petro-chemical companies, such as DuPont and Atlantic-Richfield (ARCO), you get a third distribution map.

A cartographic-demographic system linked to a customer data base would lend itself ideally to this type of application. The inclusion of color output would portray the information required for planning in a readily identifiable format.

## Proposed System Functionality

It is assumed that any system introduced to support the AT&T-C cartography application would be "state-of-the-art." Although this phrase is overused, in this case it can be interpreted as meaning that the system will utilize an open architecture, include the latest features, support graphics standards and support a wide variety of work stations. This ranges from the AT&T-C Interactive Planning Work Station (IPWS), the Tektronix 4105, 4107, 4109, 4114 and 4115B to the IBM PC and XT environment. This can be achieved by a micro-coded "termcap" that replaces device drivers at the front end of CAGES. The termcap is easily updated to include new terminals and devices as they become available. Short of this, an emulator package for a specific terminal could be used. Along with utilizing raster terminal technology, the system would support a full-color pallet, 256-color minimum, and utilize a 32-bit map data base interactively.

Since the AT&T-C operating area is nationwide, the size and precision of the graphics data base must allow the construction of a continuous base map from assorted original map sources. When constructing an integrated map from individual map segments, generation of a standard scale and storage format is essential. Both marker (latitude and longitude reference points) and edge matching procedures will electronically align the map segments while minimizing distortion.

The sources of geographic data used to create the initial continuous map digitization will come from a variety of places:

- Landsat Photogrammy (Satellite Photographs)
- Geodetic/Topographical Maps (Topos)
- Electronic Theodolite (Electronic Survey Coordinates)
- GBF/DIME Files (U.S. Census Bureau SMSA Mapping Data)
- STAMAP (State Planear Maps)
- Manually Digitized Maps (Mouse Encoded Geographic Data)

By using the transformation capability inherent to a specific graphics core, such as DI3000 or Tektronix IGL, and a least squares-elastic body algorithm, the system will have the capability to merge a variety of map segments, differing in size and scale, into a single, continuous map of the United States. A second transformation process would match various map grid systems to a latitude and longitude base which in turn would be stored as x,y coordinates for future manipulation.

Zoom and pan features along with the application of Boolean polygon generation, will allow the zooming-in on an irregular polygon area such as a state, city, zip code or a several block area. The polygon attributes can be defined in the same manner as those in the SMSA files and include tax block lot and address attributes.

The system must allow for the integration of new Theodolite or Photogrammy data into the geographic data base as well as tape file update and manual input. This would require a stereodigitization capability that would probably be contracted to regional survey corporations. This brings up the point of input standardization, which will be discussed under the next heading. However, it must be pointed out that the contracted format must match the Initial Graphics Exchange Standard (IGES) for transporting CAD data, the Graphics Kernel System (GKS) which defines 2-dimensional objects and the Virtual Device Metafile (VDM) which represents a standard file format for 2-D graphics data.

These same standards would apply to data captured by various scanning techniques. These techniques range from line followers through digital cameras coupled to optic fiber scan heads. Basically, this technology scans existing maps and plats (outside plant drawings for telephone plant and other utilities) to derive a rasterized image which is then converted to a vector format. By assigning the latitude and longitude of interlock markers on the drawings these can also be integrated into the geographic data base as x,y coordinates.

Map discrepancies, resulting from either incomplete digitized information from the file merger of the GBF/DIME file and automated conversions of other maps or from human input entry, must be corrected by human interface using a workstation. The engineer or cartography system operator compares proof plots to the original documents or files, and verifies the accuracy of graphics-coded representations. In addition, the engineer runs polygon closure routines, based on Boolean applications, which can identify any polygonal inadequacies. Interactive map editing capabilities must be provided to allow for boundary modifications, corrections and additions.

Overlaying capabilities are required that allows the system user to view an existing segment of the cartographic file or area map and superimpose geographic or demographic models for quick comparisons and "what if" study capabilities. This feature is similar to those incorporated into the Multi-user Engineering Graphics System (MEGS) which is a third generation space planning and architectural CAD system also being developed by AT&T-C. To increase the system flexibility to meet the modeling and "what-if" analysis overlay demands, linkages must be built to non-graphics data bases to allow information that is crucial for analysis to be extracted and included on the cartographic model. Once again, this points to the need for creating CAGES in an IGES format.

Maps and related icons, such as cable vaults, repeater symbols or customer-industry symbols, must have both defineable and scale dependent symbology default capabilities to allow for specific relevant details to be drawn for analysis.

The development of a thematic analysis package would allow interactive analysis of spatial relationships between complex data sets using a variety of quantitative and statistical management techniques. Non-graphics analysis (mean, standard deviation, population variance, trend, linear regression, etc.) as well as polygonial analysis (intersection, union and subtraction logic) should be developed. The resultant data set represents the multi-parent relationship between data file entities and accurately portrays complex logic relationships without redundant storage. This in turn can be used for further graphics manipulation analysis such as zone generation, point and icon overlays and common boundary removal. The calculated results from thematic analysis should be retrievable via cartographic output or via an alphanumeric report extract. Since the type of analysis will vary greatly between the various user communities, custom reports as well as standard reports will be required, therefore, a report writer linkage, such as the RAMIS® Report Writer should be included in the system development.

Since outside industry is migrating to voice recognition as an input capability, considerations should be given to this technology as a system input method as well as mouse/menu input. Voice recognition systems have developed from 10-words "untrained" vocabularies to well over 100-words "untrained" vocabularies during 1984. "Untrained" means that it will recognize specific commands from a variety of users without the system undergoing a "user-voice-specific-familiarization" training session.

## Computer Graphics Standards

Standardization clearly effects the development of graphics software packages much the same as other types of computer applications. It reduces development time and simplifies programming. Standards avoid the need for constantly reinventing the wheel by allowing a graphics drawing package or "core" to incorporate common computer graphics functions in a predefined format. Adoption of standards translates into reduced development costs and provides the ability to incorporate various vendor software packages into a graphics application.

Various graphics committees have issued guidelines as an attempt to regulate or define computer graphics formats. The committees recognized by the National Computer Graphics

Association (NCGA) and the World Computer Graphics Association (WCGA) for standards development are:

- American National Standards Institute (ANSI)
- Institute of Electrical and Electronics Engineers (IEEE)
  Computer Society
- International Standards Organization (ISO)
- Y-14 Committee
- Independent Software Information Standard (ISIS) Group
- National Committee for Digital Cartographic Data Standards (NCDCDS) - part of the American Congress on Surveying and Mapping (ACSM)

A brief description of the various standards follows:

- Initial Graphics Exchange Standard (IGES) is an ANSI standard for transporting Computer Aided Design (CAD) and Computer Aided Manufacturing (CAM) data within and between systems.

- Graphics Kernel System (GKS) is an official European standard adopted by ISO for defining two dimensional computer graphics and allows graphics software to operate independent of computer type or the graphics input/ouput devices. It provides the needed functions for a majority of applications with a minimum number of commands. ANSI has endorsed adoption of GKS as the American standard.

- Programmers Hierarchial Interface to Graphics (PHIGS) is a developing standard, similar in concept to GKS, for dynamic systems. PHIGS is currently under review by ISIS and has been proposed for acceptance for ANSI and ISO.

- Virtual Device Interface (VDI) is a two-way protocol which takes place at the lowest level of device independence.

- Virtual Device Metafile (VDM) is a standard file format for two dimensional graphics data.

- North American Presentation Level Protocol Syntax (NAPLPS) defines the method of presentation and storage for videotex graphics.

- Geographics Information Systems (GIS) is a developmental standard for capturing, editing and displaying geographic information for polygonal analysis and thematic mapping.

- Mapping Information Management System (MIMS) is a methodology for cartographic data base management.

Implementation of the above standards will allow the adaption of a wide variety of graphics software to new generations of processors. However, the portability issue can be addressed in part by developing the proposed cartographics system utilizing UNIX® System 5.2 as the operating system of choice. Portability is one area where UNIX® excels because it can be implemented on a wide range of processors from many manufacturers, such as the AT&T 3B20 processor and the DEC VAX 11/780.

End users are the driving force in making the various hardware and software vendors conform to computer graphics standards. They have a definite need to have various systems and data bases interface.

Many companies try to adhere to standards, others adhere only when it suits their company's purpose. One attitude of turnkey vendors is that if a user has data files written using the graphics Kernel System (GKS) file structure, they'll provide a utility to translate that information. However, they are not going to make files compatible to run on a competitor's machine. Software vendors take another stance and depend on their ability to create device independent programs or to develop drivers for industry leading equipment. General acceptance of standards promote the portability of their software to a wide variety of processors.

The following diagram shows the relationship between the various standards that are required to develop a versatile cartography like we are proposing.

# Computer Graphics Standards

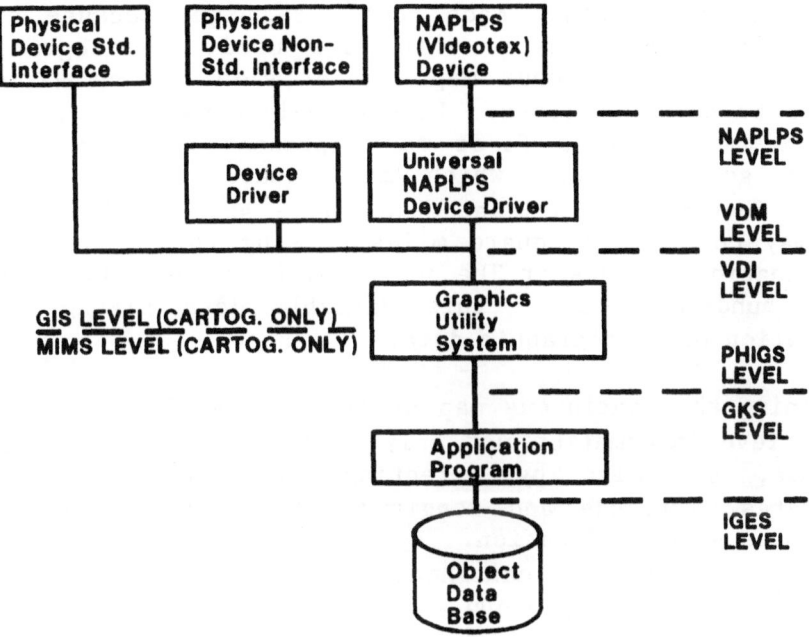

UNIX® has been the operating system of choice for many engineering and technical applications. And since it is the operating system of choice for the AT&T product and many of the new computers, we should use our own operating system. The AT&T Interactive Planning Work Station (IPWS), which is a large scale mapping system, was developed as a UNIX® system and many of the techniques learned and developed with IPWS can be used to develop a detailed cartography system. One of the advanced techniques for programming mapping systems, such as CAGES, is the use of the high level language, GRADIAL, which is UNIX® based.

## Data Base Structure

The importance of the data base structure grows exponentially with the size of the cartographic application which demands a data base structure that can effectively handle large volumes of information and can link to other systems.

The information stored in the cartographic data base must be stored as a continuous map to guarantee minimal plotting error. Plot information is stored in latitudes and longitudes

as x,y coordinates.  The data structured of the continuous map
is partitioned into user-defined geographic polygons that are
referred to as facets.  Each facet is unique because of the
associated x,y coordinates which are used to integrate the
facet into the continuous map.  Facet size can be varied to
coincide to data densities.  In extremely dense areas, such as
a center city area, a facet may represent only two to five
thousand square yards, which may equate to several city
blocks.  Conversely, in less dense areas, such as the Mojave, a
facet may cover many square miles.  Using this level of data
discrimination, a SMSA or Theodolite area may be defined by one
or one hundred facets.  This variable data sizing permits
optimization of cartographic data.

By defining the continuous map of the U.S. as facets, the user
can retrieve information not only by searching for a specific
attribute, but also by directing CAGES to specific x,y
coordinates, latitude and longitude, V and H coordinates or
approximate graphic location.  By approximate graphic location,
the data base design can home in on site, county, city,
municipal township, lakes and infrastructures.

Using the facet definition, the system response speed remains
efficient as the number of graphics polygons grow because only
a limited portion of the continuous map needs to be searched
for any given display.

All the data required to describe the infrastructure, street
numbering and municipal or company imposed boundaries, such as
LATA's, are confined to a facet and are stored separately
within the data base as specific non-graphics attributes and
graphics icons (graphical representation of an element).  In
addition, linkages to other non-graphics data bases, such as
the Planning Customer Data Base (PCDB), provide information
such as specific customer address and location code, in V and H
coordinates.

Separate data base files will be maintained for public domain
data, such as the U.S. Census Bureau's GBF/DIME files of each
U. S. Standard Metropolitan Statistical Area (SMSA).  This will
also hold true for files such as the Electronic Theodolite
Survey data.

Because of the expected size of the AT&T-C cartography system
complete data base management is required for both graphics and
non-graphics data.  The data base management capabilities

provide the means by which information is stored and organized and, more importantly, the way that the multitude of facet data, map layers, icons and other data types are manged and interconnected.

The system manager schema organizes the cartographic geo-coded data in a unique set of tables and directories that provide the flexibility to be updated or modified to meet the demands of a dynamic interactive system. By utilizing the data base schema approach, a schema conversion program can be run by the data base administrator to incorporate new concepts and new pointer programs into the directory. Any number of tables can be defined and these can easily be expanded or changed at any time.

Applications Supporting the Development of CAGES

Many of the AT&T Communications organizations have shown an interest in having Systems Engineering pursue the development of a corporate cartography geo-code system enhanced with analytical capabilities. The application areas that were identified for inclusion in the CAGES feasibility study are listed below in alphabetical order. As part of the feasibility study, an economic value will be determined for each application and they will be rank-ordered by the value to AT&T-C.

- Access Planning
- Alternative Access Studies
- Cable Route Mapping
- Chorapleth Mapping
- Customer Locations
- Direct Service Planning
- Feature Groups for Local Service Offices (LSO's)
- Indigenous Customer Grouping Studies
- Local Access Transport Area (LATA) Mapping
- NPA and NXX Boundaries and Studies
- Outside Plant Protection and Restoration
- Point-of-Presence (POP) Planning
- Political Boundaries and Jurisdictions
- Population Density Studies
- Rate Band Studies
- Real Estate Records
- Scattergram Shadowing
- Site Location Topos
- SOMS FID Mapping
- Switching Studies

- Tax Maps
- Terrain Mapping
- WATS 800 Studies
- Zip Codes – 5- and 9- Digit Maps

## Recommendation

The computer graphics environment is changing rapidly. Two years ago, there were approximately 60 to 65 vendors for both hardware and software. Today, that number is somewhere around 300 and this does not include service bureaus that specialize in engineering CAD and cartography offerings.

Along with the rapid vendor growth, processor capabilities and terminal and peripheral hardware features are increasing constantly.

Although there are many vendors offering "expert" turnkey systems, to utilize this method of satisfying the business requirements would create an atmosphere of vendor dependency. AT&T-C would be dependent on vendor for a specific processor, work station and terminal features and software releases. The latter may be the most critical because AT&T-C would not own the cartographic source code and would be dependent on the vendor for even minor system enhancements. And since an enhancement may be specifically for AT&T-C, we would incur special development costs.

To meet this changing environment, CAGES should be designed using an open architecture approach, utilize the various national and international graphics standards for maximum interface capabilities and be developed for the UNIX® environment.

This development approach will allow AT&T-C to take advantage of public domain files and software, and allow the flexibility of incorporating specific vendor software, provided they adhere to the standards. But most importantly, the CAGES programs will be portable within the UNIX® environment. CAGES will not be designed for a specific processor, nor will it be locked to a current work station design.

CAGES will use a layer structure for the system architecture. This will allow common use of the graphics GKS-type core and public domain layers by the entire user community. However, at the same time, CAGES can be partitioned to allow the creation of company proprietary layers, application data layers and private user data layers.

An important design feature of CAGES that is not easily attainable from turnkey systems is the inclusion of pointers within the various tables to allow CAGES to interface with other corporate systems and data bases, such as the Planning Customer Data Base (PCDB), and to retrieve required information. This ensures CAGES ability to stay syncronized with the latest data available.

The following drawing represents the CAGES layered architecture.

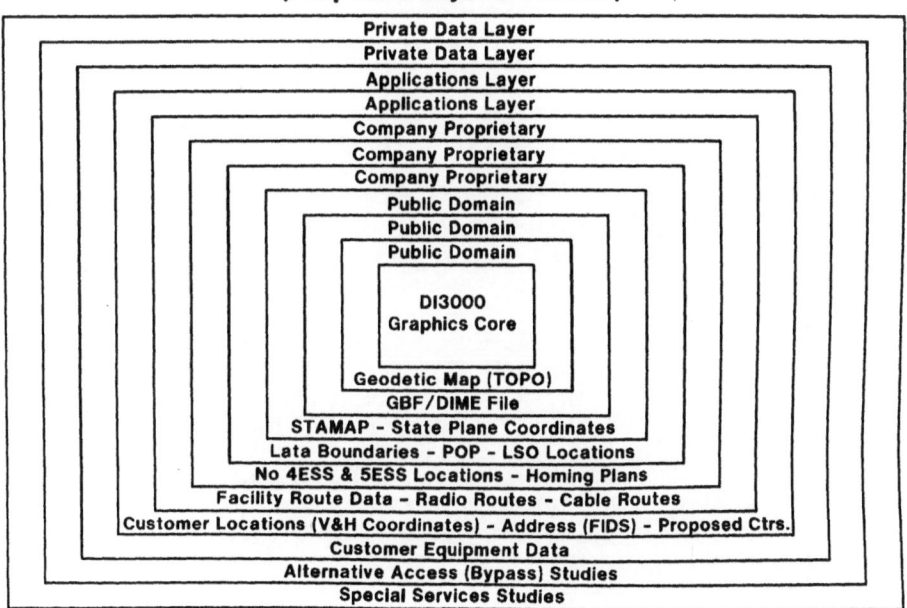

**CArtographic GEo-Coding System**
**CAGES**
**(Proposed Layer Structure)**

Private Data Layer
Private Data Layer
Applications Layer
Applications Layer
Company Proprietary
Company Proprietary
Company Proprietary
Public Domain
Public Domain
Public Domain

DI3000
Graphics Core

Geodetic Map (TOPO)
GBF/DIME File
STAMAP - State Plane Coordinates
Lata Boundaries - POP - LSO Locations
No 4ESS & 5ESS Locations - Homing Plans
Facility Route Data - Radio Routes - Cable Routes
Customer Locations (V&H Coordinates) - Address (FIDS) - Proposed Ctrs.
Customer Equipment Data
Alternative Access (Bypass) Studies
Special Services Studies

# A Raster Display Graphics Package for Education

David F. Rogers[1] and Stephen D. Rogers[2]

[1] U.S. Naval Academy, Annapolis, MD 21402, USA
[2] Annapolis Computer Graphics Consultants, 817 Holly Drive, E., Route 10, Annapolis, MD 21401, USA

## ABSTRACT

The need for a minimum suite of raster display routines is discussed. The design requirements for such a suite of routines are presented. Specifications for a package satisfying these design requirements is provided. Experience with the implementation and the use of the resulting package in an educational environment is discussed.

## INTRODUCTION

Recent successful standards efforts have resulted in both an ANSI (American National Standards Institute) and an ISO (International Standards Organization) draft standard for graphics. This is GKS (Graphical Kernal System) (Ref. 1). A standard for specification of a device independent interface between graphics software and hardware is under active discussion as both ANSI and ISO standards. Advanced graphics standards including PHIGS (Ref. 2) and extensions of GKS to three dimensions are also under active discussion by both ANSI and ISO. The existence of graphics standards is extremely important to professional and commercial programmers and organizations. However, the use of standard graphics programming environments for educational and research purposes is not always advantageous or appropriate.

In research, the standard graphics environment may not be available for the specific sophisticated state-of-the-art support computer or graphics device being used, specific required features of the graphics device may not be supported by the graphics standard, or the overhead associated with support of the complex, rich graphics standard may result in unacceptable performance.

In an educational environment, again, the graphics standard may not be implemented on the available machines and graphics devices. This is particularly true for low cost systems using third party add-on hardware and for the normally diverse mix of devices used in an educational environment. Further, even if available, procurement and licensing costs for large numbers of systems may be prohibitive. Finally, a standard graphics system is not necessarily suitable for teaching the fundamentals of computer graphics. Specifically, this is because the complexity and richness of the system requires the introduction of concepts out of logical sequence and/or the devotion of significant amounts of lecture time to explaining how to use the system. Telling students to use the system as a black box is never good pedagogy. In addition, since the system is already developed, students are discouraged from developing a personalized tool box of graphics routines.

## DESIGN REQUIREMENTS

The design requirements of any system are dependent upon the intended use. Here the anticipated use is in computer graphics courses that emphasize the underlying fundamental mathematical and procedural aspects of computer graphics rather than the use of computer graphics devices or software systems. At the completion of these courses students are expected to have developed a personal tool box of specialized graphics routines. The graphics system is also intended for limited specialized systems development including research.

Design requirements are also dependent on the anticipated available hardware. Here, it is assumed that available hardware will include medium resolution graphics boards/devices with at least ¼ million pixels on the screen and at least 256 simultaneous colors with on board/chip capability to draw lines, plot pixels, etc. Support for high resolution graphics boards/devices with at least 1 million pixels on screen and at least 256 simultaneous colors is also assumed. Downward compatibility with low resolution devices by providing dummy routines or simulation is very desirable. Support of interactive devices is not required.

The principal design requirements are

- simplicity
- ease of implementation
- speed of implementation
- minimum use of assembly language
- implementable across languages
- full use of any on board/chip capability
- separation of drawing/display functions from purely
    mathematical or procedural considerations
- variable spatial resolution
- support for multiple gray levels and multiple colors
- variable color resolution
- support for a color look-up table
- line drawing support
- support for the concept of software levels or shells

Since in an educational environment lecture time is precious, it should be possible to totally explain a simple graphics system within one 50 minute lecture period or less. Even better, the explanation should occur naturally as part of the first one or two lectures in the course.

Ease of implementation is important so that programmers with limited experience can develop a workable system. If the graphics system requires a significant amount of time to implement, then using it represents no advantage over a purchased standard system, e.g. GKS. If implementation of the system requires significant assembly language programming, then programming and debugging time will be extended and portability sacrificed. Further, the pool of available programmers will be limited.

The system should be implementable across languages, e.g. ANSI BASIC, FORTRAN 77, C, and Pascal. The only language dependent requirement is that the language should have separately compilable programming modules. The system should, of course, be implementable on top of a standard graphics environment, e.g. GKS. If a standard graphics environment is used, then the details of the environment should be totally hidden from the user.

Full advantage should be taken of any firmware/hardware routines that are available on plug-in graphics boards or at a lower level in the actual display controller chip, e.g. the NEC 7220 or the Hitachi HP63484 display controller chips. This will increase the speed of the system, decrease the

load on the central processor, and reduce the amount of assembly language programming required to implement the system. Further, the use of on board/chip capabilities reduces the work required to implement the system for various boards/chips.

There should be a definite distinction between functions that are mathematically or procedurally founded and those that are fundamentally display oriented. Specifically those functions that are mathematically and procedurally founded should be excluded from the package. Only the basic display functions should be included. In the context of an educational environment students should be required to develop the mathematical and procedurally founded functions as part of their personal graphics tool box, e.g. rotation and polygon fill algorithms. (See e.g. Refs. 3-6.)

Variable image space resolution is required. This is particularly important for complex algorithms that are computationally intensive. With variable image space resolution, these algorithms can first be tested at low resolution. Only final testing requires expenditure of high resolution computer resources. This is particularly important for hidden line and hidden surface algorithms, e.g. Warnock, z-buffer, and ray tracing algorithms, etc. (See e.g. Refs. 4-6.) In addition, variable image space resolution allows algorithms to be developed on lower cost and lower resolution machines and subsequently moved to a higher resolution, higher cost machine for final development.

Along with variable image space resolution, variable color space resolution is required. Variable color space resolution means that multiple intensities of the red, green, and blue primary colors and multiple gray levels are available. For the medium and high resolution displays used for computer image generation at least 256 simultaneous colors and at least 16 gray levels are required. Support for larger numbers of simultaneous colors and gray levels is also required. Again, variable color space resolution allows many algorithms to be initially developed on lower resolution/cost devices before final development on the higher resolution/cost device.

If variable color space resolution is allowed and if algorithms are to be transportable across implementations of the raster display graphics package and, hence, across devices, the user should not be required to have any knowledge of the specific look-up table index or of the specific binary numbers required to generate a specific color or gray level on a specific device. A simple solution to this problem is to specify all color components and gray levels on a scale of 0 to 1 with 0 being no intensity for a color component, or black for grey levels, and 1 being full intensity for a color component, or white for gray levels. The specific implementation then uses the best approximation, within its capabilities, to the requested value.

Support for a color look-up table (palette) is required to take advantage of expanded capability to display colors or additional gray levels with limited numbers of physical bit planes. Assuming that W is the width of the look-up table and n the number of physical bit planes for a given primary color ($n \leq W$) then, if the hardware allows, $2^W$ intensities of any individual primary color or $2^W$ gray levels are displayable at any given time. Further, to provide maximum flexibility it should be possible to assign any number of bit planes $n \leq W$ to a specific primary color, provided that the sum of the red, green and blue bit planes is less than or equal to the total number of physical bit planes, $N$. Essentially this assumes that the look-up table is implemented as a single contiguous table rather than as three separate tables, one for each primary color.

Line drawing support at maximum screen resolution is required because several topics in computer graphics do not require knowledge of raster display devices, e.g. curve fairing, surface generation, clipping, etc. It should not be necessary to teach students the various line rasterizing algorithms prior to use of the system for such applications. Further, in many raster applications 'thin' lines are convenient for drawing grids, axes, etc. Consequently, line drawing commands should not be affected by the pseudo resolution of the display. They should always yield 'thin' lines at the maximum display resolution. However, to avoid confusion their position should always be specified in terms of the specified image space or pseudo resolution using floating point numbers.

The raster display graphics package should support the concept of software levels or shells. By introducing these concepts, students are encouraged to organize their personal graphics tool boxes into various software levels, e.g. one level or shell might contain 2-D manipulation routines (rotation, translation, scaling, etc.), another, 3-D manipulation routines, a third, polygon scan conversion and fill algorithms, etc.

Detailed specifications for a suite of routines based on these concepts is given in Appendix A.

## RESULTS

The raster display graphics package described above and in Appendix A has been implemented in four different languages, on four different computer graphics systems: in True BASIC, IBM FORTRAN 77, DeSmet C, and IBM Pascal on an IBM PC-XT/AT equipped with a Vectrix graphics board set (672 x 480 x 9 bit planes); in IBM Professional FORTRAN (F77) on an IBM PC-XT/AT equipped with the IBM PC Professional Graphics Controller board (640 x 480 x 8 bit planes), in DeSmet C for the IBM color card, and in FORTRAN 77 and C on a VAX 11/780 under Berkeley 4.2 BSD Unix driving an Ikonas (Adage) RDS 3000 frame buffer (512 x 512 x 24 bit planes). The system is used in graduate level computer graphics courses at The Johns Hopkins University Applied Physics Laboratory and in undergraduate courses at the United States Naval Academy. Course content is essentially the same. Students are encouraged to develop personal computer graphics tool boxes through the use of selected required programming projects. Typical projects include

- developing and displaying multiple images of 2-D lines transformed in different ways (window, viewport, and 2-D transformation routines),
- developing a 3-D object manipulation program (3-D transformation routines)
- fitting curves through data (parabolically blended curves, cubic splines, Bezier and B-spline curves)
- generating and displaying 3-D surfaces (Coons and B-spline)
- comparison of the DDA and Bresenham line rasterization algorithms (line generation on a raster display)
- comparison of the Bresenham circle generation routine with an inscribed polygon approximation rasterized with the Bresenham line generation algorithm (circle rasterization)
- scan conversion of polygons (ordered edge list, edge fill/fence fill and edge flag algorithms etc.)
- polygon filling (seed/flood fill algorithms)
- clipping (Sutherland-Cohen, mid-point subdivision, Cyrus-Beck, Sutherland-Hodgman algorithms)
- hidden line/surface algorithms (floating horizon, Warnock, z-buffer, scan line z-buffer, Watkins, ray-tracing)
- rendering (lighting models, shadows, transparency, and color)

The package has proven quite adequate for all of these projects. Several of the graduate students have implemented the package with little effort on alternate hardware and successfully transferred the resulting programs to the 'officially' supported hardware. This has proven particularly advantageous to graduate students that have minimally configured personal computers of their own. A number of programs have been successfully transferred between the VAX-Unix-Ikonas system and the IBM PC-XT/AT-Vectrix system without change. The programs, of course, require recompiling and relinking. Interestingly enough, the performance difference between the IBM PC-AT-Vectrix system and the VAX-Unix-Ikonas system is only a factor of 2-3 in favor of the VAX-Unix-Ikonas system. The cost difference, however, is about 25 to 1 in favor of the IBM PC-AT-Vectrix system. Figure 1 was generated using the Raster Display Graphics Package (RDGP) on an IBM PC-XT/AT with a Vectrix Midas card set. The polygon in Figure 1 was scan converted with an ordered edge list polygon solid area scan conversion algorithm with antialiasing (See Ref. 4).

In implementing the package for the IBM PC-XT/AT-Vectrix system two assembly language routines were implemented and used to provide fast i/o to the Vectrix Midas card set. One routine puts a byte to the card set and the other gets a byte from the card set. The routines are basically the same for each of the four languages, differing only in the interface for each specific language. Each routine contains approximately 80 lines of 8086 assembly language, including comments, and required approximately 6 hours to design and implement.

The package makes full use of the Vectrix Midas card set on board functions. For example, the Vectrix Midas card set function for rectangular fill was used to implement the setpxl routine (see Appendix A) needed by the pseudo resolution requirement.

For the True BASIC implementation an assembly language interface was not available in the beta test version used (it is available in the final version of True BASIC). Consequently, the initial implementation treated the Vectrix Midas card set as a file (see Appendix A). Because of the way ANSI BASIC, of which True BASIC is an implementation, handles file i/o this lead to an apparent factor of two decrease in display performance. Initial tests with the final version of True BASIC, using an assembly language interface, yielded performance equal to the other implementations.

The FORTRAN implementation for the IBM PC-XT/AT equipped with the IBM PC Professional Graphics Controller board set was built on top of the IBM implementation of GKS. Since the details of GKS are totally hidden from the user, the RDGP for this implementation appears identical to all the others.

The implementation for the IBM PC color card required addressing the display directly as a bit map. As with the Vectrix Midas card set, extensive use was made of existing capabilities; in this case, the IBM PC BIOS video functions. About a dozen small assembly language routines (each about ten lines long) provide an interface between the RDGP and the required BIOS video functions. An assembly language implementation of Bresenham's algorithm is used for efficient line rasterization. The implementation for the IBM PC color card does not, and cannot, meet the design requirements for color capability. Its advantage is that it provides students with an implementation of the package on a low cost system for initial program development. Refinements to the program that require additional color capability are then made using less restrictive implementations. Figure 2 was generated with the IBM PC version of the RDGP. The polygons in Figure 2 were rendered with a scanline z-buffer hidden surface algorithm (See Ref. 4). The background is black. Each polygon is shown in one of the 3 possible colors available on the IBM PC color card.

The implementation on the VAX-Unix-Ikonas system was written entirely in C. These routines are callable from FORTRAN 77 under Berkeley Unix 4.2 BSD. Because the Ikonas does not have an on board line drawing function, a Bresenham algorithm is used to generate lines at full screen resolution (512 x 512). A system to convert C code to microcode for the Ikonas processor called Gia is used to download the Raster Display Graphics Package to the Ikonas. This yielded a considerable increase in display speed. Figure 3 was generated on the VAX-Unix-Ikonas system using a Warnock hidden surface algorithm (See Ref. 4).

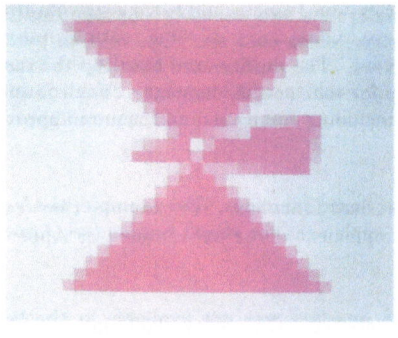

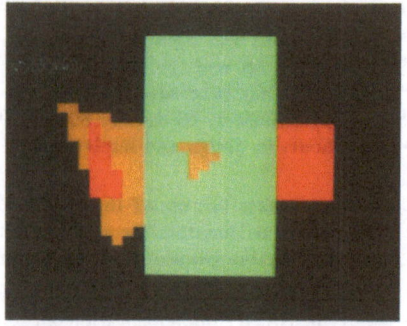

Figure 2.  z-buffer hidden surface algorithm--
IBM PC-XT with standard color board
a. 32 x 32 resolution, 128 x 128 resolution.

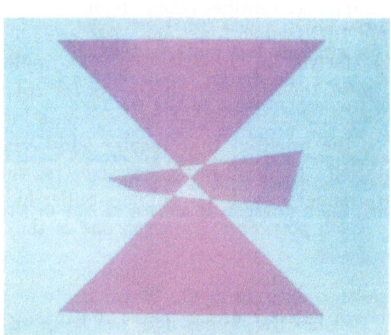

Figure 1.  Solid area polygon scan conversion
with antialiasing--IBM PC-XT/AT--Vectrix
system.  a. 32 x 32 resolution, b. 100 x 100
resultion, c. 480 x 480 resolution.

Figure 3.  Warnock hidden surface
algorithm--VAX-UNIX-Ikonas RDS
3000 system at 512 x 512
resolution.

## ACKNOWLEDGEMENT

The efforts of Linda Rybak in implementing the RDGP on the VAX-Unix-Ikonas system are gratefully acknowledged. Gia, originally written by Gary Bishop, was provided by the University of North Carolina.

## REFERENCES

1.   American National Standard Draft Proposal, Graphical Kernel System, Computer Graphics Special GKS issue, February 1984.

2.   American National Standard for the Functional Specification of the Programmer's Hierachical Interactive Graphics Standard (PHIGS), ANSI X3H3/84-40, February 29, 1984.

3.   Rogers, David F. and Adams, J. Alan, *Mathematical Elements for Computer Graphics*, McGraw-Hill, 1976.

4.   Rogers, David F., *Procedural Elements for Computer Graphics*, McGraw-Hill, 1985.

5.   Foley, James D. and Van Dam, Andres, *Fundamentals of Interactive Computer Graphics*, Addison-Wesley, 1982.

6.   Newman, William M. and Sproull, Robert F, *Principles of Interactive Computer Graphics*, 2nd Edition, McGraw-Hill, 1979.

## APPENDIX A

The material given below constitutes both a more detailed specification of the Raster Display Graphics Package (RDGP) and a user manual for the package.

### RDGP - RASTER DISPLAY GRAPHICS PACKAGE ©

The Raster Display Graphics Package (RDGP) is a minimal set of graphics routines designed to be used in teaching and in system development. The routines are available in four languages: ANSI BASIC (True BASIC), FORTRAN 77, C, and Pascal.

Specifications for all four languages are given for each of the routines. The specifications are given first for ANSI BASIC, then for FORTRAN 77, C and Pascal in that order. Command specifications are separated by horizontal lines. Variable types are indicated for each of the parameters for each routine.

Because ANSI BASIC does not have global variables, information about the state of the graphics device is maintained in a communication vector q.

The routines fall naturally into three groups: display state, pixel manipulation, and line drawing. The routines are discussed in this order.

| | |
|---|---|
| name: | rdinit (Raster display initialize) |
| purpose: | Initialize the raster display graphics package and the graphics device. |
| calling sequence: | call rdinit(q,#1)<br>q is the communication vector<br>#1 is the file designated as the Vectrix.<br><br>call rdinit<br><br>rdinit()<br><br>procedure rdinit; |
| comments: | rdinit should be called only once at the beginning of the program. |

---

| | |
|---|---|
| name: | erase (Erase the screen) |
| purpose: | Erase the graphics screen with the specified color. |
| calling sequence: | call erase(r,g,b,q,#1)<br><br>call erase(r,g,b)<br>real r,g,b<br><br>erase(r,g,b)<br>double r,g,b;<br><br>procedure erase(r,g,b : real); |
| comments: | r, g, b are the red, green, and blue components of the color.  r, g, b are values in the range 0 to 1.  (r,g,b) = (0.,0.,0.) is black and (r,g,b) = (1.,1.,1.) is white. |

---

| | |
|---|---|
| name: | setrsl (Set resolution) |
| purpose: | Set the pseudo resolution of the display raster. |
| calling sequence: | call setrsl(xres,yres,q,#1)<br><br>call setrsl(xres,yres)<br>integer xres,yres<br><br>setrsl(xres,yres)<br>int xres,yres;<br><br>procedure setrsl(xres,yres : integer); |
| comments: | xres is the pseudo resolution of the display raster in the x or horizontal direction. xres is between 1 and the maximum physical resolution of the display raster in the horizontal direction. |

yres is the pseudo resolution of the display raster in the y or vertical direction. yres is between 1 and the maximum physical resolution of the display raster in the vertical direction.

The pseudo-raster is centered in the physical display space.
Pixels are square or as square as it is possible to make them within the limitations of the physical display.

---

| | |
|---|---|
| name: | setrgb (Set rgb; red, green, blue) |
| purpose: | Set the current drawing color. |
| calling sequence: | call setrgb(r,g,b,q,#1) |

call setrgb(r,g,b)
real r,g,b

setrgb(r,g,b)
double r,g,b;

procedure setrgb(r,g,b : real);

comments: r, g, b are the red, green, and blue components of the color. r, g, b are values in the range 0 to 1. (r,g,b) = (0.,0.,0.) is black and (r,g,b) = (1.,1.,1.) is white.

This command is generally used to set the color for the drawing commands ma, pa, da, mr, pr, dr and text given below. Note, however, that calls to setpxl and setscn may change the drawing color.

---

| | |
|---|---|
| name: | setlut (Set the look-up table) |
| purpose: | Set the color look-up table (LUT). |
| calling sequence: | call setlut(table$,rbits,gbits,bbits,q,#1) |

call setlut(table,rbits,gbits,bbits)
character table(*)
integer rbits,gbits,bbits

setlut(table,rbits,gbits,bbits)
char *table;
int rbits,gbits,bbits;

rdString = string[255];
procedure setlut(table : rdString;

rbits,gbits,bbits : integer);

comments: table is a string which indicates the specific look-up table to be set. Possible values are:

default -- the default look-up table
gray   -- a gray level look-up table
color  -- a special color look-up table

rbits, gbits and bbits are the number of bit planes assigned to each of the red, green and blue components of the frame buffer. The number of pure shades for each color is $2^{bits}$. rbits, gbits, bbits must each individually be less than or equal to the width of the color look-up table (LUT). The sum of rbits, gbits, and bbits must be less than the number of physical bit planes N in the frame buffer. The total number of colors displayable at any one time is $2^{(rbits+gbits+bbits)}$ out of a possible palette of $2^{(3*W)}$ where $W \geq N$ is the width of the LUT.

For a gray level look-up table the gray bits are taken as equal to rbits. The maximum number of gray bits is W.

---

name:                 setdm (Set the display mode)

purpose:              Control the display mode.

calling sequence:     call setdm(string,q,#1)

                      call setdm(string)
                      character string(*)

                      setdm(string)
                      char *string;

                      rdString = string[255];
                      procedure setdm(string : rdString);

comments:             The default strings are

                      monitor  = the standard alphanumeric device
                      graphics = the standard graphics device

                      Other allowable string parameters are the names of the standard alphanumeric and graphics devices for any individual computer system or graphics board.

---

name:                 setpxl (Set pixel)

purpose:              Set a single pixel on a scanline.

calling sequence:     call setpxl(x,y,r,g,b,q,#1)

                      call setpxl(x,y,r,g,b)
                      integer x,y
                      real r,g,b

```
setpxl(x,y,r,g,b)
int x,y;
double r,g,b;
```

procedure setpxl(x,y : integer; r,g,b : real);

comments:  x and y are the coordinates of the lower left hand corner of a pseudo pixel as defined by setrsl. The pixel covers an area to the right and above the location x,y. r, g, b are the red, green, and blue components of the color for the pixel. r, g, b are values in the range 0 to 1. (r,g,b) = (0.,0.,0.) is black and (r,g,b) = (1.,1.,1.) is white.

---

name:  setscn (Set scanline)

purpose:  Set a group of pixels on a scanline.

calling sequence:  call setscn(y,ra,ga,ba,xstart,xstop,q,#1)

```
call setscn(y,ra,ga,ba,xstart,xstop)
integer y,xstart,xstop
real ra(*),ga(*),ba(*)
```

```
setscn(y,ra,ga,ba,xstart,xstop)
int y,xstart,xstop;
double ra[ ],ga[ ],ba[ ];
```

```
rdScanline = array[0...maxres] of real;
procedure setscn(y:integer; ra,ga,ba:rdScanline; xstart,xstop:integer);
```

comments:  y is the pseudo-scanline to be set

xstart is the starting location of the pixels
xstop is the location of the last pixel

ra, ga, ba are arrays containing the red, green, and blue values for the pixels to be set. The elements of ra, ga, and ba are in the range 0 to 1 with (0.,0.,0.) as black and (1.,1.,1.) as white. The first element in each of the arrays is used for the pixel at xstart. Succeeding pixels along the scanline use the values in succeeding elements of the array.

---

name:  getpxl (Get pixel)

purpose:  Get a single pixel on a scanline.

calling sequence:  call getpxl(x,y,r,g,b,q,#1)

```
call getpxl(x,y,r,g,b)
integer x,y
real r,g,b
```

getpxl(x,y,r,g,b)
int x,y;
double *r,*g,*b;

procedure getpxl(x,y : integer; var r,g,b : real);

comments:    x and y are the coordinates of the lower left hand corner of a pseudo-pixel as
defined by setrsl. The pixel covers an area to the right and above the location
x,y.

r, g, b are (in C pointers to) the red, green, and blue components of the color for
the pixel. r, g, b are values in the range 0 to 1. (r,g,b) = (0.,0.,0.) is black and
(r,g,b) = (1.,1.,1.) is white.

---

name:    getscn (Get scanline)

purpose:    Get a group of pixels on a scanline.

calling sequence:    call getscn(y,ra,ga,ba,xstart,xstop,q,#1)

call getscn(y,ra,ga,ba,xstart,xstop)
integer y,xstart,xstop
real ra(*),ga(*),ba(*)

getscn(y,ra,ga,ba,xstart,xstop)
int y,xstart,xstop;
double ra[ ],ga[ ],ba[ ];

rdScanline = array[0..maxres] of real;
procedure getscn(y:integer; ra,ga,ba:rdScanline; xstart,xstop:integer);

comments:    y is the pseudo scanline to be read
xstart is the starting location of the pixels
xstop is the location of the last pixel

ra, ga, ba are arrays which receive the red, green, and blue values for the pixels
to be read. ra, ga, and ba are in the range 0 to 1 with (ra,ga,ba) = (0.,0.,0.) as
black and (1.,1.,1.) as white. The first element in the arrays is the value for the
pixel at xstart. Succeeding elements of the array contain the values for succeeding pixels.

---

name:    text (Text)

purpose:    Display text.

calling sequence:    call text(string$,q,#1)

call text(string)
character string(*)

text(string)
char *string;

rdString = string[255];
procedure txt(t : rdString);

comments:        Text is displayed at the last 'cursor' position in the default character size. The 'cursor' position is the lower left corner of the first character cell. The 'cursor' is left at the lower right of the last character cell of the text string.

Note: Because text is a reserved word in Pascal the abbreviation txt is used.

Note: The text/character string in FORTRAN 77 must end with a $, e.g. HELLO$ is used to display HELLO.

---

name:        tsize (Text size)

purpose:        Set text size.

calling sequence:    call tsize(wf,hf,q,#1)

call tsize(wf,hf)
real wf,hf

tsize(wf,hf)
double wf,hf;

procedure tsize(wf,hf : real);

comments:        wf is the width factor; 1.0 is the standard text width.
hf is the height factor; 1.0 is the standard text height.

Tsize sets the text size to the nearest available hardware/firmware text size. All subsequent text is displayed at this size.

---

name:        tangle (Text angle)

purpose:        Set text angle.

calling sequence:    call tangle(angle,q,#1)

call tangle(angle)
real angle

tangle(angle)
double angle;

procedure tangle(angle : real);

comments:           angle is the text angle in degrees.

Tangle sets the text angle to the nearest available hardware/firmware text angle. All subsequent text is displayed at this angle.

---

name:           ma (Move absolute)

purpose:           Move the 'cursor' invisibly to the absolute location x, y.

calling sequence:           call ma(x,y,q,#1)

call ma(x,y)
real x,y

ma(x,y)
double x,y;

procedure ma(x,y : real);

comments:           x and y are real numbers. x and y are in absolute coordinates for the pseudo-raster set in setrsl. 0, 0 is the lower left corner of the pseudo-raster.

---

name:           mr (Move relative)

purpose:           Move the 'cursor' invisibly by the relative amounts dx, dy.

calling sequence:           call mr(dx,dy,q,#1)

call mr(dx,dy)
real dx,dy

mr(dx,dy)
double dx,dy;

procedure mr(dx,dy : real);

comments:           dx and dy are real number. Movement is relative to the last location of the 'cursor' in the dimensions of the pseudo-raster set in setrsl.

---

name:           da (Draw absolute)

purpose:           Draw a thin line in absolute coordinates.

calling sequence:           call da(x,y,q,#1)

call da(x,y)
real x,y

da(x,y)
double x,y;

procedure da(x,y : real);

comments:      x and y are real numbers given in the dimensions of the pseudo-raster set in
               setrsl. A thin (1 physical pixel wide) line is drawn from the 'cursor' location to x,
               y. x, y are given in absolute coordinates with 0, 0 as the lower left corner of the
               pseudo-raster set in setrsl.

               The current color is used to draw the line. setrgb is used to set the current color.

---

name:              dr (Draw relative)

purpose:           Draw a thin line using relative coordinates.

calling sequence:  call dr(dx,dy,q,#1)

                   call dr(dx,dy)
                   real dx,dy

                   dr(dx,dy)
                   double dx,dy;

                   procedure dr(dx,dy : real);

comments:          dx and dy are real numbers given in the dimensions of the pseudo-raster set in
                   setrsl. A thin (1 physical pixel wide) line is drawn from the last 'cursor' location
                   x0, y0 to x0 + dx, y0 + dy. dx and dy are given in relative coordinates with x0,
                   y0 as the last 'cursor' position.

                   The current color is used to draw the line. setrgb is used to set the current color.

---

name:              pa (Point absolute)

purpose:           Display a point in absolute coordinates.

calling sequence:  call pa(x,y,q,#1)

                   call pa(x,y)
                   real x,y

                   pa(x,y)
                   double x,y;

                   procedure pa(x,y : real);

comments: x and y are real numbers given in the dimensions of the pseudo-raster set in setrsl. A small dot (1 physical pixel size) is displayed at the location x, y. x, y are given in absolute coordinates with 0,0 as the lower left corner of the pseudo-raster set in setrsl.

The current color is used to display the dot. setrgb is used to set the current color.

---

name: pr (Point relative)

purpose: Display a point using relative coordinates.

calling sequence: call pr(dx,dy,q,#1)

call pr(dx,dy)
real dx,dy

pr(dx,dy)
double dx,dy;

procedure pr(dx,dy : real);

comments: dx and dy are real numbers given in the dimensions of the pseudo-raster set in setrsl. A small dot (1 physical pixel size) is displayed at the location x0 + dx, y0 + dy. dx, dy are relative coordinates with respect to the last 'cursor' location x0, y0.

The current color is used to display the dot. setrgb is used to set the current color.

# Chapter 3
# CAD/CAM

# The Interactive Interface of "CADME" System

Carlo Bizzozero and Umberto Cugini

Politecnico di Milano, Dipartimento di Meccanica, Piazza Leonardo da Vinci 32, 20133 Milano, Italy

## ABSTRACT

This work stands as a contribution in the area of the man-machine communications. In the field of Computer Aided Design the solution of such a problem has led us to the definition and realization of an indipendent interface placed in front of solid modellers accepting C.S.G. definitions. This system is able to simulate the orthographic projections of the specified part without activating the solid modeller. The illustrated interface is a part of an integrated system called CADME.

KEYWORDS: solid modelling, interaction, user interface

## Introduction

Solid modellers have the main characteristic of being able to merge in an unique mathematical model all the informations generated during the design process and necessary in the industrial process of manufacturing solid objects (typically mechanical parts). These systems are able to maintain all the geometrical and topological features of the described object, logically connected and structured.
Traditionally all these informations have to be deduced from a non connected set of geometrical and topological data represented in engineering drawings. Those data must be interpreted by an expert able to correlate them using representations, schemes, conventions and standards.
Characteristics and performances of systems can be classified following Stafford Beer [1], in terms of "capacity" and "ability". **Capacity** represents a systemic concept: it gives a value of the theoretical performances of a system, without any consideration about the constraints imposed by the environment. On the other hand, **ability** represents what we can really get from the system, noticing that an informatic system becomes more and more just a component in more complex and integrated ones [2]. A typical example of systems which join high capacity and a usually low ability is that of the Solid Modellers [3],[4]. What dramatically reduces the ability of such systems resides in the interaction process: in fact modellers mainly use command languages which lead to the use of complex sentences and describing operations in a three dimensional space: an unfamiliar job to almost all the designers [5].

## Motivations for the followed approach

This work suggests a step towards the solution of such problems, describing an interface system between Geometric Modellers and designers implemented into CADME system [15]: the interface system is able to simulate the work of a modeller, being at the same time a more natural tool for the usual user: a draftman. This system has been designed in such a way to represent an interactive graphic generalized front-end to solid modellers. The adopted point of view was the "designer" point of view who, in a design process, uses the modeller mainly with the aim to create a unique representation of a complex solid. Thus the preliminary study has been devoted to an analysis of the designer's usual ways of working and of the problems arising because of the introduction of modelling systems.

We found that the existing modellers have some disadvantages:

- there is a low level of interaction, which is mainly based on the use of sentences in a specific command language

- the system is oriented towards the modellers' problems rather than those of the users'

- the designer is forced to produce preliminary sketches in order to obtain the geometrical and topological informations needed for the model definition

- it is necessary to evaluate the model to obtain the visual feed-back assuring the user of the correctness of the specified operations

As a matter of fact a mechanical designer does want to use the modeller in a correct and simple way, preserving methods which he is accustomed to, avoiding, as much as possible, other difficulties connected with the introduction of the computer in his work. In other words the use of a modelling system needs more interaction based on procedures (as much as possible graphical ones) allowing the use of traditional drafting methods (bidimensional representations of solid objects by means of orthographic projections, sections etc.). It also needs an immediate visualization of the results of each action, operating on the graphical bidimensional representations.
The design of a system able to join capacity of the modellers with ability started from the identification of such needs. The resulting system, indipendent from a specific modeller, can be seen as divided into two main parts:

-the first one allows the user to describe the object via drafting procedures and performs the simulation of the resulting orthographic projections;

-the second one is really an interpreter, used as a code generator producing commands in the language of the modeller, starting from the generalized data structure generated during the designer interactive work and stored by the first module.

This solution also permits the descriptions of solids for the unification of the input procedures, adding freedom to the use of different modelling systems.

## A 2D drafting system as an emulator of the Solid Modeller

The tipical task of a system which models rigid solids following a C.S.G. approach is combining simple primitives in different ways to obtain complex shapes. This approach is very powerful and is widely used by designers at mental level: a mechanical part is conceived adding, subtracting or gluing simpler functional parts.
The main problem is to qualify and verify the results of the logical description via the usual representations means: different orthographic projections in an engineering drawing. The system presented is based on the concept of maintaining the power of a C.S.G. based way of part description and the need of an immediate possibility to verify the results via their representations without activating the modeller at each step. This approach was mainly due to the context of CADME project [15] aimed at the production of an integrated CAD/CAM system for small and medium industries, so with strict limitations on the power of the computers to be used. This led to the decision to reduce as much as possible the complexity of the problem so to simulate the results of C.S.G. operations in full 3-D space by equivalent C.S.G. operations in 2-D spaces corresponding to the different projection planes characteristics of each orthographic projections.
Following this approach each C.S.G. tree representing the procedural description of the object, is maintained and stored for the following interfacing with solid modellers, but is also mapped into "equivalent" 2-D C.S.G. trees corresponding to each orthographic projection as illustrated in figure 1.

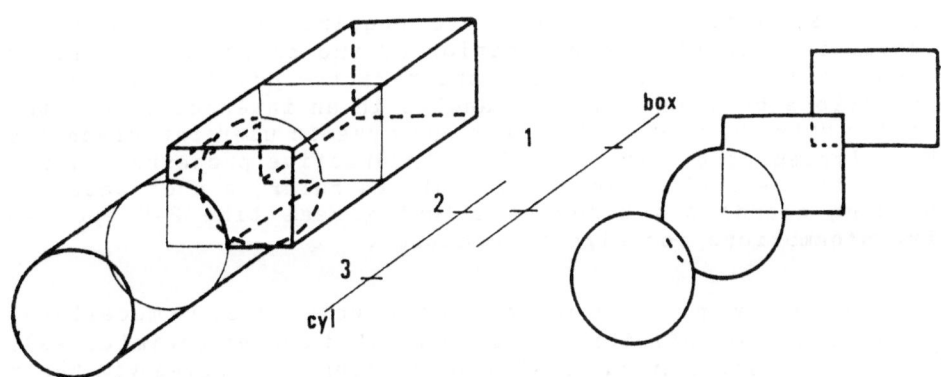

Figure 1

In this way the 3-D problem is split into parallel 2-D problems and it is possible to simulate operations between solid objects by means of a planar description, more simple from the algorithmic and computational point of view. In order to obtain these planar representations of complex solid objects the system produces the orthographic projections superimposing several planar figures, representing sections of the solid, perpendicular to the point of view (figure 2). This sections are automatically generated by the system applying logical multivalued functions of union, intersection, difference, and finally superimposition, to plane operands which represent co-planar sections of the solids to be combined.

The problem solved by the system is that of univocally represent complex shapes by means of a sequence of characteristic cross sections, parallel one to the other. In simple cases, for objects in two and half dimensions, it is easy to identify such sections; in these situations it's enough to apply the logical function (the set union, intersection, difference) to the co-planar sections of the objects, superimposing the results in a second time applying a procedure for hidden line removal.
For more complex objects, say fully three dimensional ones, the task is harder and the difficulty depends on the shape of the particular figure to be treated.

By means of the "constructive" approach [6], followed by the simulation process, it is easy to translate the graphic commands for the definition and operation of solids in the 3D space into an equivalent set of instructions for the definition of the 2D figures and their combinations.

**Architecture of the CADME user interface**

The simulation system's dialog towards its environment is mainly kept by means of two modules (see fig. 3)
    a) a user-interface system
    b) an interface towards the modelling
       system

The first module is designed to acquire the geometric and topologic data for the definition of the solid primitives in terms of dimentions, absolute and relative positions, and the operations between them; it handles in an interactive way the dialog with the user. A flexible and dynamic user interface has been implemented using graphical interactive procedures which simulate the tipical drafting tools (a ruler, a protractor, a drawing board) and hardware allowing real time 2-D and 3-D transformations for high interaction.

The interactive part of a design process coincides, in modellers, with a phase of definition of simple solid shapes (primitives). This is performed in our system describing primitives via their three orthogonal projections. These projections are defined by users with interactive procedures (graphic and alphanumeric); permits the use of graphical tools and modalities of interaction which can be chosen and activated via dynamic menus displayed on the screen.

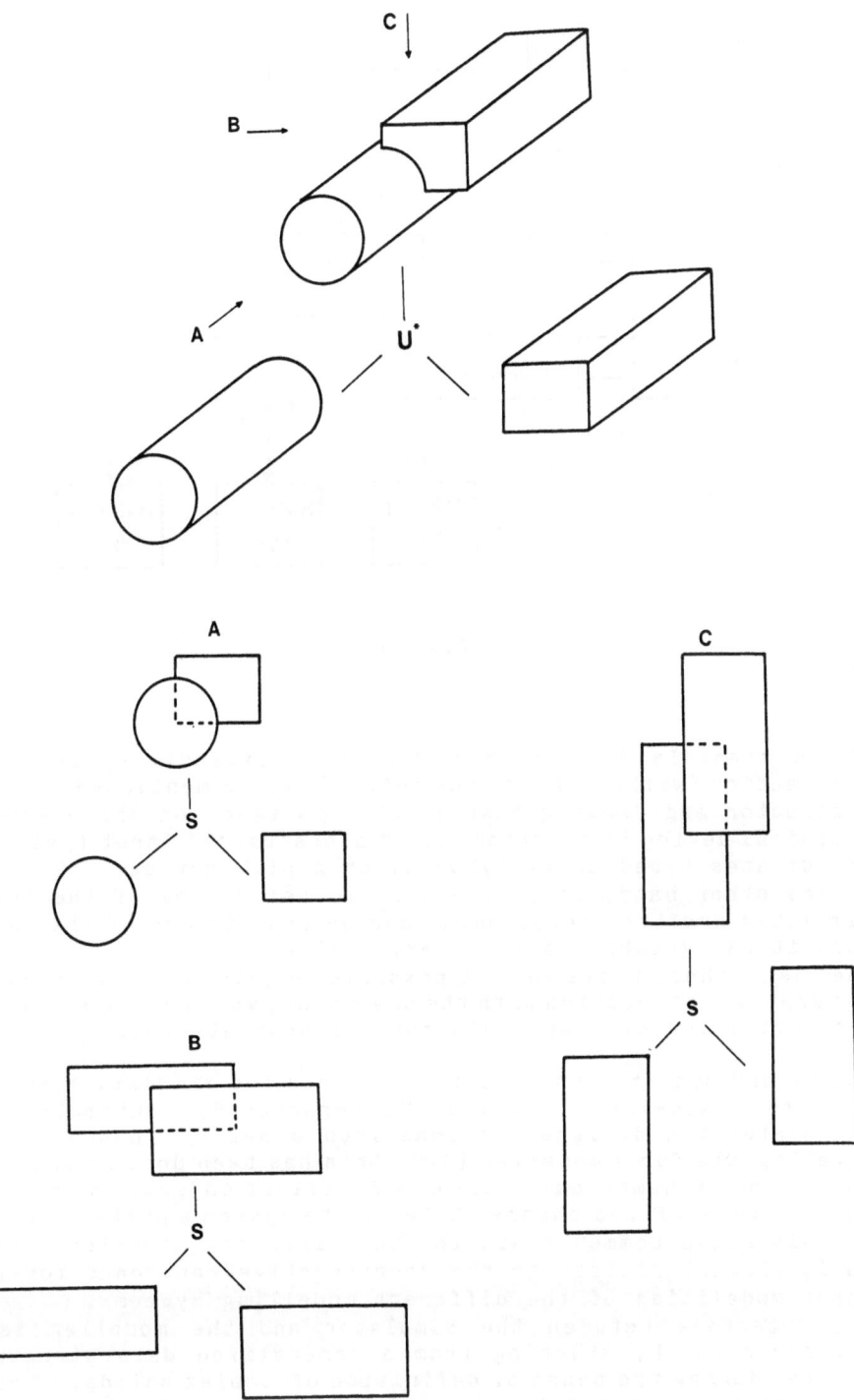

Figure 2

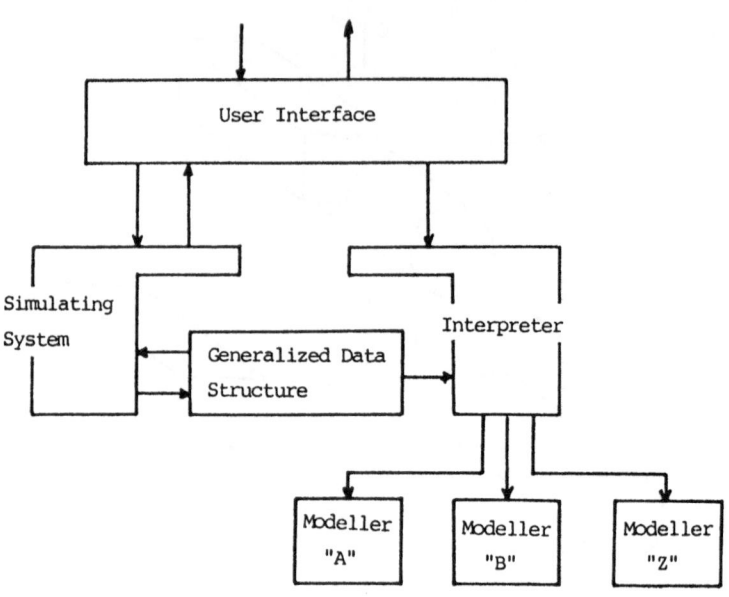

Figure 3

It is possible to select a "direct", exclusively graphic,
interaction (without any of the software tools mentioned: ruler,
protractor and drawing-board) which is based on the use of a
graphical device (a joystick) or an alphanumeric input (pairs of
coordinates typed on a keyboard) or a pick device.
On the other hand, it is possible to select one of the three
simulated drafting tools which can be used in one of the three
modalities: graphic, alphanumeric, pick.
The use of these tools make it possible to join the ease of use of
the graphic interaction with the precision, which is necessary in
the definition of shapes via their coordinate values.

The second system, the interface between the simulation system
and the modeller, called "interpreter", automatically
translates the designer actions into a set of instructions,
intelligible for a modeller [16]; this has been done in order to
obtain the mathematical model of the defined object. In order to
have a generalized channel between the system and the modeller
we maintain a common basis for the different modellers: this
basic element resides in the "constructive" approach for the
input modalities of the different modelling systems.
The interface between the simulator and the modeller is a
processor which, starting from a generalized data structure
created during the phase of definition ofcomplex solids, is able
to generate the shape (geometry and topology) of the designed
object.
This modularity lets a possibility of using the user interface
and the simulating system combined with different modellers.

Our applications deal with three different "translators", each of which related to a particular modeller. The first two modellers used are: PADL1, developed by the University of Rochester, N.Y. [7],[8],[9],[10],[11] and TIPS1, developed in Japan by a research group of the Hokkaido University [12],[13]. As a note we underline the substantial difference between the languages of this two modellers.
We have built up a third "translator", which is necessary for the system to support a modeller, based on a C.S.G. approach and a Ray Casting technique [14], developed in the CADME research group, at the Politecnico di Milano.

## An example

In the design of a simple mechanical part are defined the geometrical and topological features of the part itself. In figure 4 is shown a moment of this phase. In the picture it is possible to note the four graphic windows. The three-dimensional window maintains a wire frame echo of the object already created. The other parts of the screen are devoted to the menus (commands, instruments, swithes, figure's names) and to the alphanumeric interaction.
At the end of the interactive phase, which gives as a result the object representation via its orthogonal projections, the user may instance the chosen modelling system; this one creates the mathematical model of the solid object.

Figures 5, 6 and 7 show three results obtained submitting to three different modellers the results of the implemented interpreters; the pictures refer respectively to PADL1, TIPS1 and CADME.

## Conclusions

The present implementation is able to deal with objects in "two and half" dimensions defined using two primitives: box and cylinder. The extwnsion for fully three dimensional objects is under development and testing.

## Acknowledgments

This research was financially supported by "Consiglio Nazionale delle Ricerche" under contracts number 83.03025.97 and 83.03007.97 in "Progetto Finalizzato Informatica".

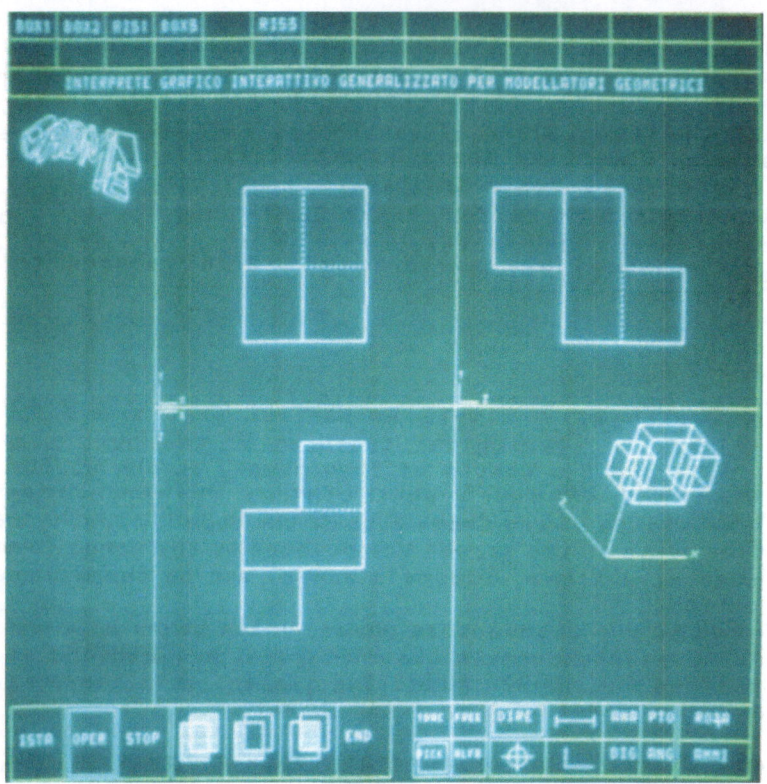

Figure 4

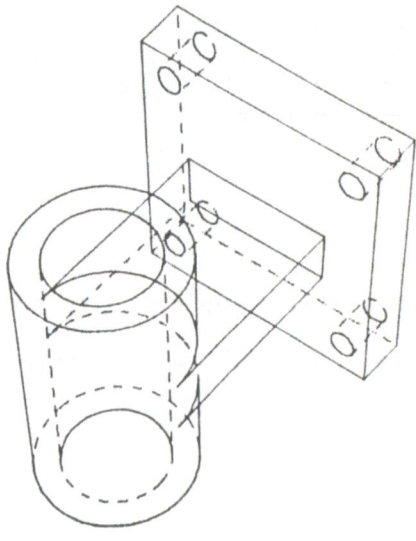

Figure 5

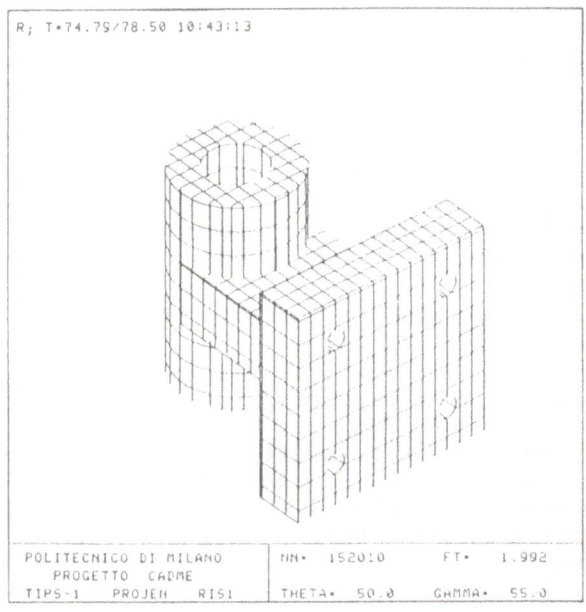

Figure 6

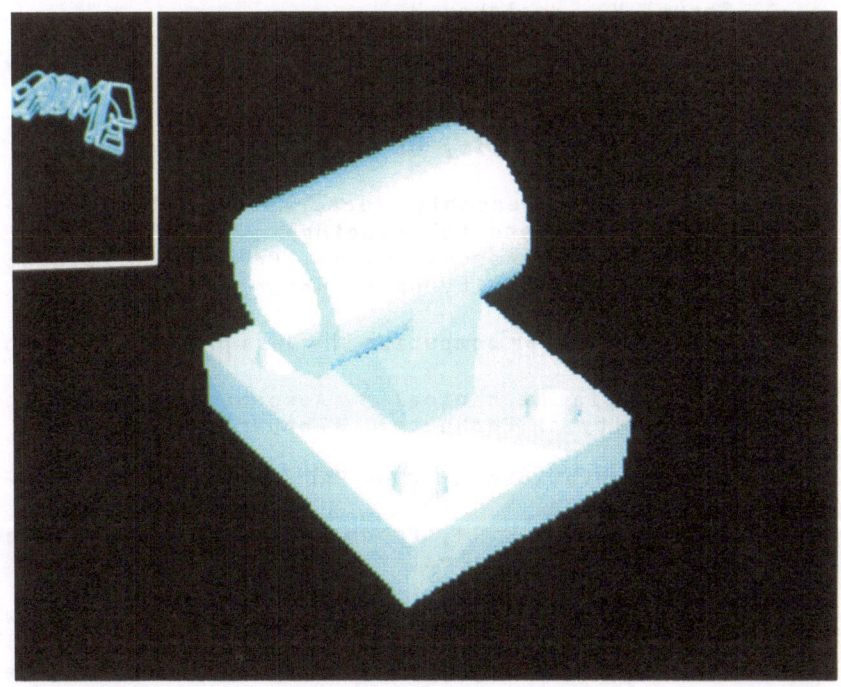

Figure 7

150

BIBLIOGRAPHY

[1]     Beer S.
        'Fanfare for effective freedom: cybernetic praxis in
        government'
        from: Beer S. 'Platform for Change'
        Wiley and Sons, 1975
[2]     Winograd T.
        'Beyond Programming Languages'
        Communications of the ACM, No 7, vol. 22, July 1979
[3]     Requicha A.
        'Representations for rigid solids: theory, methods
        and systems'
        Computing Surveys, vol 12, No 4, 1980, pp.437-464
[4]     Requicha A., Voelcker H.
        'Solid   Modelling:   a   historical   summary   and
        contemporary assessment'
        IEEE C.G. and A., March 1982, pp 9-24
[5]     Cardani A., Cugini U.
        'Analisi critica dell'impiego dei modellatori PADL1 e
        TIPS1'
        P.F.I. Obbiettivo CADME, technical report, May 1982
[6]     Requicha A., Voelcker H.
        'Constructive Solid Geometry'
        Technical  Memorandum  25  Production  Automation
        Project, University of Rochester N.Y., November 1977
[7]     Fisher W., Requicha A.,.
        Samuel N., Voelcker H.
        'Part   and   assembly   description   languages   II:
        definitional   facilities   in   the   PADL-1.0/2.n
        processor'
        Technical memorandum No. 20b, Production Automation
        Project, University of Rochester, June 1978
[8]     Requicha A.
        'Part   and   assembly   description   languages   I:
        dimensioning and tolerancing'
        Technical memorandum No. 19, Production Automation
        Project, University of Rochester, May 1977
[9]     Lee Y.
        'Algorithms for computing the mass properties of solid
        objects'
        M.S. Thesis, Mechanical and Aerospace Sciences Dept.,
        University of Rochester, February 1980
[10]    Hunt A.
        'Representations in the PADL-1.0/n processor: the
        drawing file'
        System Doc. No. 14, Production Automation Project,
        University of Rochester, August 1978
[11]    Hunt A.
        'Processes in the PADL-1.0/n processor: the drawing
        file post processor'
        System Doc. No. 15, Production Automation Project,
        University of Rochester, August 1978

151

[12]     Okino N. et al.
         ' TIPS-1 '
         Institute   of   Precision   Engineering,   Hokkaido
         University, Sapporo, Japan, 1978
[13]     Okino N., Kakazu Y., Kubo H.
         'TIPS-1: technical information processing system for
         computer aided design, drawing and manufacturing'
         in  'Computer  Languages  for  Numerical  Control',
         Amsterdam, North Holland, 1973, pp. 141-150
[14]     Scardaccione A.
         'Il modellatore solido CADME di tipo C.S.G.'
         P.F.I. Obbiettivo CADME
         Technical report, December 1984
[15]     Cosmai G., Cugini U., Rosoni R.
         'A graphic interpreter for solid Modellers'
         Proceedings  of  the  First  International  IFIP
         Conference on Computer Applications in Production and
         Engineering (CAPE) 1983, Amsterdam, the Netherlands,
         25-28 April 1983
[16]     Cosmai G., Rosoni R.
         'Studio ed implementazione di un interprete grafico
         interattivo generalizzato per modelli geometrici 3-
         D'
         P.F.I. Obbiettivo CADME, technical report, October
         1982

# A Low-Cost 2-D CAD System Based on Personal Computers

## Background of its Design and Implementation

Shunichiro Tsurumi[1] and Jiro Yamada[2]

[1] Design Department, Office Systems Development Factory, Hitachi, Ltd., 292 Yoshida-cho, Totsuka-ku, Yokohama, 244 Japan

[2] Computer Graphics Department, Hitachi Software Engineering Co., Ltd., 6-81 Onoe-machi, Naka-ku, Yokohama, 231 Japan

## 1.    Introduction

There has been amazing development in electronic equipment using micro-processors in recent years.  In particular,
the veritable flood of devices using micro-processors that
has been put on the market in the field of Office Automation
equipment leaves one truly astounded.  This has been likened
to fresh foods by some people because of a market life of a
mere six months.

Five to six years ago, when OA equipment entered the
Japanese market, there were a handful of companies manufacturing 8-bit personal computers and word processors mainly
for hobby use and they had dreams of an enlightenment coming
that would increase the demand.  This market has grown to a
yearly production of 430,000 16-bit business-oriented personal computers (afterwards called PC), 1.73 million units if
we include those built for hobby use.

The general consensus is that this type of equipment
will spread to eventually replace the pencils, pads and
calculators we have always used.  Although increasingly more
intelligent functions are added, along with complex and
communication functions, the devices are expected to become
both easier to use and cheaper.  The application fields of
PCs, considered to be the key component in office system

configuration, are predicted to be at the forefront of such developments.

We believed that the two-dimensional graph processor described in this report, GRAPHMASTER Mini (GMM), would be welcomed by all those persons involved in the tedious preparation of blueprints and design drawings. Based on the functions of a 16-bit personal computer, GMM can be provided as a turnkey system, with graph processing functions loaded in its specially designed software system. From the 1,500 sets sold in its first eighteen months on the market, it would seem that our assessment of GMM's reception was no exaggeration. Many other manufacturers entered the same field after the appearance of the first GMM, the products available including both devices with similar functions and software packages. This all attests to a sudden increase in demand. In the market, this type of device has been given the names P-CAD and Personal CAD. Table 1 shows the various types of CAD on the market at present.

We only wonder, now such a product (cheap, requiring no program creation and easy to use) is available, how people managed for so long without it. Conditions for a hit product exist and regardless of the unquestioned superiority of a given development plan, it is basic that investment can only be retrieved by making a viable, saleable product that meets the conditions. Marketing books teach us that the important thing in marketing is to know the needs of the market and be one step ahead in product development but most people find that the business world does not go according to the book.

GMM's success is due purely to lucky timing but we found the the following results of an analysis of its success. 1. The product met a hidden demand, 2. basing it on a PC made it right up-to-date, 3. it has a high quality graphic processing function and 4. it is cheap. The forecasted 60-70% annual growth of the market indicated in Figure 1 was proof that we had uncovered a potentially large market, another source of satisfaction.

2.    Background to the Revealed Market

We decided to examine the reasons for this potential market suddenly coming to light.  Most papers dealing with product development and design tend to deal strictly with the results of the development and the techniques utilized but the author believes that it is the needs and pre-conditions to the development that should be examined.

1)    Changes in the Economic Environment

Figure 2 shows the results of the Arthur D. Little (ADL) report that sparked the OA boom in Japan.  It shows trends in investment per worker and rises in the productivity rate for various industries in the United States in the decade between 1968 and 1978.  It indicates quite clearly that the investment amount in office-based businesses was very low compared to that for agriculture and industry, with the result that productivity rose by a mere 4%.

A recession came to the advanced nations because of two oil shocks and the dollar shock and economists, despite zealous attempts to explain the structure of the recession, were unable to find any real factors.  Japan could not avoid a sharp drop in its GNP and a period of low economic growth.

Japan overcame the worst effects of the first oil shock by the automation of production lines.  In this rationalization of the production process, Factory Automation (FA) was promoted.  FA is a system in which work that does not need to be done by humans is done by robots and other machines. It definitely resulted in decreased costs and improved quality. However, when the second oil shock came, industries were forced to look at rationalization of other departments of the company's operations in order to survive. The release of the ADL report mentioned earlier at about that time led to improvements in office productivity, in particular, the speeding up of all office information processing and higher quality of work done. This brought about an actual decrease in indirect costs and proved to be the starting point for the entire OA boom.

But let there be no mistake about it, humans are still central to office work. Much of the criticism of OA hinges on the misconception that, as had happened in factories, automation of offices will lead to less jobs for people. The ideal of OA is to allow human beings to concentrate on and thus perform to the best of their abilities the tasks that really belong to them, namely those requiring imagination, judgement, instructions and commands. This is achieved by making machines do all the mechanical office work stemming from these intellectual activities, i.e. the information gathering, reference, calculation, separation, printing, contact and communication etc. This results not only in an increased information processing volume per hour but also in increased intellectual productivity and in the final analysis, increased profits for the company.

People working in design offices also want to improve productivity and to escape from the drudgery of having to sit in front of the drawing board doing the tedious work of design drawing. They craved for the appearance of a device that could do this work for them. This was the first major feature behind the realization of GMM.

2) The Change from an Industrial to an Information
   Society

The second major factor I want to discuss is the sudden change from an industrial society to an information society. This change has already been covered in detail in Alvin Toffler's famous work "The Third Wave"[2] and John Naisbitt's "Megatrends"[3]. The basic thesis is that the mainstream of economic activity is switching from regular industries to the information industries and that our sense of values is changing from pure materialism to a scale of added values based on the presence of information. According to J. Naisbitt, 60% of the workforce in the United States was, as of 1982, involved with information and knowledge services and connected in some way with the production, processing and distribution of information. (Agriculture was 3%, manufacturing 13% and services 11-12%). Design is no more than the production of information to help people build things and so we believe that there is a definite need among the people in this industry for this type of device.

3) A Changing Social Environment

Japan's recovery after the devastation of World War II was achieved by an all-out effort, the greatest efforts being in the acquisition of the essentials, namely clothing, food and housing. This led to the Japanese economic miracle, focus of the world's attention, which definitely succeeded in building a peaceful and plentiful society. But people's desires have changed and they prefer to wear and eat different and better things, and this strong desire to express individual character and personality has led to a diversification of consumer demand.

The industrial society as we knew it was based on an ideology of mass-production and mass-consumption. We can say that the mass public demand that led to mass-consumption was the supporting pillar of the industrial society. So when this demand diversified, there was really no choice for companies but to accept a policy of small-production of a wide range of products. I mentioned earlier the importance of understanding consumers' need. Getting and comprehending this information as quickly as possible is really the only way for a company to survive in today's extremely competitive society. It also serves as an explanation for the speed and truly international scale with which the transformation to the information society I touched on earlier is being carried out.

The author feels that production will be just as dynamic as before but with a major difference. Rather than being promoted purely according to the producers' theory, the producers are going to have to take the users' opinions into account far more than previously. When technology starts being used to produce goods that the consumer really wants to use, then, and only then, can companies look forward to real sales growth.

4)   Technical Revolution

The transistor has been called the greatest invention of the 20th century. Techniques in the ability to integrate on a silicon wafer only a few millimetres square semiconductor elements developed astoundingly, to such a degree that they have become "the staple diet of the industry." Quite definitely, without today's semiconductor technology the electronic industry, and all related industries, would not have been able to develop as they have. It was thanks to this technology that we were able to realize small, light, cheap yet high precision equipment. A good example is the computer. Only ten or so years ago, even a reasonably large company hesitated before paying rental for the use of a computer with only the same functions as those in the personal computers used by individual people today.

The famous Moore's Law, that holds that the degree of semiconductor integration doubles every year while the price drops by 40%, is on the verge of becoming true and this is probably the major factor behind the promotion of the information society.

The various background factors mentioned here combine with each other in that sector of the business that is presently under the most pressure. I refer to the people in the development design sections. They sit chained to the drawing board but no matter how hard and fast they work, they can never keep ahead of the seemingly endless stream of orders. This is understandable when we consider the speed with which information arrives from the sales outlets and the extremely short life of most products. But if the job is even slightly rough, sales plummet alarmingly.

3. Motivation for Development

The idea of using a computer's functions in design operations is not new, models and simulations as part of information, reference and product image and attempts to systematize the graph operations in detailed drawings having been looked at since the early 1960's. They never got past the draft stage then but Computer Aided Design (CAD) systems are now quite close to full realization, almost, in fact, to the stage of popularization.

In Japan, these systems were originally developed for the shipbuilding and automobile industries but tended to be used exclusively in those industries and never spread to become an all-purpose system. At the start of the 1970's, CADAM®, developed by the Lockheed Corporation, was marketed by IBM and achieved a certain degree of sales. However, there were a number of drawbacks with this product when viewed from the users' position.

1.  Used with a large-scale computer, it was too expensive to be easily purchased by the people with the real demand, the medium and small-scale companies.

2.  It was too complicated to be used by amateur operators, needing a full-time specialist. The people who really want to use it are computer-amateurs.

3.  Restriction on number of terminals make it impractical.

4.  Too expensive for simple graphs because of unit cost.


An analysis of design department operations, Figure 3, showed that many of the operations are two-dimensional graph preparation. A further analysis, Figure 4, showed that 80% of all graph preparation work was alterations to or tracing of existing graphs, with only 20% being preparing absolutely new graphs.

That being the case, most of the problems facing people working in these departments would be solved by the provision of a tool enabling an increase in the productivity of these operations. This conclusion is what led us to commit ourselves to the development of GMM.


4.  The Hitachi GRAPHMASTER Mini GMM-30 Graphic Processor

Figure 5 shows the configuration of this system. In order to enable the user to select input requirements matching his actual job, all input commands are options. The system uses a 16-bit personal computer with the i8087 high-speed calculation processor installed, a 640kbyte memory and a twin $5\frac{1}{4}$-inch floppy disk drive. The main unit consists of a 14-inch color graphic display, a 5-inch, 13Mbyte (unformatted) hard disk, a keyboard and a system rack. Input can be done by either a tablet or a digitizer, the digitizer being able to be connected randomly to paper size from A3 to A0, while output can be done by X-Y plotter, facsimile or dot matrix printer from A3 to A0. The graph created can be stored on either a $5\frac{1}{4}$-inch (0.3Mbyte) or 8-inch (1Mbyte) floppy disk. Data transfer between GMM and the computer described above is supported by the DES (Data Entry System) protocol.

Facsimile output is suitable for transmission to remote locations and because output from GMM is by means of direct electric signals, the reception is extremely clear. Tests done by transmitting A1-size graphs for A4 reception gave high legibility.

GMM software consists of the following three programs and is operated by MS-DOS®, an all-purpose OS for personal computers. System generation is a program for execution of the preparation required to operate the equipment configuration used in GMM and file allocation and alteration etc.The basic program is central to the operation of GMM because it is this program that controls definitions, alterations, deletions,· sectional shapes, storage and positioning of drawings. The utility program controls the menu data not requiring interface processing and storage and deletion of the kanji (Chinese character) font, line font and macro. In consideration of ease of maintenance and translation, most of the software uses MS-PASCAL® and some MS-ASSEMBLER®.

Input usually takes a lot of time in drafting.
Particularly in graphic processing work stations, there is a
tendency for the designer himself to be the operator and
input is done as he thinks, with alterations being made from
the display as he goes along.  Thus the device must have a
function permitting frequent interruptions and restarts.  It
also needs a function to save the work in progress in case
of power failure and to give rapid recovery.  Providing
these functions in GMM has enabled us both to satisfy these
demands and to enhance the reliability of the system.

(1)  Graph Creation Functions

Table **2**   gives an outline of the different functions
available with GMM-30.

(2)  Geometric Analysis

Although GMM is actually a graphic processor, it also
has some geometric analysis functions that enable it to
calculate coordinate values, distances, angles, circumfer-
ences and areas.  When the user specifies the graph he is
seeking and enters the command, the calculation result is
displayed in the upper left corner of the graphic display.

(3)  Function for Writing in User's Program

The user wants his work station ready for him to use
whenever he wants to start work.  In addition to the obvious
requirements for a high-performance and cheap device, it is
also necessary that it have a function permitting the user
to facilitate the creation of his own operating program.

GMM provides, for the user's convenience, sub-routine
groups that can be called from either PASCAL or FORTRAN.
Because the user can access both the display board file and

the parts file using these sub-routine groups, GMM can be used in conjunction with a unique user's program. Thus using sub-routine groups for the user interface has the advantage over the conventional method, in which the file configuration was opened up, that the program is easier to create. An additional advantage is that the user can continue using his own program even when the manufacturer changes the file configuration.

(4) Macro

Macro is a function whereby a series of GMM commands and numerical formulae are given a designation which can then be used as a new GMM command in its own right. The operator can use not only parameter definitions in Macro but also variables (undefined parameters), making this function perfectly suited for parametric drafting in which the shape itself doesn't change, only the dimensions. In a case such as this, the operator creates Macro data with the dimensions to change entered as variables or numerical formulae and stores this data. When required, he recalls the stored Macro and merely replaces the necessary values.

5. Applications

Figure 6 shows a breakdown by industry of purchasers of GMM. As mentioned earlier, GMM is extremely user-friendly and was designed so that even a person with no knowledge of computer technology or operations could use it freely and master drafting after only a very short time. Thus we were able to attract to GMM a very wide range of users, these ranging through people doing serious design operations, preparation of proposals and documents, on-the-spot creation of kitchen or furniture layouts as a service to

housing display customers and even those making block copy
originals for printing.

Making it able to support IGES V.2.0 means that it can
carry out    drafting    data transfers directly with large-
scale CAD systems and this enables it to be used as an
online terminal.  In response to many recent demands to make
it possible to control machinery directly by the results of
the graph created, we developed a paper tape support application.  Another application is calculating estimates from
the elements of the lines in the drafting. But the largest
number of users is, quite naturally, those people who need a
means right now of creating accurate graphs quickly and
efficiently.

Although it may be just as quick to draw the basic
graph by hand as by using the GMM commands, there is usually
some degree of alteration or addition to a graph before it
is finished.  When these are taken into consideration, we
calculate that GMM is approximately 30-50% faster than hand
drawing.

Our 1,500-strong customer base has suggested various
methods of using GMM to increase its user-friendliness.
Some technically-inclined users, as a means of achieving
faster, more accurate and more efficient    drafting,
have modulized those parts they use with the highest frequency and are using them much as a    drafting    database.
Some users have stored as figure data which they know will
not be altered.  When GMM is used in these ways, the savings
can reach as high as 80-90%.

Taking a hint from these comments, we are presently
working on the development of a kit containing a specialist
parts file for different industries and a menu sheet for use
with digitizers.  Figures 7 and 8 show the menu sheet for

use in design of electrical panel boards and an example of a graph respectively.

6.    Conclusion

I have covered the background to and motivation behind the development of a two-dimensional graph processor based on a personal computer and would like, in the conclusion, to examine the future problems we foresee.

I mentioned earlier that the designer's job was to produce information in order for something to be manufactured but the job does not simply entail designing things. A good product can not be developed unless the developer is directly involved in each facet of the business, from marketing research, product planning, production planning to sales. Although GMM was developed as a low-cost drafting system, you will better understand why people want it to be able to be run in tandem with a host computer or connected to NC operational machinery if you consider the designer as one unit in a large entity that takes in marketing, development and production.

OA equipment began with single-function devices but gradually became more complex as more intelligent functions were added later. These devices are now on the verge of becoming work stations in larger network systems in connection with a host computer and other electronic equipment. In the same way, we believe that GMM will develop in a number of areas within the design operation field.

One trend already evident is for GMM, as a work station for development and planning staff, to utilize to the full all the many functions of a personal computer by being used as a complex terminal. Another is for GMM to support information retrieval and analytical functions as well as supporting functions for image sketching, rendering, layout and tracing.   Another is having GMM supported by wordprocessor and electronic mailing functions.   While we realize the main function of GMM as a work station for detail designers is graph processing, GMM can be made to support a powerful graphic database by having functions enabling the transfer of figures both inside and outside the company and the sharing of large capacity optical disks for electronic drawing filing and high-speed plotters.   Or given a function enabling easy connection with operational machinery.   And of course the cost must be kept as low as possible.

Estimates put the number of drawing boards in Japan at about 3.5 million and there must be tens of millions throughout the world.   Of course, it is not wrong to count in the potential demand for GMM the more double that number of architects who are involved in design work.

We are committed to giving priority to the needs of all these people in our development of systems that are easy to use.

Bibliography

1)   Norman S. Zimbl, Robert L. Fronk and Anne M. Mayfield
     "The Emerging Real World of Office Automation"
     Arthur D. Little, Inc., 1979
2)   Alvin Toffler
     "The Third Wave"
     W. Morrow & Co., New York 1980
3)   John Naisbitt
     "Megatrends"
     Warner Books, Inc., New York 1982

4)   Jiro Yamada, et al.
     "A Low-cost Drafting System Based on a Personal
     Computer, IEEE Computer Graphics and Applications" 1984
5)   Summary of 1984 CAD/CAM White Paper
     Japan Management Association CAD/CAM Center
     Japan Management Association Research Institute
     Japan Management Association Consulting

Table 1    CAD Classifications

| Type | Applicable Computers | Price Range |
|---|---|---|
| Host-type CAD/CAM | Large and medium-scale | ¥100 million or more |
| Turnkey-type CAD/CAM | Medium-scale/ super mini-com | ¥50~ 150 million |
| Work Station | 32-bit micro-computers | ¥5~ 40 million |
| DraftingSystem | Mini-computers | ¥10~ 30 million |
| P-CAD | Personal computers | Below ¥10 million |

(Japan Management Association)

Table 2    Outline of GMM-30 Functions

| Graph creation functions | Straight lines, circles, arcs, dotted lines, polygonal forms, rectangles, ovals, free curves, trace curves, kanji, English, numerals. |
|---|---|
| Editing functions | Parallel lines, rotation, mirror reflection, magnification, reduction, copy, trimming, deletion, round cutting, insertion and replacement of kanji, offsetting etc. Automatic dimension display |
| Operation functions | * Display board ... can take up to 255 sheets, create on each sheet, display optional.<br>* Line types ... solid, broken, dotted, dot link line, double dot link, line font defined by user.<br>* Menu ... standard command menu, user-defined menu.<br>* Rubber band ... graph creation, windowing, picks.<br>* Batch input ... batch processing of commands possible.<br>* Macro ... Parametric graph creation possible by using undefined parameters that can change command groups into macro commands.<br>* Grids ... Grids and isometric.<br>* Coordinates ... Direct, polar and opposite coordinates. |
| Calculation Functions | Coordinate values, distances, circumferences, angles, areas. |
| Application Programs | * Estimates and integration programs<br>* Pass graph creation programs.<br>* Shadow graph creation programs.<br>* IGES data conversion programs.<br>* Off-line plotter data creation. programs.<br>* Graph access sub-routine.<br>* File transfer programs. |

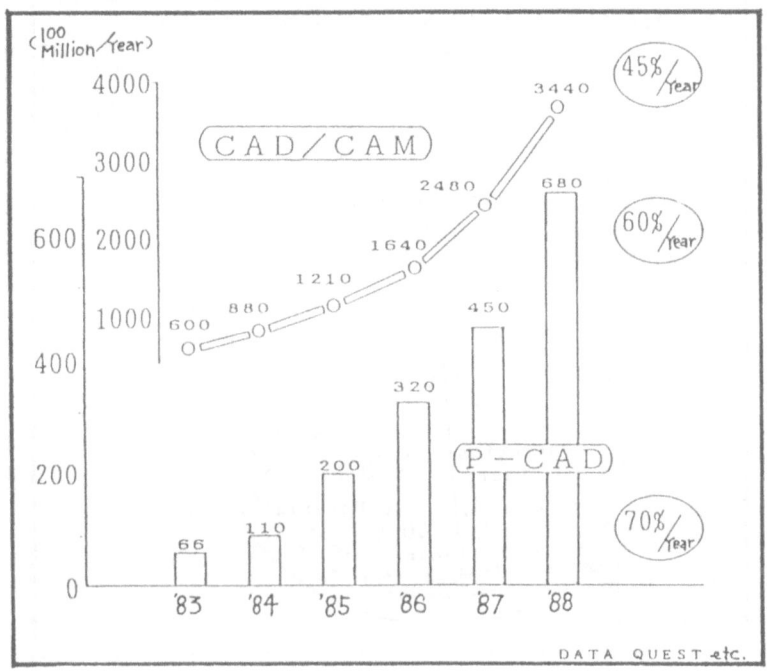

Figure 1    Scale of CAD/CAM Market

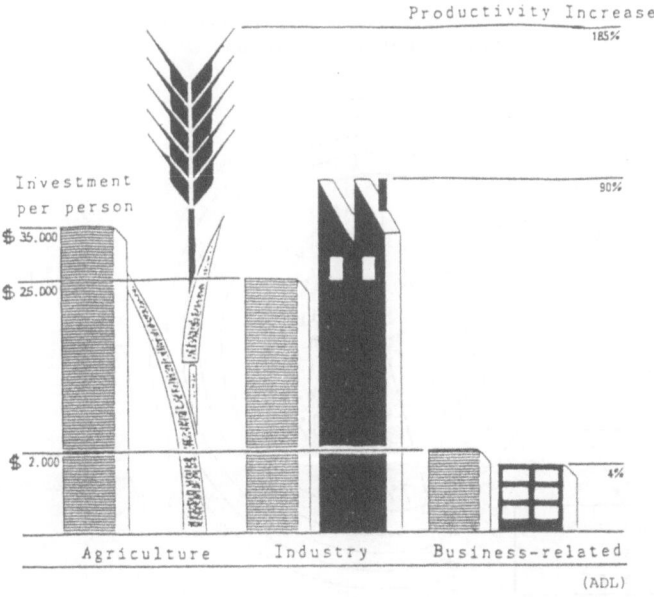

Figure 2    Investment and Productivity Increase
by Industry in the United States
(1968-1978)

170

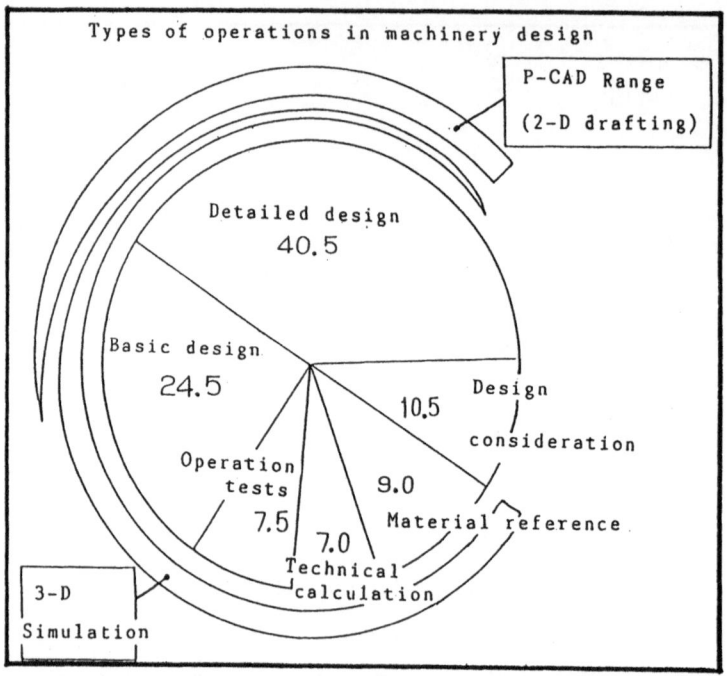

Figure 3    Analysis of Design Department Operations

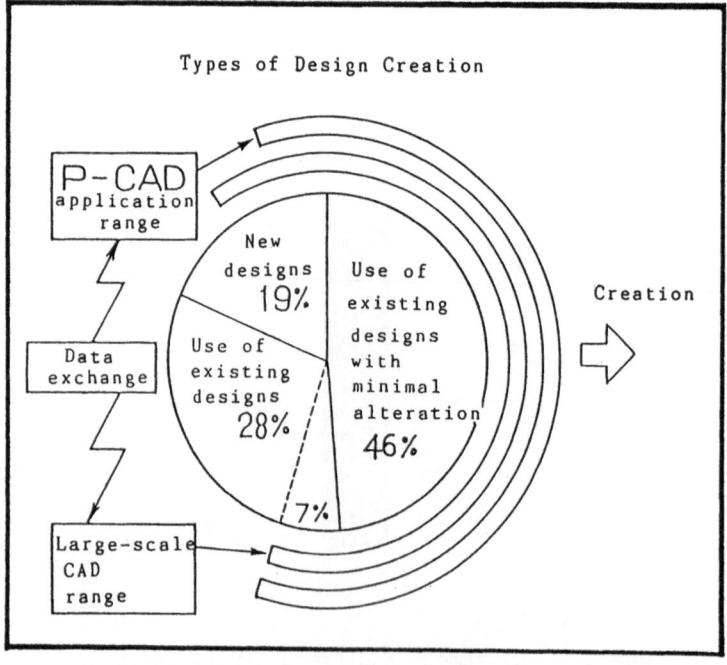

Figure 4    Applications of P-CAD

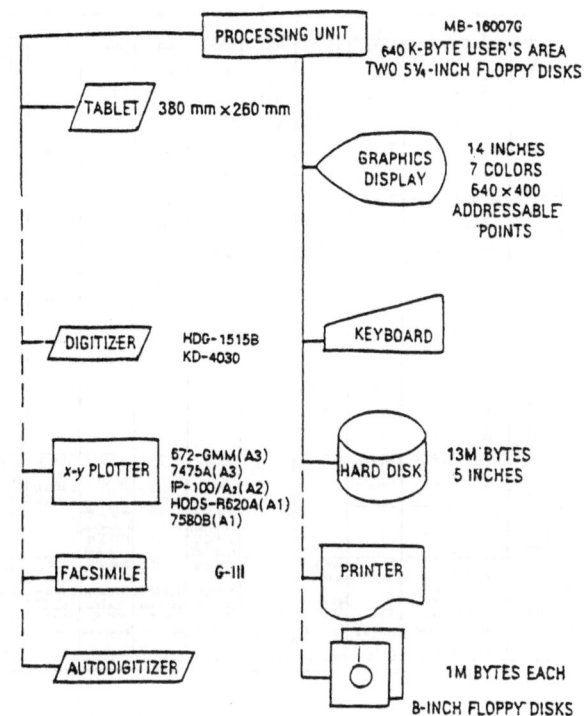

Figure 5    System Configuration

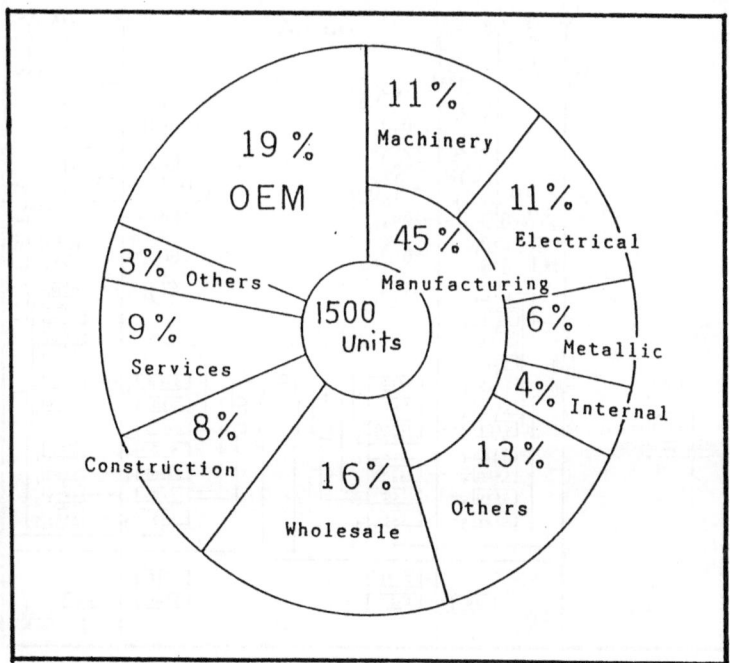

Figure 6    Analysis of GMM Purchasers by Industry

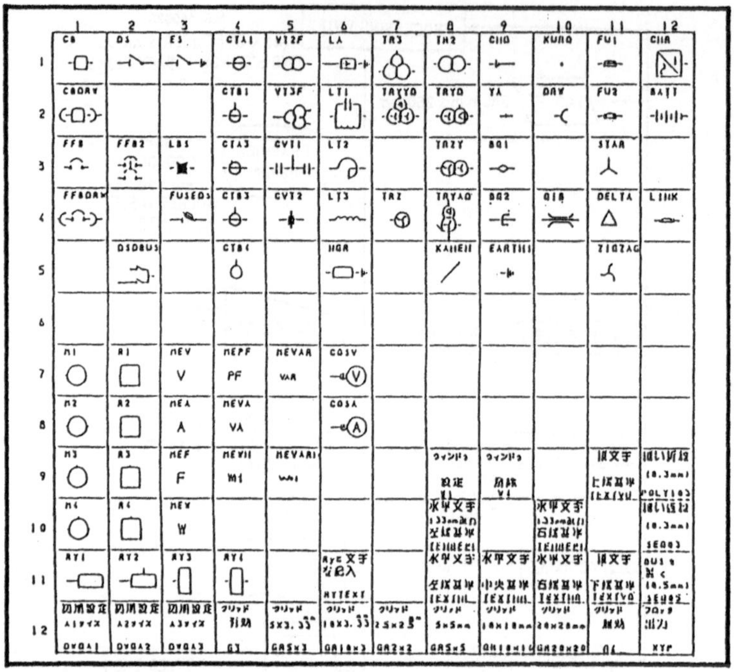

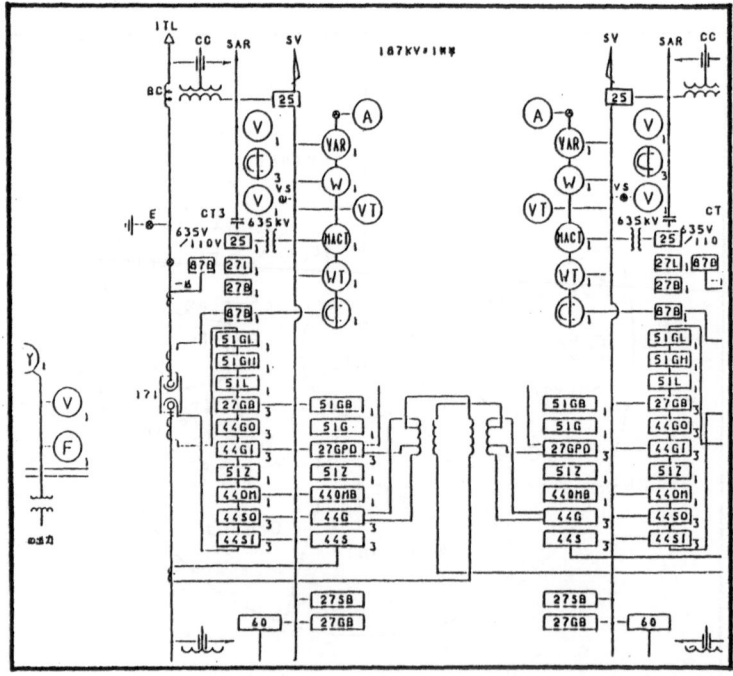

Figure 7    An Example of an Exclusive Menu
for Panel Board Sequence Design

Figure 8    One Section of Sequence Design Panel Board

# A High Performance Graphic System for VLSI Design

Sumitsugu Inoue, Takashi Watanabe and Takayoshi Nakashima

Atsugi Electrical Communication Laboratory, N.T.T., 3-1, Morinosato Wakamiya, Atsugi, Kanagawa, 243-01 Japan

## ABSTRACT

A high performance Graphic System for VLSI-CAD has been developed. A customized, 170k-gate, Graphic Processor (GP), the core component of the system, has high speed display functions with direct processing of primitives such as rectangles and cells without interpreting intermediate display formats. It supports high speed hardware editing functions and multi-user functions, with a large scale buffer memory.

The system has about 100 times, for display, and 1,000 times, for editing, as high performance as conventional graphic systems. For example, the display time of a 2,000-gate LSI (335K vectors) is about 3 seconds, all the editing times of the same LSI are shorter than 1 second, the display time of a 14,000-gate LSI (3.67M vectors ) is about 25 seconds, and most of the editing times of the same LSI are shorter than 3 seconds.

## 1. INTRODUCTION

Due to the rapid progress of VLSI technology, a highly integrated and efficient VLSI Design system is in great demand. Recent efforts in VLSI CAD have made it clear that this kind of system will be realized not with a simple combination of automatic programs but with a combination of well-designed interactive feedback processes and automatic programs. This is especially true for VLSI layout design.

The graphic system for the above-mentioned purpose should have several features which conventional turnkey layout systems don't possess. That is, high speed processing capability for a very large volume of VLSI layout data and tight connection with the main CAD system, which resides on the host computer, in terms of both hardware configuration and LSI data base.

Under these considerations, we have developed the new Graphic System which is especially tailored for VLSI layout design.

## 2. FEATURES OF VLSI LAYOUT DATA

VLSI layout data have several remarkable features as follows:

1)   Most VLSI layout data consist of straight lines such as rectangles, polygons (shapes) and polylines.   Circles or other kinds of curved lines are rarely used.   In most cases, these straight lines are placed horizontally or vertically.

Text elements are also used mainly for denoting the signal names and circuit names,   which give the basic information to the checking and routing programs.

These basic elements are called "primitive"s.

2)     VLSI layout data are constructed in a hierarchical manner. The group of geometrical data is often called "cell" and the lowest cell usually  corresponds to a basic circuit such as "NAND-gate".   Cells one level higher  are designed by using the lowest cells and other primitives.   This step is repeated until "chip", the top of the hierarchy.   A chip generally has several levels of hierarchy.   The cell which is referred in the higher cell acts as a primitive from a functional point of view,  so it is often referred to as "primitive".

3)     VLSI layout data are essentially two-dimensional.   But they have a unique concept called "layer".   Layer is a group of geometrical data,  each of which pertains to the single "mask" in VLSI fabrication process.   Every primitive has to belong to one of the layers, so that the layer acts as an attribute of each primitive.   The relationship between cells and layers is illustrated in Figure 1.

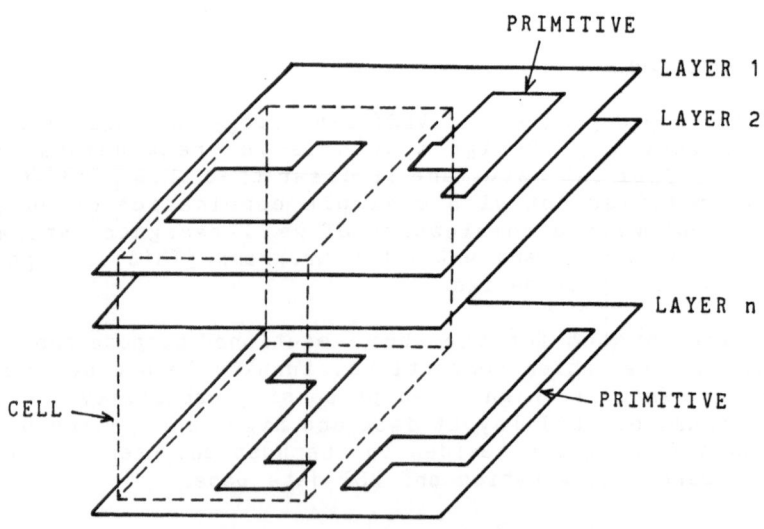

Figure 1    Structure of LSI layout data

4)      VLSI layout data require a high resolution coordinate
system.   Recently, it is not unusual that the minimum unit for
VLSI geometrical data is 0.1 micron or less.   Provided that this
minimum unit is assigned to the minimum   coordinate unit,  VLSI
chip size, which ranges from 5 mm to 10 mm, requires 50,000 to
100,000 units to represent its coordinates.   It means that 16-
bit data handling is not sufficient for a VLSI data coordinate
system.

5)      VLSI layout data have a very large amount of vector
data  which occupy several megabytes of memory as a whole.  A
20K-gate logic LSI is estimated to contain 2-4 M bytes  while
maintaining its hierarchical structure.

To summarize these features, VLSI layout data have a  very simple
structure and format but have a very large volume and high resolution.   Because of these latter features, processing of VLSI
layout data is beyond a conventional graphic system capability.
Small amount of memory capacity, low processing power of a mini-
computer and software-oriented data manipulation; all of these
don't match the VLSI level data processing.

## 3. DESIGN POLICY

Under these conditions, we have set our scenario for a high
performance graphic system as follows:

1) A special purpose graphic processor called "GP" should be
developed so as to achieve high speed processing of VLSI layout
data.   As shown in the previous discussion, its simple data
structure is expected to fit very well for hardware manipulation.
Functions such as smooth panning and zooming, clipping, vector-
to-raster conversion and text generation, are supported by hardware.

2) GP supports micro-programmed editing functions of VLSI
layout data as well as high speed display capability.  This means
that a single data format on the GP memory is used both for a
modeling data and a display file. Eventually this format supports
hierarchical structure and some flags for editing usage.

3)      It should have a large amount of memory capacity which
can contain all VLSI chip layout data at a time.   This enables
not only high speed processing on GP, but also a small number of
times of data transmission between GP and host computer.

4)      The new graphic system  consists of a GP and a system
software.  The latter part should run on a host computer where
main CAD system resides.   This software performs the data base
management such as a translation between the CAD data base and GP
data format, controls the transmission between GP and host
computer, and manages the miscellaneous supervisory functions.
The transmission rate between GP and host computer should be high
enough to maintain the interactive characteristics of the system.

A block diagram of the system is shown in Figure 2. In this figure, a color CRT means a high resolution RGB color monitor.

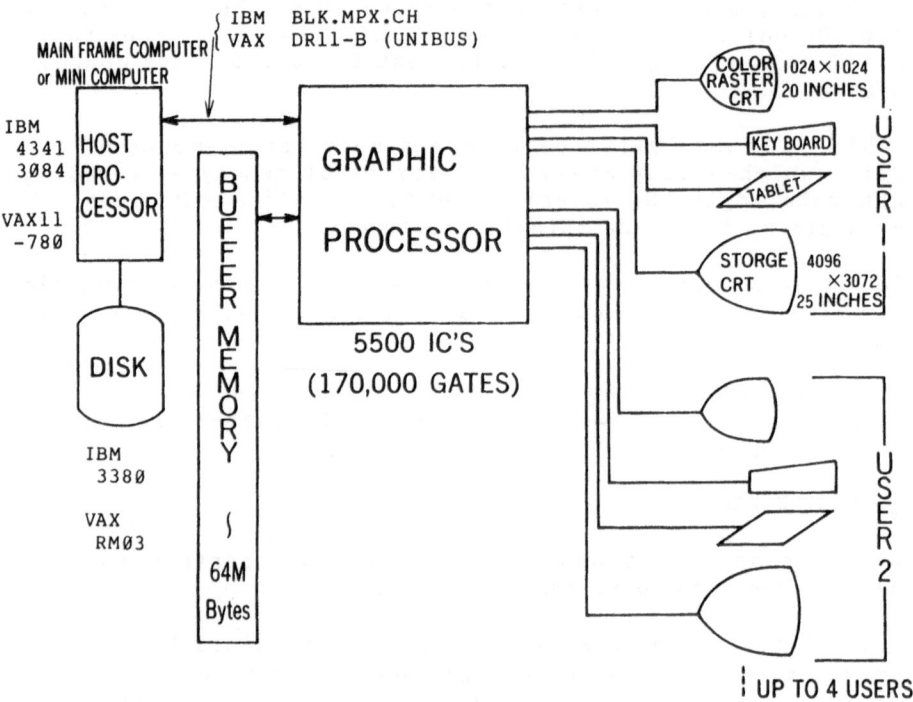

Figure 2    System configuration of Graphic System

## 4. USER INTERFACE

Our graphic system supports many interactive user commands and functions which are used for layout data input and edit.    Our discussion will be focused  on our notable features  which are not known in conventional graphic systems, and on our hardware support capabilities.

(1) Smooth panning and zooming
Versatility of the window manipulation function is one of the most important factors of the graphic system.    The high speed display performance of the GP has made it possible to realize a smooth (or continuous ) zooming and panning function on our graphic system.    In the special mode  which is initiated  by a menu key, a display window is being changed every few seconds depending on the number of vectors to be displayed.    The size and position of the window are controlled by dials,  and the zooming ratio changes within the range from 1/64 to 64 times the default window size.    The default window size is 1,024 x 1,024 minimum units.

(2) Layer and selection handling

Note that "layer" attribute in VLSI layout data plays a very important role. For example, whether a certain primitive is visible or not is decided according to which layer that primitive lies on. Generally speaking, when a user wants to edit a certain primitive, he selects the primitive among those editable primitives by specifying the layer on which it lies and the window area which contains its primitive. In fact, the select function is one of the most frequently used commands. In order to process these layer handling and selecting functions faster and easier, each primitive has on its header the information about the layer to which it belongs and about its selecting status. This also enables the system to support these functions in hardware easily.

Further details of the basic specification of the system are decided according to the above-mentioned conditions. These are listed in tables 1 - 3.

Table 1    Requirements for speed

| Display Speed | Short vector | 100,000 to 200,000 Vectors/sec |
|---|---|---|
| | Medium vector | 30,000 Vectors/sec |
| Editing | Speed | 0.4 to 1.0 micro second/word |

Table 2    Summary of display functions

| World coord. | $-2^{31}$ to $2^{31}-1$ |
|---|---|
| Layer | 64 |
| Nesting level | 15 |
| Color | 7 |
| Primitives | Line with Width, Shape,Rectangle,Text, Cell,Matrix,Return,NOP,Jump,JID |

Table 3    Hardware editing commands

| |
|---|
| Select, unselect |
| Move |
| Erase |
| Mirror |
| Rotate |
| Macro expand |
| Replicate |
| Change layer |
| Change width of lines |
| Change size of texts |

## 5. ARCHITECTURE

For future expansion and hardware efficiency, we have adopted a 32-bit world coordinate to express the layout data. In other words, the GP is a 32-bit processor.

A block diagram of the GP is shown in Figure 3. The GP is divided
into three major blocks, that is, micro-programmed Display Edit
Processor, Display Pipeline Processor and terminals.

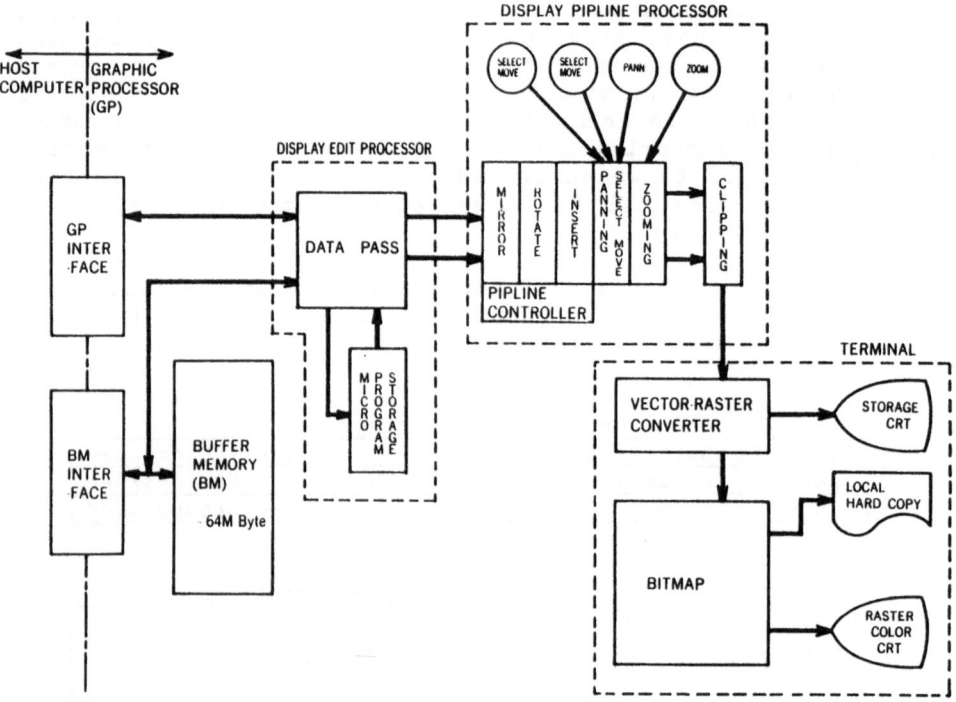

Figure 3    A block diagram of the Graphic Processor

## (1)  Display Edit Processor

### Display functions
One of the main jobs of this processor is to calculate the "primary coordinate" for each primitive datum to be handled.

This processor reads primitive data from the buffer memory and
picks out the data which are on visible layers which are set by
user commands.   In the buffer memory, each primitive coordinate
is represented by the most suitable format for modeling, depending on the type of primitive.  For example, a rectangular primitive has one coordinate of a corner point and the values of width
and height, while the polygonal primitive has one coordinate
followed by relative displacement values for subsequent vertices.
All these coordinates are changed into absolute coordinates which
represent  the actual vertex location of each primitive and are
expressed in the vector format. After this process,  the data are
sent to the next stage,   the display pipeline processor.

## Edit functions

This display edit processor supports the editing commands shown in Table 3.

Basic editing commands are "Select", "Unselect", "Rotate", "Mirror", "Erase", etc. These can be processed by hardware. In the "select" command, this processor judges editable layers, previously selected primitives, and a category of editable primitives. Then this processor reads the original coordinates, generates primary coordinates, and compares coordinates. In this comparison, before a select command controller starts sending select area coordinates, $(x_1,y_1),(x_2,y_2)$ to the register in this processor, the display edit processor compares the primary coordinate $(x,y)$ to $(x_1,y_1)(x_2,y_2)$. When the primary coordinate $(x,y)$ is included in the select area, this processor writes a select flag into the top word of the primitive. This processing is completely performed in this processor as shown in Figure 3.

In "move" command, this processor saves the moving distance at first, then searches for selected primitives at that time. When there are any selected primitives, this processor reads insertion coordinates and computes new coordinates according to the following equation:

New insertion coordinates = Old insertion coordinate
+      Moving distance

The display edit processor writes these new coordinates to buffer memory in place of the old ones.

### (2) Display Pipeline Processor

The processes of this stage are shown in Figure 3. In this processor, modeling transformation for a hierarchical structure and viewing transformation are performed.

In these calculations, we have made use of the pipeline processing technique. Because there are no conditional branches and no feedback loops in this processing, higher processing speed is expected than with the micro-programing technique.

### (3) Clipping Algorithm

Clipping speed at the end stage of the display pipeline processor is important because VLSI layout data consist of a great deal of data.

Three well-known algorithms[1] are :
1)  Direct computation of the points where lines intersect with the edges of the screen.
2)  Scissoring
3)  Midpoint subdivision.

Under the condition that 32-bit wide world coordinates are in use, these algorithms are not expected to give us the high throughput that is needed. No.1 algorithm needs a high precision divider, while no.2 and no.3 are not suitable in terms of their efficiency. Accordingly, we have developed and introduced a new algorithm.

We describe the outline of the new clipping algorithm by
using Figure 4. The principal point of this algorithm is to
bring end points of vectors into a virtual window by using a
shifter without lowering precision and to calculate coordinates
by taking advantage of the similarity of triangles.

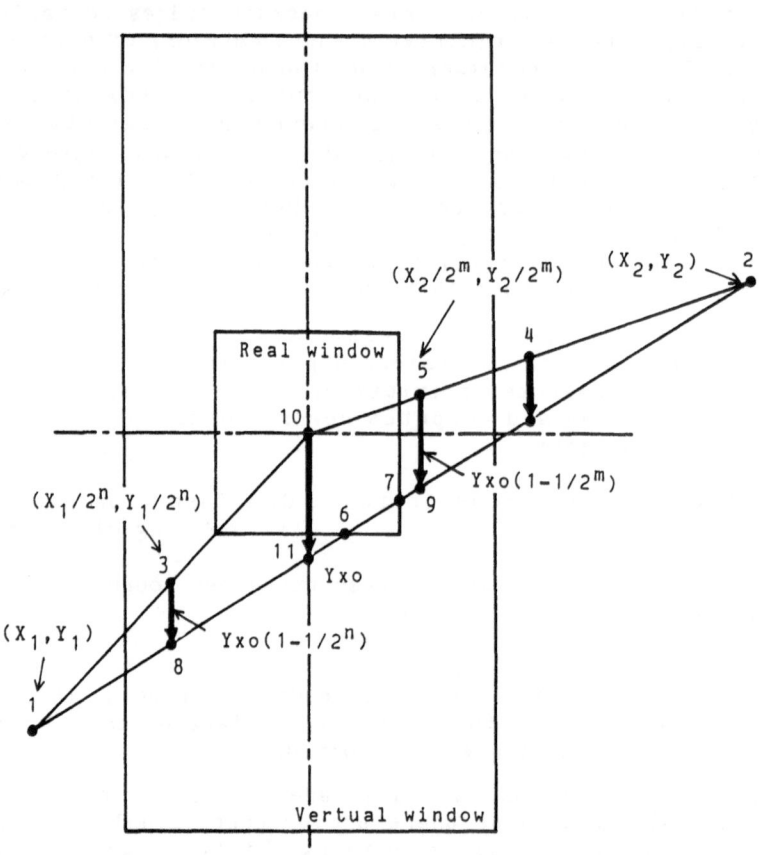

Figure 4    New clipping algorithm (slant angle $\leq$ 45 degrees)

Before using this algorithm the system processes a simple rejec-
tion test, such as judging by end point codes which are coded by
the nine regions defined by extending the edges of the screen.
And short vectors whose value of $MAX(ABS(X_1-X_2),ABS(Y_1-Y_2))$ is
less than the height of the real window, bypass this algorithm
and go to the next stage.

Suppose that a vector 1-2 in Figure 4 is being processed whose
slant angle is less than 45 degrees.

First, the y-coordinate of the point 11 (Yxo), where the vector
intersects the y-axis, is calculated. The coordinate is given by
the equation    $Yxo = ((X_2Y_1-X_1Y_2)/(X_2-X_1))$.    If the absolute
value of this coordinate (Yxo) is larger than the height of the
real window (the distance from the bottom to the top of the real

window), this vector doesn't intersect with the real window, so it is discarded.   Next, the virtual window   which is two times as wide and four times as high as the real  window, is set.   The next calculation step  is to find the coordinates  of points 3 and 5.   These points are the first points which fall inside the virtual window when coordinates of both ends  are divided by factor 2 repeatedly.

The calculation of coordinates of points 8 and 9 is the next step.  By taking advantage of the similarity of the triangle 1-3-8 and triangle 1-10-11, triangle 2-5-9 and triangle 2-10-11, the coordinates are easily calculated. Thanks to the previous steps, points 8 and 9 always lie within the virtual window so that the new vector 8-9 is generated.    The value of point 8 is given by:

$$X_1/2^n, \; (Y_1/2^n + Yxo(1-1/2^n))$$

where

$$Yxo = (X_2Y_1-X_1Y_2)/(X_2-X_1)$$

These values may be equal to the virtual window coordinate precision. As the absolute values of $Y_1/2^n$ and $Yxo(1-1/2^n)$ are less than half of the height of the virtual window, these dynamic ranges are equal to the virtual window's, and the two values may be equal to the virtual window coordinate precision.  On the other hand in the direct computation algorithm, new coordinates are given by $(X_r, \; Y_1+(Y_2-Y_1)(X_r-X_1)/(X_2-X_1))$ where $X_r$ is an x-coordinate  of the window boundary. As the two values of the y-coordinate equation $Y_1$ and $(Y_2-Y_1)(X_r-X_1)/(X_2-X_1)$ have the same dynamic  ranges as the world coordinate,  the result of this addition may be equal to the screen coordinate precision but the two values $Y_1$ and $(Y_2-Y_1)(X_r-X_1)/(X_2-X_1)$ need to be equal to the world coordinate precision.

After this, the normal scissoring algorithm or the like  is applied.  For the vector whose slant angle is greater than 45 degrees, the virtual window aspect ratio is reversed  for the x and y axes. These entire steps are repeatedly applied to all vectors.

This new algorithm has several advantages.   First of all,  it requires only four times as high as the screen coordinate precision for division operation.  Secondly, this leads to the fact that simple hardware can easily perform these calculations.   In our graphic system, a low precision divider, multiplier and subtracter are used for these calculations.   The low precision divider can be made by using PROM's which store a table of reciprocals and multipliers. Lastly, high speed calculations are easily achieved because of its hardware simplicity.   These calculators can be constructed by parallel hardware and pipeline structure. Using this algorithm with parallel and pipeline structured hardware, we have realized a high throughput clipping divider.[2]

After clipping, the vectors are sent to VRC (vector to raster converter), and are displayed on a CRT via a bitmap.

## 6. OUTLINE OF GP HARDWARE

We show IC's and LSI's used in the GP in Table 4.   We use STTL
IC's  and MSI's for the major part of the GP.   In our display
edit processor,  micro codes have a rather wide bit width in
order to reduce the processing steps for the micro-programmed
computing.   These codes are stored in Writable Control Store for
easy debugging and user coding.   High speed FPLA's which have
been developed in our laboratory are used for the implementation
of the control logic. (3)   This gives us a flexibility of the
logic design.

A photograph of the whole system except host computer is shown in
Figure 5.   Quantity of hardware is :

```
No. of boards          64
No. of IC's         5,500
No. of gates      170,000
```

Table 4    IC's and LSI's used in GP

| Block name | IC LSI |
|---|---|
| Buffer Memory | 64K-DRAM |
| Bitmap Memory | 16K-DRAM |
| Control Store | 4,16K-SRAM STTL-MSI,SSI |
| others | Multiplier (16X16 bits) FPLA,UART,ADC,S&H,etc. |

Figure 5   Photograph of the Graphic Processor

Hardware specifications are summarized as follows.

1) Display Operation
   Throughput of pipeline processor        250  nano   sec/coordinate
   Through time of pipeline processor      2.25 micro  sec/coordinate
   Clipping time of long vectors           6.0  micro  sec/vectors
   Changing time of vector to raster       125  nano   sec/pixel
   Writing time of bit map memory          752  nano   sec/pixel

2) Editing operation
   Micro  instruction cycle
          in the display edit processor    125  nano   sec
   Micro  branch and jump time             250  nano   sec
   Reading  and  computing time of entity  1.25 micro  sec/word
   Read  modify  write time of entity      2.25 micro  sec/word

## 7. PERFORMANCE TEST RESULTS AND ESTIMATION

(1)  Determining the quantity of Layout Data and Loading Time to
the Buffer  Memory
"Load" operation is the first step of every layout design procedure in the graphic system.   The layout data in the data base on
a host computer are transferred to the GP buffer memory and
become active.

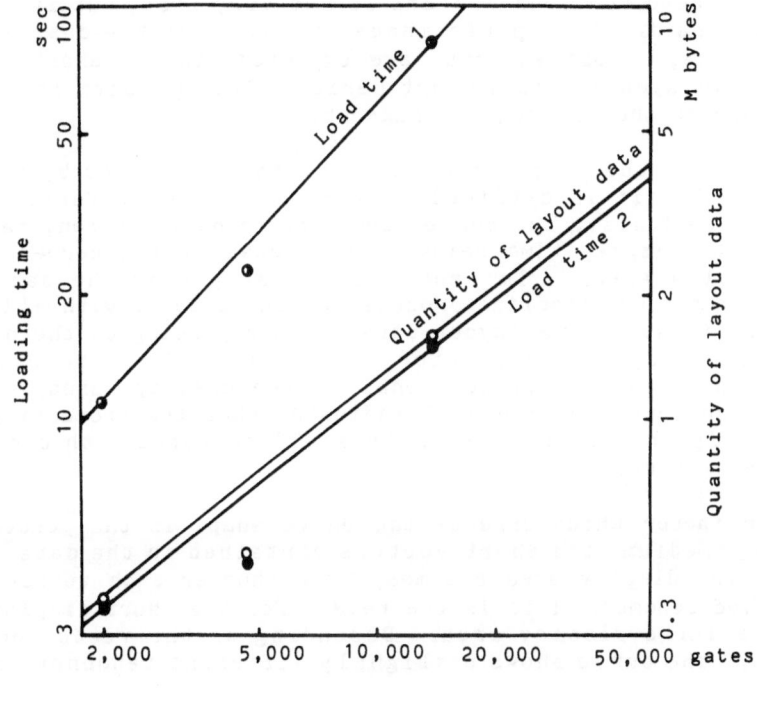

Figure 6    Quantity of layout data and Loading time

The relation of the number of gates to the quantity of layout data, load time 1 (disk - host main memory - interface - buffer memory), load time 2 (host main memory - interface - buffer memory) are shown in Figure 6.    This figure shows that GP can load VLSI layout data of tens of thousands of gates which is equivalent to 2M bytes of data within a few minutes.  This is mainly because of the high speed data transmission between the host computer and the GP.

In this figure, loading time of 4,700 gate LSI is a little bit shorter compared to its gate amount, because  it does not have the data of inside cells.  This often occurs when the layout data produced by an automatic layout and routing program are handled.

(2)  Display Time
The relationship between the percentage of display area and the display time is shown in Figure 7.  A conventional system spends 2 or 3 minutes to complete the display of 2,000 gates which has 335,412 vectors or 2,202,790 pixels as a whole.  We have obtained a display time about 100 times as fast as conventional systems.

We measured display time by using three test patterns which have many long vectors, medium vectors and short vectors, respectively.   Display time is 1,000 vectors/sec (long vectors ; 1024 pixels), 15,000 vectors/sec (medium vectors ; 32 pixels),   and 98,000 vectors/sec (short vectors ; 6 pixels), respectively. Display speed for long vectors is not very fast, but it doesn't degrade the display  performance, because, in the case of VLSI layout data,   most vectors  are expected  to be  short  enough to be displayed within a short period.  This problem is further discussed in the following paragraph.

In Figure 7, the shape of each curve is controlled by several factors  but it is difficult  to separate the effect of each factor.  Basically, the curve seems not to have a strong tendency toward the display time being proportional to the percentage of the display area.   In fact,  every step from the data read operation through pipeline processing always deals with all coordinates of the active layout data,  not depending on the display area percentage.   The vector data amount after the clipping operation is exactly proportional to the display  area.  Therefore,  the curve in Figure  7 indicates that the processing time after clipping is comparatively small compared with the whole processing time.

Another factor which effects the curve shape is the percentages of long, medium, and short vectors contained in the data.   The larger the display area becomes,  the shorter each vector to be displayed becomes. This is the reason for the short display time of  the large display area. Depending on the vector constitution,   the curve shows a slightly different tendency in each case.

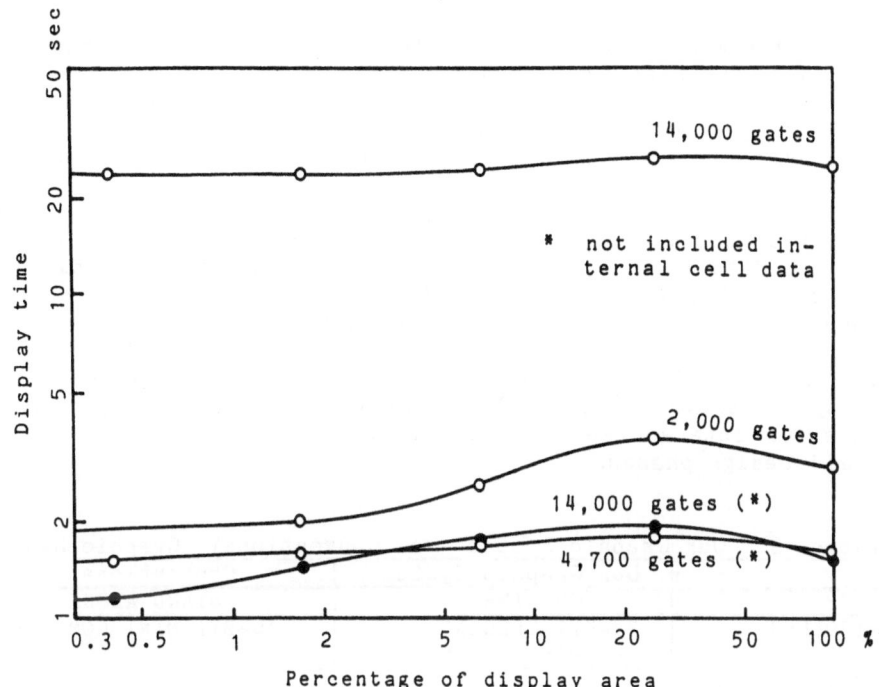

Figure 7 Display Speed


(3)  Editing Time
Editing time is shown in Table  5.    In this table, "half select"
means to select a half part of a chip and "full select" is to
select a whole chip.    This table shows that all commands except
the replicate operation can be  processed  in one  to three
seconds. The same editing operations of conventional systems
spend some minutes or some tens of minutes for these data.    An
editing time  of 100 to 1,000 times  as fast as  conventional
systems has been realized.    In the replicate function,  the GP
has to get new pages (1,024 bytes/page) to store replicated
layout data so that  it needs  much time to· process it.    Nevertheless,  the editing speed of replicate is high enough for our
requirement.    Consequently,  the interactive environment for
VLSI level layout design is at hand in its real meaning.


Table   5   Editing speed   (second)

| No | No.of gat | H.sel | F.sel | Move | Rotat | Mirr | Repl | Erase | Quantity of dat |
|----|-----------|-------|-------|------|-------|------|------|-------|-----------------|
| 1 | 2,000 | 0.4 | 0.4 | 0.7 | 0.7 | 0.7 | 0.8 | 0.7 | 18K Bytes (*2) |
| 2 | 4,700 | 0.6 | 0.6 | 1.6 | 1.8 | 1.6 | 10.6 | 1.2 | 445K Bytes |
| 3 | 9,000(*1) | 1.0 | 1.2 | 2.4 | 2.9 | 2.5 | 18.4 | 1.6 | 770K Bytes |

*1   9,000 gates data is part of 14,000 gates LSI.
*2   Quantity of data is only editing level of nesting.
H.sel = Half select      F.sel = Full select

## 8. CONCLUSION

A high performance graphic system for VLSI layout design has been developed. The features are summarized in Table 6. Pipe-line display processor in conjunction with micro-programmed layout data editing functions has enabled us to manipulate VLSI layout data a hundred to a thousand times as fast as conventional layout design systems.

A 32-bit clipping engine which adopted a new clipping algorithm, a unified data file which is used both for modeling and displaying, and a large amount of buffer memory, all together have helped this system achieve such high performance.

While emphasis is put on the layout design, it is expected that this system plays a major role in an up-coming LSI CAD system as a powerful interactive interface between designers and a system for all design phases.

Table 6  Our Graphic System  vs. Conventional  Graphic System

| | | Our Graphic System | Conventional |
|---|---|---|---|
| SYSTEM | | ON LINE | STAND ALONE |
| CONTROLLER | | 32-BIT SPECIAL PURPOSE PROCESSOR | 16-BIT MINI COMPUTER |
| GRAPHIC MEMORY | | 64M BYTES | 100K BYTES |
| DISPLAY TERMINAL | | HIGH RESOLUTION CRT (1024X1024) | CONVENTIONAL STORAGE OR REFRESH CRT (512X512) |
| PERFORM- ANCE | DISPLAY | 100,000 VECTORS/SEC (SHORT VECTOR) | 1,000-2,000 VECTORS/SEC (SHORT VECTOR) |
| | EDITING | 0.3-2 SEC/2,000 GATES | 1-30 MINUTES/2,000 GATES |

### ACKNOWLEDGEMENT

The authors would like to thank Director Hisakazu Mukai, and Deputy Director Tsuneta Sudo for their encouragement,  and Senior Stuff Engineer  Kou Wada,  Yoshi Sugiyama,  and  Engineer Kazuo Tansho for their technical  support.

### REFERENCES

(1)  W.M.Newman and R.F.Sproull "Principles of Interactive Computer Graphics" Chapter 5  page 65  ,1979  McGRAW-HILL

(2) S.Inoue  "High speed clipping algorithm for graphic display" ,1981 All  Japan  Electronic  Communication  Society Convention Record (in Japanese).

(3)  T.Takeda, et.al. "High performance Bipolar FPLAs", Review of the Electrical Communication Laboratories  Vol. 31 No. 4  1983

# Chapter 4
# Graphics Networks

# CrossoverNet

## A Computer Graphics/Video Crossover LAN System

Tosiyasu L. Kunii and Yukari Shirota

Department of Information Science, Faculty of Science, The University of Tokyo, 3-1, Hongo 7-chome, Bunkyo-ku, Tokyo, 113 Japan

ABSTRACT

A new type of audio visual network system is designed and implemented to control remote audio visual and digital devices such as TV cameras, TV displays, video discs and personal computers, through local area computer networks. This network system named CrossoverNet can handle both digital and analog information, and can mix two types of information freely through audio visual and digital workstations connected by the network.

A high level database management system called G-base (GDL) helps users create user friendly interfaces to control the network. A three layered architecture endows the system with easy extensibility and testability as well as conceptual clarity of the roles of the network managers, the workstation managers and the device managers. As user friendly interfaces, MacroMenus to control audio visual devices and a database query language named InteractiveGDL are designed. Users can freely interact with a system visually through computer graphics, and prototyping tools support end users to generate MacroMenus to control the system.

KEYWORDS: local area network (LAN), analog/digital crossover LAN, audio visual (AV) devices, remote control, user friendly interface, prototyping tool, database, GDL, G-base, example-oriented programming

## 1. INTRODUCTION

The recent progress in AV (audio visual) devices such as TV cameras, TV displays, video recorders and laser discs is remarkable, but most of them are designed in such a way that each device can be used only independently of one another. Actual uses of them require their operations to be related to each other. A little bit of insights into the applications of AV devices shows us far better use of them when used together in a coordinated manner. Such networked AV devices have wide applications especially in industrial, business and educational fields. As usual with most of end user oriented systems, AV networks have to satisfy the following requirements:

    1. High functionality,

    2. Evolutionary architecture,

    3. User friendliness.

This research is toward realizing the crossover network (<u>CrossoverNet</u>) to satisfy these requirements.

We will briefly summarize how to satisfy these requirements. The first requirement of extensibility can be realized by interfacing AV devices with computers, the interfaces being soft controlled. Current hard-wired and non-programmable interfaces do not allow complicated concurrent control of AV devices. Let us look at an example of uses of AV devices at schools. Usual school AV facilities form closed loop circuits, and prevent sharing of AV information and devices. It is generally the case that video information in a laser disc which is placed in a remote place is referred, while a TV camera shoots some target objects, and that we need to display them on many coordinated TV displays. By using local area networks to connect distributed AV devices, we can form a highly functional AV system allowing to enjoy all the functionality of AV devices connected by the network. This extends the applicability of such AV devices in schools, in offices and in factories. As the local area network for use with our <u>CrossoverNet</u>, we selected a broadband system, not a baseband system. To transmit both video and digital signals on a same communication line, this is almost the only choice.

The second requirement of extensibility is partially realized also by local area networks. Further extensibility is also realized by separating the systems into a logical layer and a physical layer. This allows the system to extend its life time beyond those of the individual devices connected to the network. By incorporating a new type of database management system into the network, we can add more extensibility to the system by allowing users to easily create new types of software, especially user interfaces.

By designing a mechanism to share and update already existing resources, the third requirement of user friendliness can be satisfied in many ways, although an ideal approach is very difficult. Significant improvements in user friendliness have been realized by designing tree-structured <u>MacroMenus</u>, menu description languages called <u>ProtoLanguage</u>, <u>InteractiveProto</u> (a programming-by-example type language), and an interactive database query language named <u>InteractiveGDL</u>.


## 2. DESIGN OF CrossoverNet

### 2.1 RESOURCES, TASKS, LOGICAL LAYER AND PHYSICAL LAYER

Definition of <u>Resources</u>

CrossoverNet has three types of resources. The first type is called the device resources. The device resources are any type of AV devices and digital devices connected to the network. The examples are TV cameras, TV displays, electonic blackboards, video recorders, robots, sensors, computers and so on. The second type is called the workstation resources. Each workstation resource consists of device resources such that they can be used to carry out a given meaningful user application. It includes a computer to control the device resources in a coordinated manner to process the application. An example of the workstation resource is an AV workstation in a classroom used to teach a course. Such a workstation includes a control device, a video projector, slide projectors, screens, blackboards, lights, curtains and so on (Fig. 1). The third type is called the network resources. The network resources consist of communication media or devices.

AV controller of an AV workstation

Fig. 1 An AV workstation in a classroom

Definition of Tasks
    The tasks of any given resource are defined as a set of input-output pairs of the resource. This definition is based on the system's function specification in [KUN70].

Let us look at some examples of a layered architecture to keep the system's architecture independent of the development of physical AV devices. Suppose we have a logical TV display. Physically, this is a usual CRT-based color TV or a modern liquid crystal display TV. It can also be a high quality digital TV which is going to be announced in a market in a few years. Independently of which physical TV display we use, by defining the tasks of a logical TV in software, these logical tasks can be converted to those of actual physical devices by tools which transform information in the database of CrossoverNet (Fig. 2).

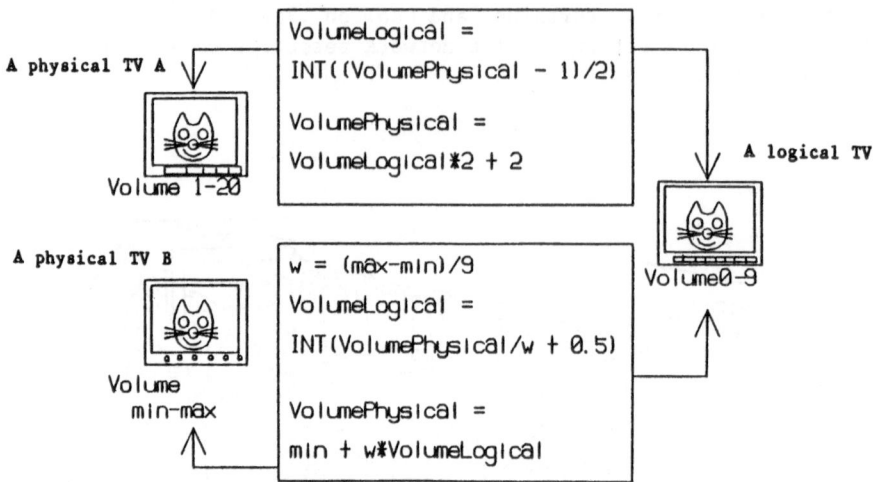

Fig. 2  Logical to physical mapping information for TV displays

## 2.2 NETWORK OPERATING SYSTEM

The network operating system model of our **CrossoverNet** is a result of the integration of a communication model and an operating system model. In general, global networks have two different types of owners, one for a communication network, and the other for computers at the communication nodes. The most popular models of data communication networks are offsprings of electro-communication technology. A typical example is ISO's seven layered model called the OSI (Open Systems Interconnection). Operating systems have been developed independently of data communication technology[KUN84].

A model for **CrossoverNet** requires a model which is higher than any data communication models and operating system models. It also has to include the models for AV devices. In the **CrossoverNet** model, we abstract all AV and digital resources, including communication resources, into two types of resources called physical resources and logical resources. We interface two types of resources by the resource mappings. We actually subordinate operating system models under network models. As a network model, we can adopt the OSI seven layered model. This simplifies the architecture of our operating system. When we have **CrossoverNet** for use at very large organizations, we have to have a hierarchy of network operating systems. Our operating system manages our AV and digital systems as a whole by abstracting them as a structure consisting of the following three layers (Fig. 3).

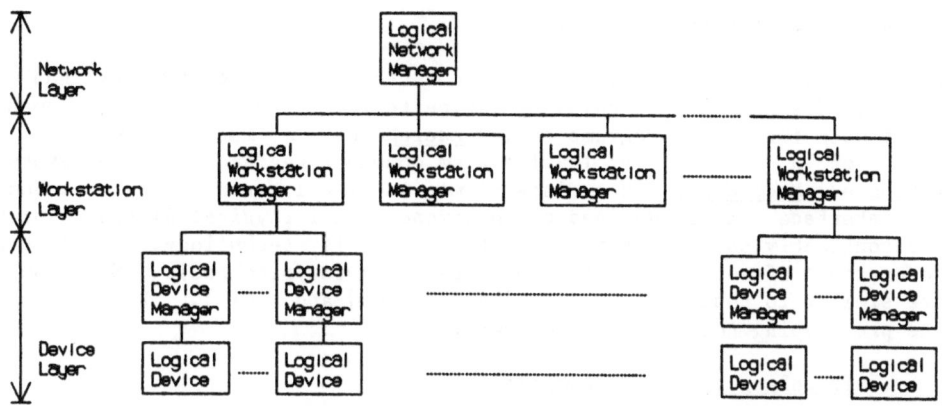

Fig. 3 A hierarchy of CrossoverNet resources

1. Network Layer

The first layer is a network layer managing the network resources as a whole. This network layer operating system has one logical network manager computer.

2. Workstation Layer

The second layer is called a workstation layer. We have one workstation manager computer for each workstation. This manages all resources at one workstation.

3. Device Layer

The third and final layer is a device layer. Any logical device in a given logical device layer has one logical device manager computer. Current physical devices are handicapped in such a way that we cannot control the most of commercially available AV devices at remote sites. In such cases, most of functions of any given logical device are handled by its logical device manager computer. This allows us to realize the idealistic AV device functions on top of commercially available AV devices.

It should be noted that any node of CrossoverNet, in principle, can be made independent of the other nodes. Namely, a workstation at a classroom, for example, can be operated independently of the other workstations at the other classrooms. This serves to increase the availability of the devices, the workstations and the network.

3. MacroMenus and ProtoLanguage

We assume a user of any workstation connected to our CrossoverNet has a graphic display and a pointing device to input a desired macro command using user interface programs called MacroMenus. A macro command consists of a set of lower level system commands registered in the system database. MacroMenus are a class of man machine interface programs. Such an interface can be defined to go beyond actual physical displays which are constantly changing reflecting the available technology. To foster generation of such interfaces we prepared prototyping tools. Such tools are similar to those reported in [WAS83],[MAS] and [MIT]. Examples of the prototyping tools are as follows :

   - ProtoLanguage cross compiler,

   - InteractiveProto,

   - AV classroom simulators.

ProtoLanguage is a general purpose menu description language.

MacroMenus consist of a set of scenarios. A scenario is a series of actions executed on a display screen. An action includes a message to send commands to a graphic object or to an AV device. A scenario consists of the following three parts.

   1. Screen Layout Part
   This defines the layout of the background objects appearing in the scenario. This part also defines the graphic objects used in the scenario.

   2. Initialization Part

   This part describes initializing actions of the scenario.

   3. Action Part
   This part executes triggers and actions of the scenario.
   A trigger is an operation executed by the system user by pushing buttons and picking some objects by a mouse.

When a scenario is executed, the actions described in the first part are executed, and then the following loop is repeatedly executed.

loop :
     - wait for a trigger
     - when any trigger is on, then the corresponding action is executed
     - goto loop.

To get out of the loop, we have to be at the end of MacroMenus or we have to move to the other scenarios.

We also designed a tool to support a user to handle ProtoLanguage. The tool is called InteractiveProto (Fig. 4). When handling AV device objects and other objects, or message menus on the screen, InteractiveProto generates necessary ProtoLanguage programs. We can simulate any part of the program whenever necessary.

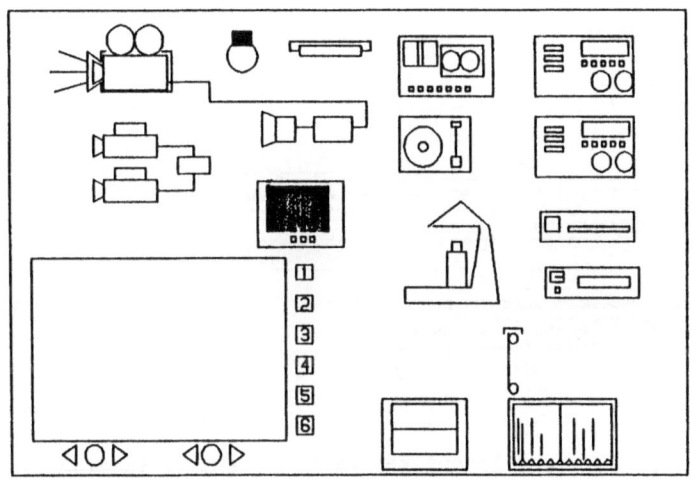

Fig. 4  A screen layout generated by InteractiveProto

## 4.  A DATABASE QUERY LANGUAGE 'InteractiveGDL'

Our CrossoverNet requires such a database management system that is capable of handling tree and network data structures explicitly and is flexible enough to modify data relations easily. In these aspects, the database management system has to be based on a data model superior to the relational data model. As such a model we use a full directed graph based data model called a graph data language (GDL) designed by H. S. Kunii [KUN83]. Another reason we selected the GDL to manage our database was the fact that it is supported as a commercial product by a dependable company, Ricoh Co., Ltd. G-base is the official product name of GDL by Ricoh.

We designed the user friendly interactive query language for GDL called InteractiveGDL. InteractiveGDL has the following two features.

1. Capability to handle various data structures explicitly through multiple windows displayed on high resolution color graphics (Fig. 5,6)

2. An example oriented programming approach

196

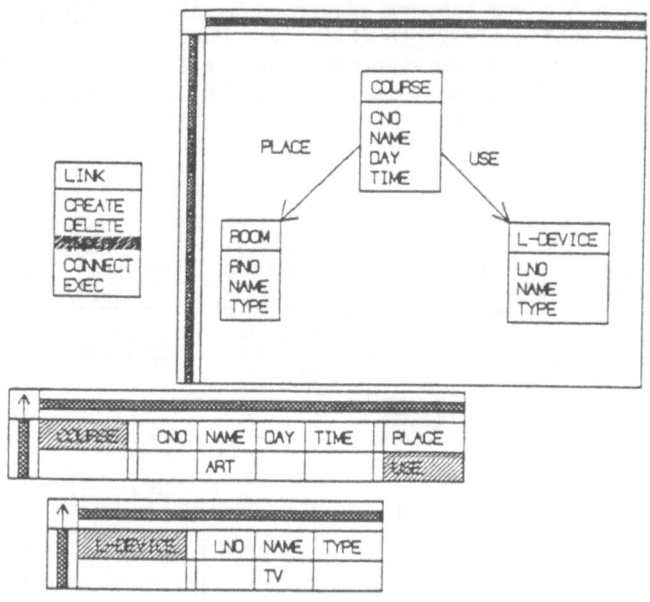

Fig. 5 A screen layout generated by InteractiveGDL

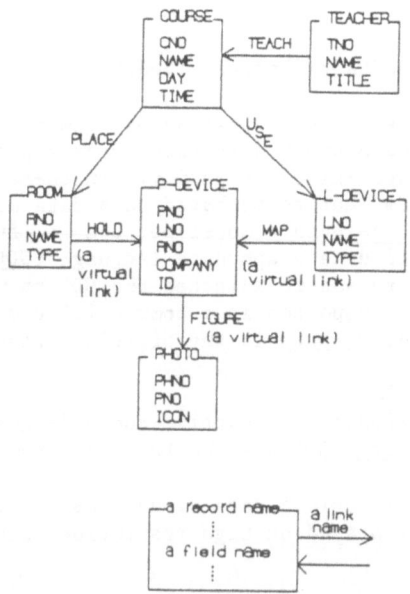

Fig. 6 An explicit structure display generated by InteractiveGDL

The example oriented approach is typically seen in QBE proposed by M. M. Zloof [ZLO82]. QBE is based on a relational model. Because GDL allows explicit and dynamic link types, to handle these types of links of GDL (actual links and virtual links), InteractiveGDL has example oriented features different from those of QBE.

## 5. IMPLEMENTATION

CrossoverNet proposed in this paper has been partially implemented at Totsuka Campus of Meiji Gakuin University. The implementation of hardware has been finished. Software implementation also has been completed at the workstation layer level and the device layer level. The implemented system enjoys the following two advantages.

1.      Frequent requests from teachers to enhance system functions are easily reflected into the systems design through software oriented (namely, programmable) AV device interfaces to control AV devices.

2.      The teachers can generate their own MacroMenus most suitable for their daily classroom works by using InteractiveProto.

We show some pictures to illustrate how the implemented version of MacroMenus actually looks.

## 6. CONCLUSIONS

We have shown the architecture, design and implementation of our local area network system which can handle both digital and analog signals. Physically they can control and utilize both varieties of popular AV devices and personal computers. Versatile capabilities of CrossoverNet have been demonstrated. We are in the course of implementing the various network level software including an AV database query language and advanced icon based menu generators.

## 7. ACKNOWLEDGEMENT

Financial support and encouragement by Dr. Hideko S. Kunii of Software Research Center of Ricoh Company Ltd. has been especially helpful for conducting this research. We are grateful to Mr. Yoshiki Matsuoka of Meiji Gakuin University for his advises while implementing the system. Mr. Tsukasa Noma, Mr. Issei Fujishiro, Mr. Kikuo Fujimura and Mr. Yasuto Shirai helped the authors summarize piles of their research results. Managemental help of Mr. Hideo Takahashi of JVC deserves our special thanks.

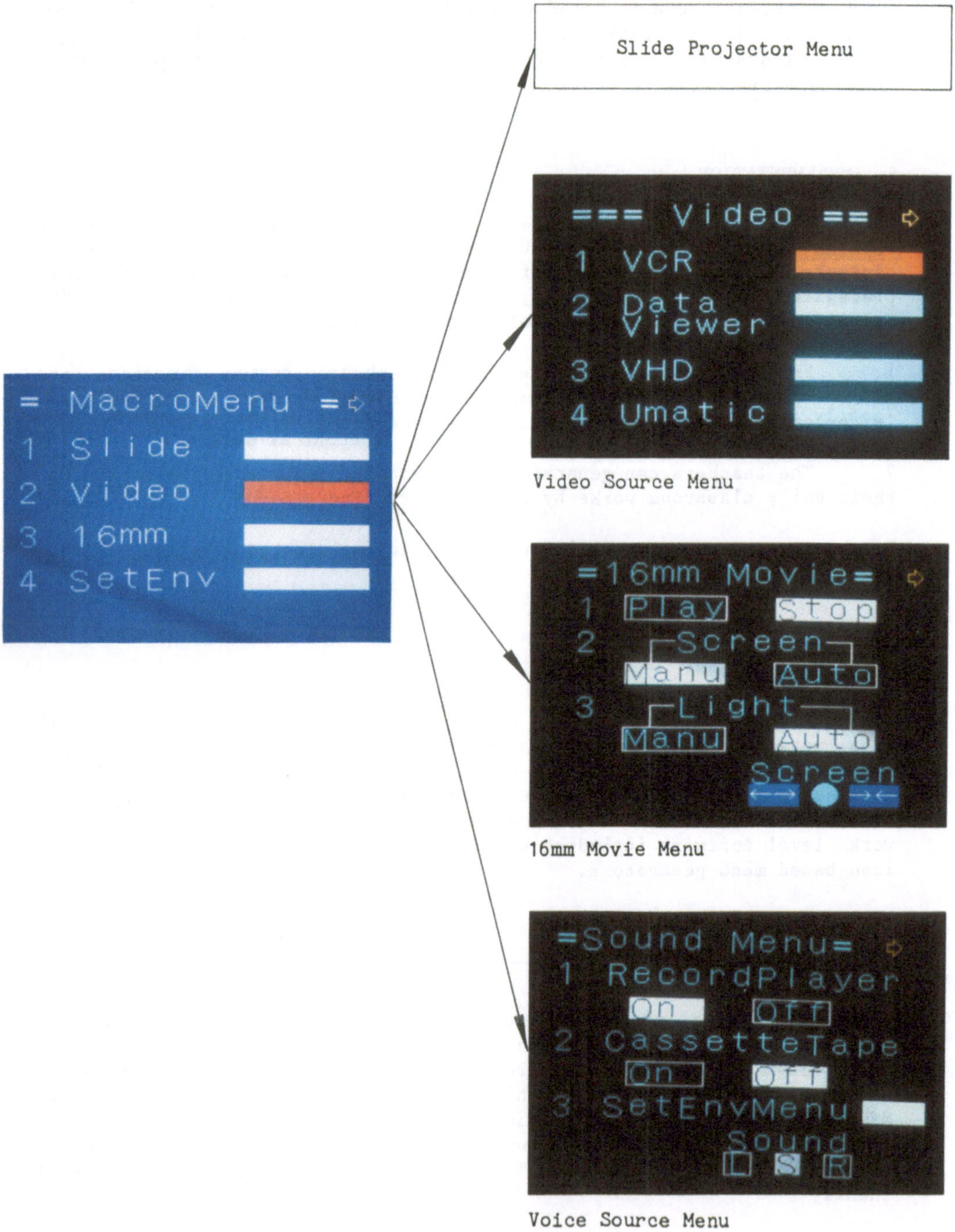

198

Photo 1  An example of a MacroMenu tree

Video Recorder Menu

Data Viewer Menu
(Video Instruction Display Menu)

Shared Devices Menu

Photo 2　A programmable
controller

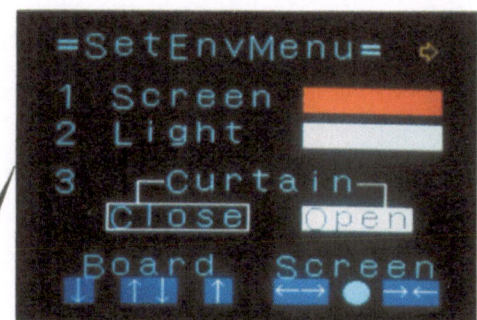

Environment Set Menu 1

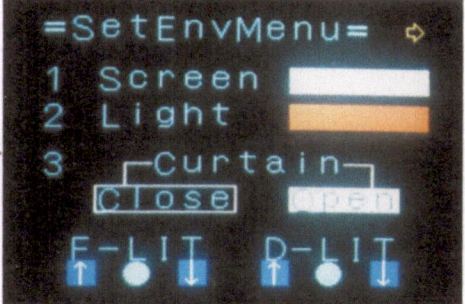

Environment Set Menu 2

REFERENCES

[KUN70] Kunii, T. L., "Introduction of General System Theory" in <u>Theory</u> <u>of</u> <u>Management</u> <u>Systems</u> ( in Japanese ), Hakutou Press, Tokyo Japan, June 1970.

[KUN83] Kunii, H., "Graph Data Language : A High Level Access-Path Oriented Language", Ph.D. Thesis, Department of Computer Science, The University of Texas, Austin, May 1983.

[KUN84] Kunii, T. L., Hashizume, H. and Yamaguchi K., <u>All</u> <u>about</u> <u>LAN</u> ( <u>Local</u> <u>Area</u> <u>Networks</u> ) ( in Japanese ), Nippon Keiei Kyoukai, Tokyo Japan, 1984.

[MAS] Mason R. E., and Carey T. T., "Prototyping Interactive Information Systems", University of Guelph, Canada.

[MIT] Mittermeir R. T., "HIBOL-A Language for Prototyping in Data Processing Environment", Institut fuer Angewandte Informatik and Systemanalyse, Technische Universitaet Wien, A-1040 Vienna, AUSTRIA.

[WAS83] Wasserman A. I. and Showmake D. T., "A RAPID/USE Tutorial", Medical Information Science, University of California, San Francisco, Nov. 1983.

[ZLO82] Zloof, M. M., "Office-by-Example : A Business Language that Unifies Data and Word Processing and Electronic Mail", IBM Systems Journal, Vol. 21, No. 3, 1982, pp. 272-304.

Chapter 5

# Visual Communication
# and Interfaces

# Graphics Interface Tool Development in a Problem Solving Environment

Kenneth I. Joy

Signal and Image Processing Laboratory, Division of Computer Science, Department of Electrical and Computer Engineering, University of California, Davis, CA 95616, USA

## ABSTRACT

A Problem Solving Environment (PSE) is an integrated system of application tools that support the solution of a given problem, or a set of related problems. Paramount in the development of such environments is the design, specification and integration of user interface tools that communicate between the application tools of the system and the user. Typically these interactions are object oriented and involve the interaction with tool parameters, which in many applications (CAD/CAM, Imaging Systems, Image Processing), are represented by graphical data. This paper describes a user-interface tool development system in which both textual and graphical display, and interaction techniques are integrated under a single model. This allows the user to interact with tool parameters in either graphical or textual modes, and to have the parameters displayed in the manner most relevant to the problem set.

Keywords : User Interfaces, Interaction Techniques, Problem Solving Environments.

## 1. INTRODUCTION

A Problem Solving Environment (PSE) [Blinn, 1982; Crow, 1982; Osterweil, 1983; NASA, 1984; DAISY, 1984] configures and manages a set of application tools, under a common manager, to support the solution of a given problem. In many scientific/engineering areas, high-level computer software has been developed that allow the user to employ the terminology of the problem area and remove the need to become involved in the design, implementation and maintenance of low level programming code. In these systems, the interface need be configured not toward the design, specification or maintenance of programming tasks, but toward the specification and modification of parameters for tools to be executed, and the management of the execution of the tool. We focus, in this paper, upon a model that allows the integration of a wide variety of user interface tools into a PSE. These tools are used to manipulate the parameters of the application tools of the system.

Interfaces have typically been centered about the command line interpreter [Blinn, 1982; Crow, 1982; DAISY, 1984; NASA, 1984; Osterweil, 1983], or a menu based system [Buxton, 1983]. Some systems have a tutor mode [NASA, 1984] or forms mode

[Tsichritzis, 1982], which are based on a limited full screen display. However, display tools in these environments are generally part of the environment tool set and not integrated with the interface.

In this paper, we present a user interface model designed to separate the interface tools from the application tool set. These interface tools are integrated into an interface system (see Figure 1), which operates as a companion to a PSE's tool manager. The interface environment now takes over much more of what is currently done in the application tool set: it takes responsibility for the user dialogue, which includes full display and interaction with all data items, and the data management for the application tools. Communication between the managers is done at a high-level [Mamrak, 1982; Liskov, 1977] which allows the user-interface system to work in a more object oriented form.

To achieve integration of different display methods, we base our system about a single abstraction, the *panel*, which will be our generalized display mechanism. A panel template is used to specify the media in which the data is to be displayed and to give the "display format."

The user interface system manages panels and the interface tools invoked by the panels. It takes as input a panel template, a parameter definition file and an instance of the data defined by the parameter definition file. It generates the display, which depends on the information in the template, and allows the user to move about and to modify data in the panel. The tool then takes the modified data (if any) and produces a data set that can be passed to an application tool.

The user interface system also is used to generate the panel templates. A panel construction tool is defined, that uses the same interface mechanism as in the production phase to allow the system manager to generate new panels, and to integrate new tools

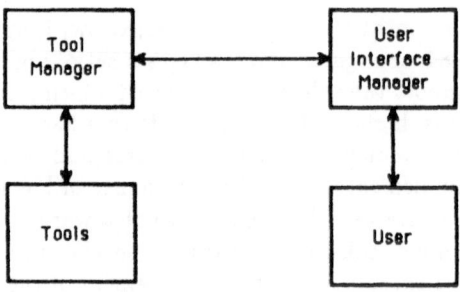

Figure 1 : The integrated PSE

```
procedure GEOTRN
   (
           INFILE :      DAISY_FILE ;
                         {Ground Control Point Data}
           OUTFILE :     DAISY_FILE ;
                         {Output Ground Control Point Data}
           TRANSFILE :   FILE ;
                         {Transformation Coefficient Data}
           TRANS :       ( bilinear, quadratic ) ;
                         {Transformation Type}
           ACC :         ( standard, extended ) ;
                         {Accuracy}
           THRESH :      REAL
                         {Error Threshold}
   ) ;

           {Generate Geometric Transformation Coefficients}
```

Figure 2 : A Parameter Definition File

into the interface environment and the application tool set. Thus, the panel management system consists of two parts: A construction tool for defining the panel templates and integrating the interface tools into the environment, and a production tool for managing the display of the data, and the interactions with the display.

In this paper, we focus on the user-interface tools and the panel model. The specifics of the interface system can be found in [Joy, 1984b].

## 2. THE MODEL

- A panel is a display of an instance of a data type, corresponding to a given panel template.

## 2.1. THE PANEL TEMPLATE

A panel template consists of

- a set of descriptors $X_0$, $X_1$, ..., $X_n$, corresponding to the data items in a given type definition,
- For each descriptor $X_i$, a display procedure $d_i$,
- For each descriptor $X_i$, a (possibly empty) set of user interactions $q_1$, ..., $q_m$, and
- for each user interaction specified, a (possibly empty) sequence of tools $t_1$, ..., $t_k$ that are be executed when the interaction is invoked.

The panel descriptor $X_0$ contains information specific to the panel as a whole. This descriptor contains the format of the panel, banner information, help information, the positioning of the underlying subdisplays, and history information. If no underlying description is present, the panel layout will default to the textual layout illustrated in Figure 3. Display procedures that correspond to this descriptor have a global affect on the entire panel. Interactions that correspond to this descriptor generally affect the entire panel or concurrent panels representing the same information. Tools associated with this descriptor also act on the entire panel. Figure 5 illustrates a parameter list for a CAD Sweep operation, of which the spine (defined by a B-spline curve) is represented in graphical form.

The descriptors $X_1$, ..., $X_n$, each correspond to a single data item from the data set. The information included in the descriptor includes prompt information, help information and local item histories. Interactions with these descriptors generally affect only the individual data items.

The display procedures, $d_i$, specify how each of the data items are to be displayed to the user. The system has a set of standard items, each of which it "knows" how to display (Integers, Reals, Simple Arrays, Scalar Types, Strings), in which case the $d_i$ will be selected automatically by the system. The model also allows the development and insertion of display procedures for special handling of higher-level data (e.g. coordinate data B-spline curves, surfaces, spheres, lists of polygonal objects, etc.). These procedures can be enacted either automatically, or by "selection." All display methods can be overridden, and the default textual data shown.

The tools $t$ are associated with user interactions $q$ on a panel. Each user interaction results in a "standard" operation. For example, the standard operation associated with the modification of a data value on a panel is to modify the data value in the data set (if certain syntax checks are satisfied). If a sequence of tools $\{t_i\}$ is associated with a user interaction $q_i$ then the tools are invoked sequentially after the standard operation has been executed.

If no tools are specified for interaction $q_i$, the corresponding operation will proceed in a standard manner.

## 2.2. THE USER INTERACTIONS

The user interactions apply both globally and locally to a panel. For each interaction, there is a standard operation and a (possibly empty) set of tools.

### Global Interactions

- Movement about the panel

  These interactions are used to move the "center of attention" throughout the panel. These operations are determined by the interaction device (e.g. mouse, light pen, or keyboard input) and capabilities of the display. These operations include commands to page through a multi-page panel, or to scroll through a single-page panel, or to track a cursor through a graphical display.

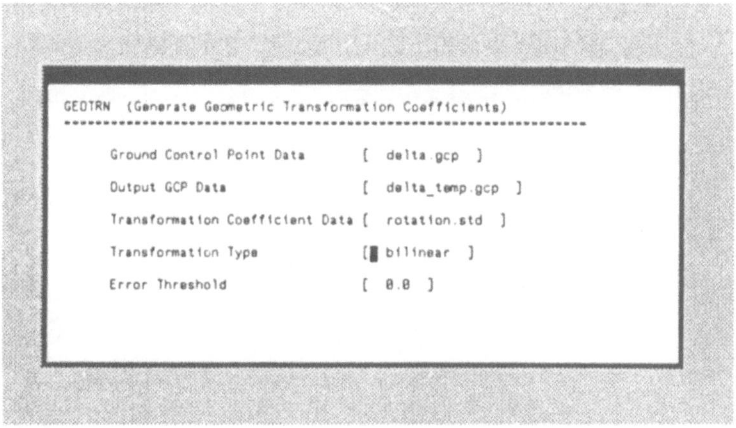

Figure 3 : GEOTRN panel

- Abort, Undo, History

  The Abort command is used to exit from the panel in a abnormal mode,. UNDO is
  used to restore the previous version of the data set into the panel display, History is
  used to review previous panels, or select a previous version of a data set for insertion
  into the panel display, and Help is used to output help information at the panel
  level.

- Global Modification

  This interaction is takes place whenever any modification takes place on a single
  data item. In the Ray Tracing Tool (Figure 4b), the a special display procedure that
  uses a quick sphere drawing algorithm on an associated frame buffer, executes
  whenever changes are made to the Sphere panel. In the CAD example (Figure 5), A
  procedure that redisplays the control points, knot vector and B-spline curve executes
  whenever changes are made to the B-spline data.

**Local Interactions**

- Selection

  This interaction allows the user to "select" a single item on the screen. This
  interaction allows the insertion of tools that use alternate display methods (e.g.
  graphical) for certain data items, special tools for browsing through data sets that
  are too large to display, or tools that allow the user to select items from a menu.
  Typically, the selection operation keys special display procedures, for selected data
  sets. Figure 5 gives the default panel produced by a CAD sweep display tool. The

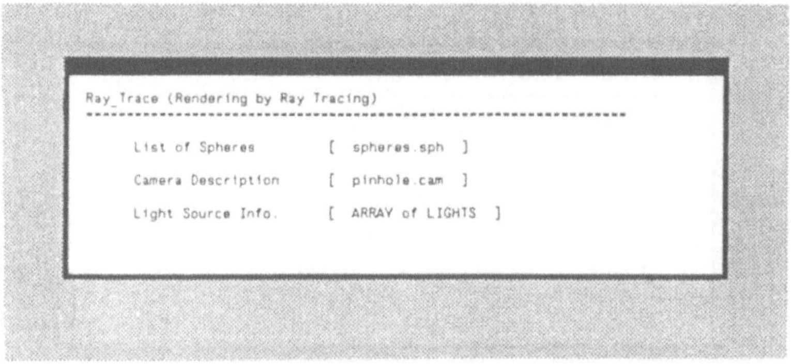

208

Figure 4a: Ray Tracing Tool Panel

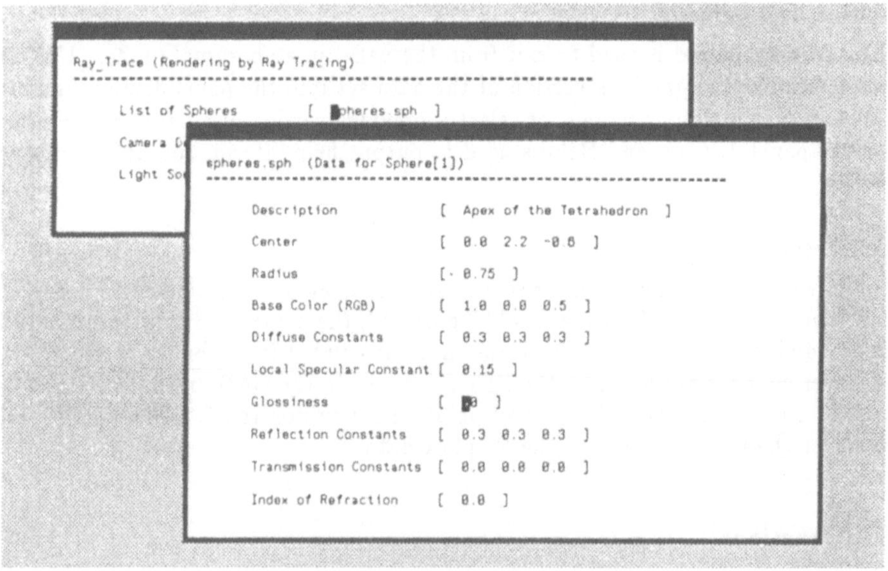

Figure 4b: Expansion of the Sphere Data Item

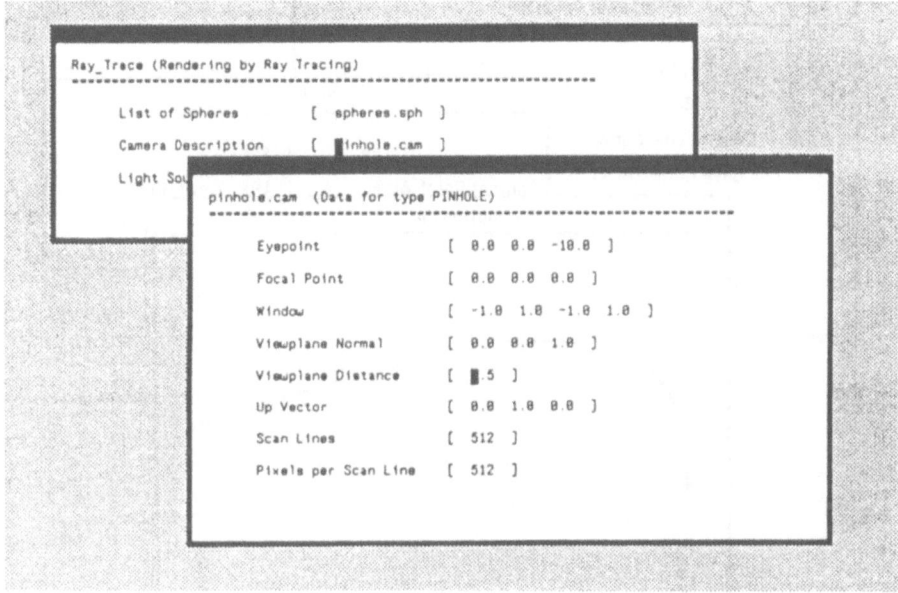

Figure 4c: Expansion of the Camera Data Item

data for the spine is contained in a file. By selecting this data item, a procedure that expands the data in a graphical form is executed. This allows the display of, and interaction with, hierarchically defined data sets.

- Entry and Modification of data values.

  This interaction is used to modify and enter data values through the panel. The standard operation associated with this interaction is the modification of the displayed data to reflect the full change (some abbreviations can be input, but appear on the display in their full form, once they are validated), and the modification of the data in the corresponding data set. The system automatically does syntax checking for known types (integer, real, etc.) and defaults to the attached tools for syntax checking for user-defined types. Modification of graphical panels is accomplished by picking detectable portions of the display, or dragging data items on the display.

- UNDO, History, Help

  These interactions correspond to the Global Undo, History and Help, however, they act on individual data items, rather than on the entire display.

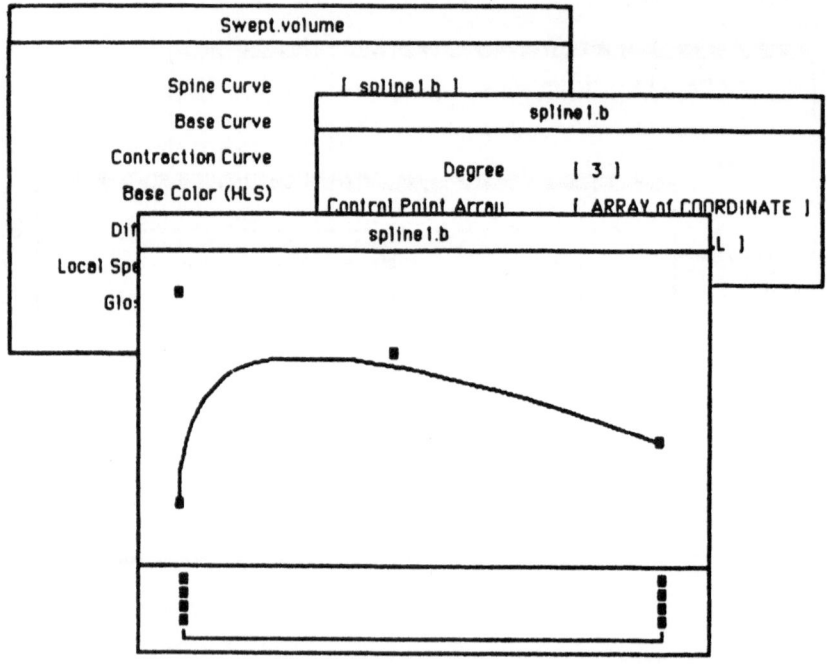

Figure 5 : Graphical Representation

## 2.3. THE INTERFACE TOOLS

Tools are attached to user interactions in the system. Generally, the tools support the entry of specific data types, the examination of data, and execution of special side effects (e.g. display of graphical images on a frame buffer). The current system includes the following tools.

- Array display mechanisms for arrays of any type. Special browser/modification tools for two-dimensional arrays have also been implemented.

- domain checking of parameter modifications

- Special display procedures for graphical representation of data.

- Communication between concurrent panels representing the same data.

## 3. EXAMPLES

Our initial panel model has been integrated into the DAISY system [DAISY, 1984, Fisher, 1984, Joy, 1984a], a software executive used for Image Processing Applications. The system is generally based on one expanded data type -- the image file. Most of the tools of the system focus on the manipulation of a single image.

Our full model is being integrated with DIMAGE - a prototype imaging system, developed at UC Davis for the testing of CAD/Rendering algorithms. Nearly all data in the system has a graphical representation. Primary output devices are a bitmap screen and a frame buffer for color images.

The GEOTRN panel (Figure 3) is developed from the Geometric transformation tools of the DAISY system. The first three data types are all files (two-dimensional arrays of reals). The Transformation type is a scalar type, as is the Accuracy. Error Threshhold is a real. The first and third parameters can each be selected, at which time they are displayed with an "array modification tool." The system uses pop up menus when modifications of the scalar types is attempted.

The ray tracing tool panel (Figure 4), illustrates the selection mechanism of the system. The user may select and display and of the three items in the data set. The Light Source Information is not contained on a file, but is defined with the parameter list, thus only its type is displayed.

Figure 5 illustrates the CAD sweep display tool panel of DIMAGE. The spine item has been selected. The panel for the B-Spline data type is automatically displayed in both textual and graphical format. The user may manipulate the control points of the graphical display, or may elect to have the spline data displayed textually. The system will all more than one representation of the same data set, and will communicate all changes between the displays.

## 4. CONCLUSION

We have described a User-Interface tool management system that is designed to interface with a Problem Solving Environment. This system, constructed under a single underlying display abstraction, the panel, results in an interface environment that is simply defined, simple for the user to control and expandable in its capabilities. It gives a separation of the tools that relate to the display and modification of data, and the application tools that use the data. It allows the system designer to configure a PSE about a number of small tools, and to combine these tools to represent high-level abstractions of data items. The system is capable of displaying and interacting with data through both textual and graphical means, and can display concurrent panels representing the same data in different formats.

Future work with this system includes the further refinement of our graphical format, full integration of the system into a large scale imaging system, and integration of the system into several specialized CAE/CAD environments.

## 5. ACKNOWLEDGEMENTS

I thank both the Computer Research Group and Engineering Research Group at Lawrence Livermore National Laboratory for support during the work. I also thank Professor M. Blattner for many enlightening discussions during this project's inception. Mark Detweiler, Frank Leahy and Jay Govind did most of the programming on the project.

This research was supported in part by Lawrence Livermore National Laboratory - Contract 5607805.

# 6. BIBLIOGRAPHY

[Beretta, 1982]. Beretta, G. and others, XS-1: An integrated interactive system and its kernel, IEEE Software Engineering Conference Proceedings, 1982, 340-349.

[Blinn, 1982]. Blinn, J.F., Systems Aspects of Computer Image Synthesis and Computer Animation, presented at SIGGRAPH 1982, State-of-the-art in Image Synthesis, tutorial notes, 1982.

[Borufka, 1982]. Borufka, H.F. and H.Q. Kuhlmann, "Dialogue Cells: A Method for Defining Interactions," *IEEE Computer Graphics and Applications*, July 1982, 25-33.

[Buxton, 1983]. Buxton, W., M.R. Lamb, D. Sherman, and K.C. Smith, "Towards a Comprehensive User Interface Management System," *Computer Graphics*, Vol. 17, No. 3, July 1983, 35-42.

[Crow, 1982]. Crow, F.C., A More Flexible Image Generation Environment, *Computer Graphics*, 16(3), July 1982, 9-18.

[DAISY, 1983]. DAISY User's Manual, Signal and Image Processing Laboratory, SIPL-84-10, University of California, Davis, 1983.

[Fisher, 1984]. Fisher, G., DAISY II, A General-Purpose Applications Executive, Computer Science Division Technical Report, CSE-84-2, University of California, Davis, 1984.

[Foley 1982]. Foley, J.D., The Design and Implementation of User-Computer Interfaces, Tutorial Notes, Given at ACM SIGGRAPH, 1982.

[Foley, 1981]. Foley, J.D., V.L. Wallace and P. Chan, "The Human Factors of Graphic Interaction: Tasks and Techniques," Institute for Information Science and Technology, Department of Electrical Engineering and Computer Science, The George Washington University, Washington, D.C., GWU-IIST-81-3.

[Goldberg, 1984]. Goldberg, A., *Smalltalk-80 : The Interactive Programming Environment*, Addison-Wesley Publishing Company, Reading, MA, 1984.

[Joy, 1984a]. Joy, K.I., A Model for User Interface Tool Development, submitted for publication, also Technical Report, CSE-84-4, Computer Science Division, University of California, Davis, 1984.

[Joy, 1984b]. Joy, K.I., Specifics of the DAISY User Interface Model. Technical Report, CSE-84-7, Computer Science Division, University of California, Davis, 1984.

[Liskov, 1977]. Liskov, B.H., and S.N. Zilles, "Specification Techniques for Data Abstractions," *IEEE Transactions on Software Engineering*, SE-1, 1(7), 1975.

[Mamrak, 1982]. Mamrak, S., R. Dunnington, and B. Shaffer. Installing Existing Tools in a Distributed Processing System, submitted to *ACM Transactions on Computer Systems*, March 1982.

[NASA, 1984]. NASA, User's Reference Manual for the Transportable Applications Executive (TAE), NASA 82-TAE-USRVIE, NASA Goddard Space Flight Canter, 1984.

[Osterweil, 1983]. Osterweil, L., Toolpack -- An Experimental Software Development Environment Research Project, *IEEE Transactions on Software Engineering*, Vol. SE-9, No. 6, November 1983, 673-685.

[Tsichritzis, 1982]. Tsichritzis, D., Form Management, *CACM*, Vol. 25, No. 7, July 1982, 453-477.

# ICONS and User-Interface Communication

Alice Bernhard

Bernhard Design, Rhinebeck, NY 12572, USA

ABSTRACT.

Icon based interfaces offer a new dimension in human-machine
communication.  An overview of man's attempts to communicate in the
past, particularly through forms of writing, examines how and why
certain methods developed and what purposes they served.  Observations
may be made of these communication symbols as to their intention and
effectiveness; relating apparent insights to the purpose and process of
the User-interface.  Historic information on the development of iconic
representations of familiar objects is given.  Much can be synthesized
and applied to the design of today's icon-based user-interface.
Advantages in using an iconic-based interface in software application
packages are discussed; the nature of this interactivity being one which
indicates a decrease in learning time and a potential increase in
productivity.

INTRODUCTION.

It is interesting to note that man has developed the alphabet during the
past five thousand years, giving up pictures for sparse, streamlined
symbols.  Today with computer technology our sleek, carefully designed
characters seem cumbersome...they slow us down. With the requirement for
a simple, yet clear, End-user interface, the need for a new, more
efficient and effective language becomes apparent.  We are not going
backwards to pictures, but are going back to study pictures.  Analyzing
and synthesizing these written forms of the past, with an understanding
of today's End-user requirements. Given hardware/software capabilities
and limitations, creating an appropriate interface dialogue or
communication, is pursued.

USER INTERFACE DESIGN.

For the User, interface design continues to move in a direction which permits interaction requiring less learning and less User-expertise.

The development is briefly listed:

1. FIXED FIELD INPUT.
The user must learn both the order of input and the specific fixed fields involved.  The Programmer or System Developer structures and organizes according to their own view of the world, not that of the User.

2. QUESTION AND ANSWER.
Limited need for the User to learn order of input and maintain fixed field input requirement.  The beginning of system/user interaction, but not being able to change the order of the input sequence, i.e. to correct errors, and the problem of verbose screens, inhibits interaction.

3. COMMAND LANGUAGES.
The User supplies both the question and answer and can vary the order of input.  However, a rigid syntax and accuracy, in remembering the syntax, typing commands and arranging data is essential.

4. MENU-DRIVEN COMMAND LANGUAGES.
The User selects from the list of commands on the screen. Hierarchical menus make for a much richer syntax, but some of the command language interface problems continue.

5. PICTORIAL MENUS.
A graphical symbol, which represents the verbal command is often easier to recognize than the literal symbols.  Reduces the likelihood of information overload.  However, the same level of syntax as command language interface is used.

6. ICON-DRIVEN INTERFACES.
Rather than provide syntax, the icon represents semantics.  The object, process or meaning is represented by a symbol, which is not distinguishable from that which it represents.  The User is manipulating the thing itself.

Icon-based interfaces are profoundly different from the command based interfaces that preceded them.  Command based systems, of necessity, revolve around processes, which are verbs.  Icon based systems are oriented towards the objects or nouns that are identified with the icons.(2)

The ICON and what it represents
are one and the same.

An ICON for a computer interface
is far more than a pictorial representation of a thing or process.

The ICON...IS...what it represents.
The User is manipulating the thing
itself.

Such an orientation implies that the
interface will model some part of
the real world, relevant to the task.

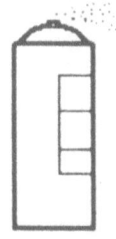

DEFINING.
An icon may be defined as an example or manifestation of the archetype.
The icon and what it represents are one and the same.  Similarly, an
icon for a computer interface is far more than a pictorial
representation of a thing or process.  In effect, the icon IS what it
represents.  Such an orientation implies that the interface will model
some part of the real world relevant to the task attempted.

CREATING ICONS.
For those who wish to create and use icons successfully and
satisfactorily, the history and theory of writing, both of the West and
other cultures, is examined. This brings an informed awareness of the
tradition in written forms, which may be applied toward an original
approach of icon design appropriate for today.
The history of writing may be studied chronologically.  However, in
seeking evidence of a developing practice and style, one looks for
parallels and analogies among historical examples of writing.  The work
of the American Indian, less than a hundred years ago, may be discussed
in relation to similar ideas thousands of years before the Christian
era, which we may in turn relate to the use of icons today.(1)

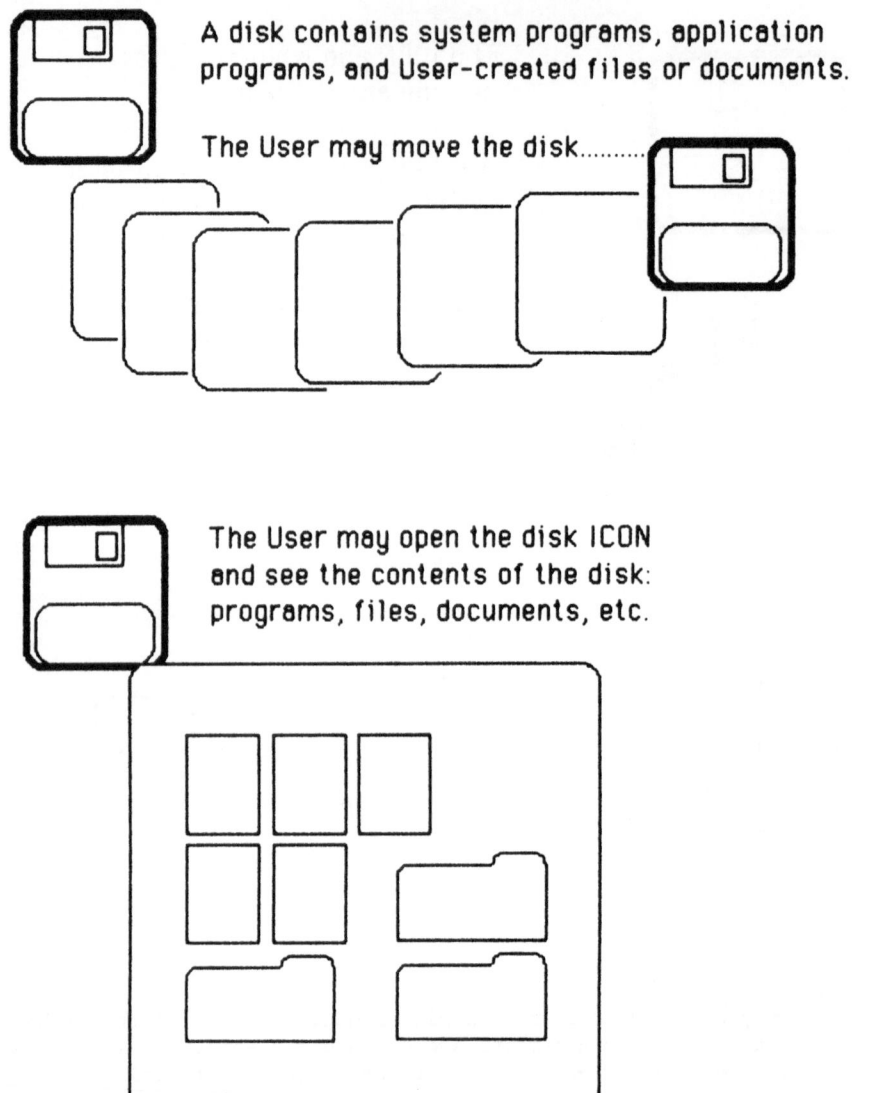

A disk contains system programs, application programs, and User-created files or documents.

The User may move the disk..........

The User may open the disk ICON and see the contents of the disk: programs, files, documents, etc.

MAN COMMUNICATES WITH SPEECH.
Man became skilled in tool making and in the use of language about 500,000 year ago.  When man began hunting, speech was necessary to teach how to make tools and weapons.  Teaching requires language.  Hunting also indicates the need for planning, such as the group of men discussing the strategy for the next day's hunt.  Through language, every member of a group may profit from another member's experience.  Words enable man to sum up what happened yesterday, analyse and plan for tomorrow.  Language gives man a means to solve and create problems and also to consider possibilities.

MAN PAINTS PICTURES.
Twenty thousand, or more, years ago in what is now France, Spain and
Italy, man rendered drawings and paintings of animals with no less skill
than painters of today.  The great cave art of Lascaux and Font-de-Gaume
is considered fully developed in terms of color and composition.  Thus,
thousands of years before writing was practiced, the races of the
Magdalenian culture were constructing, in terms of drawing and painting,
a visual record of high sophistication.  Most of the graphic works are
considered to be of a cryptic nature.  Man believed that through the
painting of an animal, such as a horse, deer, bison, etc., that power
over the animal was secured. Although enhanced with magic, the purpose
of the painting was quite serious.  The illustrated animal was always
within range of a spear throw.  A deer may be painted in the wall or
ceiling of the cave to make the next day's hunt successful.  Similar to
the Congo Pygmies trying to win the favor of the forest through song,
with pictures, man tried to engage with nature and in the process win
some control over the environment or surroundings.  The Australian
aborigines continue to make animal drawings which they believe have
magical powers.(4)

MAN COMMUNICATES WITH PICTURES.
The attempt to communicate specific information may be considered the
first stage in the development of writing.  In this first prewriting
stage, emphasis is on the recording of objects and events and attention
is not given to esthetic considerations.  However, today pictographs are
admired for these qualities. Pictographs, the term used to describe
prewriting records, from its roots, means "picture writing".(3)
Although this is somewhat misleading, because the signs do not stand for
speech values, the term is in wide use. Aside from what they tell of a
culture in terms of its religious and social habits and its technology,
pictographs are important to the development of writing in several ways.

    1. They exhibit a strong tendency toward abstraction or extreme
simplification of natural form.  When alphabetic signs were developed
they reflected this same sparseness in graphic form, a necessity in
graphic communication, particularly in the keeping of records.  It is
obvious that to record the ownership of forty sheep by drawing the image
of a sheep forty times is too complicated.  Some economy of means is
required.

    2. They demonstrate the effort to establish a sequence of order
within the the pictographic message.  Some Paleolithic cave works depict
tribal episodes by drawing them one on top of another.  In certain works
by American Indians, the events were drawn in sequence, one event next
to another.  These could be "read" for a specific meaning. Random order
and specific meaning are incompatible.  Consider our system of writing;
when we write or print, we make one sign or character at a time.

    3. A thorough understanding of sign and meaning is involved in
pictographic communication.  Communication requires language, which may
be defined as any set or system of such symbols as used in a more or
less uniform fashion by a number of people, who are thus enabled to
communicate intelligibly with one another. A hungry tribesman cannot
afford any misunderstand in his signs that read "nothing to eat".(1)

IDEOGRAPHS.
As man developed the need to communicate abstract thoughts in writing,
symbols took on a broader meaning and might require two pictures.  Ox
might also mean food.  Abstract thoughts could be communicated by
combining different pictographs.  The action of eating or drinking might
require the picture of "mouth" and picture for "bread or water". Pairs
of pictographs meaning idea + graph are ideographs.  Symbols no longer
represent objects, but ideas. The Chinese ideograph meaning "east" is
formed from two pictographs "sun" and "tree".  "Tear", as in crying, is
made from pictographs "eye" and "water".  A contemporary ideograph is
the warning symbol for poison. The skull and crossbones are not seen for
what they are, but for what they represent, death.(3)

MAN COMMUNICATES WITH MNEMONIC DEVICES.
Signs which function to prompt the memory of an event or place are
called mnemonic devices.  An example is a calendar kept by an American
Indian tribe, the Dakota.  Each of the seventy-one years of the tribes'
existence is represented by a graphic sign which calls to mind a
memorable happening for that year.  Another example, also from the Dakotas,
is a detailed story of six Indians who eat rotten buffalo meat, proceed
to become violently ill and die.  A single, stereotyped graphic sign
illustrates this phenomenon, the story being easily recalled. Mnemonic
characters are used to preserve the remembrance of the Ojibwa Indians
songs or traditional poetry.  The words of the songs are memorized and
the pictographs, rather than suggest exact words, give a general
interpretation of the song. Since a stereotyped sign always identifies
the same object or phenomenon, the approach is toward a sign
representing a word, considered the key to advanced systems of writing.
Also, graphic signs that have a verbal counterpart point toward a
connection between graphic signs and speech.(1)

WORD SIGNS.
The second stage in man's search for efficient systems of communication
through symbols or signs is that in which graphic mark and spoken word
are equated.  Since pictograph is also used in connection with such
writing systems as Egyptian and Chinese, there is danger of confusion.
The Chinese writing system, is basically a picto-graphic word-sign
system.  Most early writing systems use the most visually significant
part of human creatures, animals, and objects, that is, the profile
view.  Examples from the Western Chou period of the eleventh century
B.C., show this in the figure of man, and the "Egyptian" eye.  Early
Egyptian stonecutters freeze the view in perpetuity, but the Chinese
capture the essence of character in movement, using brush or pen. In
early Chinese, a hand holding a brush designates a "scribe", "woman"
plus "broom" means "wife", "woman + woman" means "quarrel", and "woman,
woman + woman" means "falsehood", "mother" and "child" means "suckling".
Compound signs were used frequently, indicating the inherent talent of
the Chinese for creating signs that meet the need for economy of means
and grace of expression in one swift action.  Logogram, the term used to
describe a sign which represents one or more words in a language, is a
stage through which the Chinese and all great historical systems of
writing passed.  Today, we continue this concept in our use of, for
example, "Rx" for prescription and "$" for dollar.(4)

ABSTRACTION.
The tendency toward abstraction in pictographic communication often
demonstrates that later forms become quite divorced from the natural,
originally quite explicit, form.  Communication can survive a change in
signs as the thread of meaning is passed on to succeeding generations
within the culture.  There is difficulty for scholars of a later time,
who may be left with the abstraction without a before and after to
explain its original meaning.  Thus, many enigmatic configurations may
appear that suggest pure invention.  In all probability the signs had a
rather specific origin and meaning to the people who made them. These
tendencies in the pictographic arts indicate that communication is a
social phenomenon.  Where two people agree on the meaning of a sign
message, the inclusion of a third requires the education of that person
and subsequently of many others.  The breakdown of communication is
inherent here.  Indeed, it is the complexity of
society that forces the abandonment of picture methods.  The number of
people involved, the number of transactions to be recorded, the number
of names to be given signs, the number of events to be
commemorated...these are the factors that eventually produce systems of
writing that can be translated and passed on to various civilizations.

SEQUENCE OF ORDER.
The prewriting graphic forms executed by the North American Indians are
particularly rich in storytelling techniques and are often interesting
for their artistic form.  For example, a hunting trip report or story
proceeds from left to right with eleven signs, each of which involves
the speaker: 1. indicates himself and points a directions: 2. holds a
paddle, indicating the method of travel; 3. denotes one night's sleep;
4. draws an island with two huts; 5. same as 1.; 6. another island; 7.
indicates two nights' sleeps; 8. holds a harpoon and gives the sign for
a sea lion; 9. shooting with bow and arrow; 10. boar with two persons,
paddles extending downward; 11. habitation.

Of particular interest is the quality and completeness of abstraction.
There is an orderly sequence in the presentation of the message.  All
superfluous details are omitted, as are esthetic considerations.  In
terms of efficiency, it is clear that the stereotyped signs are
indispensable to the orderly presentation of large amounts of material
to a large group of readers. Throughout the history of writing,
exceptions to the rule of efficiency/economy occur.  As soon as a system
of writing becomes current, esthetic considerations are established, not
so much on the old basis of picturemaking, but on esthetics involving
the form of the letters and space these letters occupy.(1)

PHONETIC TRANSFER.
In a strict logographic approach to writing, a separate sign would have
to be developed for each word.  As a group moves its economic base from
hunting and agriculture to trade and manufacturing, with the expansion
of urban living, the number of words increases sharply. Due to the
complexities of modern living, the number of word signs grew from 2,500
in the Shang dynasty in 1765-1123 B.C., to the 50,000 graphic
characters, which the Chinese language has.  However, on the average,
not even a small fraction of these are utilized.  Early Sumerian used
2,000 different signs, in the later Assyrian period 600 were used,

Egyptian used 700 and Hittite culture used 450. The Sumerians built the
first advanced civilization.  They also developed the first adequate
phonetic system of writing.  The Sumerians, being the original keepers
of records, had to find a quicker writing method.  All Sumerian writing
came to be interpreted through a few shapes that could be cut from the
end of a native reed.  Wedge-shaped, these original pictographs, subtle
in curve formation, were reinterpreted through the use of a few tools
stamped into clay in a number of positions and the direction of writing
changed from vertical to horizontal. It was the principle of phonetic
transfer that enabled the various languages to halt or reduce the
proliferation of word signs.  This is the most
important principle on the history of writing.  All modern alphabetical
languages are dependent on it.  This third stage in the development of
writing results from a general pattern of increasingly involved social
problems, especially record keeping and the designation of proper names,
especially foreign, and those involving abstract qualities.(1)

REBUS PRINCIPLE.
The principle of phonetic transfer is often called the rebus principle.
Although the rebus principle of word-sign substitution in situations
where there are like sounds was discovered by many diverse civilizations
it was not fully exploited by most. The well know Egyptian "eye" is used
for words and syllables of similar sound.  In the rebus principle or
phonetic transfer the "eye" sign is substituted for the pronoun "I", for
which there is no sign.  The "eye" sign then has two functions: 1. as a
word sign for "eye" and 2. as the pronoun "I" and/or each time the
diphthong written "I" appears where there is no appropriate word sign.
In terms of the double function of a sign, context indicates how it is
to be read. The Sumerian symbols, which were originally logographic,
became syllables through utilizing the rebus principle.  Many Sumerian
words were monosyllabic and were composed of signs ending in a vowel or
a consonant.  For example, the logogram for "ox" is substituted for the
first syllable in occidental.  The approximate 500 original logograms
came to stand for syllables.(1)

SYLLABARY.
When such a phonetic substitution is fairly complete, the system of
writing is called a syllabary.  In principle, the Sumerians achieved
this.  The graphic signs and speech sounds are so codified as to permit
reasonably accurate translations after a span of four or five thousand
years. The advantages of this system are beyond calculation, providing a
method of recording foreign names, words, and objects in interculture
trading and in the invention of new words.  Through the
vowel-plus-consonant combinations and the consonant-and-vowel
combinations, the total number of graphic signs involved is reduced to a
number that can be handled in printing processes and in teaching.
Egyptian hieroglyphic writing did not attempt to completely replace the
pictorial elements with phonetic elements.  It remained a
picture-writing with the phonetic elements supplementing or completing
what might be lacking.  Much of the European tradition, i.e. ruled
lines, flush margins, large initial letters, stems from Egyptian
writing.(1)

The Egyptian syllabary, the phonetic part of the language, consisted of 24 signs of a single consonant plus any vowel, and about 80 signs with two consonants plus an admixture of vowels between and after. The Hittite syllabary consisted of about 60 signs, with the number of word signs about 450. Greater economy in the number of signs used is not to be found in ancient writing. It appears however, in syllabaries especially designed for a specific language, like that of the Cherokee Indian sound structure in the nineteenth century. Logographs are eliminated and invented signs stand for syllables needed to record the spoken language, which indicates a sharp break in method. The Cherokee Indian syllabary, invented in modern times to reproduce Cherokee sounds, numbers approximately 80 signs and is quite manageable. The principle of economy in signs was an important factor in the structure of early syllabic writing. Imperfections, such as a symbol having several sounds, as in our 26 signed alphabet the "a" in fate, fat, father, and fall, are tolerated in exchange for the facility to work with a minimum of signs.(1)

DESIGNING.
There is an inverse relationship between the ease of using an interface and the ease of writing the interface software. In the design of icon based interfaces ergonomic efficiency must be ensured and consistency maintained. A principle of external interface design of the screen accounting for positive learning curve results is consistency of design.

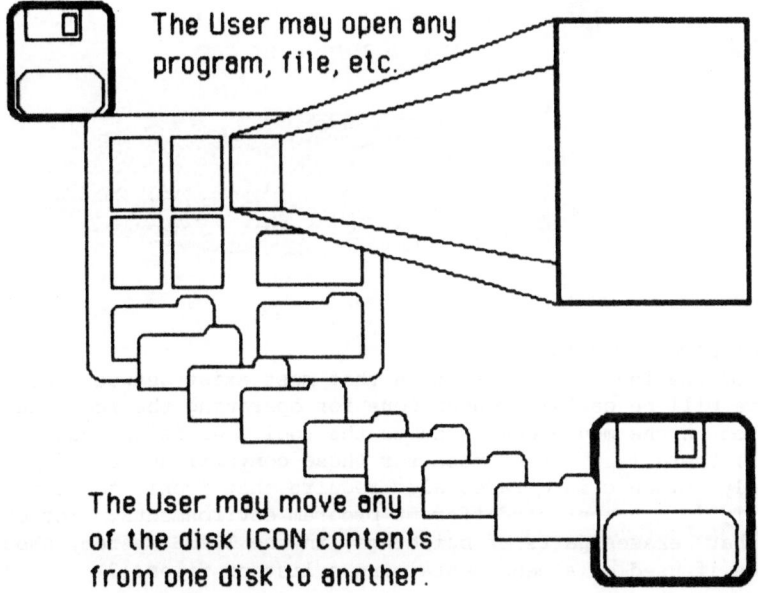

The User may open any program, file, etc.

The User may move any of the disk ICON contents from one disk to another.

This is the primary and critical reason people are able to capitalize on previous knowledge and apply it to new tasks, thus increasing their expertise in task performance.

CONSISTENCY WITH THE REAL WORLD.
The objects in the interface rely on their being consistent with the objects in the real world on which they are based.  The icon should include the most significant and distinguishing feature of the object it represents, so that the relationship between the two is immediately obvious.  Care should also be taken that icons be clearly different from each other, even if the objects they model are similar.  For example, the pen and pencil in the ICADS interface are similar tools in reality. However, the pen is shown in black, signifying its permanence, while the pencil is in white, which appears less substantial on the white background.  The pen is more angular, since it is a more machined tool, and the pencil more rounded.(2)

CONSISTENCY WITH THE REAL TOOL.
The operation of each icon must also be consistent with the real tool in order to capitalize on the User's knowledge of that tool.  Because of the strong link established between tool and icon, any inconsistency requires not only learning of the icon's behavior but also unlearning of the real tool's behavior.

This ICON is about filling an area
or shape, with a particular pattern.

It floods or fills an area very fast,
as only a computer can.

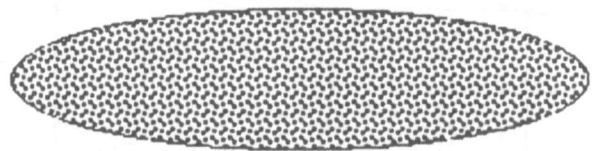

CONSISTENCY WITHIN THE INTERFACE.
By virtue of the level of abstraction that must exist between tool and icon, there will be certain conventions for operating the icon, such as which button on the mouse does what to the tool.  As is the case in all interfaces, there is a strong need for these conventions to be applied consistently.  Iconic interfaces also require that iconic tools behave consistently in a number of different program environments.  For example the icon that  erases parts of buildings, in the ICADS system, should erase files if used on a menu containing a list of files.(2)

LEARNING.
Icon based interfaces are much easier to learn.  By virtue of their orientation towards visual rather than verbal representations of objects, icon based interfaces benefit from the greatly increased efficiency in recognizing and remembering information.  Verbal and

visual information are thought to be processed in different parts of the
brain: verbal information in the left hemisphere of the brain which
specializes in language; visual information in the right hemisphere. As
a result, verbal information is processed serially whereas visual
information is processed holistically. Holistic recognition and
comprehension is much faster where there are a range of things to be
recognized. Verbal information is remembered in short term memory which
is strictly limited in capacity whereas visual information is stored in
long term memory which is virtually limitless in its capacity. People,
thus, have much greater ability to recognize, comprehend and remember
the visual information built into iconic interfaces. It is again
emphasized that one principle about the external interface design of the
screen accounting for positive learning curve results is consistency of
design.
Because they are fun to use there is a real incentive to learn how to
use icon-based-interfaces. By modelling objects with which the user is
familiar in such a way that they behave in the way he expects, there is
much less for the user to learn. He should already know how to use most
of the tools at his disposal. Based on a general knowledge of what
should happen and the immediate visual feedback inherent in iconic
interfaces, the user is free to experiment and learn by discovery. What
is learned by seeing and doing rather than just hearing or reading will
be retained much more easily.

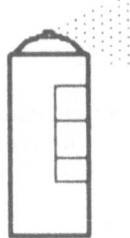

The User may direct the spray using
the ICON, assisted by the familiarity
with the tool in the real world.

The difference, as also in the eraser
and other ICONS, is with the computer.

The computer permits the User, direction
with control, accuracy, and speed.

Comparably, these tools in the real world,
are often restricted in these areas by their
mediums.

USING.
The first impression of any object oriented interface is that it is a
lot of fun to use. It is very important that work should be enjoyable,
but the corollaries are even more important. As much as possible, it is
desirable that the functional screens, i.e. those on which work is
performed, be self-evident. For example, they should not require much
external assistance to make them productively useful. When the
usability of the screen is high, with minimum need for supporting
documentation, on-line tutorials and help screens, clarity and ease of
use may be evident. Although we shall continue to produce User-manuals,
the layout and design concepts of the manual need to reflect the
"functional-screen" and use of an icon-based interface.

Novice Users want easy-to-use interface screens. However, after gaining
experience, they do not want to be slowed. When the more experienced
User continues to consider the screens, easy-to-use, productivity levels
may continue to increase. It is of interest that given easy-to-use
screens, novice users, in spite of moving through the tasks at a fast
rate, may view the program as hard to use. The more expert user, or one
who understands the computer environment, perceives the program as easy
to use. While Users objectively might not have difficulty performing
tasks on the functional screens in terms of time and errors, they may
perceive their work as difficult due to a lack of understanding about
the work, i.e. program tasks, themselves. This is significant in
assessments of usability form both a psychological perspective as well
as methodological. Often usability methodological assessments are made
only on the basis of subjective feedback. To get an accurate and
complete picture, objective testing is required before a true assessment
of the usability of a software interface can emerge.(5)

SEMANTICS.
The language and instructions on screens may be very clear and the
dynamic operations simple and straightforward, so that even novice Users
can perform the tasks easily from a psychological perspective. However,
if the semantics, that is, the understanding of why one is doing what
one is doing, is not made clear, the subjective perception of
ease-of-use suffers, in spite of the objective evidence suggesting
otherwise. Perceptions of usability therefore, may not be tied to the
objective reality of easy-to-use screens and dynamics thereof, so much
as to the psychological understanding of what one is doing. An
objectively simple and easy-to-use interface may be a minimum
requirement and absolutely necessary for subjective perceptions of high
ease-of-use, however it appears that the understanding of the function
determines acceptability subjectively. The designer must make this
concept an inherent part of the design. In addition to understanding
and utilizing organization, unity and structure, the designer must
"understand the program", that is the "rules of the game" and what it is
"about". Even with a formula for straightforward "screen design" with
principles of design and readability in terms of type style and size,
blocks of text and space, colors, etc. or a format for conventions,
messages, etc., there is an indication of something missing. The entire
program, i.e. application, must be designed with the functionality or
use of the program and the end-user in mind. Without this awareness, a
subtle but overall(pervasive) static, disjointed, stiffness and lack of

clarity, continuity and flow may permeate throughout the screens, having considerable negative effect on the User. Also considered in the designing of the User interface, is objective task performance, i.e. times and errors, learning curve, and subjective user attitudes.

CONCLUSION.
A serious problem in introducing computer graphics to non data processing persons, is that as users, they may experience emotions ranging from apprehension to hostility. A system which has an interface which attracts people to use it has overcome such hostility. Number of panel transitions and amount of data entry must be carefully monitored. The requirement that objects modelled in an iconic interface be general in their operation usually leads to a small number of powerful tools. Apart from the advantages of a smaller number of things to remember, these powerful tools require fewer physical operations on the part of the User.

Icon-based interfaces offer a new dimension in human-machine communication. The nature of this interactivity is one which indicates a decrease in learning time and a potential increase in productivity.

REFERENCES:

1. Anderson, Donald,M. THE ART OF WRITTEN FORMS: The Theory and Practice of Calligraphy. Holt, Rinehart and Winston, Inc., New York. 1968.

2. Cornell, David; Sambura, Andrzej; Gero, John. ADVANTAGES OF ICONIC INTERFACES FOR DRAFTING SYSTEMS. Computer Application Research Unit, Department of Architectural Science, University of Sydney. Computer Graphics '84: Online Publications, Pinner, UK. 1984.

3. Craig, James. DESIGNING WITH TYPE: A Basic Course In Typography. Watson-Guptill Publications, New York. 1980.

4. Gallant, Roy A. MAN MUST SPEAK: The Story of Language and How We Use It. Random House, New York. 1969.

5. Teitelbaum, Richard, C. A HUMAN FACTORS TEST of the TSO/E Information Center Facility Screen Interface. IBM Technical Report TR 00.3306. October 19, 1984.

# Video-Graphic Query Facility for Database Retrieval

Nancy H. McDonald

Computer Technology Planning, 10014 N. Dale Mabry Hwy, Suite 101, Tampa, FL 33618, USA

ABSTRACT

The goal of this project was to develop a prototype to demonstrate the use of video and graphic techniques applied to the human-machine interface for data retrieval from a typical computerized database. Data is presented to a user via video and graphic means; queries are formulated in one of several graphic formats; control operations are handled through joystick, touch panel, or single-keystroke maneuvers. To accomplish this, we made use of videodisc, interactive computer graphics, and relational database technologies. Still pictures, video segments, and pictures of text are used as visual cues to a user who indicates interest in a data item in a pointing gesture by touching the panel through which the item may be seen. The user may find the actual data item s/he desires, then pose a query for additional information in one of four graphic query formats. A specially designed database was developed to handle the video and graphic data needed for this user facility.

KEYWORDS: videodisc technology, interactive graphics, human factors, query language interface, database.

## INTRODUCTION

The purpose of the video-graphic query facility (VGQF) project was to investigate the feasibility of using video and still pictures of data to assist a user in formulating queries for retrieving information from a database. Rather than have a user express retrieval operations in a specially structured database query language or vague and lengthy English-like text, we try for a more natural approach by allowing the user to browse through video pictures of data at levels of increasing detail; flip through still pictures of data items and text; or view two simultaneous images of various views of similar or associated data. The user's interactions are mainly performed by menu-select and touch-select operations. After the user finds the items and attributes of interest, s/he may compose a more precise query.

Others have used computer graphics in expressing database queries [MCD75, ZLO75, CHN80]; some have used video data in a database [HER80]; but few, if any have attempted to combine computer graphics, motion pictures, still photographs, alphanumeric information, and pictures of text in a user facility front-end to a database. Additionally, this project demonstrates the use of presenting simultaneous, differing images at times to aid the user's natural, visual, associative process.

A major goal for this effort was to make the human-machine interactions as natural as possible. Therefore, we made heavy use of browsing, pointing, picture flipping, and positioning operations. One underlying assumption of this type of facility is that a human often knows what s/he is interested in only when s/he sees it, alone or in some physical or geographic context.

The purpose of this paper is twofold: 1) to describe the prototype project which was completed to prove the feasibility of video-graphic concepts; and 2) to discuss some issues which should be studied in future projects to better understand human interactions with computer controlled pictures of all types. Therefore, the paper is divided into two sections: VGQF Project; and Future Directions.


VGQF PROJECT

This section will describe the application selected to demonstrate the concepts, the functions which were implemented, and the hardware and software components of the system.

In order to present a realistic data environment for the concepts, we selected a hospital supply database as the application. A special videodisc was produced for this project. The videodisc was designed to contain motion sequences of the general hospital's warehouse, a single department's storeroom, as well as still pictures from both locations and from catalogs, computer printouts, textbooks, and order forms.

The user is initially led through a set of menus to define how s/he wishes to begin. This action takes place on the center computer monitor (see Fig. 1), which we call the instructional screen. The mode of operation to accomplish this activity is selection from a menu using a joystick or keyboard. The feedback to the user is primarily graphic to suggest what the user will see on the video monitors. If the user has requested video information, then s/he will interact with that video material on one or both of the video monitors which are covered with touch panels. Should

the user wish to express a specific query, then the
interactions are centered on the instructional screen.

The five types of interactions a user employs are:

1.  Manu-select (joystick or keyboard) to define the
operation of browse, locate, or query.
2. Menu-select (joystick or keyboard) to specify the type
and level of detail to be shown on each screen.
3. Screen-touch to stop the action and select something.
4. Screen-touch to manuever (e.g. reverse, fast forward) the
videodisc so that the desired view is shown.
5. Menu/graphic manipulations to express a query.

The three basic functions which a user may perform are:

1 Browse -- The VGQF's browse feature presents sequences of
motion or still pictures continuously. In our hospital
supply database application, the user may browse through the
following information:

* Overviewing the warehouse by traversing the perimeter
* Scanning a specific aisle by strolling down the
  center of the aisle
* Scanning random aisles
* Viewing a specific shelf
* Perusing random shelves
* Scanning a shelf area near an item
* Viewing pictures of items being used in applications
* Flipping through text pages
* Seeing inventory listings
* Scanning views of individual items

The user may define the browse function to view on either
video screen or both. When s/he selects both screens, the
system requests that s/he decide if the screens are to be
coordinated. Coordinated video segments in this project are
defined to be sequences of video photography concerning the
same subject from differing views or differing contexts.
This coordination capability is made possible by the
underlying database. A detailed description of the
relational database designed for this project can be found
in [MCD81].

Another interesting concept we chose to employ in the browse
mode to achieve further naturalness was what we called
"levels of hierarchical detail". We noticed that it is not
unusual to visualize objects first in an environmental
context, then in a more specific area of interest, focusing
eventually onto the specific object itself. Therefore,
there was an implicit level of detail for each level of
browse. In other words, when a user was browsing the
warehouse from the periphery, the only type of selection
possible was an aisle. After touch-selection of an aisle,

the proceed operation would continue the browse down the next level of detail -- the aisle. From this level of detail, the user could select a shelf unit, then a specific shelf, and, finally, an item.Alternating between the two video screens for each new level of detail provides an interesting visual effect. We leave the last level of detail frozen on one monitor while presenting the full motion video on the other monitor to provide a frame of reference.

2. Locate -- The VGQF locate feature permits the user to immediately view a static picture of a particular item. In this warehouse application, the user may locate one of the following:
 * A specific item.
 * A specific aisle.
 * A specific shelf.

The user specifies the item to be located either through menu selection or by keyboard entry. S/he then may utilize this located view to begin a browse operation or to develop a query.

3. Query -- The VGQF's query function assumes the user has decided what specific information s/he desires via browse, locate, or other means. The system leads the user through the query composition. The video images, system supplied menus, and graphic format assist the user in the query composition task. We identified four possible query motifs (see Fig. 2) for query expression, but only developed part of the puzzle motif for this feasibility study. Our rationale for identifying more than a single motif is for personal preference and the realization that certain ideas may be more easily expressed in certain formats.


To provide the reader with some understanding of the visual effect, Figure 3 is included at the end of the paper. In these photographs one can appreciate some of the potential of this type of interface.

In Figure 3a we see the monitor configuration with a user interacting with the right video monitor to assist in formulating a query on the center monitor. The second, or left, video monitor is partially blocked by the user's left shoulder.

Figure 3b provides the view of a coordinated browse in which the user asks to see the warehouse periphery on the left and a still shot of each aisle as its passed on the right. The instructional screen in the middle presents the graphic of that operation.

In Figure 3c, the user has progressed down several levels of detail until s/he has a shelf-unit on the left and a specific shelf on the right. At this point, the center screen depicts a specific query that has been processed by the system.

Figure 3d demonstrates a locate capability. The left screen is showing a photographed map from which the locate operation was initiated. The right screen shows the video result of that location.

The puzzle query motif is shown in its formative stage in Figure 3e and in its final stage in Figure 3f. Pieces are selected and drawn in any random order and the system assembles them and performs further interpretation. Figure 4 provides the BNF formal description of the retrieval portion of this query language.

To accomplish this effort we assembled the hardware configuration depicted in Figure 1. The controlling mechanism was an Apple II Plus computer with 64K memory. The computer was directly connected to its own monitor (instructional screen), two videodisc players, two touch-sensitive panels, and a joystick. In addition to the instructional screen used to assist the user in performing the operations of the system, there were two video monitors for users to interact with views of video information.

The software system developed to perform the necessary functions was composed of six components:

1. Data presentation subsystem -- depicting the data presentation as graphically as possible on the instructional screen.
2. Query language composition -- using a finite set of graphic components, menu items, and pictorial data from the database to build a meaningful query.
3. Query decomposition -- deciphering the structure representation and producing access strategies to display and/or obtain required information for the interface to a database's access methods.
4. Multimedia access control -- coordinating and controlling all of the above components.
5. Database -- relational database design with storage positioning and usage information.
6. Instructional screen presentation -- interacting with the user to define the video presentation desired.

Most of the software was developed in UCSD PASCAL with a small portion developed in assembly language to control some hardware interfaces.

## FUTURE DIRECTIONS

This project has begun to make contributions in the areas of human interactions with video and graphics, pictorial presentation for assisting the human associative process, and picture language development. Our efforts towards these ends have suggested such future activities as:

Graphics: For the very near future, we would present more graphics and video mixed than was possible in this initial effort. One of the medium range goals of this effort is to make greater use of graphics in the queries themselves. The long range goal of this type of interface entails the user pointing to an object in a photograph and obtaining a graphic outline or duplicate picture of the object to use in a pictorial query--so that no words need be typed.

Linguistics: In our attempts to describe this project, we have found a lack of sufficient language or languages to use for the human-machine interface. In this case, there is a need for a storyboard-like language to describe the various interactions a user may have with graphics, video, text, and data.

Audio: We would like to utilize the audio tracks on the videodisc. Although we recorded both English and Spanish words, we did not have enough resources to develop a verbal capability.

Human Factors: The concept of personal preference for the way in which a user expresses a request to the computer will become more important as computers become more and more commonplace. For that reason, as well as the fact that certain functions and/or data structures lend themselves to certain graphic depictions, we believe additional work in human factors for graphical interfaces will be important.

Database: We believe that we have only begun to develop some of the possibilities and necessities for handling alphanumeric, graphic, and video information as well as their combinations and associations. There may be better data organizations and algorithms for handling certain types of information in certain situations. We believe dynamically defined relations should be investigated for user-defined functions. There may also be good reason to consider storing some data on the videodisc. Deciding which data and how to best position the data is an interesting topic.

Hardware improvements: We know that a production system will need a great deal more RAM and secondary storage. This may mean a more powerful processor also. Similarly, as graphic technology improves, we will wish to make use of split screen and other special video effects which are presently very costly.

Experimentation: With a more fully functional system, we would like to perform human factors experiments to evaluate the effectiveness of this facility.


Summary

This project has demonstrated that a video-graphic query facility is technologically feasible. From the reactions we have received to our videotape of the system, it also appears to be quite attractive to many potential users. From a three-screen setup, a user receives instructions and naturally interacts with video and graphic data, to browse, locate, and query a computerized database. Although there is much work to be done, this effort begins to analyze how a user may interact with various forms of data. Some areas which might benefit from this type of system include inventory databases, picture recognition training systems, psychological studies, and office automation.

BIBLIOGRAPHY

[CHN80]    Chans, N. S. and Fu, K. S., "Query-by-Pictorial-Example", IEEE Transactions on Software Engineering, Vol.1 SE-6, No. 6, IEEE, Nov., 1980, pp. 519-524.

[HER80]    Herot, C. F., "Spatial Management of Data", ACM Transactions on Database Systems, Vol. 5, No. 4, Association for Computing Machinery, Dec., 1980, pp. 493-514.

[MCD75]    McDonald, N. H., "CUPID:    A Graphics Oriented Facility for Support of Non-programmer Interactions with a Database", Memo No. ERL-M563, Ph.D. Dissertation, University of California, Berkeley, Nov., 1975.

[MCD81]    McDonald, N. H. and McNally, J. P., "Video-Graphic Query Facility Database Design", presented to and in the proceedings of the SIGMOD Workshop on Small Database Systems, Oct, 1981, Orlando, Fla.

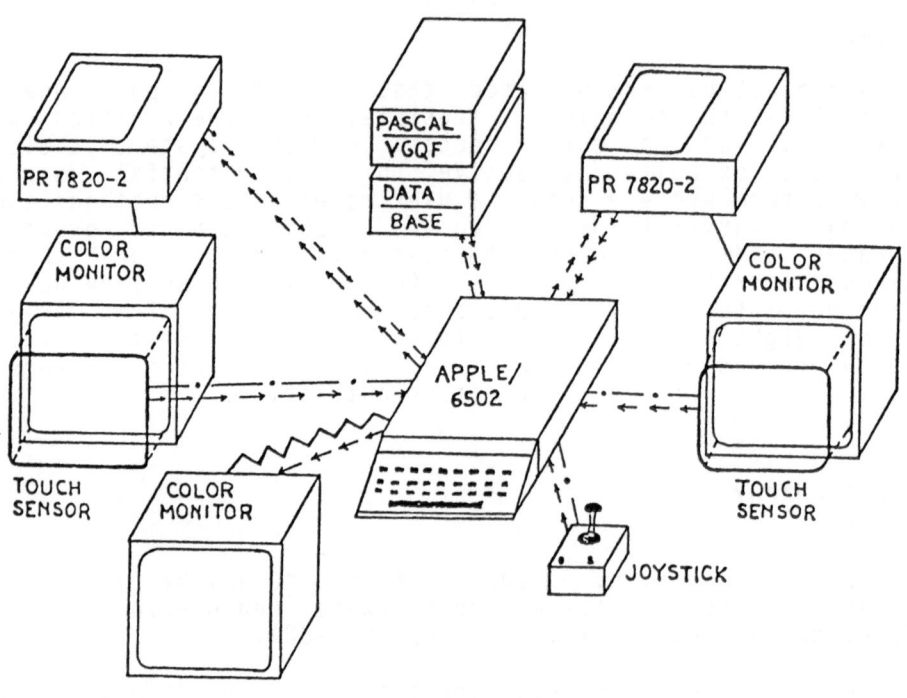

PR 7820-2

COLOR
MONITOR

PASCAL
VGQF

DATA
BASE

PR 7820-2

COLOR
MONITOR

APPLE/
6502

TOUCH
SENSOR

COLOR
MONITOR

JOYSTICK

TOUCH
SENSOR

LEGEND:
VIDEO ———
GRAPHIC ∿∿∿∿
DATA →→
CONTROL —·—·

Figure 1   Hardware Configuration

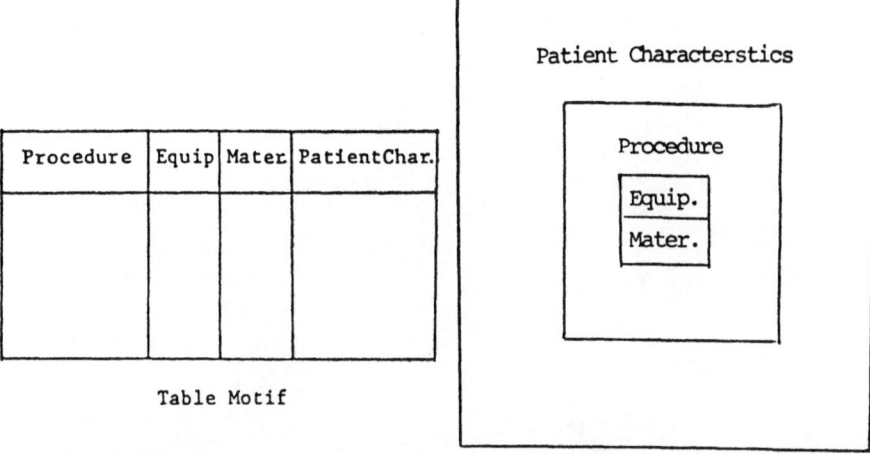

| Procedure | Equip | Mater | PatientChar. |
|---|---|---|---|
|  |  |  |  |

Table Motif

Patient Characterstics

Procedure

Equip.

Mater.

Bullseye Motif

Procedure

Equipment &
Material

Patient
Characterstic

age        weight    allergies

Tree Motif

Equip.          Patient
        Procedure
Material          Charact.

Puzzle Motif

Figure 2    Query Motifs

Figure 3a   User at VGQF system.

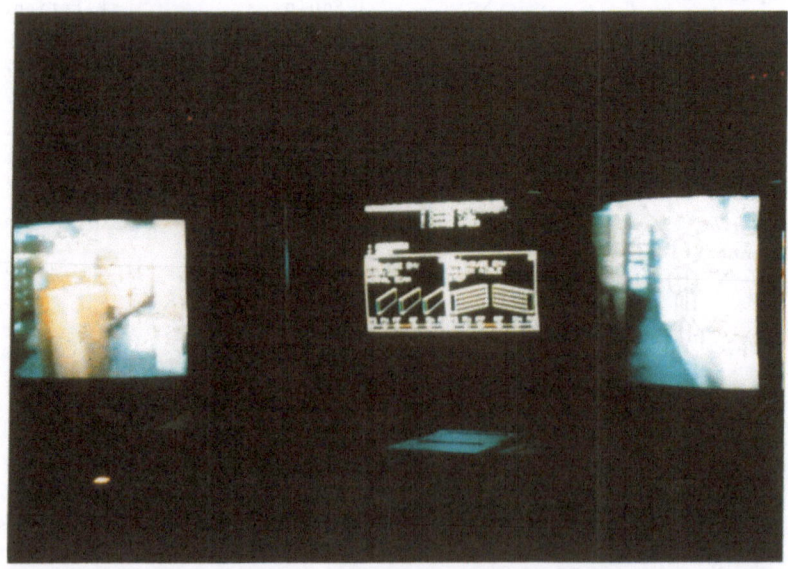

Figure 3b   Coordinated browse of warehouse periphery
            (left) and aisle (right).

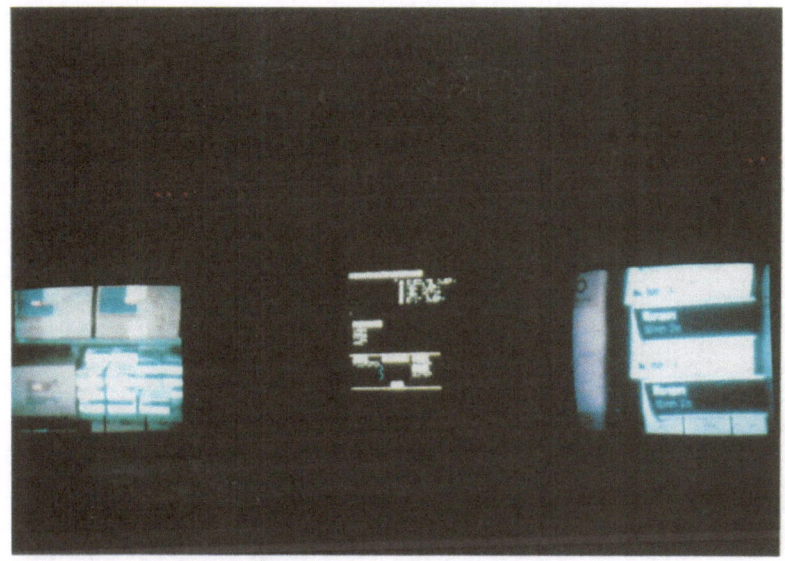

Figure 3c   Shelf-unit (left) and shelf (right) with
specific query on the center screen.

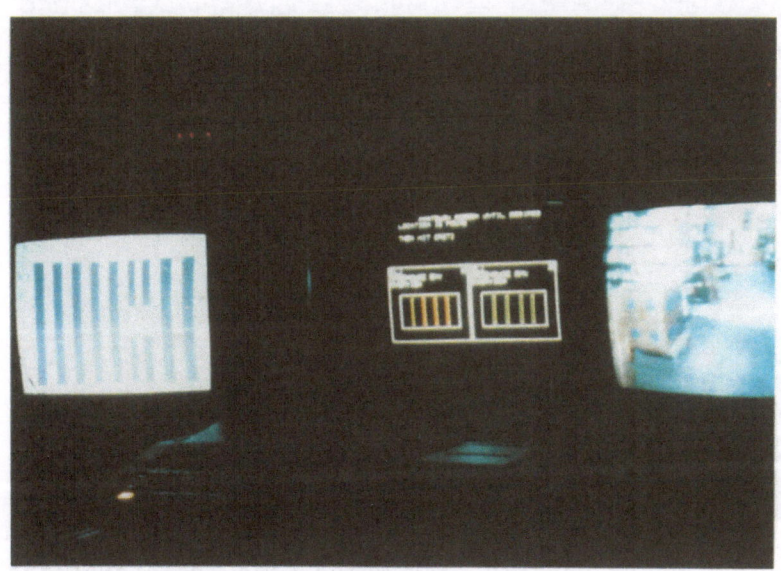

Figure 3d   Locate operation with warehouse map (left)
and the video view of the location (right).

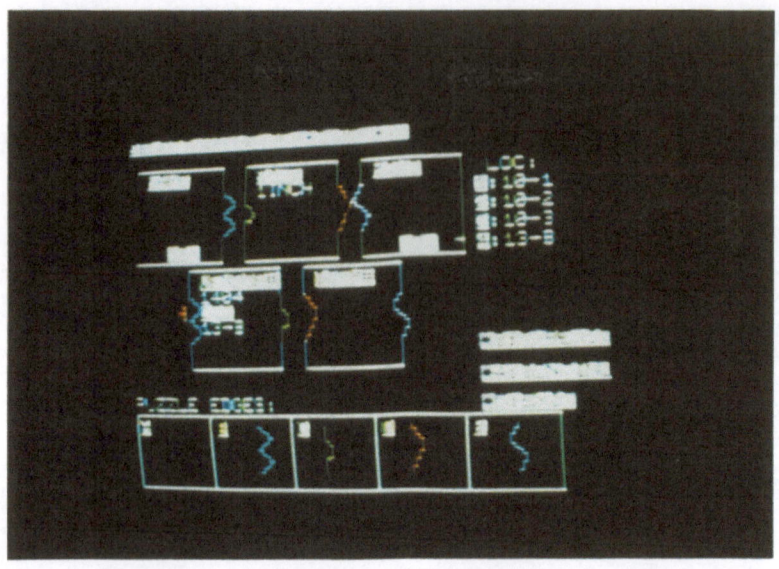

Figure 3e   Query puzzle pieces being defined individually.

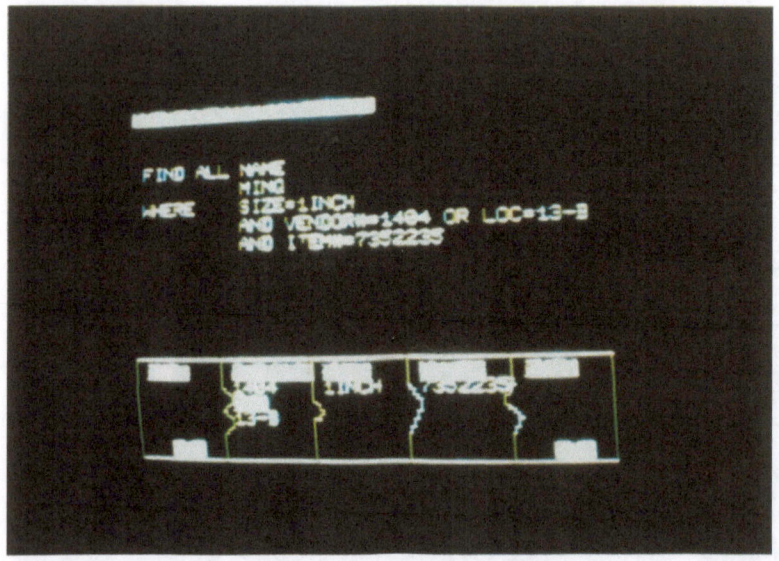

Figure 3f   Query puzzle assembled and reinterpreted to request the system to "Find all names and minimum-quantities where the size is 1 inch and the vendor identification is 1404 or the location is 13-3 and the item has an identification of 7352235".

Figure 4 Description of puzzle motif query language with BNF notation for retrieval.

Since this is a specialized query language for an inventory database, we have made several simplifying assumptions:

All information concerns the objects in the inventory and, therefore, there is a consistent set of attributes which can be named uniquely. This means that all queries may be expressed in terms of attributes, relationships among attributes, and operations on attributes. No identification of special entity types or relation names need be used.

Insert and modify operations can be made to follow the retrieval syntax very closely. Set functions may be handled like aggregate functions.

Each puzzle piece is intended to represent a simple phrase in the query (e.g. either the target phrase, or part of the conjunctive qualification.

The pieces are placed together into one or more rectangular puzzles (i.e. no jagged vertical edges) for associative clarity. As an example, should a user wish to ask for a list of all tape-type products with the unit cost which is less than the average cost of Micropore tape, we would develop the following configuration:

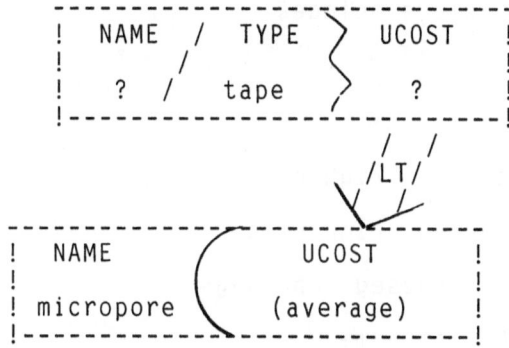

If we had not developed two puzzle segments, the association of the attribute cost with the two different query parts would have presented a problem. Many queries may be stated as one puzzle.


Notational Meanings:

Puzzle pieces contain attribute names with either ? for target identification or operators and/or values, which may or may not be computed.

Pieces may be linked by thick arrows which contain operators describing special actions to be taken on the attributes linked.

Vertical positioning of attributes/values within a puzzle piece implies the OR relational operand; while the horizontal positioning of pieces implies the AND relation among attributes.

The special symbols devised to express picture positioning include:

a C b:  a contains b within it.
a ≈ b:  a and b are anywhere in the query.
a ➔ b:  a has a relationship to b as specified within
        the arrow.
a ∧ b:  a is ontop of or below and attached to b.

The Grammar

attname:   attribute name selected from a menu or typed

value:     constant typed by user

ques:    ?

piece:

pieces;    piece ! piece  pieces

leftpiece:  [

rightpiece:  ]

anypiece:    leftpiece ! rightpiece ! piece

puzseg: leftpiece  pieces  rightpiece

puzsegs: puzseg  !  puzseg  puzsegs

targ:    anypiece  C  attname
                       ques

attribute:     attname    !   attname
                 value          (aop)

orquals:   attribute
             --
           attribute
           orquals

rop:

```
bop:    ⤴ + !  ⤸ - !  ⤴ * !  ⤷ ⌐

uop:      +    !  -

luop:   |NOT|

by:     | BY |

aop:    |SUM|  !  |SUMP|  !  |AVG|  !  |AVGP|  !
        |MAX|  !  |MIN|

aop2:   |CNT|  !  |CNTP|

tl1:    targ  !  a_fcn  C  ques

t1:     tl1   !  tl1     t1

qual:   luop  qual  !  attribute  !  attrib_pce  !
        clause

qualification:  qual  !  qual  qualification

clause: a_fcn ⟨rop⟩ a_fcn !  a_fcn ⟨rop⟩ clause  !
        Tuop ∧ clause

a_fcn:     attrib_fcn  !  aggr_fcn  !  ag2_fcn  !
           a_fcn ∧ bop ∧ a_fcn  !  uop ∧ a_fcn

attrib_fcn:  attrib_pce  !  uop ∧ attrib_pce

aggr_fcn:    attrib_pce C aop  !  aop ∧ attrib_pce

attrib_pce:  anypice C orquals

query:   t1  !  t1 qualification
```

# Communications and Graphics

Mark G. Rawlins and Vince Uttley

Visual Engineering, 2680 N. First Street, Suite 200, San Jose, CA 95134, USA

Until recently, computer graphics has been used as an "end" and not so much as a "means". As an "end", graphic output ranges from simple bar charts to three dimensional surface charts to CAD/CAM layouts. Applications have long existed to convert data into graphics. There have been many sophisticated libraries and stand alone products which draw these charts on any number of devices and in a multitude of resolutions. There never has been any serious consideration of graphics as a general communication tool until the recent introductions of both hardware and software technology that made the throughput acceptable and visibly clear.

In today's economy, and with the competitive forces that exist in the engineering, research and business communities, one no longer has the freedom to draw a bar chart just for the sake of doing graphics. If the chart or design does not convey more information than using some other display technique, then the use of graphics has been wasted. Fortunately, this is not the case, as graphics offers the ultimate as a communication tool.

Before we look at a few areas of technological advances which have allowed the use of graphics to obtain it's stature as the ultimate communication tool, it is worth while looking at the concept of graphics and the physiological process that we use to understand it.

Mankind first started to communicate in concepts. Cave drawings exist where in a single picture an entire day's hunt might be depicted. This general overview or "information presentation" was devoid of specific data, but it none-the-less communicated the essence of the day's experience.

As we advanced in our civilization, the need to communicate data as opposed to information prompted the creation of language and the spoken word. It is easy to see that the translation process in communicating from one person to another can be extremely complex. The anxieties of someone who has never flown in an airplane before can be taken as an example. The passenger would first experience this new sensation. He would then try to understand the sensitivities or level of understanding of the targeted listener. Next, he would translate his emotion with flying into words that have somewhat the same meaning for the listener and hope that the listener can in turn translate those words into an emotion. Through all these translations of emotion to words then back to emotion, it is hoped that the listener will respond similarly to the novice passenger.

The above discussion is not unlike the problem in initially communicating with information and then breaking down this information into raw data, hoping only to again reconstruct the initial information from its "data components" without a change in meaning.

The above analogy should point out one of the primary problems in the data/information processing environment. One would be very lucky, indeed, to reconstruct the whole from all of the parts. It is also because of this refocusing that the term information processing is now replacing the older concept of data processing. The role which graphics plays in this data/information process has until recently been an historically based "end", not a "means".

During the Sixties, when more data erroneously meant more information, computer graphics was used to act as a vehicle by which mounds of data could be fathomed. The success of graphics both in data representation and in geometric representation applications lies in the inherent ability of man to suffer from "through-put" overload. There is a finite amount of information that can be processed by any of the body's receptors. The body shuts out too much light by squinting. The first sip of a hot cup of tea is always hotter than the second sip. This is not because the tea has gotten cooler, but because the body acknowledges the fact that the tea is hot and so it need not process this information further. Other examples include the placing of the left hand in cold water and the right in hot water. After a minute, both hands are placed in a cup of warm water. The hand originally in the cold water thinks that the water is hot, while the hand which was in the hot water now thinks that the same warm water is cold.

The human understands new, different or unusual environments or information based on a previously understood foundation. In the case of the cold hand in warm water, the base foundation was cold and so the new information said it was hot; likewise, the hand in hot water chose "hot" as the foundation, and therefore, determined the warm water was cold.

The proliferation of data during the 1960's required the use of graphics as a vehicle for adding "understanding" to the data. So much data was being extracted that noone could make proper use of it. A vehicle needed to exist that would keep the understanding process from being overloaded and represent the data in forms that could be reassimilated into its original form -- Information.

The fact that this data had initially come from information, was at the time unimportant. It was felt that the initial information was only a vehicle which contained the data. The computer and subsequent use of graphics was the best if not the only mechanism to put that data back into meaningful information. This unfortunately was not the case.

It wasn't until recent software advances and the development of better man/machine interfaces that the processing of information as opposed to data was possible. As graphics lent itself so beautifully to the presentation of data and its comparison to known basics, it was obviously used in the presentation of information. Concepts beyond simple bar and pie charts were invented to add more meaningful dimensions so that the charts would hopefully contain the subtleties of the original information base. Multiple dimension charts, multiple charts on a page, new and original charting elements (bubble charts) help add to this process. Though the examples initially cover data representation charting, we will see how the same concerns have led to advanced software and hardware technology in the area of design or geometric representation.

As the process proceeded to keep the information base intact, a bottle-neck quickly became apparent. That bottle-neck was the use of words or fixed terminology to determine what information needed to be extracted from the global information base. The initial analogy of the first-time airline passenger is a point worth bringing up again. With the airline passenger, the information was his emotion with flying. He had to then extract this information and break it down into data or words in order to communicate it to the listener and in turn the listener had to take these words or data and reconstruct it, hopefully correctly, back into the initial information. The use of command driven applications to select or classify subsets of information for viewing or decision making was tantamount to breaking the information back down into its original data.

Man/machine interfaces became the first area to be addressed in this new world of information processing. If the information was of a conceptual nature, couldn't the extraction and manipulation process of that information also be conceptual? The extension of this conceptual manipulation extends further into the realm of artificial intelligence and on into further areas of technological breakthrough. The first and major step, though, was developing techniques for conceptualizing communication. It might seem obvious in retrospect, but it was rather a significant breakthrough when someone realized that graphics could be used as this communication tool. In more basic terms, how can symbols or icons be used to express internationally accepted ideas?

One needs to first start with either intuitive or easily learned symbols. The symbol of a man might be considered intuitive, but in reality it is probably learned. Only those societies where man wears western garb would this symbol be immediately understood. It is perhaps not an important point as to whether symbols are intuitive or learned; it is more to the point that they can easily be understood within the realm of normal existence.

Symbols, like the concepts they represent, can be combined to form new concepts. The case in point is the international symbol of "not". That symbol superimposed on any other symbol negates its information. A door containing the symbol of a man with the "not" symbol superimposed is a clear indication that men are not welcome.

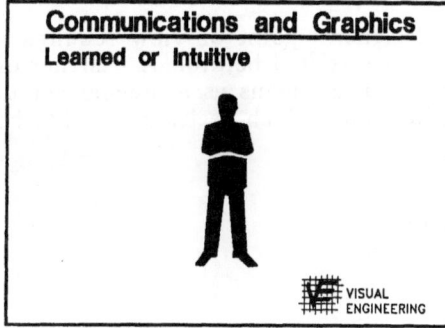

It is interesting to note that some words take on symbol or icon stature. In the western society, the word "exit" is used to indicate passage out of a building. In reality, the word "exit" is third person singular for "he leaves" in Latin. It is no longer important what the dictionary meaning of "exit" is, but rather its global information or conceptual content.

With the assumption that we now know the mechanism by which concepts can be communicated (an assumption which may not be quite valid), we need to look at the technology at hand by which these conceptual indicators or icons can be selected, manipulated or generally used.

How do you use a keystroke depression to select an icon which represents "shut down the nuclear reactor, we're having a melt down"? As we are now using symbols, one can't type in the command. It is also inefficient to hit the space bar so many times to position an alpha-numeric cursor to the proper symbol or icon on the screen. New technology needed to be invented that would allow the extension of human communication to select these concepts. Areas of selection cover both tactile pointing and ocular pointing. The tactile pointing is in some way the moving of the hand, or some other part of the body, and the striking of a surface to indicate the selection point or item. Work is being done in the areas of eye movement so that one merely needs to glance at an item for selection or placement.

Nowadays, one can use touch screens, trackballs, mice, joysticks, digitizers as well as function keys, and the ever-present keyboard. Other areas of input that are considered in standards-based software tools, such as GKS, cover control knobs and valuators.

It is important to match the application or selection process with the physical device. Using a digitizing tablet to control the applications flow of a word processer is probably not the best use of a selection device. On the other hand, a keyboard to control a video game is also not ideal. In fact the keyboard is a good case of "too much of a good thing". If you consider a keyboard as a "choice" input device, you can see how it is less effective than one with only two keys. The decision of which of the ninety-five keys on a keyboard to select requires more "user" thought processing than the application might call for. Going back to the analogy of the emergency in the nuclear reactor, the selection criteria in that case should not be one out of ninety-five. The wrong key might be chosen. In this scenario, perhaps one out of one, or one out of two buttons might be indicated. The button for turning off the reactor would have a clear and concise symbol which indicated danger. This button would be in a position so that it would not be confused with any other function.

The use of these icons from a software designer's point of view requires a different perspective than one which might have existed before. A designer of a communications based product might want to use icons as a mechanism to control application flow. In selecting three items for which decisions need to be made, we can consider the setting of:

    baud rate
    choosing the use of colors for hi-lighting
    function keys definition for certain actions

Though these three elements need to be under user control, the random use of arbitrary icons to depict their activity could be confusing. Also, having these icons represented on the screen at one time could create visual clutter and, thereby, render the application useless.

An application designer wishing to put the control of these capabilities under icon selection needs to perhaps change his thought process. The designer needs to understand the psychology of the user and prioritize the selectability or availability of these functions in the overall spectrum of the application. Again, going back to the ability of the human body to turn off or ignore extraneous input, the designer needs to be aware that there are perhaps just certain times during the running of the application that the selection of this information is necessary.

In pursuing this logic down one more path, we can see perhaps that these capabilities might be reserved for either occasional use or an expert. In thinking of the latter, a new category of selection might be created that could be chosen with the concept of a mortar board. As mortar boards connote college graduation, the items contained or controlled by this symbol would constitute advanced features and one which significant training might be required. This information, or this concept, can be easily presented with the properly selected symbol. Whether or not that symbol is a mortar board is irrelevant, the point is that just the presence of this symbol signifies three things. The first is that there are further actions to be pursued upon the selection of the symbol. The second is that these actions are advanced features, and thirdly that the user needs to pursue an educational process in either on-line help or other documentation so that he can familiarize himself with the functionality of these features. All three points can be communicated by one symbol.

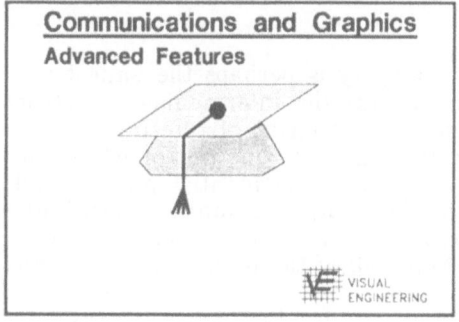

During this discussion we've been touching on the importance of "conceptual communication" with its value lying in its ability to communicate more than one point without ambiguity. This comprehension factor is very important because in real life, one is never breaking decisions down into nondivisible binary choices. Application software packages that extract and manipulate information typically require a number of linked decisions. The more decisions one needs to make, the more potential confusion exists in the selection process. Again, using the analogy of the nuclear reactor, the keyboard is clearly not the best way of shutting down the system. The confusion over which of the ninety-five keys to strike may clearly cause an incorrect decision.

In looking at the optional types of selection categories, we can construct three models:

> essay
> menu choice
> fill in the blank

The "essay" category is exemplified by a command front-end. This essay input requires a stream of concepts to be entered before a final action is taken. Though application command processors make it easy for the expert to quickly produce results, it presupposes the knowledge of those commands as well as their actions. This is a classical case of "easy to use" versus "easy to learn" and has brought the command front end or "essay" category of application input under fire as more and more nontechnical users start to use the computer.

The "menu choice" category corrects some of the problems inherent in the essay type. The menu itself acts as a coherent structure to minimize "user overload" and keep information to a relevant minimum. It also offers an immediate feedback mechanism as the user sees what selections are possible. By selecting or entering the wrong choice in a menu, the application can immediately respond and thereby help in the learning process. "Menu choice" can be used for both the entering and selection of textual, as well as graphical information. More importantly, an application can use a combination of the two in order to optimize clarity. The primary drawback of using a "menu choice" front end lies in the nesting of the menus. As long as all the information is visible on one menu, the options are very clear. In the distribution of the choice process over multiple menus, the user may not know fully what options are available and thereby spend too much time going from "page" to "page". Several techniques exist which correct for this deficiency. In fact, it is now unusual to find "menu choice" front ends without some time of short-cutting technique.

The "fill in the blank" category is perhaps the easiest to use for the beginner, but the most cumbersome for the intermediate or advanced user. "Filling in the blank" is a sequential mechanism of offering one decision at a time, and quite often basing the responses to "one out of n" options. As every selection must be evaluated in order, the sequential process makes it impractical for information processing where large amounts of decisions are necessary. Quite often one wants to proceed to the last few selection items and to do so with a "fill in the blank" front end, all of the preliminary questions must be answered.

This spectrum of "easy to use" for the expert ("essay") through "easy to learn" for the novice ("fill in the blank") gives the application writer an insight as to how a front end must be designed for his targeted user. The "menu choice" category, which has the benefit of both being "easy to use", as well as "easy to learn", is the most flexible and widely accepted.

It is interesting to realize that the success of "menu choice" still lies in the use of words as opposed to symbols. Though technology exists today (with the availability of rastor based screens) to display highly complex symbols and icons,; there have been few, if any, commercially successful applications which are symbol based.

Perhaps today's generation of computer user has been too programmed to accept symbol oriented applications? Perhaps people just can not handle concept driven programs? Perhaps the ultimate pointing device has not been invented?

Some of the problems lie in the fact that rastor icons are machine specific and it is important for an application writer to make sure that his software runs on a broad spectrum of machines. Using rastor based icons, every machine adaptation would have to be individually tooled. There also has been less than full acceptance of input devices such as a mouse. As was discussed earlier the use of the keyboard to control symbol selection is not adequate. A great number of people find pointing devices still awkward. Whether symbol selection or icon interfaces coupled with the "menu choice" front end will be widely acceptable as a mechanism for communicating concepts still has yet to be fully resolved.

Extrapolating the obvious importance of graphics and communications into the design and CAD/CAM world, we are starting to see more imaginative uses of graphics. Graphics is being used more and more to get an exact rendition of a designed structure. Due to computational barriers, many designers would only use mesh or stick diagrams in visualizing their projects. With the advent of sophisticated computer simulation, more structural and design information could be processed and perceived electronically than mechanically. The problem existed in the visualization of this analysis and because of that, the analysis produced pages and pages of output instead of a clear picture. Again we see the destruction of information into its data subsets and the attempt to reconstruct that information graphically. Sometimes the creation of the graphic was too mathematically intensive.

Mechanisms did exist for exact rendering and simulation graphically with the original information intact. Dedicated IBM or CRAY computers would spend tens of hours producing one picture. The cost and time in some cases was a viable tradeoff for the information gained, but there were many circumstances where it was not worth it. The fallback was again the use of data components.

The latest advance comes in the area of constant time rendering. Anti-aliased, smoothed, ray-traced images with multiple cameras and light sources are now available on UNIX based workstations and small computers. How viable is this new software? The highest quality image of an item composed of 10,000 polygons takes about an hour and a half on a VAX 780 to render with the highest mathematical accuracy. Increasing the number of polygons from 10,000 to 100,000 has minimal impact (less than 3%) on the time of computation and output. These same images with older algorythms have taken up to 100 times more CPU resources. It is plain to see now that with the full ability to render a model as accurately as possible and see the results as clearly as possible expidites the design process and opens up more analysis possibilities due to the shortened time and accurate representation.

In summation, all graphics designers and users need to start rethinking their use of this graphics communications as a "means" and not an "end". Information needs to be kept intact, and graphical techniques, whether they are graphical user front ends or more optimized three dimensional representations for modeling an analysis, need to be used to communicate this information, not just present a pretty picture.

# Advanced Systems Integration Management via CAD Graphics

Robert T. Bannon

AT&T Communications, Bedminster, NJ 07921, USA

## Abstract

The purpose of this paper is to explain the creation of an Electronic Data Processing Architecture using a Computer-Aided Design (CAD) System. The EDP Architecture includes the interrelationships and data dependencies between EDP systems required for effective systems integration management. For purposes of illustration, this paper will use the functional relationship required to support telecommunications engineering.

By using computer graphics to define EDP architecture, the following advantages become evident:

- Graphic mapping of interfaces inform EDP systems designers of user requirements. An example of this is the access of equipment requirements for determining floor space requirements.
- Inform both users and upper management of proposed EDP design activity.
- Color display and output capabilities provide the capability to highlight major impact items.
- Graphics structure allows the EDP Architecture to clearly convey the maximum information required for a specific application function.
- Dynamic graphics teleconferencing allows for immediate viewing from remote locations.

A suggested methodology of preparing an integrated EDP Architecture using Computer Graphics is described and can be applied to other technologies and industries.

## Introduction

In a Booz-Allen study conducted in 1983, it was estimated that almost half the United States workforce was engaged in information processing. Since that study was conducted, information processing requirements and computing graphics output of this information has grown rapidly. There is a increasing number of companies and research institutions becoming more deeply involved in data manipulation, processing and information management. Because of this rapid growth, it is not uncommon to find that similar or redundant functions are being performed in various departments. In extreme cases, EDP systems within the same department may even store and manipulate the same data. This is caused by poor EDP system design, changing user requirements, parochial interests or proprietorship of information. Organizations do not want to disseminate their knowledge if this causes additional work or loss of total control of their system.

System integration architecture is a complex planning procedure that does not lend itself to analytical treatment of its effectiveness. Therefore, to plan system integration and an efficient data flow between systems, with a minimum of human interfaces and functional duplications, the establishment of an EDP Planning Organization is required. This group can reside within either the user or design organization. Its function is to create an integrated EDP System Architecture which depicts both the functional work flow and the interrelationship between systems. The basic thrust of the EDP Architecture is to provide an automated coordination and mechanization of interfaces for better data consistency and information management.

This paper discusses the use of a Computer-Aided Design (CAD) System to create the EDP system integration layout and to manipulate the EDP Architecture. By using the CAD system for these purposes, we are able to map the changes in information developed in one system and passed downstream to another. Also, we are able to convey, with a high degree of clarity, major impacts on the EDP system architecture. This in turn results in better system design for a new system or set of programs that will be integrated into the overall functional work flow.

## CAD System Selection Criteria

The selection of a computer graphics system to support the design of an EDP system architecture is similar in nature to selecting a graphics system to support either circuit board or building design.

Human interfaces with the graphics system is via a workstation. Today's workstations are ergonomically designed to relieve eye strain and body fatigue from working for prolonged periods. The operator creates, modifies, and refines the architectural layout interactively, viewing the emerging work on a graphic display. With a single command, the architectural designer can manipulate and change the proposed data flow highlight impact areas in the output format or change the relational view.

A typical workstation will consist of a terminal (CRT), a hardcopy device and a variety of peripheral hardware that enhances a system's flexibility and responsiveness the EDP architectural designers need.

To construct the EDP architecture and map functional relationships, you may choose to use either an existing in-house computer graphics system or opt for a new system. When using existing hardware and software, the initial economic outlay is less than that of a new system, however, there are some trade-offs that must be considered:

- What is the volume of work already residing on existing graphics systems?
- Is the processing environment a Mainframe or Mini-computer or workstation micro-based?
- Is access time readily available, or is it on a special priority or allocation basis?
- Is the workstation convenient for the architectural designer, such as in a common terminal area? Or will access be dependent on purchasing a new separate workstation?
- Does the existing workstation design meet the user requirements of the architectural designer without modification? And if modifications are required, how extensive are they?

- Is the software in a programming language, such as Fortran-77 or "C", supported by the potential designer organization? If software changes are required, does it require the vendor to make changes?
- Does the system support the Initial Graphics Exchange Standard (IGES) and the Graphics Kernal System (GKS) standards?
- Was the graphics system designed to be menu driven only, or does it have the flexibility to allow the creation of special symbols, line manipulation and alpha-numeric text input and editing capabilities?
- Is existing documentation sufficient to allow the existing CAD system to be manipulated for EDP Architectural integration?
- What are the operational costs of the existing system?
- How extensive is the EDP Architecture you intend to create? Does it support only one department, or does it encompass the entire EDP resources of your entire company?
- Will your EDP Architecture include only the function and system level? Or will it branch into schemas and subschemata for functions and systems?

After investigating the capabilities and limitations of your existing CAD system you may decide that it will meet your requirements or a majority of them effectively. If there are legitimate concerns about its efficiency and usefulness you may want to investigate a new system.

It should be remembered that most CAD graphics systems are designed to allow interactive manipulation of symbol location and associated text. Business graphics systems and statistical graphic packages do not have the flexibility required for this aspect of EDP architectural design, therefore these systems are unsuited for an EDP architectural design application.

In investigating the purchase of a new graphics package to support the design of an EDP architecture, some additional considerations should be evaluated:

- Total package price?
- Cost/performance comparison?
- Processor features - Micro-, Mini-, or Mainframe?
- System Capacity?

- Interface Compatibility?
- Quantity of workstations system can support?
- Expandability?
- System performance specification?

## CAD Selection

Based on an evaluation of our Engineering Department requirements, the time constraints associated with introducing a new graphics system and the versatility of an existing system, we choose to initially implement the EDP Network Systems Architecture on the Telephone Office Planning and Engineering Sytem (TOPES). Since the original decision to use TOPES, we evolved into replacing TOPES with a third generation CAD system, Multi-user Engineering Graphics System (MEGS). As a spinoff to MEGS, we are developing a UNIX®, System 5.0-based CAD graphics application to support the EDP architectural design. This application is known as the Mini Unix® Graphics System (MUGS).

TOPES was an interactive computer aided design (CAD) system that was developed by Bell Laboratories (BL), Western Electric Company, and AT&T Long Lines personnel to assist office planning engineering in the layout and design of telecommunications and computer equipment offices. It was also used to size and layout administrative space requirements, support systems and building elements. TOPES was not a commercially available system. At the time of initial development, because of limited display capabilities, TOPES was developed around storage tube technology to accommodate the large number of drawing elements required to support space planning. However, high resolution refresh and raster scan terminals allowed TOPES to achieved device independence and it can be access from a variety of terminals. The TOPES software utilized PLOT-10 software for its basic graphics subroutine package, and for object manipulation and transformations, however this software was greatly enhanced by Bell Laboratories. TOPES operated on a DEC 10 computer, therefore approximately 16 concurrent users were supported without response time deterioration.

The development of MUGS will allow the EDP Architecture to migrate from a 36 bit processor to a 32-bit environment and to utilize new workstation features that have become available during the second half of 1984. In addition, the PLOT-10 graphics core is being replaced with the new version of Precision Visuals, DI3000 which will be Graphics Kernal System (GKS) compatible. MUGS runs on either a DEC VAX 11/780 or the AT&T Technologies 3B20 processor. MUGS use INGRES as its database management system (DBMS).

As with my company, time constraints will weigh heavily upon your evaluation and will influence your decision to use an existing in-house system, permanently or for an interim period, or opt to implement a new system.

## EDP Systems Architecture

EDP System Architectural Design is a discipline that evolved out of a combination of engineering and EDP program documentation criteria. It is based upon the CAD technology that evolved from schematic drawing layout for printed circuit boards and building design. At the same time, EDP architecture utilizes techniques associated with data flow and system documentation. The motivation for developing an EDP System Architecture is the creation and documentation of a logical model of system interrelationships for a functional or engineering technology. By using CAD graphical techniques it enables engineers, users, analysts and designers to develop a concise picture of the various system dependencies and data access requirements existing between functional groupings of systems.

Ironically, system designers and programmers have relied on manual drafting techniques for system documentation, even while they                                                     were designing computer graphics systems. The use of a CAD system has eliminated this manual bottleneck in developing and publishing an EDP Systems Architecture. These non-creative and error-prone procedures can be costly and contribute to the untimeliness and inaccuracy of an EDP Architecture which must be a dynamic transition document.

Implementation of a CAD system in the EDP planning environment has eliminated much of the frustration incurred while making changes in a complex EDP Systems Architecture which contains a maze of engineering support systems that integrate functionally on information processing levels. Manual modifications that reflect system interconnection can be tedious, but with computer graphics the process will be expedited and the EDP Architecture will become a dynamic tool that can reflect transitional impacts from subschema level through functional level in a timely fashion. This allows the EDP Planning Organization to answer "what if" questions concerning downstream impact if the generation of certain data is eliminated or the format is modified.

With the old method of manually drawing system interrelationships, the input was usually a hand-drawn sketch prepared by the EDP planner, which was then redrawn into an understandable format that met corporate standards. This included the drawing of each system symbol separately, interconnection of these symbols based on the hand-drawn sketch, and finally annotating flow lines and placing an EDP system name within each symbol. Allowing for correction of errors and changes in subschema flows as projects become more defined, this process went through several reiterations before final distribuiton. This was a very time-consuming task, requiring constant interaction between system designers, EDP planning staff and the drafting department.

The use of the CAD system should not require the user to be familiar with a programming language, however our EDP planners have both an engineering and programming background. Therefore, the introduction of CAD system into this process was an easy transition. The need for the development of a rough sketch and the drafting department translation into a corporate format that underwent multiple revisions were eliminated. The EDP Planner now creates an integration architecture directly in the CAD system. Our CAD system has become the electronic scratch pad for the EDP planner, and consistently produces high-quality drawings. The transition to MUGS will allow an expansion of the user community because the command language can be either at the conversational level or at a more advanced level for frequent users.

The creation of an EDP System Architecture is usually created by repeating the following steps for functional engineering clusters:

- Create a drawing grid or call up a standard grid from a symbol library, including border and legend generation.
- Placement of individual system symbols in functional clusters on the grid. Symbols are drawn once and stored in a library from which they can be recalled from a menu or by a simple command.
- Interconnection of system symbols. This is accomplished with line segments and arrows used to depict direction of interface flow or by use of connector symbols which are drawn adjacent to each system symbol. As a drawing convention, the connectors are used when the interconnection crosses three interface lines or 5 horizontal units. Each connector symbol uses and alpha-numeric code, i.e., A or B2, and is recorded on an interface connector table for reference ease.
- Reposition systems for functional cluster interface or interface with other systems.
- Annotation or printing text on the EDP Systems Architecture.

## CAD Library and Symbol Retrieval

The establishment of an EDP-oriented symbol library is one of the major factors contributing to the cost effectiveness and dynamic flexibility of using a CAD system to develop EDP architectural interrelationships. The storage of frequently used symbols greatly simplifies the preparation of the EDP Architecture drawing. These symbols may be simple, such as an arrowhead or extremely complex, such as the EDP architectural symbol for a mechanized non-engineering interface process, which includes border shading. Once these symbols are created and stored in the library or database, the symbols can be recalled and incorporated into the drawing at the proper coordinate points. The method of retrieval is dependent upon the terminal hardware employed.

The use of mouse in conjunction with a menu is synonymous with current CAD technology. This peripheral input device allows a symbol to be inserted into a drawing in seconds with just the touch of a button. Prior to 1982, systems based on raster terminal output were limited to fairly simple displays because of limited screen resolution. However, availability of high resolution color displays (up to 1240 x 1240) at reasonable prices have now allowed complex drawings to be presented.

With TOPES, the initial drawing symbol was added on the drawing using a four-letter command after the terminal crosshairs are positioned at the desired X- and Y- coordinated. MUGS will use a menu and mouse to place symbols on the drawing. Symbols can be moved and relocated via the mouse or the symbol can then be copied at other drawing locations by repositioning the crosshairs to a new set of X- and Y- coordinates via the thumbwheel cursor controls or via a joystick and then issuing a single letter command (i.e., "c") to copy.

## CAD Input

The EDP Planner can design the architectural layout "on-line" or within a local, down-loaded micro-processor which stores the drawing coordinates and associated symbols on either a floppy or Winchester disk for block transmission to the host processor. The drawing input capabilities are inherent to the CAD system selected. Both modes of operation allow the system to respond immediately when compared to manual methods. A major advantage to the introduction of CAD systems into this area of EDP engineering is that as the architecture and associated data is being stored in the processor, visual feedback is drawn on the CRT which allows immediate on-line editing and rapid error correction.

When creating this type of drawing, many system symbols are the same, however, system titles are different which require the individual key entry of the associated text. Standard annotations, such as flow notes and test strings, can be stored in the library for recall. The test string can then be placed at the appropriate X- and Y- coordinates via the cursor/command sequences already described.

## EDP Architecture Functional Geometry and Integration

CAD systems use the computer's processing capabilities to eliminate many of the problems associated with the placement and interconnection of the various symbols utilized in an EDP Architecture drawing. However, for these features to be utilized the EDP planner must establish a placement grid and a functional geometry.

Once the grid is established, the EDP planner functionally divides the grid for system placement. By functional division, it is meant that an area that serves and engineering discipline is reserved on the grid. For telecommunications engineering these functional disciplines might include:

- Network Planning
- Switching Planning
- Equipment Planning
- Internode Planning
- Facility Planning
- etc.

To establish an EDP System Architecture for other than telecommunications technology, substitute the appropriate engineering function or industrial responsibility for the functional division. An advantage of the functional division is that it allows the establishment of boundary coordinates for "zooming-in" on a portion of the overall Architecture. This allows small areas of the drawing to be copied in an enlarged state for the purpose of clarity or if higher management's interests are focused on impact areas within a specific functional discipline.

Once the functional strategy and grid geometry are established, the various system symbols, i.e., network engineering symbols or non-network interfacing system symbols, are placed on the drawing in the manners previously described. The system symbol placement utilizes a strategy to minimize total length of the interface connections and limit line bridging once the systems are interconnected. This "mapping" technique is one of the most difficult for the EDP planner to apply. The planner must take into account the various drawing standards and physical constraints imposed by the functional grids and engineering clusters. Using the CAD system, the EDP planner must arrive at a functional placement that optimizes subsequent interface routes on the drawing without creating an undecipherable congestion. This is a matter of experience that may require multiple iterations, however, based on PC board and cartography applications, the use of a CAD system has a potential of a 5 to 1 time savings over manual drafting.

Some PC board graphics systems are equipped with an automatic router software which can be adapted for preparing the EDP Architecture. This is accomplished by assigning a location and zone to a symbol, similar to gate assignment. For example,

B7R3 to D4T1 would mean to connect the third right zone of the symbol in "B" vertical, seventh horizontal to the first zone on top of the symbol in "D" vertical fourth horizontal. However, if your system is not equipped with an automatic router, and the input method is by terminal input, the interconnections are drawn by cursor control/command methodology.

If the CAD system selected for creating the EDP Systems Architecture utilizes either refresh or raster technology, there are several features that can be utilized to expedite drawing the interrelationships without abnormal congestion. Once the systems (symbol and system name) are placed on the drawing, a PC board design feature referred to as "RATS NEST" can be utilized. This feature allows the computer to determine interconnections paths and provides the EDP planner with a graphic representation of the proposed mapping. From this graphic display the planner can determine whether a system must be moved to provide a cleaner interconnection route. At this point in the Architecture layout, the EDP planner can activate another PC board graphics design feature, "Rubber-banding." The planner places the graphics system into a dynamic mode which allows the EDP system and symbol to move or track across the screen and positions the symbol at potential locations. While tracking, the system interfaces stretch or bend while conforming to drawing standards, i.e., lines do not cross symbols but route around them. This gives the EDP planner the opportunity to select the optimum location. An adjunct standard that could be added to the "Rubber-banding" feature is the use of drawing connectors. If the interconnection line is forced to bridge across 3 or more system interconnections, or if the interconnection must pass thru 5 or more horizontal grid areas, then the CAD system will default to the automatic selection of the next available connector, i.e., B2. The B2 connector would subsequently be placed adjacent to both the upstream and downstream systems and arrows would be drawn to show flow direction.

## Editing and Flow Checking

Throughout the layout process, it is necessary to perform various editing functions. The editing features are powerful commands that are incorporated in well designed CAD systems, whether they run on storage tube, refreshed or raster terminals. Interactive editing functions include commands such as layer or overlay discrimination and transfer. They may also include a color highlighting or a glow command which allows the EDP planner to highlight major impact areas and systems. Another editing feature is the ability to change line type and weight, i.e., solid, dotted or dashed, heavy, etc. This feature conveys a high degree of clarity and information about a specific function. An example of this would utilize one line type and weight to show an interface between two IBM mainframe based systems, while another line type and weight could be used for a proposed interface between a system run on a AT&T 3B20 processor and one run on a DEC mini-computer.

Additional editing commands exist that control functions such as moves, deletions, text edits and symbol and job renames.

If the EDP Systems Architecture is driven by an associated database, then a base exists to check the interconnections between systems. This can be approached either by manual inspection, or if your system is so equipped, by using the data extract process along with the default or "not-equal-to" linkage to print discrepancies.

At the same time, when a new system or interface between systems is added the database design can flag additional changes and deletions and generate a CAD input report. For our non-graphic telecommunications engineering systems database we use RAMIS® as our data manager and report writer. This was employed in conjunction with TOPES, however as stated earlier, we will be using INGRES as our DBMS with future developments.

## Color Enhancement

With the availability of high resolution raster workstations (1240 x 1240), color becomes an important feature for highlighting many different types of data. When creating an EDP Architecture, color can be used to show the telecommunications functional disciplines, i.e., Equipment Planning, system developmental status, Systems Management Organization (SMO) or even annual operational costs.

Advances in color output devices, coupled with the device independence attainable through GKS conversion, allows our EDP architecture to be outputted to a wide variety of devices. Initially, color output was limited to either pen plotters or expensive film recorders.

Cost effective color output is now available from the Seiko
Color Hardcopy unit, which uses thermal ink transfer
technology, and low cost ink jet plotters from Tektronix, ACT
and Diablo. In addition, inexpensive screen cone systems are
avialable for color slide production from either Kodak or
Polaroid. These are usable for peer presentation.

Good resolution, presentation quality slides can be processed
on the Samuri and Polaroid Palette systems. These units are
far less expensive than slide generation systems of 2 or 3
years ago.


## Graphics Teleconferencing

If the CAD system is run on a mini-computer as its only
processor, between 4 to 16 remote terminals is the maximum
configuration. This limitation is a function of engine size,
access and processing capabilities. One advantage of a
mainframe environment is that there can be a significantly
larger number of available ports for individual users access.
However, depending on the number on concurrent users, response
time may deteriorate to an unacceptable level. Drawings can be
downloaded to microprocessors located at the workstations for
local graphic processing and transferred to the mainframe for
drawing archival.

One of the most significant features of our CAD system is that
of graphics teleconferencing from remote locations. Depending
on port and conferencing bridge capabilities of the operating
system and the CAD systems, it is not uncommon to have 4 to 16
simultaneous remote conferees watching the same graphics
output. By design, manipulation of the drawing symbols can be
relinquished to remote locations, however the initiating
drawing control ID maintains the ability to issue permanent
overwrite or storage commands.

An advantage of graphics teleconferencing is that an EDP
planner can be at a remote location and still make a
presentation to upper management who may be at a remote
management information and monitoring center.

An enhancement that we are investigating includes linking color
code capabilities and subschema logic. The graphics
teleconferencing when coupled with color capabilities and

editing features allow "what-if" questions to be answered in an interactive mode. For example, if the long range (beyond 5 year) circuit input requirements from a forecast conditioning system were eliminated, what is the resulting impact on Space and Power Planning?

To answer this, the current path is depicted in one color. Analysis of functional schema tasks performed in various Equipment Planning systems show that the circuits must be converted into orderable equipment quantities which are then converted to full bay equipment compliments. The full bay compliments are the basis for Space and Power Planning.

When the deleted input is shown, the subsequent functions glow or flash repetitively to indicate an engineering function jeopardy. The functional schema and subschema level must be searched to see if a modification or change can produce the required data. If it can, the "RATS NEST" feature can be activated to map the new interconnection path. When this is accomplished the line color, type and glow frequency can be changed to indicate the answer to the "what-if" question. The EDP planner who has the drawing control ID will determine if the new input should become a permanent part of the EDP Architecture.

Conclusion

As in many technical fields, the design of Telecommunications EDP Systems Architecture requires multi-discipline expertise. This position requires a strong technical background in engineering function as well as an understanding of EDP System design and development. The need for people with these special skills is consistently outpacing the personnel available. Examination of business opportunities are frequently postponed until an EDP Planner is available to address the EDP solution and incorporate it into the Architecture. This is even more apparent if the entire planning process is manual and computer graphics are not applied.

Therefore, it become essential that the EDP Planner's knowledge be recognized as a resource that can be enhanced with a CAD system and result in a productivity increase.

The advantages of introducing a CAD system into the EDP Planning environment are increasingly obvious. The CAD system rapidly produces an overall view of EDP systems interrelationships and functional dependencies.

The CAD system enables a human-computer synergism to exist. The system supports the creative abilities of the EDP Planner and the interaction of the two produces an Architecture that neither is capable of producing alone in a timely fashion. Clearly, a CAD system can produce a significant time savings over manual methods.

Additionally, an up-to-date Architecture can provide a method for tracking EDP development projects and map their overall impacts. This keeps both the user and upper management informed of EDP activity.

Color graphics and editing features inherent to the CAD design allow the Planner to highlight major impact items and perform architectural "what-if" studies if a subschema level of detail is available.

If the CAD resides on a processor that allows remote access another benefit of using a CAD system to develop an EDP Architecture is the dynamic graphics teleconferencing capability which allows immediate viewing from multiple locations.

CAD systems and applications are constantly being improved and enhanced and we have not yet discovered their technical limitations. The only suggested limitation is the human imagination. EDP Planners should be at the forefront of CAD system usage and take advantage of the mechanized capabilities they have created for other functions and technologies.

# Chapter 6
# Computer Animation

# Single and Multiple Virtual Movie-Cameras for Special Cinematographic Effects

Nadia Magnenat-Thalmann and Daniel Thalmann

MIRA Laboratory, HEC/IRO, University of Montreal, 5255, avenue Decelles, Montreal, P.Q. Canada H3T 1V6

ABSTRACT

The term "virtual camera" is well-known in Computer Graphics. But, it usually represents a mere abstraction for labelling the projection mechanism from 3D to 2D. We believe, on the other hand, that a virtual camera should be a software entity that can be manipulated in the same way as cameramen manipulate real cameras. First, we present a integrated camera model which includes not only typical characteristics like the eye, interest point, zoom and spin but also other functions which we consider to be part of the camera definition like viewports and clippings. Then we introduce a model of a virtual movie-camera. Typical effects used by cameramen are described using this model - such as panning, tilting, tracking, zooming and spinning. The use of a stereoscopic virtual camera is also discussed. The second part of the paper presents the use of several virtual movie-cameras for special effects like wipe effects.

KEYWORDS
Computer animation, virtual camera, director, special effects

## INTRODUCTION

One of the most impressive effects in computer-generated films (1) is the possibility of rotating around a three-dimensional object or entering into any complex solid. Although people generally find these effects very spectacular, they are in fact quite easy to produce. Typically these effects are obtained by simulating a camera, called a virtual or a synthetic camera and by moving it. In fact, a single virtual camera consists only of a pair of vector characteristics known as the eye of the camera and the interest point. The model may be completed by a zoom. These features are very convenient for all wire-frame drawings and most shaded images. A more realistic camera model has been introduced by Potmesil and Chakravarty (2); it approximates the effects of the lens and aperture function of an real camera. It allows the generation of synthetic images which have a depth of field and can be focussed on an arbitrary plane.

In fact, the term "virtual camera" is frequently used by authors in Computer Graphics, but it is always an abstraction.

A virtual camera is generally defined as a procedural software responsible for the transformation from 3D space to a 2D projection. It may consist of a set of subprograms as defined in numerous graphics packages like those based on GSPC (3) or it could be reduced to a few matrices which are applied to objects. The virtual camera is not considered as an object which may be directed by a set of commands. For us, on the other hand a virtual camera is a software entity that may be manipulated exactly in the same way as cameramen manipulate real cameras. For this reason, we propose a virtual camera model which integrates well-known functions like zoom, spin , viewport and clipping. We then introduce a model of a virtual movie-camera. Typical effects used by cameramen are described using this model (e.g. panning, tilting, tracking, zooming and spinning). The use of a stereoscopic camera is also discussed. The second part of the paper presents the use of several virtual cameras for special effects like those produced by optical printers in conventional animation. In particular, scenes with wipe effects are emphasized. All examples are described using our MIRANIM (4) director-oriented animation system.
MIRANIM is a complex and advanced system; however, only commands to define virtual cameras are discussed in this paper. Typically, a command is characterized by its name and parameters. The first parameter is generally the camera identifier; the other parameters are constant values or state variables (animated variables), which drive the camera motions according to evolution laws. Constants, variables and laws are also defined by using interactive commands.

## AN INTEGRATED CAMERA MODEL

A virtual camera is a software entity that uses a few input parameters and displays a 2D view of a 3D scene. This means that the role of a virtual camera is to perform all geometric transformations needed to convert three-dimensional points into points in the two-dimensional image plane. Our basic virtual camera has a name and it is characterized by at least two parameters: the eye and the interest point. For exemple, we may define a camera called MYCAMERA by:

    CAMERA MYCAMERA,EYE,INT

The eye is a point (or vector) and it represents the location of the camera. The interest point is the point towards which the camera is directed. In our system, both points are defined as vectors and if they are constants (option C) their values are for example entered as:

    VECTOR EYE,C,-10,-20,100
    VECTOR INT,C,0,0,0

### zoom

A zoom lens permits the cameraman to quickly adjust the size of the field being filmed by the camera. In a virtual camera, a zoom may be defined by changing the ratio between the dimensions in the image space and the display space. This generally consists of modifying the window. In our animation system, a zoom may be added to any camera, by just specifying:

    ZOOM MYCAMERA,ZOOMVALUE

where ZOOMVALUE has been previously defined as a constant real
number by for example:
    REAL ZOOMVALUE,C,2.5
Fig. 1 and 2 show two views with two different values of zoom.
spin
The eye and the interest point define a line and a direction
on this line, which is in fact an axis. However, there is
still one degree of freedom i.e. the possibility of rotation
by a given angle around the axis. This characteristic of a
camera is called spin. The default spin corresponds to a zero
angle. Fig.3 shows a virtual camera with eye, interest point
and spin. In our approach, a spin is associated with a camera
by defining:
    SPIN MYCAMERA,SPINVALUE
where SPINVALUE may be defined by:
    REAL SPINVALUE,C,1.5
Fig.4 shows an image with such a spin.
viewport and clipping
This term has been introduced as a standard term in all
graphics software and textbooks (5,6). It is generally defined
as the portion of the graphics display corresponding to the
window in the image space. In fact, we consider that a
viewport should be defined as a characteristic of a camera and
may be described as:
    VIEWPORT MYCAMERA,V,VIEW1,VIEW2
where VIEW1 is the lower-left point of the viewport and VIEW2
the upper-right point. For example:
    VECTOR VIEW1,C,0,0
    VECTOR VIEW2,C,0.5,0.5
Note that sometimes, it is useful to automatically modify the
size of the window when changing the size of the viewport.
This is possible by specifying a viewport with the option T
(television) instead of the option V (visual). For example:
    VIEWPORT MYCAMERA,T,VIEW1,VIEW2
As we shall see in the section on special effects with
multiple movie-cameras, clipping is also an essential camera
characteristic. Generally, a clipping of all drawing outside
the viewport is performed corresponding to a window clipping.
However, it could be very useful to suppress this automatic
clipping or to clip everything that is inside the viewport
instead of outside. For exemple, we define:
    CLIPPING MYCAMERA,I,CLIP1,CLIP2
or
    CLIPPING MYCAMERA,E,CLIP1,CLIP2
to associate with a camera a clipping inside or outside the
rectangle defined by the lower-left point CLIP1 and the
upper-right point CLIP2.
stereoscopic virtual cameras
Images produced on a terminal using a single virtual camera
model have a defect because only one eye is simulated. In
reality, the brain receives two pictures one from each eye. As
the eyes are not exactly at the same location, this gives a
depth-perception. With only one eye, depth-perception is
suppressed and this is especially limitative for wire-frame
drawings. One way of solving this problem is by the

introduction of stereoscopic virtual cameras. Such cameras are defined in the same way as other cameras, but they are declared as stereoscopic by for exemple:

   STEREOSCOPIC MYCAMERA,2

This means that the camera MYCAMERA will have two eyes separated by 2 units. The two eyes are located on either side of the location of the eye as defined in the camera. Fig.5 explains the principle of a stereoscopic camera. Now, for any scene that is viewed with such a camera, two views are produced, one for each eye. The first view corresponds to the left eye and is colored in red. The second view represents the view from the right eye and is colored in blue. Fig. 6 shows an image in stereoscopy. In fact, to view this stereoscopically it is necessary to wear special glasses in which the left glass does not allow the green color to pass through and the right glass blocks the red color.

### A MOVIE-CAMERA MODEL

The difference between a normal camera and a movie-camera is that the movie camera takes several pictures of a scene during a period of time in order to record the motion. The speed of a movie-camera is defined as the number of images (or frames) taken in one second. Typically this is 18 or 24 frames per second. For TV and video cameras there are generally from 30 to 60 frames per second in North America and Japan and from 25 to 50 in Europa. Our movie-camera model is considered as a virtual camera with a speed. However, in order to easily change the context when necessary, we define a general speed which is the speed of the physical camera that takes the picture. For example, we may define:

   SPEED 24,1

In this example, the speed is at 24 frames par second. The second number indicates how many duplicates of each frame is produced. For example, it is possible to simulate a speed of 12 frames per second with a physical camera that runs at 24 frames per second by using:

   SPEED 24,2

In this case two identical pictures are taken 12 times.

The speed of the virtual movie-cameras are specified relatively to the speed of the physical camera by using the command SLOWDOWN. For example:

   SLOWDOWN MYCAMERA,0.75

corresponds to a virtual movie-camera with a speed of 32 (24/0.75) frames per second. When recorded at 24 frames per second the motion will effectively correspond to a slowdown of a factor 0.75.

When we talk about camera motion, we are in fact referring to the motion of the eye. In our model, this means that camera definition is not affected, but the eye point is not constant, but variable. For example, we have:

   CAMERA MYCAMERA,EYE,INT
   VECTOR INT,C,0,0,0
   VECTOR EYE,A,-10,-20,-100,10,15,30

The last command means that the eye moves from the point $\langle-10,-20,-100\rangle$ to the point $\langle10,15,30\rangle$. The question is : how does it move ? In fact, the eye may follow any motion, however classical camera motions should first be described.

## panning, tilting and tracking effects

A panning effect is an effect in which the camera is moved horizontally from one point to another one. In a tilting effect, the camera is moved vertically from one point to another one. Tracking corresponds to moving the camera towards the interest point. We may define these motions by specifying laws of variation for the eye.

1)    VECTOR EYE,A,10,30,50,50,30,50
       LAW PAN,LINEAR
       EVOLUTION EYE,PAN,0,10

This defines a panning effect from the position ⟨10,30,,50⟩ to ⟨50,30,50⟩ which varies linearly over in 10 seconds

2)    VECTOR EYE,A,10,30,50,10,100,50
       LAW TILT,ACC
       EVOLUTION EYE,TILT,0,8

This defines a tilting effect from ⟨10,30,50⟩ to ⟨10,100,50⟩ in 8 seconds with an acceleration

3)    VECTOR EYE,A,10,30,50,1,3,5
       LAW TRACK,ACCDEC
       EVOLUTION EYE,TRACK,0,6

this defines a tracking effect from ⟨10,30,50⟩ to ⟨1,3,5⟩ in 6 seconds witn an acceleration followed by a deceleration.

## zooming and spinning effects

In a movie-camera model, it is possible to change the zoom or the spin continuously. This means that we must define a zoom value or a spin value which is time-dependent. For example:

1)    REAL ZOOMVALUE,A,1,3
       LAW VARIATION,LINEAR
       EVOLUTION ZOOMVALUE,VARIATION,0,10
       ZOOM MYCAMERA,ZOOMVALUE

This defines a zooming effect from 1 to 3 with a linear variation during 10 seconds.

2)    REAL SPINVALUE,A,0,6.28
       LAW VAR2,ACC
       EVOLUTION SPINVALUE,VAR2,0,8
       SPIN MYCAMERA,SPINVALUE

This defines a spinning effect where the angle varies from 0 to 360 degrees in 8 seconds with an acceleration.

Note that it is possible to combine several effects for the same movie-camera. For example:

     CAMERA NEWCAM,EYE,INT
     ZOOM NEWCAM,ZOOMVALUE,
     SPIN NEWCAM,SPINVALUE

where all parameters may be time-dependent

## arbitrary camera path

Although classical camera motion are often used, there are many situations where it may be more attractive to design a non-linear trajectory for the camera. We call such a trajectory a camera path. In our approach, there are three ways of defining such a path.

1) We apply to the eye variable one of the predefined laws of the ANIMEDIT animation editor (4) system: harmonic motion,

circular motion, fuzzy motion, penduluum motion. For example, we may define a camera that moves circularly around a vertical axis (<0,1,0>) passing through the point <5,6,7> with an angular velocity of 1 radian per second and no angular acceleration by:

```
VECTOR EYE,A,10,20,30
LAW TURN,CIRC,5,6,7,0,1,0,1,0
EVOLUTION EYE,CIRC,0,10
CAMERA EYE,INT
```

2) We apply the law FOLLOW to the eye variable. This law consists of defining a curve the vector should follow. The curve must have been previously read from a file. For example:

```
READ CURVEFILE,CURVE
VECTOR EYE,A,12,15,20
LAW PATH,FOLLOW
EVOLUTION EYE,PATH,0,10
```

This curve is in fact a P-curve (7) that contains time and space information. The curve may have been created by digitizing, using parametric equations or beta-splines (8,9). This task is performed in our case with the BODY-BUILDING object modelling system (4).

3) We apply a procedural law programmed in the CINEMIRA-2 sublanguage (2,4). The law is applied as follows:

```
VECTOR EYE,A,5,3,2
LAW MOTION,PROCEDURAL,HELICOIDAL
  0,0,0,10,30,4,0,1,0
EVOLUTION EYE,MOTION,0,10
```

moving interest point

Not only the eye of the camera may vary, but also the interest point. For example, a camera may look at a person moving from the feet (<10,0,30>) to the head (<10,1.8,30>) by the following sequence:

```
VECTOR INT,A,10,0,30,10,1.8,30
LAW MVT,LINEAR
EVOLUTION INT,MVT,0,5
```

Fig.7 shows two frames of a sequence where the eye and the interest point are moving.

camera assigned to an actor

The main purpose of a camera is to look at a scene. Until now, we have only considered the motion of this camera. This means that we have assumed that the scene is only composed of a decor (static objects) or that there is no interaction between the camera and the dynamic objects called actors. In our approach, an actor is as defined by Reynolds (10) as an object that posseses its own animation. This animation is specified by a list of transformations as in the Mudur and Syngh notation (11). Transformations are driven by variables like these used in camera definitions. For example:

```
ACTOR BALL,BALLOBJ
ROTATION BALL,Y,PY,ANGLE
MOVE BALL,POS
```

where BALLOBJ is a spherical object, PY is a moving point, ANGLE is a time-dependent angle and POS is a moving point.
When an actor is moving, the motion of the camera may have a

similar motion. More accurately, the eye or the interest point
of the camera may follow the actor. This is possible in our
model by using:
      DEPENDENT MYCAMERA,E,BALL
or DEPENDENT MYCAMERA,I,BALL
where the first command means that the eye follows the actor
BALL; in the second command, the interest point is moving with
the ball.

### MULTIPLE VIRTUAL MOVIE-CAMERA EFFECTS

The use of several cameras allows the simulation of special
effects like those traditionally produced by optical printers.
An optical printer is a movie camera which is focussed on the
gate of a lensless movie projector to duplicate one piece of
film onto another. Optical printers are used for
superimpositions and multiple-image effects. They are also
very useful to provide fade and wipe effects. A fade-in is an
effect used at the beginning of a scene: the scene gradually
appears from black. A fade-out is an effect used at the end of
a scene: the scene gradually darkens to black. With the wipe
effect, one scene appears to slide over the preceding scene.
Fig.8 shows different possible forms for the dividing lines
between the scenes.
We now give an example of a wipe effect using two virtual
cameras CAM1 and CAM2. Fig.9a and Fig.9b show the views picked
up by both cameras. Suppose we would like to obtain the
situation presented in Fig.9c. This can be obtained with the
following commands:
   VECTOR EYE1,C,-8,8,-8
   VECTOR INT1,C,5,14,0
   VECTOR VA,C,0.25,0.25
   VECTOR VB,C,0.75,0.75
   VECTOR EYE2,C,-3.5,1012,-3.5
   VECTOR INT2,C,5,1016,0
   CAMERA CAM1,EYE1,INT1
   CAMERA CAM2,EYE2,INT2
   VIEWPORT CAM2,VA,VB
   CLIPPING CAM1,I,VA,VB
To obtain the situation presented in Fig.9d, we have to
replace
      VIEWPORT CAM2,VA,VB
by  CLIPPING,CAM2,E,VA,VB
Now we may produce a wipe effect by changing the size of the
picture taken by the camera CAM2 from the complete screen to
the center point of the screen in 10 seconds. This is
performed by redefining the vectors VA and VB as variables:
      LAW VARY,LINEAR
      VECTOR VA,A,0,0,0,0.5,0.5,0
      EVOLUTION VA,VARY,0,10
      VECTOR VB,A,1,1,0,0.5,0.5,0
      EVOLUTION VB,VARY,0,10
Fig.10 shows two frames of this wipe effect.
We now give a final example involving three virtual
movie-cameras that display three different views of the same

scene. The first camera shows a tracking effect with clipping, the second camera performs a zooming effect and the third one a spinning effect. The script is listed in Fig.11 for camera operations and results are shown in Fig.12.

CONCLUSION

This paper has shown how special effects may be produced in computer animation using a model of virtual movie-cameras. The approach used is artist-oriented because the commands are very similar to the actions performed by conventional cameramen. Traditionnal effects like tracking, spinning, zooming, panning, fade and wipe effects are possible and innovative effects may also be produced, limited only by human creativity.

ACKNOWLEDGEMENTS

The authors are grateful to Ann Laporte who revised the English text. The research was supported by the Natural Sciences and Engineering Research Council of Canada. and by the Quebec FCAC foundation.

REFERENCES

1. Magnenat-Thalmann N. and Thalmann D. Computer Animation: Theory and Practice, Springer-Verlag Tokyo, 1985
2. Potmesil M. and Chakravarty I.," Synthetic Image Generation with a Lens and Aperture Camera Model ", ACM Transactions on Graphics, Vol 1, No2, 1982, pp. 85-108.
3. Bergeron R.D., Bono P.R. and Foley J.D. "Graphics Programming Using the Core System" Computing Surveys, Vol.10,No4,1978.
4. Magnenat-Thalmann N., Thalmann D. and Fortin M., " MIRANIM: an Extensible Director-Oriented System for the Animation of Realistic Images ", IEEE Computer Graphics and Applications, Vol.5,No.3,1985,pp.61-73
5. Newman W. and Sproull R. Principles of Interactive Computer Graphics, McGraw-Hill, 1973
6. Foley J.D and Van Dam A. Fundamentals of Interactive Computer Graphics, Addisson-Wesley, 1982
7. Baecker R.M. " Picture-driven Animation", Proc.Spring Joint Computer Conf., AFIPS Press, Vol.34, 1969, pp.273-288
8. Barsky B.A. "A Description and Evaluation of Various 3D Models", IEEE Computer Graphics and Applications, Vol.4, No1, 1984, pp.38-52.
9. Barsky B.A. Computer Graphics and Computer Aided Geometric Design Using Beta-splines, Springer-Verlag Tokyo, 1985
10. Reynolds C.W. "Computer Animation with Scripts and Actors", Proc. SIGGRAPH '82, 1982, pp.289-296.
11. Mudur S.P. and Singh J.H. "A Notation for Computer Animation", IEEE Transactions on Systems, Man and Cybernetics, SMC-8, No4,pp.308-311

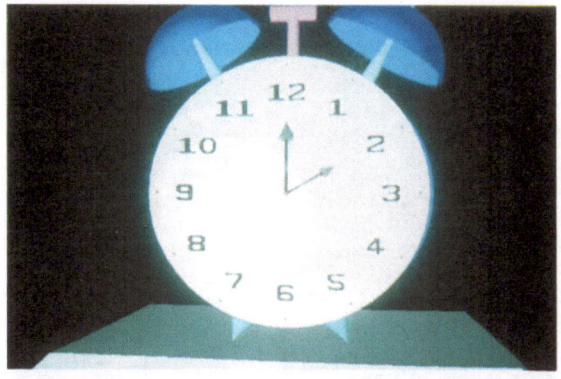

Fig.1 A clock

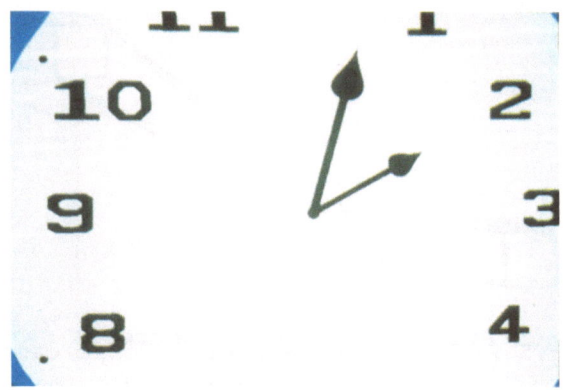

Fig.2 A zoom effect

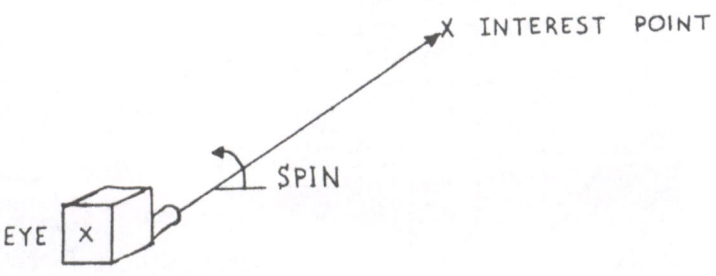

Fig.3 Principle of a virtual camera

Fig.4 A spin effect

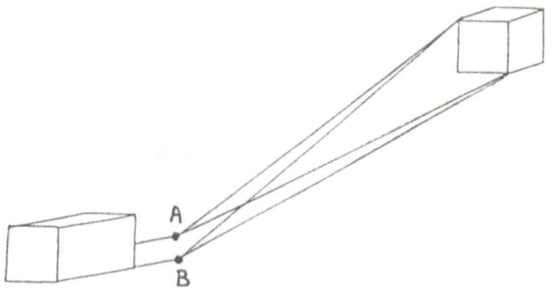

Fig.5 Principle of a stereoscopic camera

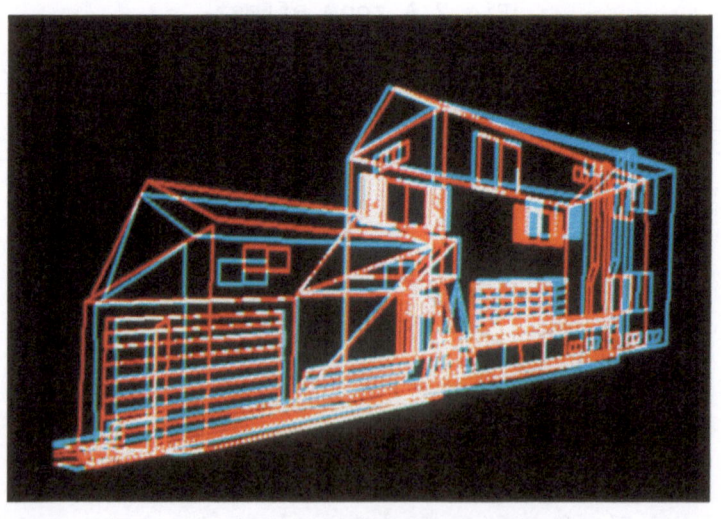

Fig.6 A stereoscopic view

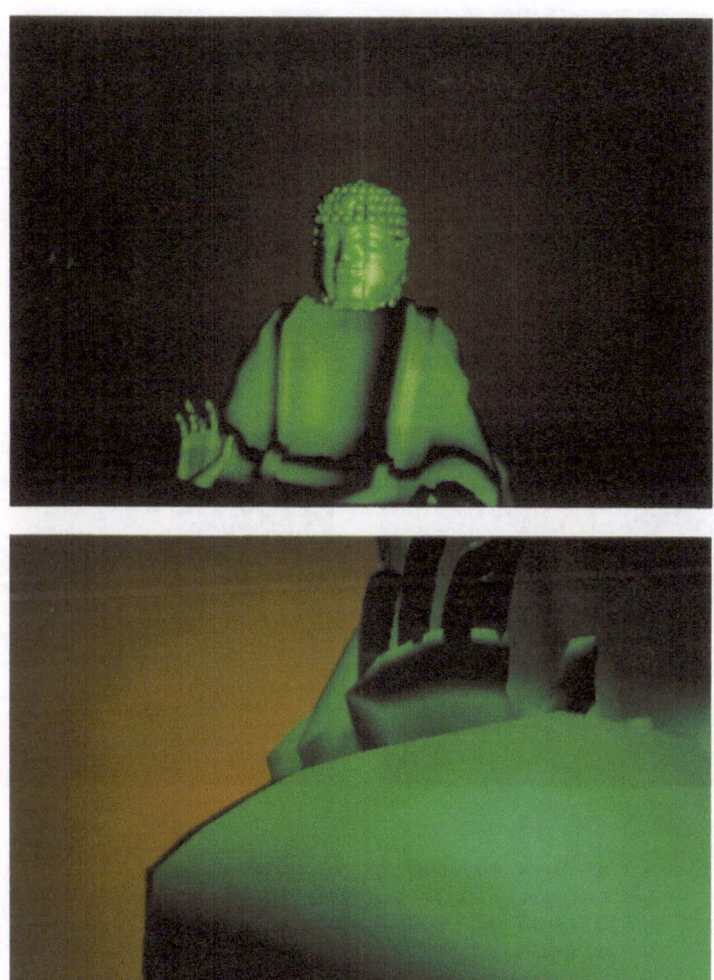

Fig.7 Two views of Bouddha
      (eye and interest point are animated)

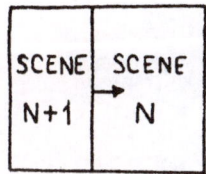 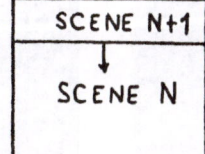 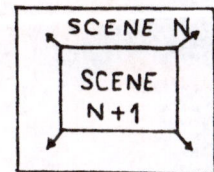

Fig.8 Wipes

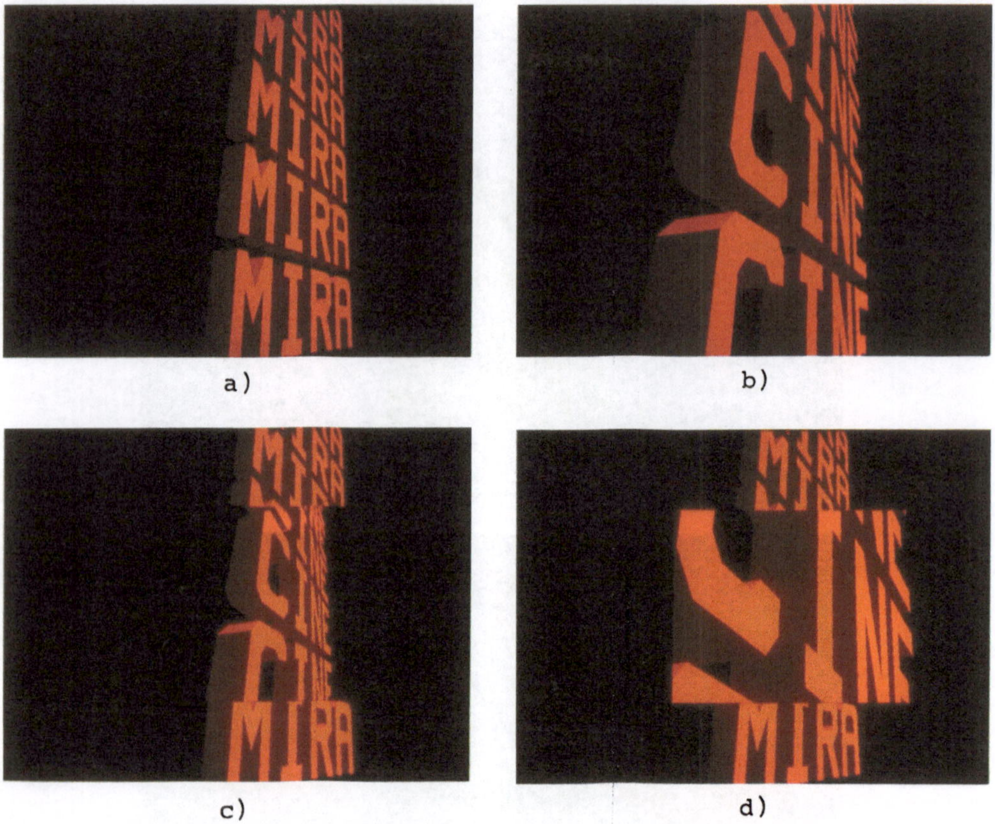

Fig.9 a) a view picked up by one camera
     b) another view picked up by another camera
     c) effect of both cameras (using VIEWPORT)
     d) effect of both cameras (using CLIP EXT)

Fig.10 Example of a wipe effect

Fig.11 A script with 3 cameras

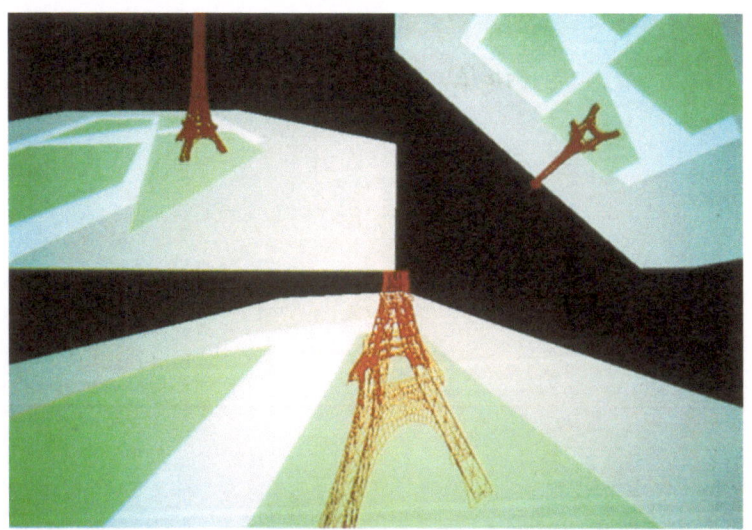

Fig.12 Effects with 3 cameras:
      left up: zooming effect
      right up: spinning effect
      down: tracking and clipping effects

# High Performance Calligraphics
## Union of Hardware and Software

Donald R. Jones, Gary L. Marchant and Michael B. Stephenson

Civil Engineering Department, Brigham Young University, Provo, UT 84602, USA

**ABSTRACT**

Dyna-MOVIE.BYU combines software and Evans and Sutherland hardware providing a highly interactive program with instantaneous feedback of object transformations; therefore, real time, dynamic calligraphic display capabilities are possible. All transformations are updated continuously by use of three interactive devices: a keyboard with function keys, the control dials and a data tablet. Two methods are available to remove hidden surfaces. Animated sequences can be produced by defining a series of frames. The frames are calculated and down loaded from the host computer to the PS330. The sequence can be previewed by three different methods. Since, the PS330 is a calligraphic display device, the final picture can be saved in a MOVIE.BYU format file. This allows the user to choose a number of continuous-tone raster devices on which the model may be rendered.

## INTRODUCTION

The MOVIE system of general purpose computer graphic programs facilitate the display of three-dimensional mathematical, topological, and architectural models as line drawings or as continuous-tone shaded images. The complete system includes the capability to clip and cap three-dimensional systems; modify geometry, displacement, and scalar function files; generate new models or title representations; and convert contour line definitions into polygonal element mosaics[1]. This paper describes the latest addition, Dyna-MOVIE.BYU, which advantageously uses the powerful real-time transformation capabilities and interactive devices of the Evans and Sutherland (E&S) PS330 graphics system. The combination of MOVIE software and E&S hardware provides a highly interactive user environment.

The above brief description of the MOVIE system is intended to allow the reader to understand the overall capabilities of the MOVIE system. To try to implement all of the capabilities mentioned above is an overwhelming task. In fact only one program, DISPLAY, of the system was converted.

DISPLAY is the heart of the MOVIE system and produces the graphical output. It is the display program for polygonal element models. Since the PS330 is a calligraphic display device, the line drawing capabilities in DISPLAY will form the basis for the research presented in this paper.

One may question the use of MOVIE.BYU as the software medium. The reasons are:

1) The graphic features are fairly comprehensive for a graphics package.

2) The source code is available instead of the executable at a relatively low cost.

3) MOVIE.BYU is used by many different institutions throughout the world.

4) The authors know the code better than any other code available.

The second part of this union is the required display device. The PS330 was selected. The reasons are three fold:

1) At the start of the research, the PS330 was the "state of the art."

2) The peripheral devices, data tablet, control dials, function keys, are provided with equipment.

3) The equipment was available at the University.

The E&S PS330 is a data-driven, interactive computer graphics system. It provides the capability to define and display two and three dimensional mathematical models that may be translated, rotated, and scaled dynamically. The model can be displayed while maintaining an orthographic or a true perspective view.

An important capability of the PS330 system is the ability to operate in a distributed graphics processing environment. Distributed graphics processing refers to the sharing of the program processing between the host and the PS330. The PS330 handles the graphical updating of the model while the non-graphical tasks are distributed to the host. This eliminates graphical processing by the host.

Display data structures define the geometric transformations that orient and position the objects, and the viewing transformations, that specify how the objects are to be viewed (Figure 1). The lowest elements of the display data structures are vector lists or character strings. The commands above the vector lists or character strings perform transformations on the defined data or provide a means to control references to the data. Each of these commands forms a node and provides a user-programmable connection point into the data structure. For instance, a rotation command node could supply new angles of rotation to be applied to all elements below that node.

The Display Processor traverses the data structure and transforms the data to be displayed each refresh cycle (30 times a second). This traversal occurs from the top of the structure to the bottom. The order of the commands or nodes in the data structure is important to insure the proper concatenation of all transformations.

Function networks provide the connections into the display data structure. A function network consists of one or more elementary functions (Figure 2). They have certain inputs and outputs that connect into the data structure or other

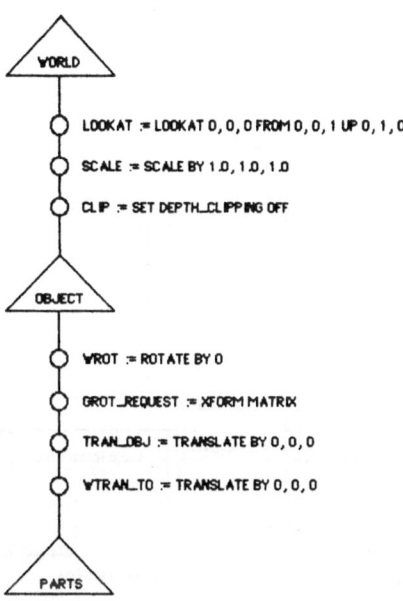

*Fig. 1. Display Data Structure used in E&S PS330*

function networks in order to perform a desired operation. They also process input data from an interactive peripheral device provided with the PS330.

How important are the peripheral devices? Foley and Van Dam [2] and Newman and Sproull [3] give lengthy discussions on the importance of such input devices and on how these devices relate to interactive graphics. These devices are the parts of the graphics package that link the user to the computer and enable the operator to control it. All of the input devices provide the necessary requirements for visual feedback, another requirement for a good interactive program. If the user can "interact" with the data presented in a orderly and efficient manner, then the users learning time for the program is reduced, and the time spent in learning is a satisfying experience.

## COMMAND INTERFACE

Dyna-MOVIE.BYU is based heavily on the DISPLAY program in the MOVIE.BYU system with modification and extensions to take advantage of the unique capabilities of the PS330. The interactive devices provided with the PS330 allow the user to interact with the displayed data. All of the devices are programmable. They include a keyboard with function keys, a data tablet and a control dial unit. Each of the twelve function keys and the eight control dials has an eight character LED display that can be dynamically labeled.

The overall design of Dyna-MOVIE.BYU has tried to considered the ergonomics (human factors) for interactive systems as discussed in Foley and Van Dam[2] and Newman and Sproull[3] with some reservations. First, the user has to be somewhat familiar with computer graphic terminology. This is quickly overcome due to the

288

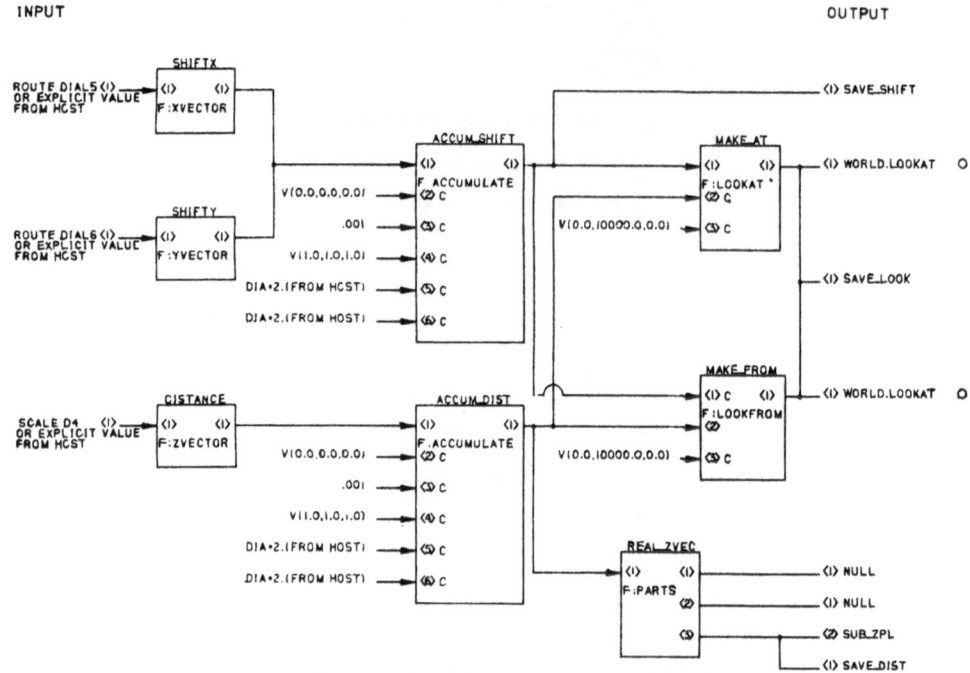

*Fig. 2. Function Network for shift and distance control*

instantaneous updating that is provided by the system. Each command can be executed, and if the displayed result is not what was expected, the system can be reset without any loss to the data structure or model information. Second, the interrogative prompts have been abbreviated, but enough of the prompt has been retained to convey the information requested by the prompt. If the user inputs erroneous values, the program will still process the information but will not "bomb" and in most cases re-prompt for the correct information. Dyna-MOVIE.BYU has been used by people both experienced and inexperienced in computer graphics. Even the inexperienced user had little or no problem in learning Dyna-MOVIE.BYU in 30 to 60 minutes[1].

The command syntax is a two level menu/keyword system with interrogative prompts forming a third level. The keyword input includes the first four characters of each command or labeled keys. The keyboard provides the main interface between the user and Dyna-MOVIE.BYU. An integral part of the keyboard are the function keys which are programmed to communicate with the data structure. The function keys are set up to provide a labeled menu set. Because of the limited number of labeled function keys, a multi-level menu system was designed. The shift function keys correspond to the first level or main menu and the function keys to the second level or sub-menu. Each sub-menu call dynamically updates the function key labels. All program input can be entered from the keyboard. This provides a means to still use the equipment if a portion or all of the other input devices fail.

---

[1] Graphics Utah Style - 84, A workshop on interactive computer graphics emphasizing the MOVIE System by Hank Christiansen and Mike Stephenson.

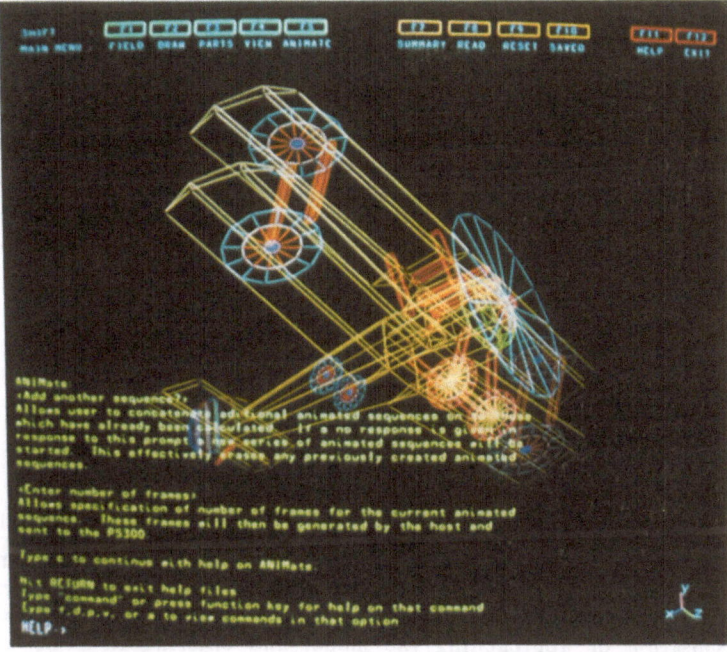

*Fig. 3. Dyna-MOVIE.BYU Display Screen Layout*

The control dial unit contains eight continuous turn, digital shaft-encoder dials. The dials are programmed to send numeric values to the data structure and the program for dynamic and incremental data updates[4]. For instance, the digital values can be accumulated and used to control global and local transformation of the displayed data in real time. The eight dials are not sufficient to handle all of the desired types of interactive input. For this reason the labels are dynamically switched with each sub-menu call in the same manner as the function keys. Some of the function keys control dial input; when the key is depressed the dials become active. Dial control is always cumulative. Most of the explicit input from the keyboard is also cumulative to imitate the control dials.

The display screen layout (Figure 3) contains the main menu, the axis triad, the prompt/input lines, the viewport for display of the model, and the alphanumeric screen. The main menu is displayed on the upper portion of the screen at all times for quick reference, but can be removed from display at any time by depressing the function key labeled "menu". An axis triad is also displayed in the lower right corner of the display screen. The triad is affected by all global rotations input either by the control dials or via the keyboard. The triad continuously shows the global orientation of the model. Removal of the triad is also possible by depressing a function key labeled "triad". The bottom three lines of the graphic display screen are reserved for the interrogative prompts, program warning/error messages, and echoing of input from the user. The model viewport displays all data both 3-D and 2-D depending on the options chosen. When the main menu has been removed from the display, the model viewport is expanded to fill the whole display screen. The entire alphanumeric screen is used for the on-line help documentation and model summary information.

The main menu contains three groups of commands--display, utility and system commands. The display commands include all of the sub-menu commands. These display commands operate on the model in specific ways to help the user understand the information presented. The utility commands do not call any sub-menu, rather they display model information to the user or help the user to run the program. The system commands allows the user to view on-line help documentation of the display and utility commands. Each of these categories will be discussed below.

## DISPLAY COMMANDS

Sub-menu Field

An important part of all 3-D computer graphics is perspective. Perspective is even more important with real-time transformations such as those of the PS330. For this reason Dyna-MOVIE.BYU allows a wide range of perspective modifications.

The user has complete control over his position with respect to the model. The distance from the user to the model can be changed at will. In fact, the distance from the observer to the model can be dialed to zero. This gives the user the sensation of approaching the model and entering it. The user can also shift his position in both the x and y screen directions. This allows the user to examine some part of the model in more detail. Dyna-MOVIE.BYU also has the ability to automatically center the model on the screen. If the user passes through the model or loses it in the x or y directions, he can reset the distance to the model and center the model by simply depressing a function key.

The user has the ability to specify his angle of view. The normal angle of view for someone in front of a graphics display is about 28 degrees and is therefore the default value[5]. This value can be changed in real-time to give the user his desired angle of view.

The PS330 also has the ability to do depth cuing. Depth cuing is tied to the z-clipping planes; lines in front of the near z-plane have maximum intensity while those behind the far z-plane have minimum intensity. Lines between the z-planes vary linearly from maximum to minimum intensity. Dyna-MOVIE.BYU allows the real-time movement of the z-clipping planes. This allows the user to have control over the depth cuing of his model. The intensity of the back face of the model can range from full intensity or zero depth cuing to zero intensity or full depth cuing. The amount of depth cuing depends upon the location of the z-clipping planes. The z-clipping planes can also be moved into the model producing a cross-section effect.

Sub-menu Draw

The DRAW sub-menu provides control over the object as a whole with no part distinctions. The coordinate triad displayed in the lower right corner of the screen responds only to rotations given in this sub-menu.

Dyna-MOVIE.BYU provides a wide range of global transformations. These include rotation, translation, and scaling (Figure 4). With these commands, the user can

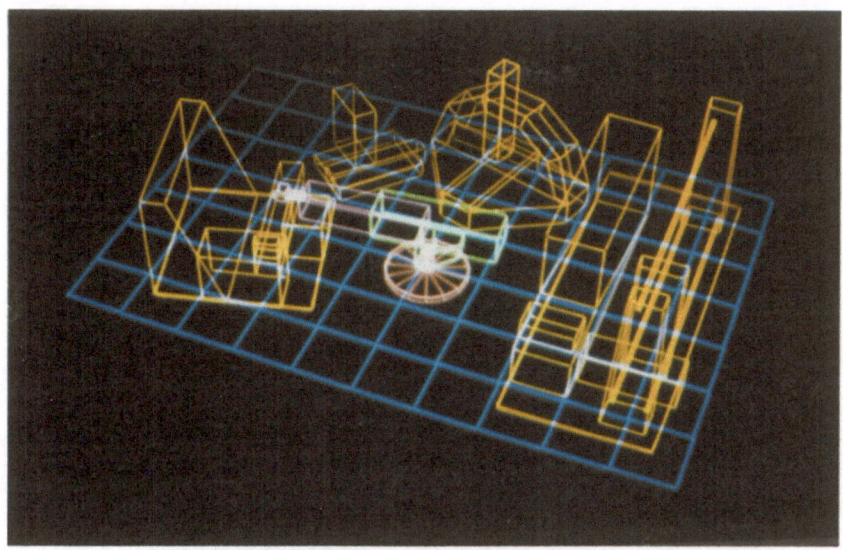

*Fig. 4. Wire Frame Model*

look at the model from any desired orientation. These commands closely approximate what the user would do if he actually had the model in hand[6].

At times the user may enter undesired rotations or translations. The rotations or translations can be reset individually without effecting any other transformations by simply depressing a function key.

Often a user may desire to know the node or polygon number corresponding to a particular graphics entity. By depressing a function key, the polygon and node number picking can be enabled. The user can then zoom in on a particular section of the model through the use of the scaling, rotation, and translation commands (Figure 5) and pick the polygon or node he wishes to identify. When the user has obtained the desired information, the node and polygon numbering can be disabled, and the identifiers can be cleared so they do not interfere with the model.

Sub-menu Parts

The PARTS sub-menu allows for transformation of individual or selected groups of parts. Because of the nature of the control dials only one group of parts may be manipulated at any one time. The group to be manipulated is referred to as the active parts list.

All the global transformations available in the DRAW sub-menu are available in PARTS on a part by part basis. This means that parts may be translated, scaled, and rotated individually (Figure 6). The rotations may occur about the origin of the part or about any user supplied origin. Reset keys, like the ones in the DRAW sub-menu, are also available to reset local translations and rotations.

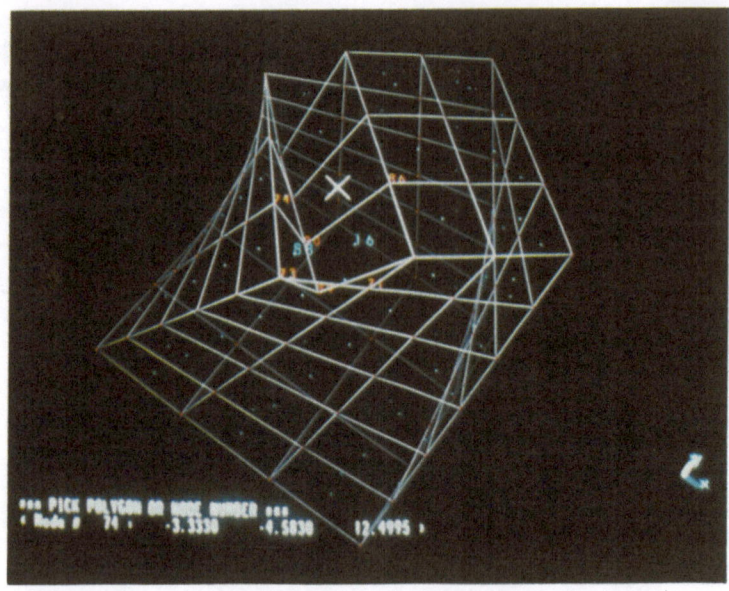

*Fig. 5. Picking of Node and Polygon Numbers.*

If the user has a large complicated model made of many different parts and wishes to work only with a subset of this group of parts, some of the parts may be removed from the display. When work on an individual group of parts is completed, the entire model can be returned to the display by depressing a function key.

Sub-menu View

The VIEW sub-menu contains most of the commands that require the host to compute a new vector list. When the user has selected the desired options, the necessary information is sent to the host which computes the new vector list and "down loads" the information to the PS330 for display.

Most of the commands in this sub-menu can be used together or separately with two exceptions. Watkins hidden surface algorithm is required whenever "contours" and/or "feature" has been specified. "Contour" allows the plotting of contour lines of supplied scalar values, while "feature" removes all shared edges between two polygons (Figure 7).

All hidden surfaces may be removed through use of the Watkins algorithm. The Watkins algorithm has been modified to display the image in color (Figure 8). This modification allows for the operator to specify color by parts and the image displayed with the specified color. In addition, a color fringed image specifying the nodal scalar values is also available (Figure 9). The user also has the choice of selecting one of four different scan line resolutions when computing a hidden line picture. The choices are 256, 512, 1024 and 2048 with 256 being the default.

293

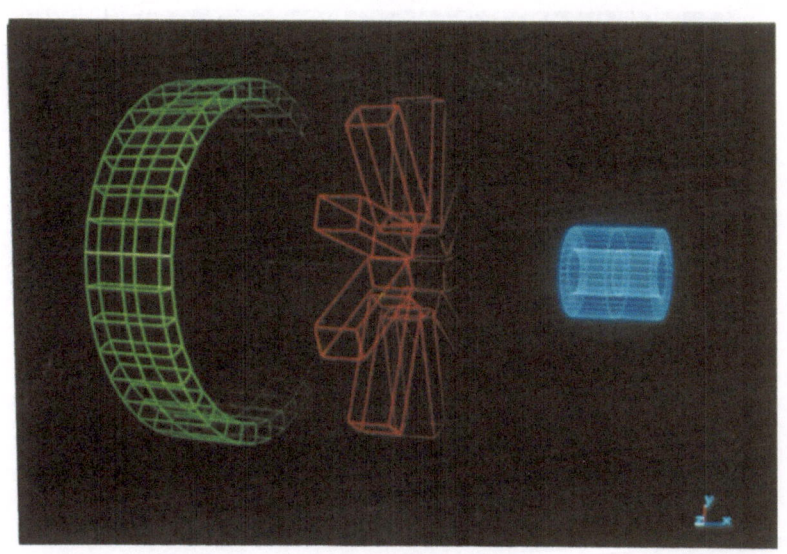

*Fig. 6. Individual Part Transformations.*

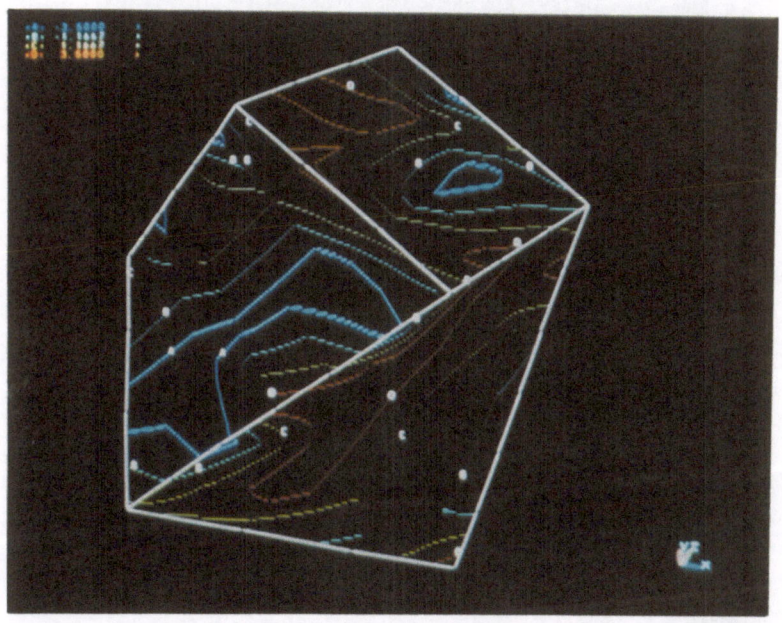

*Fig. 7. Contour and Feature*

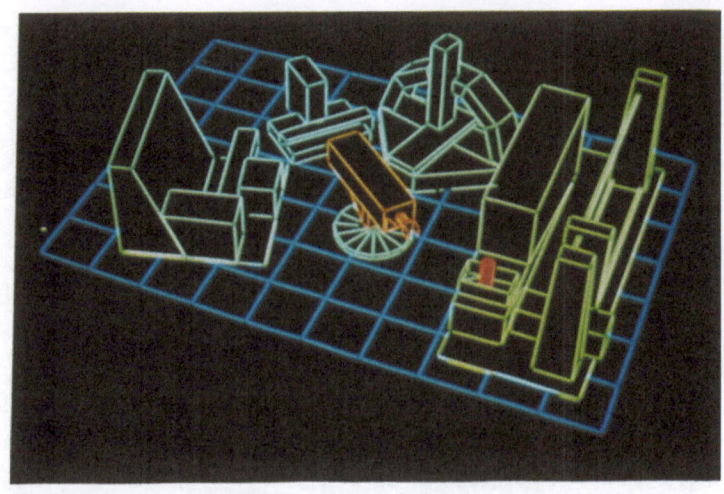

*Fig. 8. Color with hidden lines removed.*

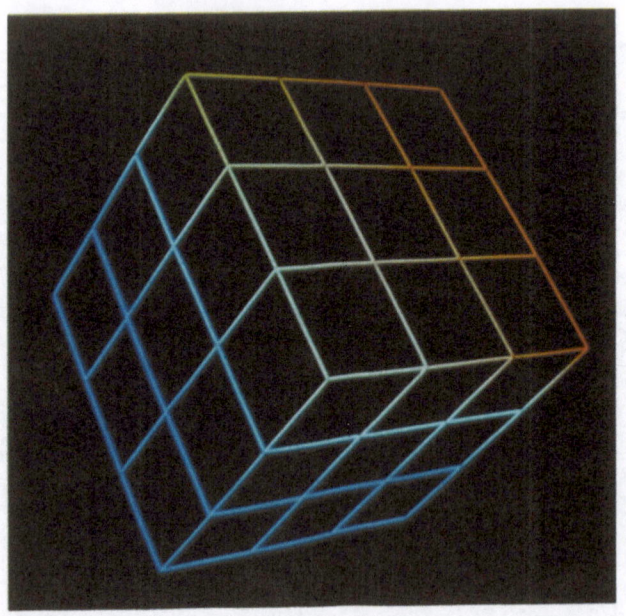

*Fig. 9. Color fringed image with scalar values at nodes.*

Elimination of back facing polygons, called "Poor Man's" hidden surface procedure, is also possible. When invoked with the Watkins algorithm, all back facing polygons will not be processed; this significantly reduces time and data storage. Another option moves the nodes of the polygon towards the element centroid. This shrinking of the elements away from each other allows for the verification of elements in the model.

Other options in VIEW allow the user to modify the geometry with displacement and scalar function files. Nodal displacements can be scaled and added to each node. A function of two variables can be displayed by warping the surface in the x, y, or z directions. Finally, the user can linearly interpolate between two displacement and scalar function files.

Sub-menu Animate

The ANIMATE sub-menu is divided into two portions according to whether the host must generate new vector lists or not. The PS330 can perform object transformations in real-time without impacting the host. The automatic portion of this sub-menu takes advantage of this feature. When animation is desired that involves computation of new nodal coordinates, this must be performed on the host. The resulting vector lists are "down loaded" to the PS330 from the host. This series of previously calculated vector lists are then cycled through to produce an animated sequence.

The local portion of ANIMATE allows automatic control of the global and local transformations that are described in the DRAW and PARTS sub-menus. This automatic control can be set to run for a specified length of time or can be turned on and off at will.

Because greater animation capabilities were desired than those that could be calculated locally, the second part of ANIMATE was written. In this portion of ANIMATE, individual frames are calculated on the host and "down loaded" to the PS330. The calculated frames may be cycled through at any specified rate and stopped or started at will. If a particular frame is desired it can be specified and viewed. The user also has the capability to dial through the frames by hand--stopping and starting at any desired frame.

The capabilities of host-generated animation include all of the transformations that can be handled in the automatic local portion of ANIMATE. In addition, smooth animation, displacement scale factors, vibration cycles per second, transient data, and shrink factors can all be specified. In Figure 10 a robot work station has been modeled. A series of frames were cycled through during the exposure to produce the movement of the robot in the work station.

Smooth animation more closely approximates real movement by allowing accelerations. This is accomplished through the use of a cosine variation rather than linear interpolation. A displacement file can be specified which allows linear interpolation between two geometrically similar models during the animated sequence. If the number of vibration cycles per second is input along with a displacement scale factor, harmonic motion can be simulated. A third type of displacement and scalar function file known as transient data allows the interpolation between two complex scalar and function files which are not periodic in nature. This allows the use of a wide variety of input data that would not normally be possible.

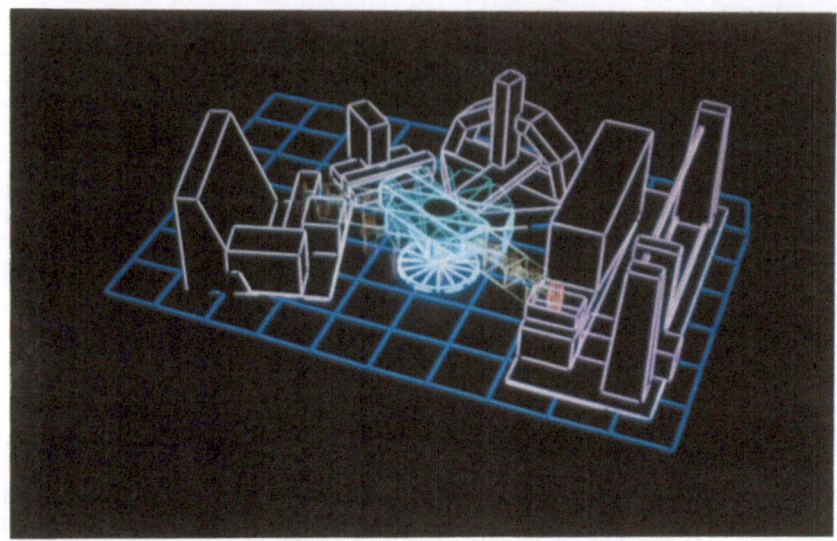

*Fig. 10. Animated Robot Work Station.*

Finally, an animated shrink factor can be specified which shrinks the polygon edges toward the center of the polygon during the animated sequence.

One additional feature which greatly enhances the animation capabilities of Dyna-MOVIE.BYU and makes many complicated animation sequences possible is the concatenation of animated sequences. During one sequence, only a limited number of transformations are possible, but with the capability to concatenate sequences, scenes as complicated as the working of a robot in a CAD/CAM lab have been modeled successfully.

## UTILITY COMMANDS

The utility commands include RESET, READ, SUMMARY, and SAVEO. The RESET function initializes all of the local and global transformations and all parameters to their default values. READ allows the user to input new displacement and scalar function files for the current geometry. SUMMARY calculates and displays several ranges and parameters pertinent to the model. SAVEO writes the current model orientation into a disk file in MOVIE.BYU format for a later continuous-tone rendering (Figure 11).

## SYSTEM COMMANDS

The system commands include just HELP and EXIT. The HELP command allows the operator to enter the help mode of the program. The help mode provides on-line documentation to all commands in the display and utility menus. The EXIT command terminates the program and performs all necessary operations to clear and reset the system.

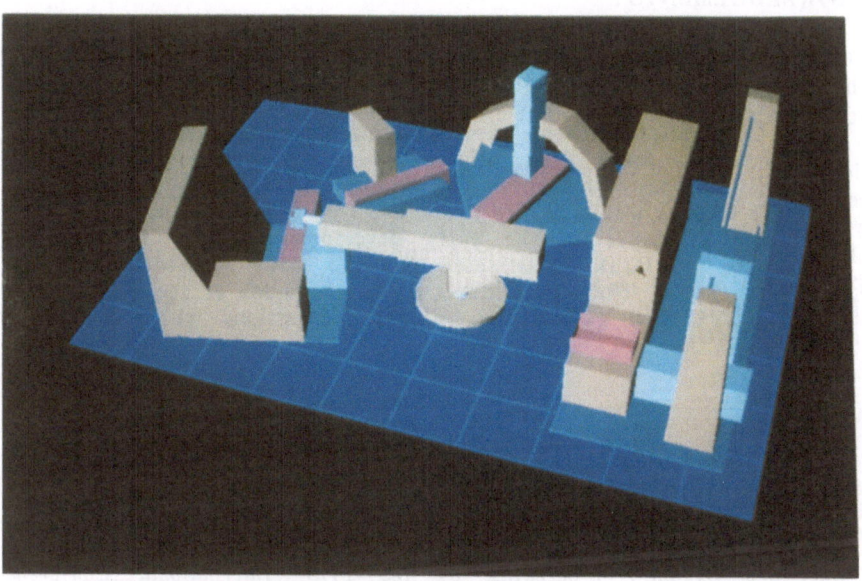

*Fig. 11. Continuous-Tone Rendering*

## FUTURE DEVELOPMENT

Dyna-MOVIE.BYU does not take advantage of all of the many capabilities of the PS330. This version is a rework of the DISPLAY program in MOVIE.BYU system and takes advantage of the real time transformation and referencing capabilities of the PS330. As the authors continued with the software design and became increasingly more familiar with the hardware, it was evident that the program could become more efficient in many areas and the program could be expanded to include many more capabilities offered by the PS330 hardware.

Greater use of the data tablet and stylus will be implemented. Dynamic picking of menus to execute commands, dragging of parts, rotation of parts, editing of the geometric structure, and viewporting and zooming will all be implemented using the data tablet and stylus.

Another area of future research will be the inclusion in the PS330 package of other MOVIE.BYU programs, such as MOSAIC. MOSAIC is a program that converts contour line representations of objects into polygonal meshes. Dyna-MOSAIC will be a stand alone program similar to Dyna-MOVIE.BYU. It will allow rotation and translation of the object using the control dials and editing of the contours and resulting polygonal mesh with the data tablet.

E&S has introduced the PS340. It has an optional raster display with hidden surface removal implemented locally. Dyna-MOVIE.BYU will be expanded to take advantage of these additional features.

## ACKNOWLEDGEMENTS

The authors would like to thank Sandia National Laboratories who sponsored much of the development work. A great deal of thanks must also go to Evans and Sutherland Corporation, without whose generous donation, this project would never have been possible. Much of the original design layout was performed by Spencer Magleby. His original design saved the authors many hours in the implementation process. The authors would like to thank Dr. Tom Sederberg and Mel Spencer, who gave valuable assistance in the early development work. Finally, a special thanks goes to Dr. Hank Christiansen and the many individuals who attended Graphics Utah Style. These individuals performed much of the original testing of Dyna-MOVIE.BYU and gave many valuable suggestions which helped improve Dyna-MOVIE.BYU.

## REFERENCES

[1] Christiansen, H. N., and Stephenson, M. B., "Overview of the MOVIE.BYU Software System", *Proceeding of the Fifth International Conference on Vehicular Structural Mechanics*, Detroit, Michigan, pp. 177-85, April, 1984.

[2] Foley, James D. and Van Dam, A., *FUNDAMENTALS OF INTERACTIVE COMPUTER GRAPHICS*, Addison-Wesley, Reading, Mass., 1982.

[3] Newman, W. and Sproull, R. F., *PRINCIPLES OF INTERACTIVE COMPUTER GRAPHICS*, McGraw-Hill, Hightstown, N.J., 1979.

[4] *PS300 User's Manual*, Evans and Sutherland Computer Corporation, Salt Lake City, Utah 1983.

[5] Christiansen, H. N., and Stephenson, M. B., *MOVIE.BYU Training Text*, University Press, Brigham Young University, Provo, Utah, 1983.

[6] Magleby, S. P., "Design of a Computer Graphics Display System for The Evans and Sutherland PS 300", Unpublished MS Thesis, Department of Civil Engineering, Brigham Young University, Provo, Utah, Sept. 1983.

# Computer Animation in Engineering

David W. Muir

Failure Analysis Associates, 2225 East Bayshore Road, Palo Alto, CA 94303, USA

## ABSTRACT

Computer animation provides the next leap in extending and enhancing the engineer's ability to communicate with others. This is a concise overview of the advantages, uses, and features available in computer animation. The discussion covers the areas such as design, sales, product litigation, advertising, and entertainment where computer animation can and is being used. The features discussed include site "walk-thru," object examination, mechanisms, vehicle dynamics, structural behavior, and pilot/driver/operator trainers.

## INTRODUCTION

Communication is important, everyone agrees. Communicating is especially important in engineering where highly technical ideas must sometimes be communicated to people with little or no technical training (managers, sales people, and clients). Even the transfer of ideas between engineers is difficult when restricted to a purely verbal level. Here, pictures and graphics gain importance. From the word level we progress to pencil sketches, where clarity is limited to an individual's artistic ability. The next level is either engineering drawings, an artist's conception, or both. In these cases however, the engineer has the difficult task of communicating the idea in words to a draftsperson or artist.

Computer graphics can bridge the communication gap. With the multitude of computer software and hardware available today, an engineer can illustrate his ideas directly. Computer pictures are often as accurate as engineering drawings and as life-like as an artist's conception and allow engineers to communicate much more effectively with both peers and non-technical people. But static computer pictures, like still photographs, are more restrictive than motion pictures. Computer animation makes ideas come to life and provides another magnitude in an engineer's ability to communicate effectively.

Computer animation also provides a method to apply engineering constraints to evaluate products, even before a prototype is built. As will be discussed later, computer models of vehicles, linkages, robots, etc., can be moved on the screen using engineering equations as the control. In this way, models can be evaluated under controlled conditions to determine their behavior long before manufacture begins.

The discussion that follows is divided into two main areas: a) advantages and uses of computer animation and b) some features of computer animation.

## ADVANTAGES AND USES OF COMPUTER ANIMATION

The advantages of computer animation are multiple. One advantage is the illustration of complex physical phenomena such as complicated motions in mechanisms or the assembly of complex components. Computer animation can also display, in real time, the results of engineering analyses. Animation helps to sell ideas. Most of us are in the business of selling ideas whether we are engineers, sales people, or managers. An engineer may need to convince his manager that a new design is feasible and must then demonstrate that new product to the sales force. The sales force can then market the company's new products to customers and clients, sometimes before the products are available.

The important point is that an engineer's ideas and imagination can be expressed and communicated more effectively through animation than through static media. Let's take a hypothetical situation. An engineer for a robotics company has an idea for a new linkage system for existing robots that will increase the robot's capabilities, decrease moving parts, and lower their cost; thus, a more efficient system. The engineer builds a computer model of this new linkage and applies the motion constraints and the degrees of freedom possible at each of the joints. By defining and testing a sample task for the robot, the computer animation will confirm or dispute the ability of the robot to perform the function. In addition, the engineer can evaluate load stresses in various parts to confirm the robot's ability to withstand the loads through the entire motion.

This system can be proposed to a new customer who has a specific task for the robot to perform. The customer's task can be programmed into the data base, and the animated computer model can move through the task. The ability of the system is confirmed, based on engineering data. Of course, in our hypothetical situation, the customer is convinced and buys the new robot.

Computer animation has an important role in the courtroom. Product litigation and accident cases often use graphic displays. Exhibits have usually been photographs, artist sketches, or models to show how mechanisms work. Sometimes actual products are brought into the courtroom. Computer animation has advantages over those traditional courtroom exhibits. A computer image can be produced and shaded to match photographic quality, and with animation can surpass the static limits of a photograph. The computer model can be built to an accuracy of several decimal places more easily than can a physical model. Computer-generated models are easier to transport and display than many actual products. A computer animation can display difficult-to-observe events like the inner workings of an engine or the reconstruction of a car accident.

In the courtroom, engineers have time and resource constraints when communicating highly technical subject matter to an audience (judge and jury) that may have a limited technical background. Computer animation displayed on video monitors can capture the jury's attention and help them understand engineering phenomena. Computer animation is a technique by which an engineer can explain the results of a complicated program. Animations that show a part deforming under load have been produced using results of finite element programs. For most people it is easier to understand a "picture" of a stress plot or a deformed plot (as shown in Figure 1) than to understand the significance of numbers that result from finite element analysis calculations.

Computer animation is widely used in entertainment and advertising. Many television station logos and program introductions are computer-generated images.

In the same manner that animation can communicate technical ideas to a jury, it is being used to sell new projects to management, new ventures to capitalists, and new products and ideas to the general public. In an article in the January 1985, IEEE Computer Graphics and Applications Magazine, John Whitney, Jr., of Digital Productions states, *"The computer is no longer a motion graphics tool; it is a tool to simulate live action, and this is changing the way advertising agencies are thinking about how to use the computer."* The use of computer animation in advertising and entertainment is growing dramatically. As software and hardware innovations become more available and less expensive, other industries are rapidly adapting computer animation to their needs.

## FEATURES OF COMPUTER ANIMATION

Although customized animation is still expensive, the computer animation features described below are commercially available and economical.

"Walk-Thru" -- A "walk-thru" can take the viewer around, over, and through almost anything that can be modeled on the computer. The viewer can walk along a road or can follow the path that someone might drive. Floor plans and architect's drawings come alive with three-dimensional images of both exterior and interior views of buildings. The viewer can "pass through" the walls of a machine and observe the inner workings of that machine.

Object Examination -- Object examination covers three areas: outside examination, exploded, and cutaway views. Outside examination entails rotating and translating the model in space so that the entire model can be examined from numerous angles (see Figure 2). Exploded views separate the model into individual components. Complex or multiple-component assemblies are "broken" or "exploded" to observe individual components in closer detail. Cutaway views entail removing portions of an outside surface of an object to allow the viewer to examine the inside, something possible with animation that is not always possible in real life (see Figure 3).

Mechanisms -- Animation can be invaluable in facilitating the design, analysis, and demonstration of how both simple and complex mechanisms work. Engineering equations of motion can be used as input to evaluate the limits and capabilities or products like robots and linkages (Figures 4 and 5 are examples).

- Vehicle Dynamics -- The dynamics of nearly any vehicle can be observed with computer animation. Vehicle-dynamics computer programs can generate reams of numbers describing center of gravity, yaw, pitch, roll, etc. Computer animation can use these engineering calculations to graphically illustrate in minutes information that would require hours of reading and analyzing numbers (Figure 6 is an example of this).

- Structural Behavior -- Civil and mechanical engineering analyses can be animated to show how a structure is stressed, heated, or deformed as a result of either static or dynamic loading. Animation can be a valuable aide in examining the results of finite element and modal analysis programs and in viewing the complex motions that may lead to failure of a component.

- Pilot/Driver/Operator Training -- Aviation training programs for military and commercial pilots have used computer animation for many years. Lower costs make computer-animated programs economical to train machine operators and automobile and truck drivers.

## SUMMARY

Computer animation greatly enhances an engineer's ability to accurately and quickly communicate highly technical ideas to both peers and non-technical personnel. Current uses of computer animation include sales and marketing, management presentations, and exhibits in the courtroom.

Today's features already allow computer animation to perform tasks and to examine features that are difficult or impossible in real life. The computer can provide a macroscopic view of a microscopic product part. Products can be tested, evaluated, and redesigned on a computer screen before they are built. Without leaving the courtroom, juries can ride along the path of an accident vehicle.

Future uses of computer animation are probably limited only to the imagination of the user.

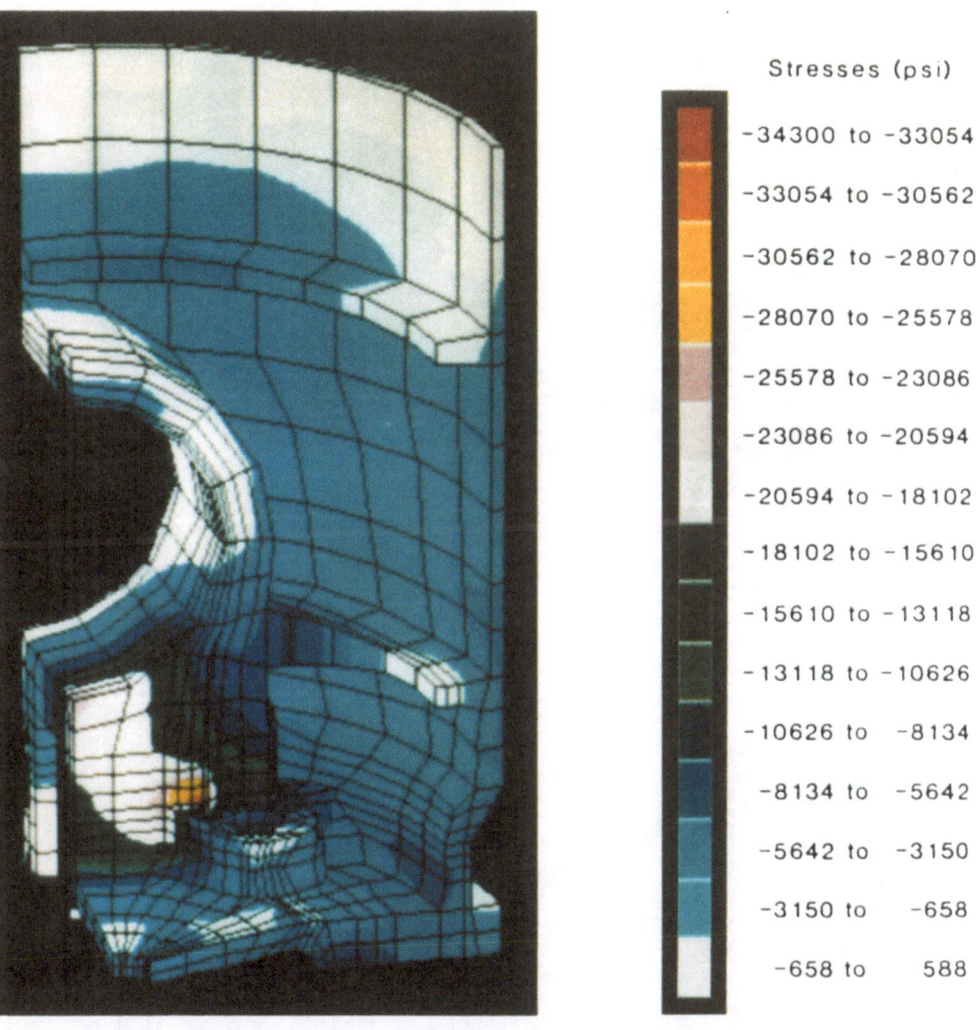

Figure 1.  Color stress plot of quarter section model of diesel engine piston.

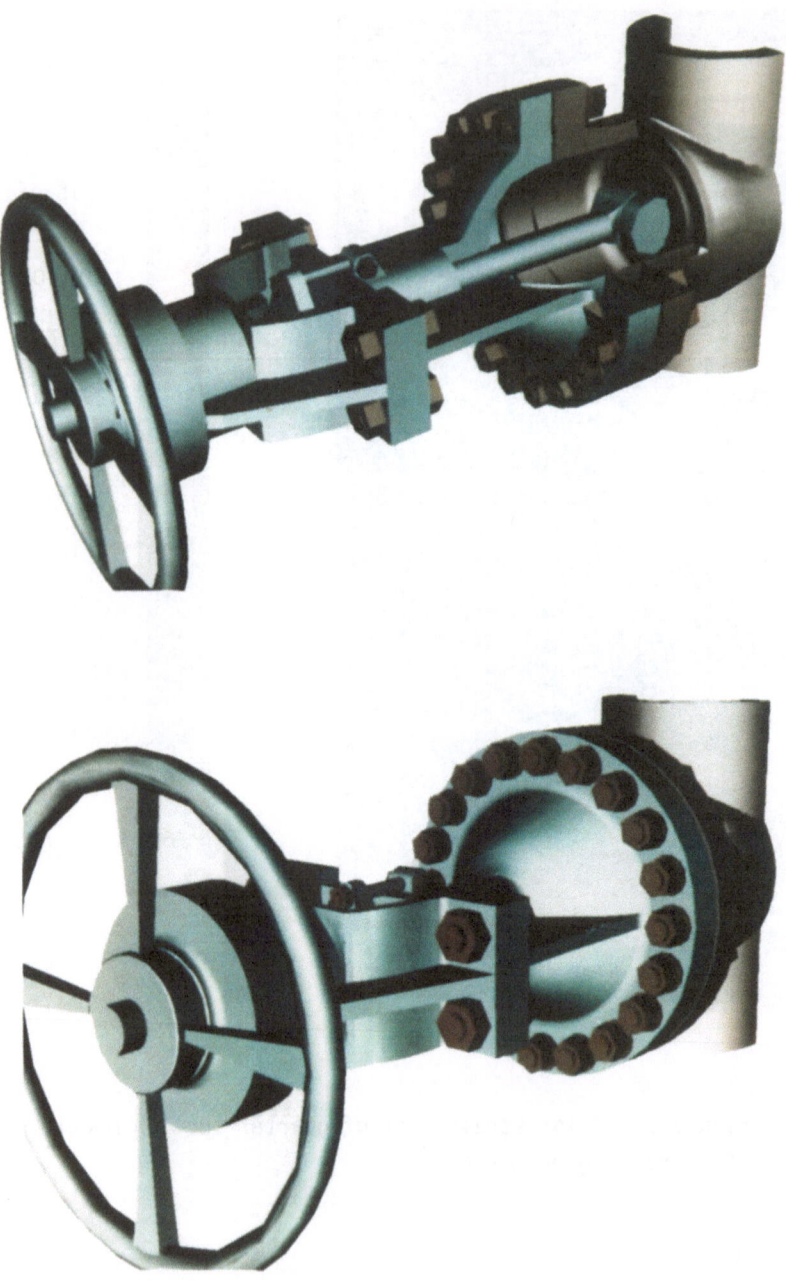

Figure 2. Frames from rotation and cutaway view of steam valve animimation.

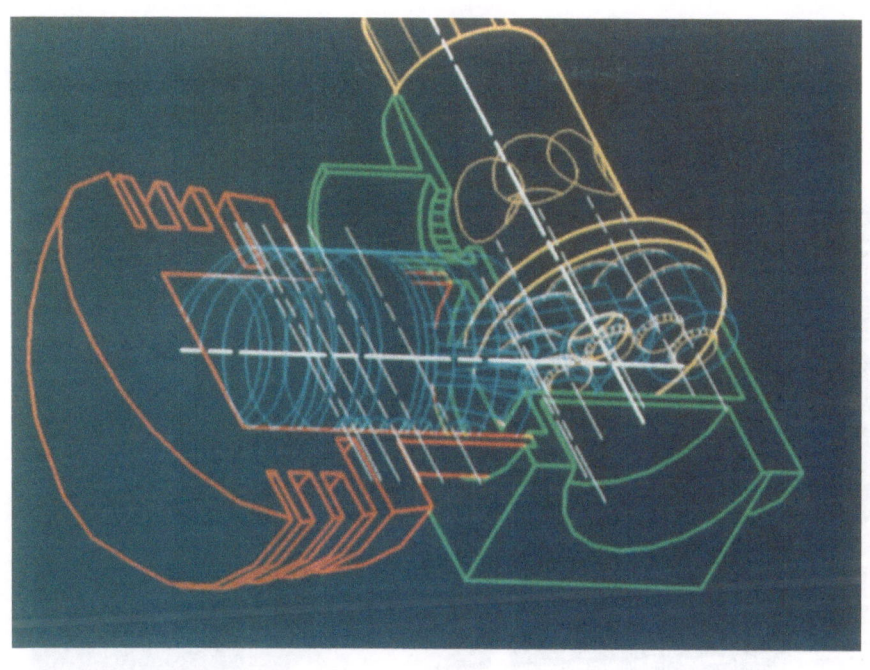

Figure 3b.  Animation of piston traveling
inside engine in wire frame model.

Figure 3a.  Solid shaded image with cutaway
of inside of engine.

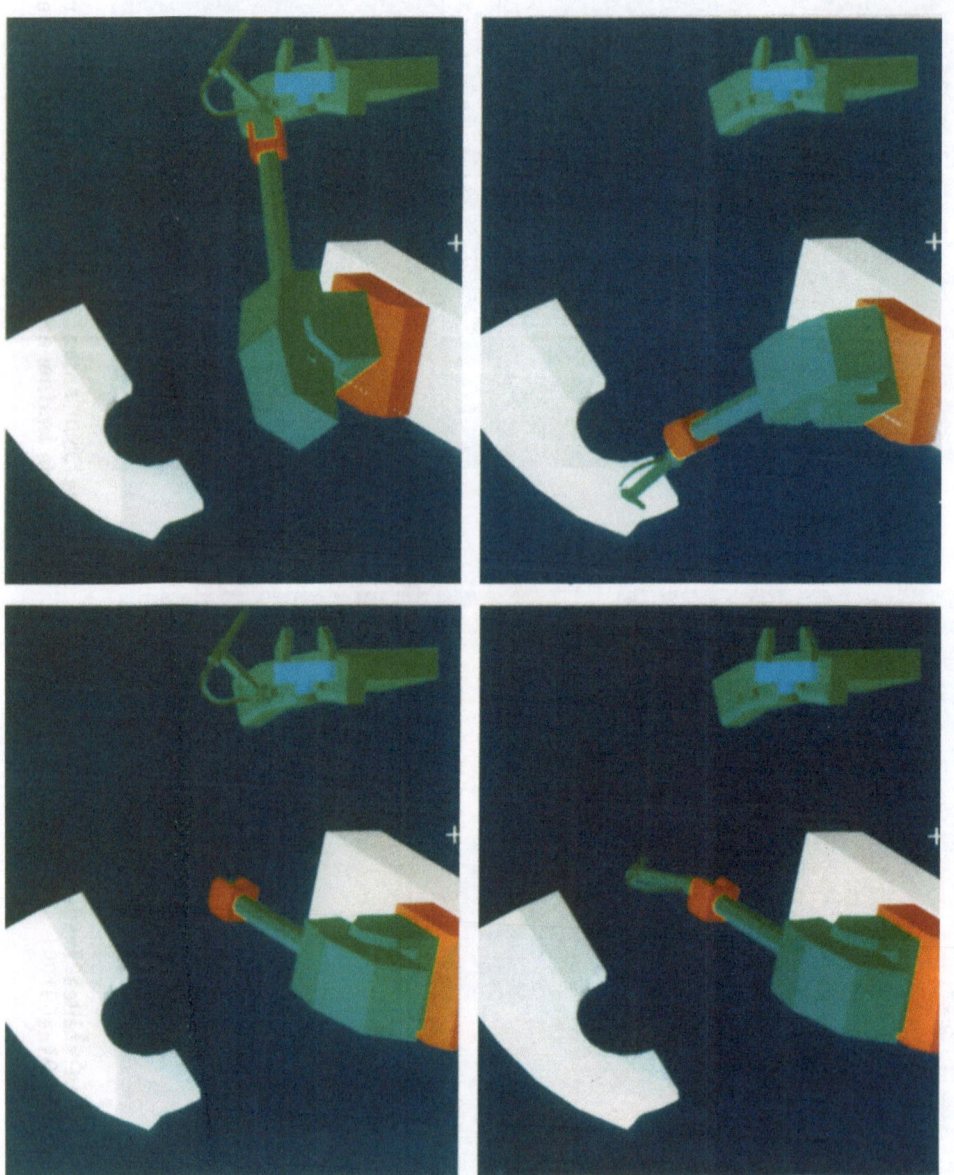

Figure 4. Animation of industrial robot.

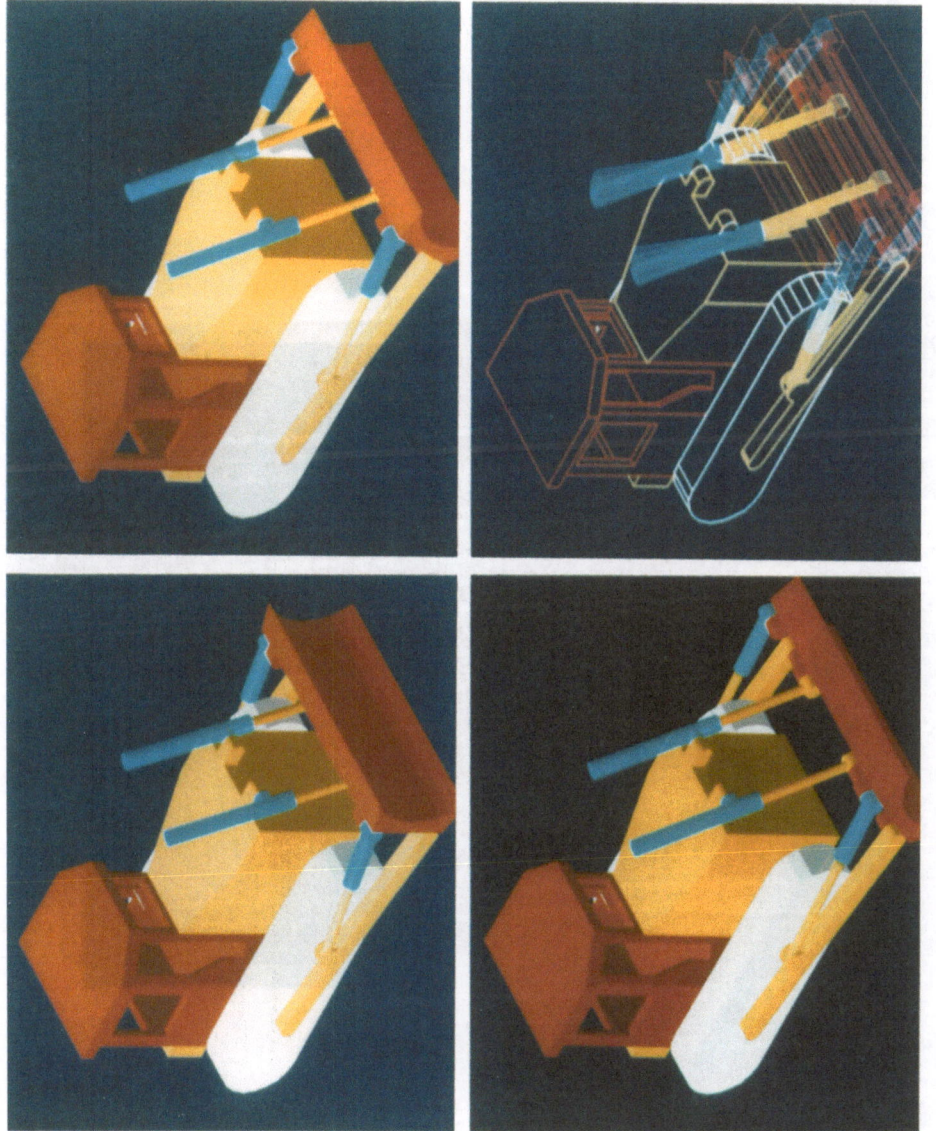

Figure 5.  Animation of shaded and wire frame bulldozer blade mechanism.

308

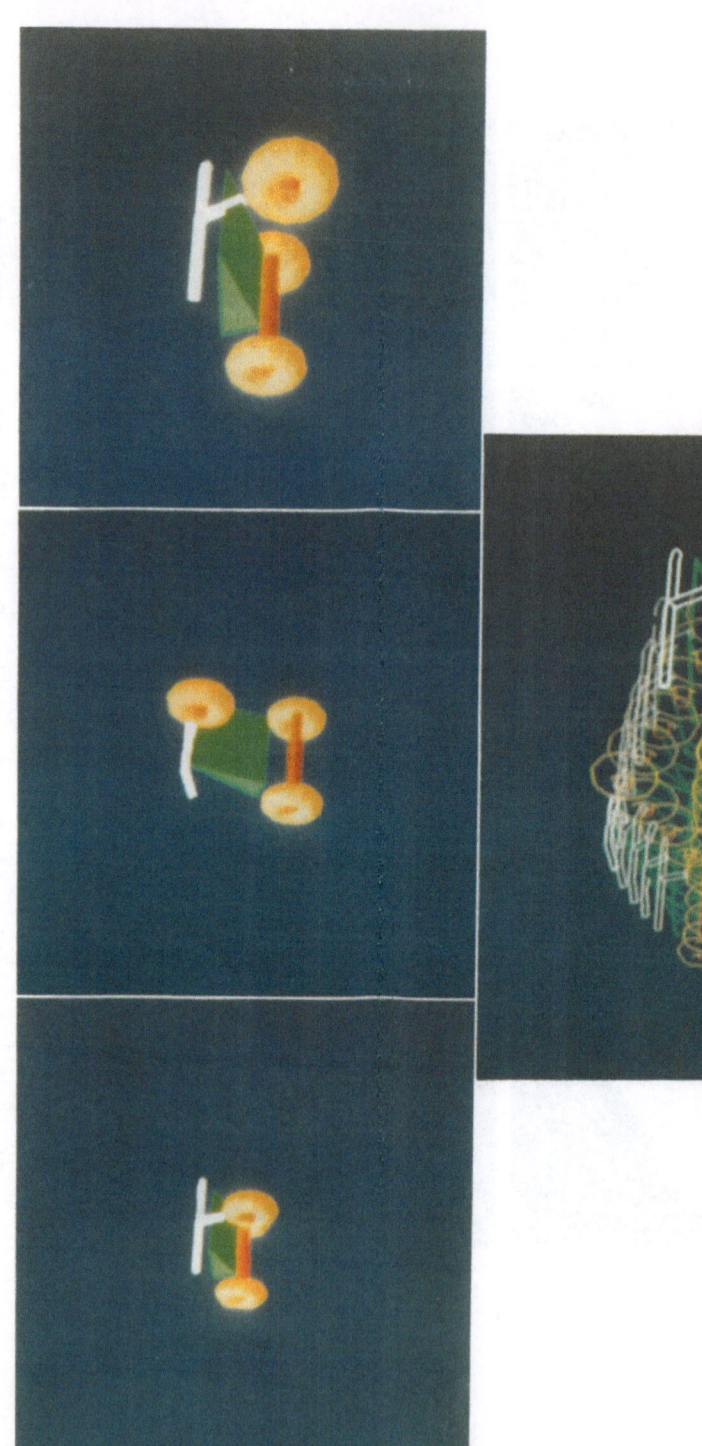

Figure 6. Frames from animation of shaded and wire frame image of three wheeled vehicle.

Chapter 7
# Computer Art

# Techniques in Computer Art

Mutsuko K. Sasaki and Tateaki Sasaki

The Institute of Physical and Chemical Research, 2-1, Hirosawa, Wako, Saitama, 351 Japan

ABSTRACT

The major techniques in computer art so far are classified into six categories and evaluated. Among these categories, we discuss the function method in details by showing pictures generated by our system ART-3, a small system based on the function method. By this, we want to show the usefulness of mathematics and to demonstrate the enormous possibilities of computer art. Furthermore, the role of artists in the technology-aided art is briefly discussed on the basis of our experience of using ART-3.

## CLASSIFICATION OF THE TECHNIQUES

Current computer art is not so highly advanced that the computer controls the composition of a picture automatically. In generating pictures so far, the computer is used essentially for transforming the input data and for "painting" a given area in various ways. Therefore, current major techniques may be classified from the viewpoint of data transformation and area painting as follows (listed approximately in the appearance order. For the actual works, see [1,2]):

1) wire-frame method,
2) data transformation method,
3) patchwork method,
4) function method,
5) algorithm method,
6) fractal method.

The wire-frame method draws a net of lines, not only curves but also freehand figures, and a superposition of the lines constitutes a picture. This method is quite simple but can generate beautiful pictures which often represent fascinating moire patterns. In the data transformation method a picture, such as a photograph of a human face, is digitized and transformed to represent another picture by a simple mapping function. Transforming a linear figure to another continuously is also classified in this category. Although these two methods are widely used in commercial art, the resulting pictures are now given only low values because the methods are so simple.

In the patchwork method, the canvas is assumed to be divided into small regions, which are usually uniform rectangles, and the computer patches many of these regions according to a simple program written by the user. The patchwork method gained fame when Knowlton generated circuit-like abstract patterns by his system EXPLOR [3]. (The EXPLOR is equipped with several techniques other than the patchwork method.) However, as an art technique, the patchwork method has not been developed as much as expected in the early days, because the pictures generated by this method so far are not much different from each other. In the function method, a pattern is generated by drawing many element patterns on the canvas, where the type, size, and even the location of each element pattern is controlled by a mathematical function. We call the pattern generated by this method a functional pattern. Note that most computer art works are generated by using mathematical functions in some ways, but such utilization is not called the function method unless the pattern is a direct mapping of a function.

Many people developed their own algorithms for generating pictures such as an area dividing algorithm, a stereographic algorithm, and so on. We summarize their methods the algorithm method. The different algorithms generate quite different pictures, and some simple algorithms are now used in commercial art. The algorithm method contains a weakness that one algorithm generates mostly similar pictures. Furthermore, the resulting picture is often not beautiful although it may be interesting. Among many algorithms for generating pictures, the fractal method invented by Mandelbrot [4] was given a special status because it can generate complicated and irregular patterns which were considered to be hard to generate by computer. Therefore, we listed up the fractal method independently.

Several comments are necessary on the above classification. Computer artists often use random numbers for determining the type, size, and location of the element pattern. We omitted this technique in the above list because it is rather trivial. The second comment is that, in many cases, the picture is generated not by a single method but by a combination of several methods. Thirdly, we can observe a common feature of the methods listed above: input data are made as small amount as possible and the pattern is generated by repeating elementary procedures quite many times. Therefore, the size of each system is not large except for some algorithm-based systems.

The authors themselves love the function method best and they used it to generate pictures for long time. The largest worry about the function method is that it may be unable to generate complicated and various patterns. One of the aimes of this paper is to show that this anxiety is unnecessary and the function method is really promising in computer art.


ACTUAL PICTURES BY THE FUNCTION METHOD

Although many functional patterns are quite beautiful, only a single pattern is not enough to constitute a picture and some complications are necessary. One of such complications is to divide the canvas area into several parts and "paint" the parts with different patterns. If we use figures of natural things to divide the canvas, the resulting picture will appeal to our hearts strongly. The series of ART systems (Artificial Realistic Technician) were based on this idea, aiming at combining natural beauty and mathematical beauty.

The ART-3, the latest version of ART systems [5,6], accepts hand-drawn figures such as flowers or mountains, and it is equipped with hidden-surface elimination capability. The procedure of picture generation in ART-3 is a repetition of outlining a figure and painting the inside of the figure by a functional or uniform pattern. In order to generate a functional pattern, we assume the canvas to be spanned by the x-y Descartes coordinate system and consider a mathematical function $f(x,y)$ on the system. The ART-3 calculates the value of f on each lattice point ($x=i, y=j$), with i and j integers, and if $f(i,j) > 0$ then it draws an

element pattern on the lattice point in the following way:
  1) When the size of an element pattern is controlled,
      the element pattern of size f(i,j) is drawn;
  2) When the type of element pattern is controlled,
      the element pattern of type [f(i,j)] is drawn,
      where [n] is the maximum integer not greater than n;
  3) When the density of the distribution of element pattern is controlled,
      the element pattern is drawn with the probability f(i,j).
If $f(i,j) \leq 0$ then no element pattern is drawn at the lattice point (i,j). The
function f is constructed by elementary functions such as "sin" or "exp", and each
function contains three parameters. The ART-3 contains a database of mathematical
functions which seem to be useful for computer art.

In painting the canvas, the ART-3 allows the following three modes:
  1) The figure is treated as opaque, i.e., once a figure is painted it is not
      painted any more;
  2) The figure is treated as transparent, i.e., multiple painting is allowed;
  3) The figure is treated as semi-transparent, i.e., a lattice point can be drawn
      an element pattern only when the point is not drawn yet.
In addition to these complications, the ART-3 has several other capabilities such
as utilization of random numbers and figure transformation. However, the motif
making such as the determination of figures and their locations, selection of
pattern functions, etc., is fully dependent on the user, and the system is very
simple compared with modern computer graphics systems.

Let us show some pictures generated by ART-3. All the pictures shown were printed
as monochromes by a CALCOMP plotter or a FUJITSU laser printer.

Fig.1: "Nemophila", appeared in Computers and People, Vol.25, No.8 (1976), p.23.

Fig.2: "Maples in Storm", exhibited at Huntsville Museum of Art (Intn'l Invitation of Computer Graphics), Alabama, Jan.14 – July 30, 1978.

Fig.3: "Mandarin Ducks ⋯ I", appeared in Computers and People, Vol.27, No.8-9 (1978), p.14.

Fig.4: "My Portrait", appeared in Computers and People, Vol.31, No.1-2 (1982), p.17.

Fig.5: "Mt. Fuji with Kokuryu (black dragon)", made in 1984.

Fig.6: "Mt. Fuji in Cloud Sea", made in 1984.

Fig.7: "Mt. Fuji in Storm", made in 1984.

Fig.8: "Mt. Fuji in Eruption", made in 1984.

For illustration, we show the mathematical functions $f_1(x,y)$ and $f_2(x,y)$ used for generating patterns in pictures 1 and 2, respectively:

$f_1(x,y') = -2 \exp(-br) + c \cdot \cos(ar/(1.2 - |\cos(4 \, \mathrm{atan}(y'/x))|))$,
　　　with $y' = 2^{1/2}y$ and $r = (x^2+y'^2)^{1/2}$,
$f_2(x,y') = c \cdot \cos(a \times (\mathrm{atan}(y'/x) + br))$,
　　　with $y' = 2^{1/2}y$ and $r = (x^2+y'^2)^{1/2}$,
where a, b, and c are parameters to be specified by the user.

We want to emphasize that the above pictures were generated by the ART-3 only and the outputs were not handicrafted. We explain how the pictures in Figs. 5 and 6 were drawn by ART-3 which accepts only two dimensional figures and not three dimensional ones. In Fig. 5, we drew the larger Kokuryu and the upper half of the smaller Kokuryu at first, then Mt. Fuji, thirdly the lower half of the smaller Kokuryu, and finally the background cloud. In Fig. 6, the lower half of the cloud was drawn at first, then Mt. Fuji, and finally the upper half of the cloud. We further note that the input figures for these pictures are the signature, the outline of Mt. Fuji, and a square as the outline of the canvas.

We cannot value the above pictures as highly as the pictures by professional artists; in particular, our pictures lack complication of the composition, delicate texturing, and local variations. However, we may value the computer-generated pictures considerably highly because of the unusual quality and fascination of their patterns. The unusual appearance is a result of using mathematical functions and the fascination is due to the high accuracy of machines which is very hard to simulate by human hand.

In our early years of using the function method, we were not good at generating the functional pattern and we could not imagine the great possibilities of the function method. Now, our skill of generating the pattern has been improved largely, and we have changed our prospects accordingly. Mathematical functions are now used widely in computer art, not only in the function method but also in other methods. However, we think that we have pictured only a very small number of many possibilities so far with most beautiful, impressive, and fascinating patterns left unpictured. In fact, we may say that the variations of the functional patterns in our pictures shown above demonstrate the validity of our prospects. That is, we are now at the entrance of mathematical art and many new types of patterns which nobody has seen before will be created in future. We ourselves want to improve our ART system for generating more variety of patterns. One improvement will be the implementation of capability of partially automatic determinantion of composition of the picture, which we think is an interesting problem of mathematics [7].

## THE ROLE OF ARTISTS IN THE TECHNOLOGY-AIDED ART

About the middle of twentieth century, technology began to invade the art world and is now making a revolution in the technique of art. The technology invasion has created and will create many new genres of art. In this sense, technology is obviously beneficial for art. However, we must notice that each technique in the technology world is usually fated to be short-lived; the progress of technology is very rapid and invention of a new and/or superior technique makes the previous techniques outmoded and often unused. For example, twenty years ago, computer art was an extremely modern genre of art. Nowadays, the position of extremely modern art is occupied by the laser art etc., and they themselves will be unable to maintain their position long time. As for computer art, the development of output devices is astonishing, and the artists using plotters are now only minors. The texturing technique in computer graphics is a typical example of the development of software techniques: the random number method in early days has been made obsolete completely by the appearance of the fractal method (realism) and the ray-tracing method (super realism).

Then, the following serious questions will happen, which may be called the technology dilemma. Is the invention of new techniques most important in the technology-aided art ? Yet, is every new technique fated to be short-lived ? The answers to these questions are inevitably be YES if the technology-aided art is such that it can generate only restricted types of works which will be exhausted in a short period of time or such that it becomes an art because it utilizes a new technique and nothing else. Even if these reasonings are wrong, what role can artists play if the answer is YES ?

Fortunately, more than two decades history of computer art revealed that the possibilities of computer-aided art are so enormous that we can never exhaust them within several decades. Our feeling is actually that the utilization of computer is making the art world much richer than before. In particular, our one decade experience of using ART systems gave us a strong confidence that mathematics is a very useful tool for pictorial art. Our experience gives us also an instruction that generating a good art work is not easy and it requires both experience and skill. Furthermore, new techniques, which obviously enlarge the possibilities of art, do not always generate good works but even the old-fashioned techniques are quite useful because of their special roles as art techniques. That is, the quality of the art work depends not on the specialized techniques but on the artist's idea and how to use the techniques. For example, the ART-3 is an old type system using a plotter or printer as the output device and based on the outmoded function method. Yet, we can generate good and fresh works by ART-3. In this sense, what is desired most eagerly at present in the world of computer art is the collaboration of artists and engineers.

In the world of technology-aided art so far, art works have been created mostly by engineers or mathematicians, and they were usually evaluated by the people in the technology world. Consequently, not the quality of the works but the media and the techniques of art making have been paid a strong attention, as the names of computer art and laser art indicate. If we look at the sides of media and techniques mostly, we will fall into the trap of the technology dilemma. The media and techniques are, however, nothing from the viewpoint of art and the art work is everything. Therefore, we must look at the side of art mostly, and artists can play essential roles in this side. From now on, the works of the technology-aided art must be evaluated by ordinary people from the viewpoint of art. Probably, this is the best way to make the technology-aided art a genuine art. Then, artists and engineers, and even mathematicians, will collaborate with each other to creat high quality works.

## REFERENCES

[1] Computer Graphics and Art, 1980-81 year book, Ed. G. C. Hertlein. This book contains many computer art works.
[2] Proceedings of Exhibition of Computer Graphics, SIGGRAPH '83. This book contains many art works generated by computer graphics techniques.
[3] K. C. Knowlton, "EXPLOR - A Generator of Images from Explicit Patterns, Local Operations, and Randomness," Proc. 9th Meeting of UAIDE, 1970.
[4] B. B. Mandelbrot, "Fractals - Form, Chance, and Dimension," Freeman and Company, San Francisco, 1977.
[5] M. K. Sasaki and T. Sasaki, "Computers and Beauty," Creative Computing, Nov-Dec issue, 1976, pp.48-51.
[6] M. K. Sasaki and T. Sasaki, "Computer Art System ART-3," Computer Graphics and Art, Aug. 1978, pp.4-11.
[7] M. K. Sasaki and T. Sasaki, "Towards an Intelligent Computer Art," Picture Engineering, Springer-Verlag, 1982, pp.286-302.

# Production of Artistic Images with "ART PROCESSOR"

Masaki Takakura, Yoji Noguchi, Hideo Takemura, Keisuke Iwasaki, Yasukuni Yamane, Kenji Hatakenaka* and Noritoshi Kako

Computer Software Research Center, Corporate Design Center*, Sharp Corporation, 2613-1 Ichinomoto, Tenri, Nara, 632 Japan

ABSTRACT

"ART PROCESSOR" is a compact image processing system using a microprocessor. It can produce artistic pictures like oil paintings from realistic pictures like photographs. We will present the image processing system and the algorithm to create artistic pictures in this paper.

INTRODUCTION

Because of a large volume of data to perform image processing, it was necessary to use a large computer than a micro computer. But, recently, the LSI technology has made remarkable progress, and a microprocessor has been much improved in functions and speed. A semiconductor memory has also become larger in capacity and lower in price. Thanks to these improvements, image processing can be now performed using a microprocessor instead of a large computer. (1)

We have now developed a new image processing system which can produces various images. We named this system "ART PROCESSOR". Characteristics of the system are as follows;
1. Compactness
2. Ease to use ( with 2 TV monitors, 4 keys, and a tablet )
3. Image input from video signal
4. Pictorial output by a color ink jet printer
We have also developed the new technique, "combined image processing method". By this method, "ART PROCESSOR" can change a realistic image such as a photograph into an artistic image such as oil paintings.

First, this paper will present the concept and hardware OF "ART PROCESSOR". Secondly, the algorithm of "combined image processing" will be described. Thirdly, the paper will describe how "ART PROCESSOR" produces an artistic image. Some examples of works will be shown which are produced from an original picture.

BACKGROUND

Up to the present, drawing images has been done mostly by illustrators or artists because it needs various skills. But, if a computer has those skills, any one will be able to have a chance to create images by help of the computer. The purpose of our studies is to develop such an aiding computer. Now, before explaining the concept of "ART PROCESSOR", we will present three kinds of tools which are commonly used to create images with a computer. , shown as table 1 .

The first kind is "3-D Computer Graphics". This technique is used in engineering and animation. The study of texture synthesis has achieved good results to produce "organic" textures or artistic images.(2) The main purpose of computer graphics is the simulation of the nonexistent scene. Therefore a user of the computer has to input all the data of the scene. Then the computer converts the data to images. The user has to use a large computer for that; it usually costs much time and money. It can be said that "3-D Computer Graphics" is not a personal tool.

The second kind is a "Painting System".(3) A painting system doesn't contain three dimensional data. A user imagines almost complete images by himself and inputs them to the painting system with a tablet or a light pen. Therefore images are produced interactively. The system is also small in size and it doesn't cost much. But a user must have a certain kind of skills for this system; because he inputs images by his own. It takes rather long time to input his images. Of course a scanner or a camera can be used to make the time shorter.

The third kind is "Digital Video Effect".(4) It is used in the field of broadcasting, for example TV titles or commercial films. This technique produces new images by converting original images input from video signal. The conversion takes less than 1/30 second. The DVE system consists of the special hardware to convert images in real time. It's very expensive, and not a personal tool.

The three kinds of techniques shown in table 1 doesn't match our purpose to develop the aiding personal computer. It needs the functions shown in table 2. Our idea to produce images are described as follows; A user doesn't have to input images with a tablet or a light pen. He just gets an image with a TV camera. A microprocessor converts an input image into a new image. He decides appropriate parameters for the conversion. Various images can be produced, if the system has enough parameters. He doesn't need so many skills to draw images. He only has to have responsibility for selecting the original images and evaluating the results.


HARDWARE

"ART PROCESSOR" hardware consists of the following components;

    1. Processing unit
    2. Two color TV monitors
    3. Flexible disk drive
    4. Color ink jet printer
    5. Tablet
    6. Switchbox with four keys
    7. Various video equipments (video camera, VTR, video disk, etc.)

Fig.1 shows the block diagram of the system of "ART PROCESSOR". The processing unit consists of a microproccessor (Z80A), 12KB ROM, 18KB RAM, and 384KB video RAM (two frame memories). Fig.2 is a photograph of the system. The ivory-colored box in the left part of the photograph is the processing unit. Two color TV monitors are set in the right side of it. By these monitors, the operator can always look at two images of the frame memories at the same time. The frame memory can provide 256 X 256 pixels as resolution and 256 gray scale levels about each R, G, B, and each frame memory capacity is 192 KB.

"ART PROCESSOR" is controlled by selecting commands in the menu, which is displayed on one of the TV monitors. To select the commands, we use a cursor which is pointed by the tablet. The switchbox is used for changing the menu or starting the command selected by the cursor. "ART PROCESSOR" can get images from various video equipments and save them in the flexible disk drive.

## SOFTWARE

We have developed the new technique, "combined image processing method". This method is a combination of three processes, such as scanning, checking conditions for processing, and basic image processing. The concept of this method is as follows.

i) Scanning point
The scanning point is scanned in the area of image. It generates "operating points" by using various "texture elements".

ii) operating point
This is the point where various kinds of operations which are described later are performed.

iii) Texture element
The texture elements simulate the pattern of painting tools. Fig. 3 shows some examples of the texture elements.

The flow chart of the combined image processing method is shown in Fig. 4. We describe the contents of this method in detail.

A. Initialization

The co-ordinates of the scanning point are initially set. The methods of initialization of the point can be classified as follows.

1. Set the first scanning point at the fixed point.
2. Input the first scanning point by cursor which is pointed by the tablet.

B. Check conditions for processing

Three conditions for the scanning point, which are defined previously, decide whether the image processing is performed at the point or not. If the scanning point doesn't satisfy any conditions, the processing described later is omitted. The conditions to check here are classified as follows.

1) Condition : area
This condition is checked after the command "Cutting" is performed. The command "Cutting" devides the whole area of an image into two parts, i.e. inside area and outside area, by the closed curve. It is checked whether the scanning point is inside or outside. Using this "area" condition after operating the command "Cutting", the image processing can be performed in special areas.

2) Condition : density
This condition gives a distance between a scanning point and the next scanning point. If Nx and Ny are given as parameters, the condition is expressed as follows;

$$( \text{Xs .and. Nx} ) \text{ .or. } ( \text{Ys .and. Ny} ) = 0$$
or
$$( \text{Xs .and. Nx} ) \text{ .or. } ( \text{Ys .and. Ny} ) \text{ not} = 0$$

( Xs,Ys ) is the co-ordinate of the scanning point. ".And." indicates a logical "and" bit operater. ".or." indicates a logical "or" bit operater. Changing parameters Nx,Ny, the scanning points which satisfy the "density" condition generate various patterns.

3) Condition : Color data
This condition checks two quantities about color data of the scanning point. The first quantity is the co-ordinate in the three dimensional space of color (Red, Green, Blue) of the scanning point, as shown in Fig.5. The region of the color for processing is defined as the inside of rectangular parallelepiped in the three dimensional space of color. It is checked whether the color data of the scanning point is inside the region for processing or not. By checking this "color data" condition, we can pick up the special same color area without using the "area" condition from the color image stored in frame memories. The second quantity of the color data is the changing rate in color at the scanning point. Checking this quantity, it can extract the outline of figure from the image.

C. Processing

Processing is constructed by two process, such as generating some operating points and operating at the points. The operating points are generated from the scanning point according to the "texture element". If the texture element is one dot, only the scanning point is operated. The texture element consists of several points varies impression of image. The point shown in Fig.6 (1a) is a scanning point. The arrow in Fig.6 (1b) shows the motion of the scanning point . If the texture element is one dot, operation is performed at the point ( Fig.6 (2a) ), or along the line ( Fig.6 (2b) ). But in the case that the texture element consists of five points, the operation is performed at five points. The results are shown in Fig.6 (3a),(3b). Fig.6 (4a),(4b) show another type of "texture element". In this case the operating points are separated from each other, and the same operation is performed at different places.

The basic image processing of "ART PROCESSOR" is an operation which is performed at one point. There are seven types of operations described as below. In the numerical expressions, (Xs,Ys) and (Xo,Yo) indicates the co-ordinates of the scanning point and the operating point. (Ar,Ag,Ab) and (Br,Bg,Bb) indicates the color data in red, green, and blue of the frame memory A and B. Suffix 'i' is a substitute of r,g, and b.

1) Artistic drawing :
Move color data from the scanning point in the frame memory A to the operating point in the frame memory B.

$$\text{Bi}( \text{Xo,Yo} ) := \text{Ai}( \text{Xs,Ys} )$$

2) Realistic drawing :
Move color data from the operating point in the frame memory A to the operating point in the frame memory B.

$$\text{Bi}( \text{Xo,Yo} ) := \text{Ai}( \text{Xo,Yo} )$$

3) Averaging :
Average color datas at the operating point in the frame memory A and B, and put the product of averaging at the same point in the frame memory B.

$$Bi(Xo,Yo) := (Ai(Xo,Yo) + Bi(Xo,Yo))/2$$

4) Multiplying :
Multiply color data at the operating point in the frame memory A by color data at the same point in B, and divide it by 128. Then put again the product of multiplying at the same point in B. If the product becomes larger than 255, 255 is put at the point.

$$Bi(Xo,Yo) := (Ai(Xo,Yo) * Bi(Xo,Yo))/128$$
$$:= 255 \quad (\text{if the product is larger than } 255)$$

5) Black and white :
Change color data into black and white data at the operating point in the frame memory B.

$$Bi(Xo,Yo) := 0.5 \quad g(Xo,Yo) + 0.33\ Br(Xo,Yo) + 0.17\ Bb(Xo,Yo)$$

6) Color changing :
Change color at the operating point in the frame memory B.

$$Bi(Xo,Yo) := Fi(Bi(Xo,Yo))$$

Fi( x ) is a function to change colors.

7) Blurring :
Average color datas at the operating point and the previous points in the frame memory B, and put again the product of averaging at the operating point in the frame memory B.

$$Bi(Xo,Yo) := (Bi(Xo-],Yo) + Bi(Xo,Yo-]) + 2 * Bi(Xo,Yo))/4$$

## D. Scanning

The co-ordinate of a scanning point is changed in three modes to scan. The first one is manual scanning. We input the co-ordinate and the action of the scanning point interactively by using a cursor. We use this mode, when we want to modify the image data delicately or want to add letters in the image by hand. The second mode to scan is automatic scanning. In this mode the scanning point is moved in the image according to raster scanning. The third mode to scan is line scanning. In this mode we only have to input several points and then the microprocessor computes the co-ordinates and moves the scanning point along the line which connects these points.

## PRODUCTION OF OIL PAINTINGS

As stated above, many parameters of conditions, texture elements, operations, and scanning method can be set. And if we set appropriate parameters, "ART

PROCESSOR" can change a realistic image like photographs to an artistic image like oil paintings. The parameters should be set as follows;

1) Conditions
    Area              : Don't care
    Density        : Don't care
    Color data    : Changing rate of color data at the scanning point must be less than an appropriate value.
2) Texture elements : Various figures such as shown in Fig.3
3) Operation        : Artistic drawing
4) Scanning method  : Automatic scanning

The theory to produce an image like oil paintings is as follows. When we paint pictures with a brush, we paint many points in the same color at the same time. Because the shape of the brush is changeable and many regions are often painted again in another color, the shapes of the regions which are painted in the same color are numerous. But all of the shapes have the same characteristic depended on the painting tools, for example, painting brushes, pens and crayon. It is called "touch of the pictures". This model of oil paintings is shown in Fig.7.

"ART PROCESSOR" produces various "touches" by using a "texture element". "Texture elements" correspond to painting tools. We will explain the processing by using Fig.8. An original picture is stored in the frame memory A. Color data at the scanning point is taken out from the memory A. Then a "texture element" of that color is made, and it is put into the frame memory B. This process is equivalent to drawing with a brush. If this process is executed on different scanning points, the color of the "texture elements" becomes different. And if several "texture elements" are put close, some part of them is erased by another "texture element", as shown in Fig.8. Now the shape of the same color region is characterized by the shape of the "texture element". It also depends on the action of the scanning point.

EXAMPLES OF WORKS

Fig.9 (a) shows an original picture of a red sports car. The results of "Combined Image Processing" are shown in Fig.9 (b-f). The difference in the touch of Fig.9 (b-d) results from the difference of their "texture elements". Their "texture elements" are shown at the end of menu in the pictures. The picture shown in Fig.9 (e) was produced from the picture of Fig.9 (d) by changing colors. Color is important to atmospher of images. Therefore, images become more artistic when they are changed in color besides in touch. The picture shown in Fig.9 (f) is produced by manual scanning. The "texture element" is a character 'C'.

Other examples are shown in Fig.10. The picture shown in Fig.10 (a2) was produced by a big "texture element". A black closed line shown in Fig.10 (a1) devides the original image into the inside area and the outside area. Artistic drawing operation was performed in the inside area and the same 64 images were produced. The picture shown in Fig.10 (b2) was produced by multiplying operation. The original image shown in Fig.9 (a) was multiplied by the color gradation image shown in Fig.10 (b1). The picture shown in Fig.10 (c) was produced by using the density condition.

The "texture element" is a square. Artistic drawing operation was performed at the points which satisfied the density condition. The picture shown in Fig.10 (d) is an output by a color ink jet printer.

## CONCLUSION

We have developed a new image processing system "ART PROCESSOR" which produces various images. We have also developed the new technique, "combined image processing method". By this method, "ART PROCESSOR" can change a realistic image input from video signal into an artistic image such as oil paintings. By this function, even if we don't have enough skills to draw an oil painting, we can draw one easily and enjoyably.

As a personal computer and a digital TV becomes more popular, it's appropriate to say that the technology of image processing will be applied to OA and home video equipments in the near future. "ART PROCESSOR" is such an equipment which can help us to draw various artistic images.

## ACKNOWLEDGMENT

We are grateful to Miss Fumiko Tsuji for her helpful advice. We would like to thank Dr. Ikuo Nishioka, the general manager of Computer Software Research Center, for his encouragement during the course of this work.

## REFERENCES

(1)    H. Mitui, S. Onishi, K. Hirono, "Gazo Kakumei" (Image Revolution), Seibundo-Shinkosha, 1983
(2)    John-Peter Lewis, "Texture Synthesis for Digital Painting", Computer Graphics, Vol.18, No.3, July 1984
(3)    "Paint System no Genjo to Doko" (Circumstances and Trends of Painting Systems), Pixel, No.19, 1984
(4)    Kinji Kodaka, "Computer wo mochiita video effect to computer graphics" (Video effects by computers and computer graphics), Pixel, No.30, 1985

Table 1.

|  | Inputting tool | Images are produced by | Interactivity | Cost |
|---|---|---|---|---|
| 3-D Computer Graphics | Tablet Key board | Computer | Bad | High |
| Painting System | 1. Tablet 2. Scanner | Man | Good | Low |
| Digital Video Effect | 1. Video 2. Tablet | Computer | Good | High |

Table 2.

|  | Inputting tool | Images are produced by | Interactivity | Cost |
|---|---|---|---|---|
| ART PROCESSOR | 1. Video 2. Tablet | Micro-processor | Good | Low |

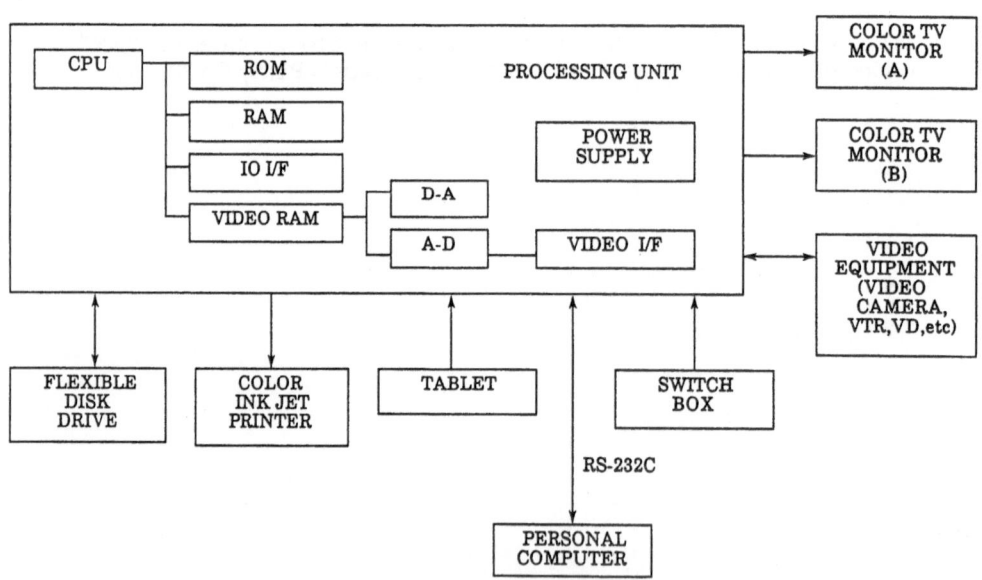

Fig.1 System of ART PROCESSOR

Fig.2 System of "ART PROCESSOR"

Fig.3 Examples of "texture elements"

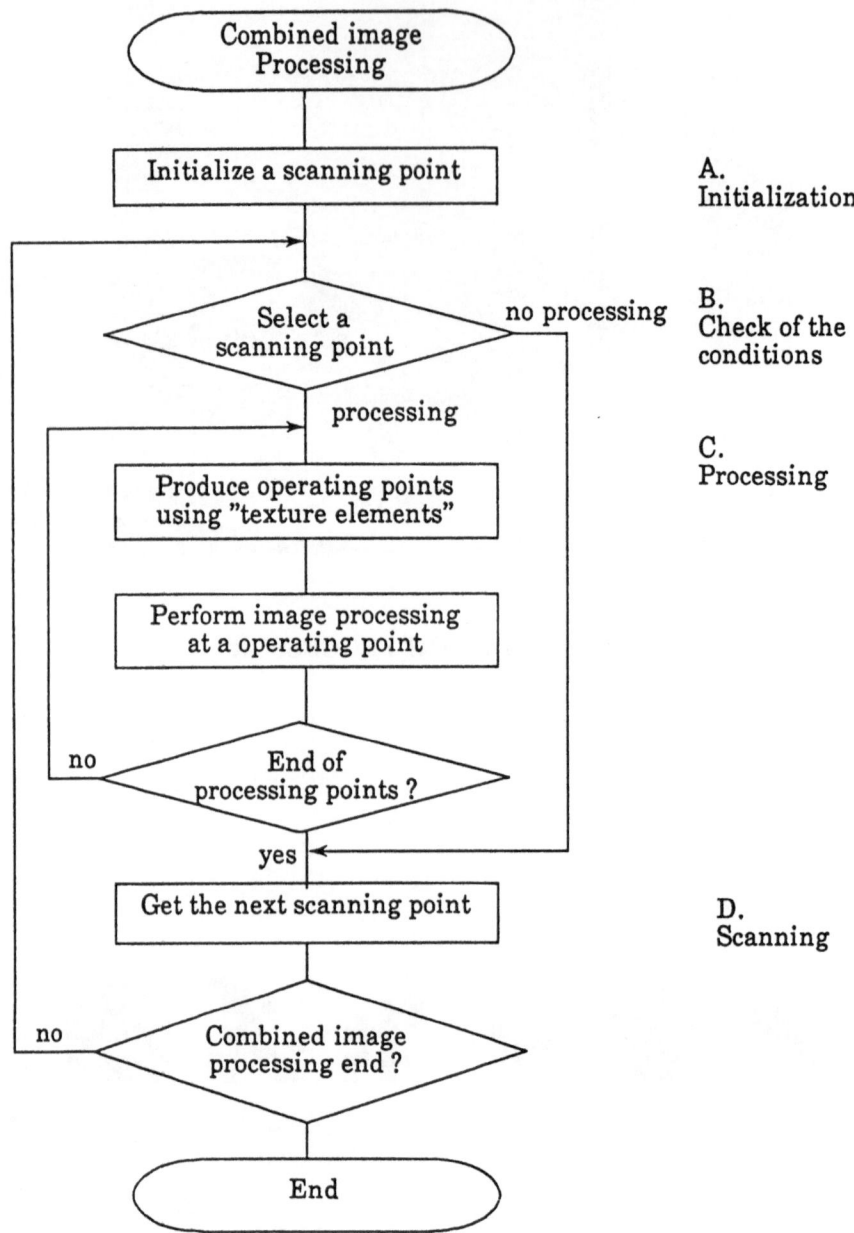

Fig.4 Algorithm flow chart of the "combined image processing".

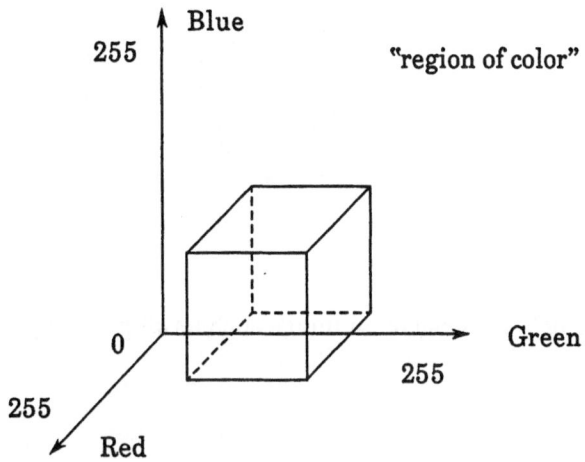

Fig.5 Three dimensional space of color Red, Green, Blue.

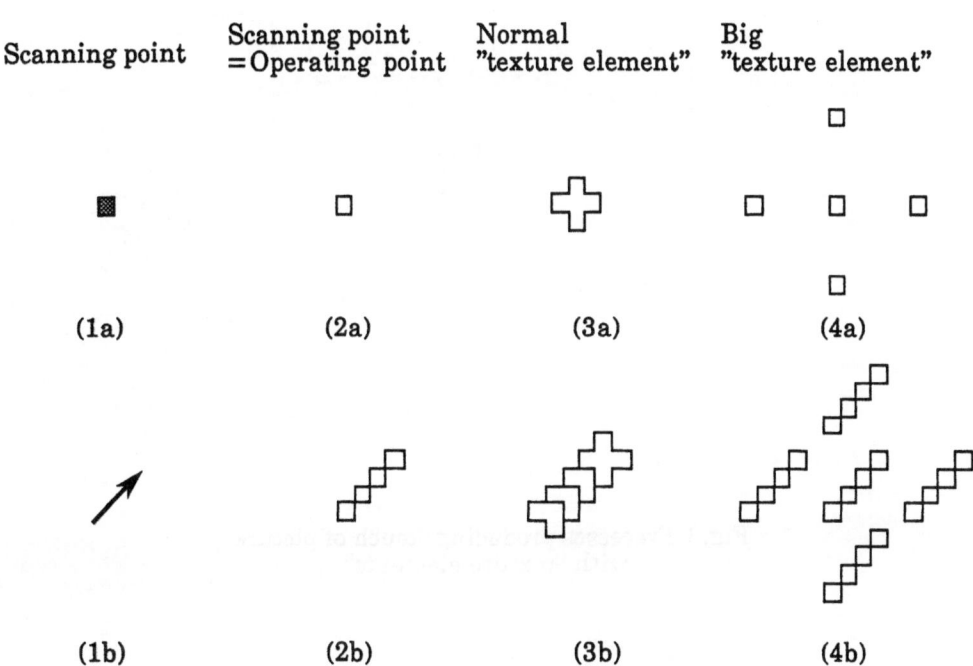

Fig.6 Effects of "texture elements"

Fig.7 A model of an image such as oil paintings.

Frame memory A   texture element   Frame memory B

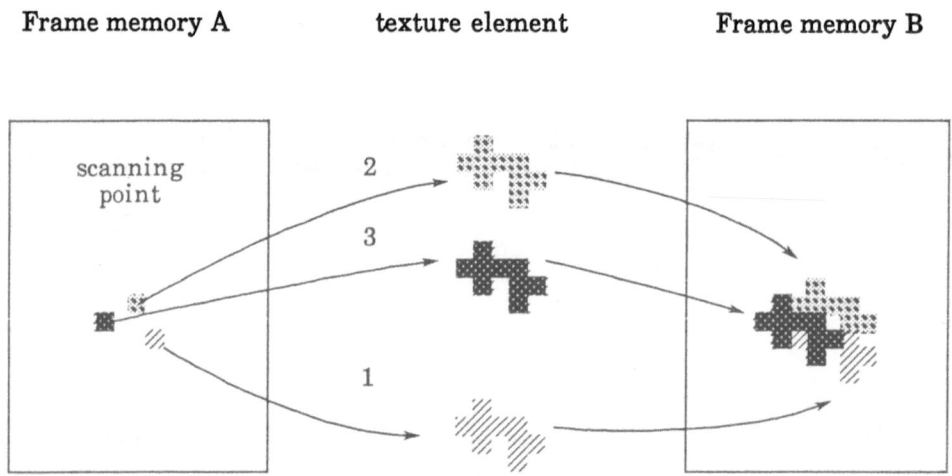

Fig.8 Processes producing "touch of picture"
with "texture elements"

333

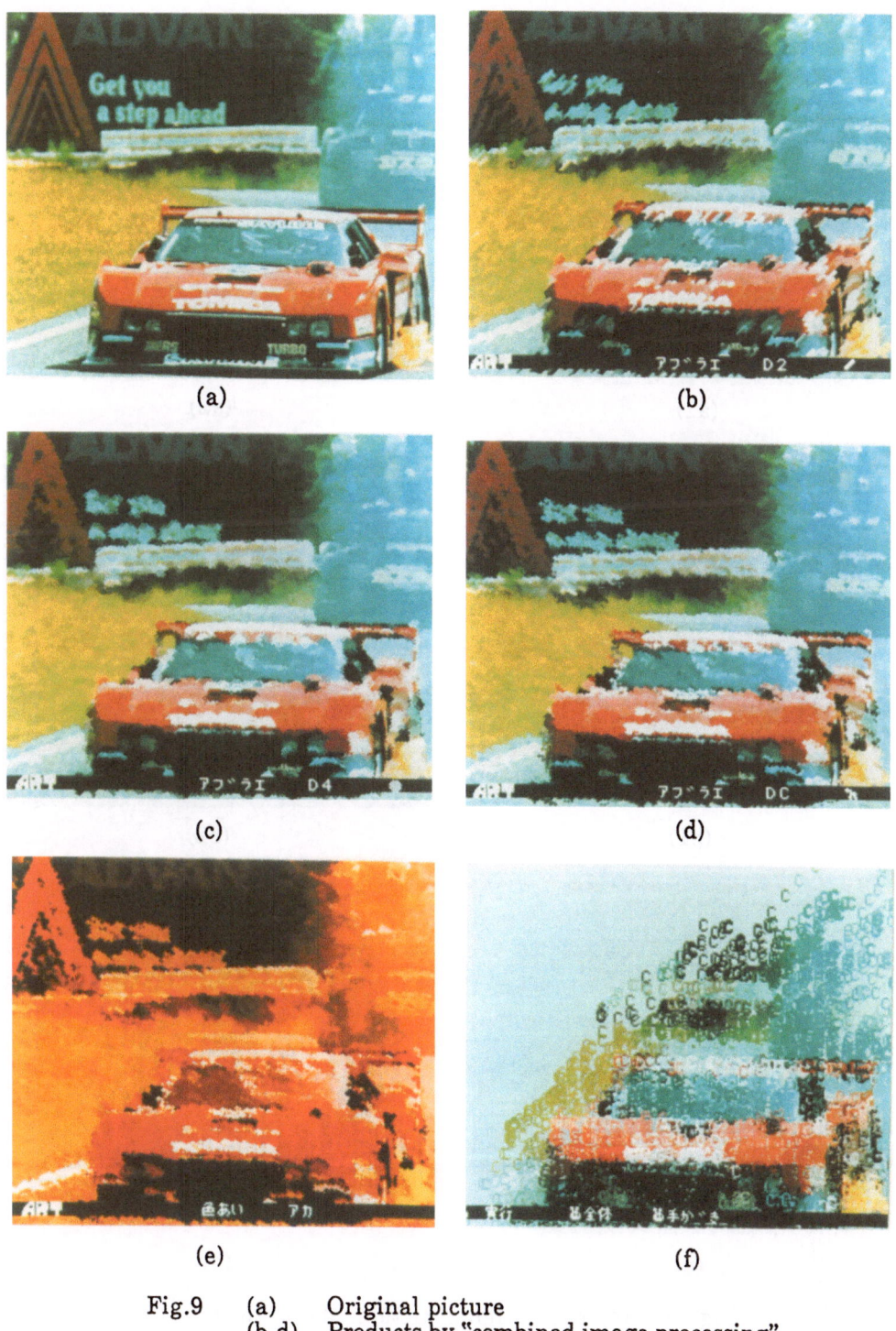

Fig.9  (a)  Original picture
    (b-d)  Products by "combined image processing"
       "texture element" is shown at the end of menu
    (e)  By changing colors of (d)
    (f)  By using manual scanning

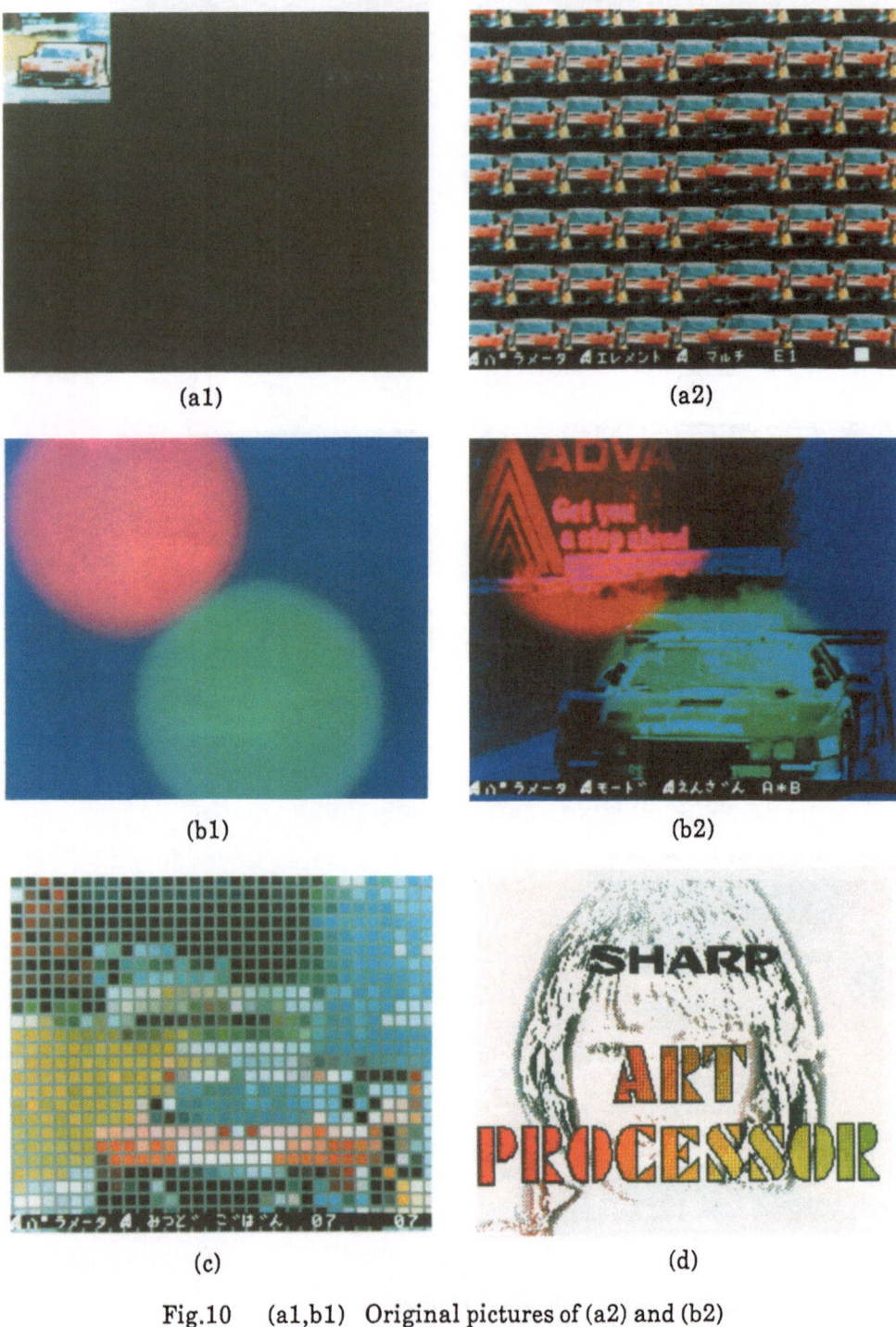

(a1)　　　　　　　　　　　　(a2)

(b1)　　　　　　　　　　　　(b2)

(c)　　　　　　　　　　　　(d)

Fig.10　(a1,b1)　Original pictures of (a2) and (b2)
　　　　(a2)　　By using a big "texture element"
　　　　(b2)　　By using multiplying operation
　　　　(c)　　　By using the density condition
　　　　(d)　　　Output by color ink jet printer

# Vector Graphics
# for the Graphic Designer and the Artist

Christa Schubert

2924 Ladoga Avenue, Longbeach, CA 90815, USA

Abstract

Vector graphics for the graphic designer and artist with applications
in trademark design, as graphic elements such as screens, rules, typo-
graphical ornaments and borders, textile and wrapping paper patterns,
animation and fine art. This paper illustrates how the hard-edged medium
of the straight line can be used to create solid shapes, curved, flowing
forms, and airbrush like appearance not usually associated with it.


Key words: Vector, shape, pattern, design.

Introduction

The computer images discussed in this paper are based on limited structures and elements which under the influence of a number of parameters
yield similar to widely diverging, different, and new forms, patterns
and textures with applications in applied as well as fine art.

The high resolution ink line and paper hardcopy features of this medium
with wide choice of colors made it an attractive subject for investigation by a graphic designer on a limited budget as myself.


Background

My first exposure to computer graphics happened through images on corporate annual reports as featured in graphic design annuals like GRAPHIS
(1) during the sixties and following that through the first books on
computer generated art in the early seventies as the publication following the CYBERNETIC SERENDIPITY show by Jasia Reichardt (2). This is
when I first saw the plotter designs created for Dutch postal stamps. (3)

All these created in me an early association of computer graphics with
line. The acquisition of a plotter was therefore natural at the time my
husband opened a timesharing business. In 1980 we settled for a product
of a mature technology over at most mediocre raster technology that was
within our reach. Without his extensive background in hardware and
software and his constant support I would not be here today.

Now I had to decide on the directions my work should take. In the past I had thought of a library of shapes. From close observation I knew what effort and time programming required and I did not want programs that generated only one effect. The software should be a tool not just for my artistic self-expression but have general and practical application in art and design. A recent volume on computer drawing featuring artists from Europe and the US with many approaches to the computer - mostly in fine art and of a narrower scope - reaffirmed in my mind the decision on my direction in computer graphics toward broad exploration and application of line to art and design. (7)


Hardware

The programs were first developed on a 128 K Ampex computer of the Data General Nova family. In 1984 we converted them to a 192 K Zenith Z100 micro for greater independence, speed, and relief of the timesharing system. To this is connected a CRT for input and a high resolution (.01mm) flatbed ink pen plotter by Soltec ( now also known as IBM XY 750 ).


Software

The language of the Ampex is Business Basic ( Iris operating system ), on the Zenith it is Microsoft Basic with CPM and MS/DOS. The plotter has a number of built-in functions such as lines, circles, limited scaling, and alphanumerics. The driver used is for Teletype.

The software uses prompts and keyboard entry to guide the user through all possible parameters. The graphs are not stored (only primitives) but before execution of the drawing the plotter prints a two-line summary at the edge of the paper with date, time, name of program, primitive, commands used, and copyright notice for complete documentation and quick reference without the need for keeping track of hundreds of names and for lengthy searches of directories.

Programs are written inhouse by my husband and junior programmers. Usually built around a geometric shape such as circle, star, zig-zag, digitized primitive, they are arranged on variable polar or square grids with parameters manipulating them in translation, scaling, rotation including +/- incrementation for all. An initial version is written which I then begin to test for its possibilities.

Of the dozen small programs, each with about five parameters, two were develeped using twenty and more. "Star" is, as the name suggests, based on polar coordinate grid structure. Each of the lines making up the star figure can, during concentric repeat, be manipulated to move almost in any directionn with end points involved in the same or separate moves. ( Fig. 1 to 6 )

The second large program is based on a variable square grid inside which units of a digitized primitive are placed that have been manipulated using over twenty parameters: "Trace". This program has only undergone initial explorations and needs extensive testing. It may well be even richer than the "Star". ( Fig. 7, 8 )

## Using the Tools

I was one of the artists who looked at early computer images like those in the "Serendipity" show (2) and wondered what I would do with such a tool. I have since often felt frustrated at seeing this tool in hands that could well create it, not use it. But more and more there are those visually "literate", who somehow manage to get near the machine after surmounting computer phobia and other obstacles to get their hands on it and make it sing. Whitney, ( we seemed to have explored the same star ), Ken Knowlton, Collette and Charles Bangert who did the seemingly impossible: Make the computer draw with the sensitivity of a live hand, connected to the artists eye, mind. ( 4,5 )

Like them I am less interested in realistic representation and literal content as I am in line and form and movement and what can come of a combination of these. Yet how different are the paths we are travelling!

Now that I have my own tools I have become aware how they reflect the limitations of the inceptor. It is only through continuing testing and working that I can push them beyond first concepts. As they expand they become pliable to my ideas, responsive to my probing.

Early in my work on the plotter I got tired of the "lacy" look, the purely linear character of the graphs. I needed to see solid color, have some weight. The repetition of the line to any number with any spacing before moving to the next was a feature that grew from this frustration. ( Fig. 9 )

The richness of the "Star" program becomes more clear when I describe how for three years this program, following new leads or through mistakes, typos, miscalculations, or the asking of a new question ('what is a star with one tip?') led me into new "neighborhoods" of shapes that would take me days, weeks, and, in the case of the spirals, nearly nine months to explore. Results might be very hard-edged and high-tech, or soft flowing, three dimensional, organic or even ethnic like a design from an antique broach. ( Fig. 10 )

The permutations that the straight-edged star shape undergoes in the concatenation of the parameters is probably the most exciting feature of this program with endresults that seem to all but have lost memory of their origin.

As an artist I have no special predilection toward line. But the plotter is the tool I have and I have no choice but to make the best of drawing with lines. But I have prefered ways of using it. In my efforts to get away from the straight and hard-edged I have pushed it to give me effects such as tone and even airbrush softness through skillful use of the narrowest angles and the play with parallel lines. ( Fig. 11 to 15 )

In conclusion I want to sum up my experience in computer graphics this way: If it was not for the constant experimentation and experience of discovery I would not persue it. It is the mathematical-generative component of the software that not only works on my ideas but feeds me new ones continuously. This makes it appear to be like a vehicle I drive and steer into terrain where I could not go alone. Because the new territory

is often outside my capacity to envision it enlarges the horizon of
graphic possibilities for me and, hopefully, for others.

References

1)  Herdeg, Walter, "Graphis" annual, Graphis Press, Zurich
                  1968 and others.
2)  Reichardt, Jasia, "Cybernetic Serendipity", W.&J Mackay
                  Co. LTD, London 1968.
3)  Diethelm, Walter, "Form and Communication", ABC Editions,
                  Zurich 1974.
4)  Leavitt, Ruth, "Artist and Computer", Creative Computing
                  Press, Morristown N.J. 1976.
5)  Bangert, Charles and Collette, "Some Algorithms for
                  Generative Computer Art",
                  Proceedings of the NCGA, Anaheim Ca. 1984.
6)  Csuri, Charles, "Computer Graphics and Art",
                  Proceedings of the IEEE Vol. 62 No. 4
                  April 1974.
7) Franke, Herbert W., "Computergrafik-Galerie", DuMont Buch-
                  verlag, Kologne 1984.

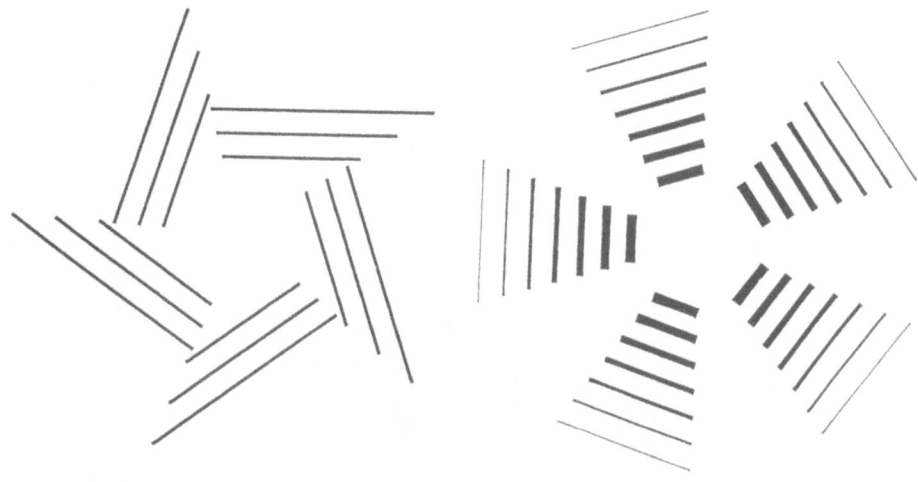

Figure 1

Figure 2

Figure 3

Figure 4

341

Figure 5

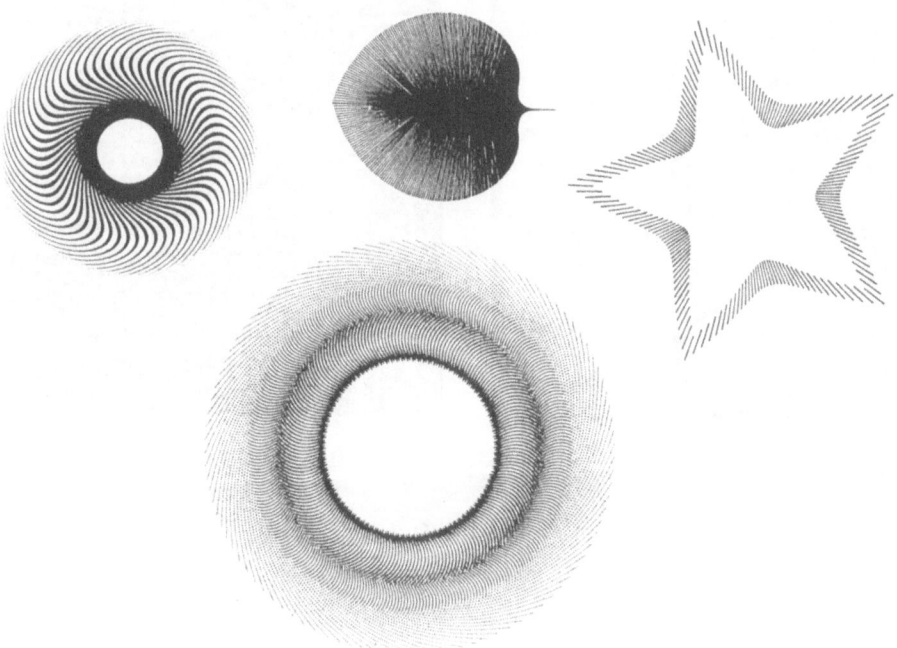

Figure 6

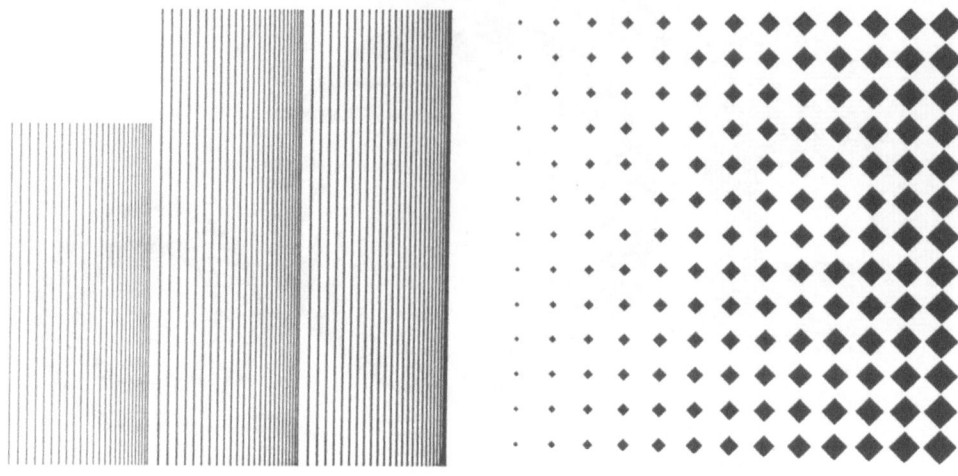

Figure 7

Figure 8

Figure 9

Figure 10

Figure 11

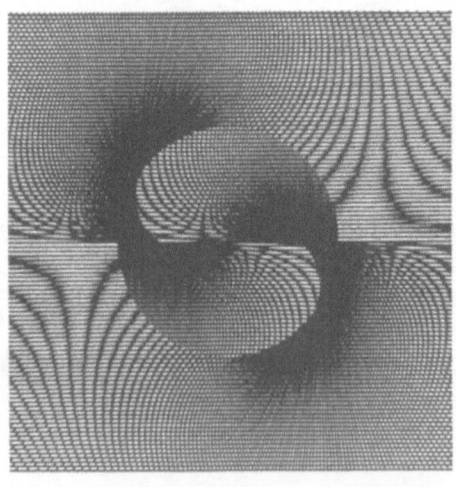

Figure 12

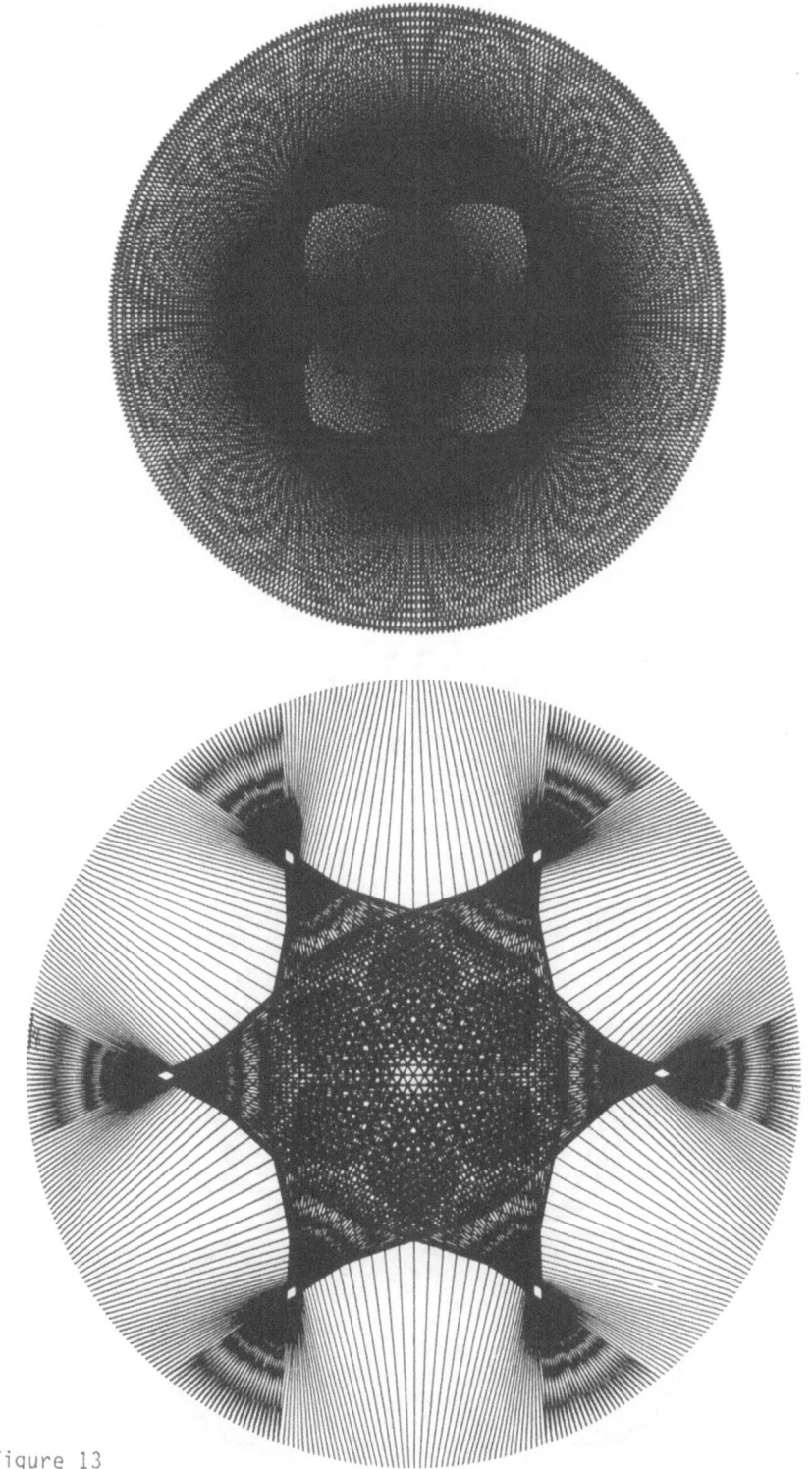

Figure 13

346

Figure 14

Figure 15                    ©1984 C. Schubert

Chapter 8
# Medical Graphics

# Three-Dimensional Display of X-Ray CT Image
## Extraction and Display of Cerebral Ventricle

Yasuzo Suto[1], Masao Kato[1], Takeshi Ozeki[1], Masami Ueda[2], Tsutomu Izumida[2] and Kimio Tarora[2]

[1] Toshiba Corporation, 1-1, Shibaura 1-chome, Minato-ku, Tokyo, 105 Japan
[2] Kozo Keikaku Engineering Inc., 38-13, Honcho 4-chome, Nakano-ku, Tokyo, 164 Japan

ABSTRACT

Multislice images obtained by X-ray CT essentially have a three-dimensional data structure. They are useful for diagnosis and treatment through three-dimensional display.
The surface display of organs is one of the effective methods of three-dimensional display. However, although completely automatic processing of contour extraction is desirable it is very difficult.
For this surface display, it is very important to extract contours of organs.
Accordingly, by using an interactive method, we have developed an algorithm that permits accurate three-dimensional display after extracting images of the cerebral ventricle. Satisfactory results have been obtained.

## 1. INTRODUCTION

Three-dimensional image processing for medical purposes is extensively studied in the world ((1) ～ (7)). Substantially, some multi-tomographic images (multi-slice images) such as those of X-ray CT images, MRI-CT and ultrasonic C mode images, and some X-ray images are obtained as a three-dimensional configuration. However, almost all of the conventional image diagnostic apparatuses conduct only two-dimensional image processing because of limits to the processing time, storage capacity and cost. Recently, as the electronic technology such as semiconductor technique advanced rapidly, latent needs became more realizable, and the three-dimensional image processing for medical purposes is going to enter the stage of practical use.

Needs of the three-dimensional image processing for medical purposes are roughly classified into diagnosis and medical treatment, including surgical operation.

To satisfy these needs the following factors need to be taken into account.

1) Since the human body has a complex three-dimensional configuration, it is necessary to display this in a easily diagnosable form. If a system for supporting such a display process could be realized, it would be very advantageous for diagnosticians.

2) Before performing surgical operations and medical treatment, it is necessary to grasp accurately the internal configuration of the human body and the spatial relationships of the various organs. For this purpose, information on the shapes and sizes of organs and tumor, and their positional relationships including those to the surface anatomy should be given. Beside the display method, three-dimensional measurement is also necessary.

To meet these requirements, the authors developed a system for extracting a cerebral ventricle image from X-ray CT multi-slice images of the head and for displaying it three-dimensionaly.
Three-dimensional image display for the cerebral ventricle has previously been performed by some research organizations. In display of the surface of such organ, it is very important to extract accurately contour lines of the organ from each slice image. However, in general, contrast information sufficient to discriminate the object organ, in this case, cerebral ventricle, from the other organs or background is not necessarily to be found in every slice.

Therefore, it is very troublesome to extract the contour information for the organ. To achieve completely automatic operation of this process, interpolation of the complicated shape must be performed by curvilinear approximation or similar process, which make accurate three-dimensional image display of the shape difficult.

On the other hand, the approach by voxel (volume element) ((2), (3)) is substantially for a solid model, and shading is suitable for high-speed processing. However, since the surface shading is limited to only three grades, it is impractice difficult for this method to delineate smoothly and accurately a body in realistic form.

In another method, all pieces of contour information are traced manually by the operator. In this method, however, processing efficiency is low.

Accordingly, the authors developed an algorithm wherein the range of processing conducted automatically is extended as much as possible and a conversational system is applied to the other processing items. The outline construction of this algorithm is as follows.

1) First, the density level of the cerebral ventricle is specified conversationally, and a continuous cerebral ventricle region is obtained by 8-directional connectivity as a binary image for each slice.

2) The binary image is of a highly complex shape and is not suitable for connecting the slices by patches when a surface image is formed later. Therefore, the boundary of the regions is smoothed in advance.

3) Finally, the cerebral ventricle regions between the slices are connected to each other. This process is performed manually.

By this method, it becomes possible to display a three-dimensional image of the cerebral ventricle with considerable accuracy and efficiency.


## 2. ALGORITHM

In the system developed by the authors, three-dimensional images of not only the cerebral ventricle but also the head surface and the cerebral ventricle can be displayed simultaneously. The procedure (Fig. 1) and the algorithm for creating three-dimensional display images of the head surface and the cerebral ventricle is described subsequently.

### 2.1 Creation of Head Surface Data

In the X-ray CT image of which the data is in this system, the head bone appears clearly. Therefore, a contour image of the head surface can be obtained by a simple linear differentiation. The contour image (linear differentiation image) is converted into a binary image by use of a threshold value specified by the operator, and a contour binary image of the head surface is created. On the basis of the binary image, a contour point sequence representing the head surface data is automatically obtained by a sampling system using the cylindrical coordinate system proposed by Yorozu and other (4)).

The head surface data of all slices are stored in the form of a contour point sequence for each slice, and used in subsequent processing. For example, when a cerebral ventricle image is created, the data are used for selection of the projection transformation center and calculation of scaling factor. When a head surface image is created, the data are used for generation of patches of the head surface. The processing flow for creation of head surface data is shown in Fig. 2.

### 2.2 Extraction of Cerebral Ventricle Image

The processing procedure for extraction of the cerebral ventricle image from each slice, that is to say extraction of the contour line of the cerebral ventricle region is shown in Fig. 3. The method utilising the cylindrical coordinate system for creating the head surface data cannot be applied to contour extraction of an organ like the cerebral ventricle, having a complicated shape. However, it is very time consuming to input a contour line manually from all slices for an organ such as the cerebral ventricle, having a density difference from other tissues. Accordingly, in this system, extraction of the contour of the organ is semi-automatically performed as described.

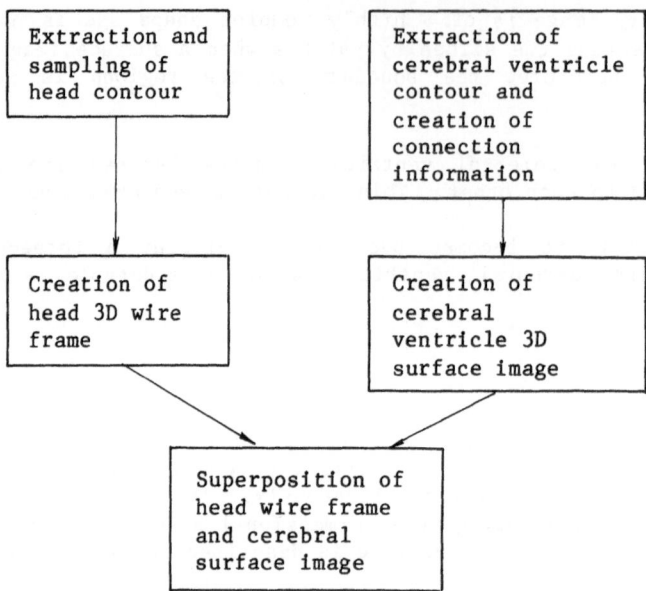

Fig. 1  Processing' flow

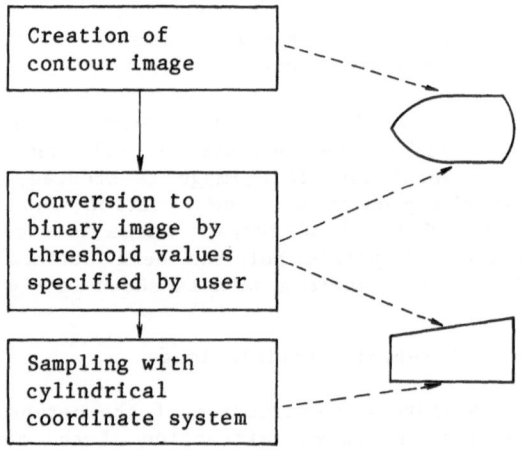

Fig. 2  Extraction and sampling'
of head contour

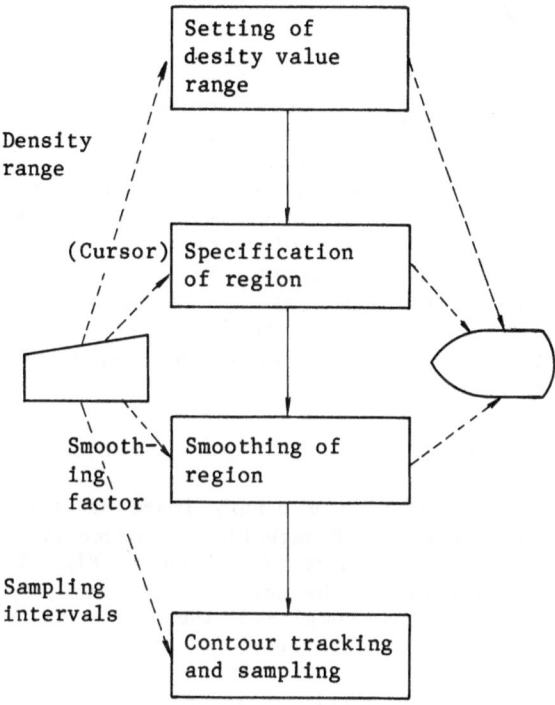

Fig. 3 Extraction of cerebral
ventricle image

1) Setting of density value range

The density level (CT value) of the cerebral ventricle in the X-ray
CT image is differenciated to some extent. Even when it is less
well differentiated, it is possible to grasp easily the density
level of an organ, which should be extracted, by developping a
utility program for investigating the density range in a
rectangular region of interest (rectangle ROI) specified by the
user in a slice image, and by using the utility. For this purpose,
this system is designed so that the density value range of the
organ, in this case the cerebral ventricle which should be
extracted as desired by the operator. To achieve this, the
following functions are provided:

① Display of corresponding slice image; monochromatic image by
density value

② Indication of only those picture element within the specified
density value range

③ Restoration of slice image when the density value range is
corrected

2) Specification of region

In general, tissues other than those of the objective organ will lie within the specified density value range. Therefore, the region of the object organ should be specified by the operator. Picture elements within the specified density value range extend into other regions, as shown in Fig. 4 by the aforesaid functions. In this system, when the specifies one point within the region of the target organ, picture elements constituting 8-connection components of the specified point are selected from the group of picture elements within the specified density value range, and a region constituted by the selected picture elements is converted into a binary image as the region of the target organ which it is intended to extracted.

3) Smoothing of region

Since the organ region of the binary image obtained as previously described is determined by 8-directional connectivity, it may have a whisker-like picture elements as shown in Fig. 5. In order to remove whiskers and smooth the contour, a technique, utilising the equation shown below, is employed whereby n is specified as a smoothing parameter by the operator.

$$IP(i,j) = \begin{cases} 0 & (\Sigma\Sigma \ IP(i+I, \ j+J) < n) \\ & IJ \\ 1 & (\Sigma\Sigma \ IP(i+I, \ j+J) \geq n) \\ & IJ \end{cases}$$

Where $\Sigma$ indicates the sum by K = -1, 0, 1.
   K

The operator must check visually whether the smoothed organ region is devided into two or more selection, or is deformed.

4) Contour tracking and sampling

The process of obtaining a contour point sequence at specified intervals from the organ region converted into a binary and smoothed image is performed fully automatically.
The contour line of the organ region is readily determined by arbitrarily determining one point on the contour line of and searching the vicinity of the point as shown in Fig. 6. Processing proceeds by taking the first located point in the organ as the next point on the contour line. In processing, the length is measured by a chessboard distance of the controur line, and sampling is performed at specified intervals, thereby obtaining the organ contour point sequence.

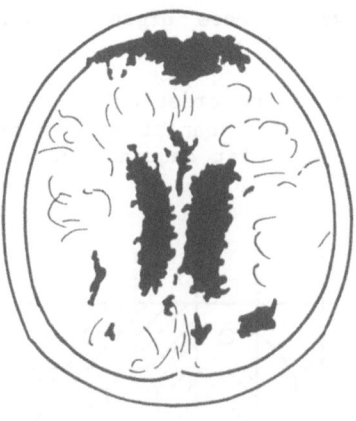

Fig. 4　Example of region of
specified density range

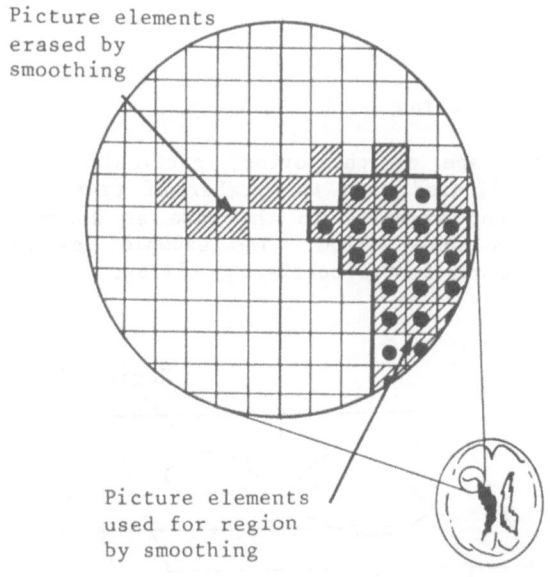

Picture elements
erased by
smoothing

Picture elements
used for region
by smoothing

Fig. 5　Smoothing

When there are two or more organ regions on one slice, this
processing is performed for each of the organ regions, and the
obtained contour point sequence is labelled sequentially.  The
operator must memorize the order of the organ region of each slice
in order to create the connection information.  The number of
points in the contour point sequence may differ between slices or
regions.

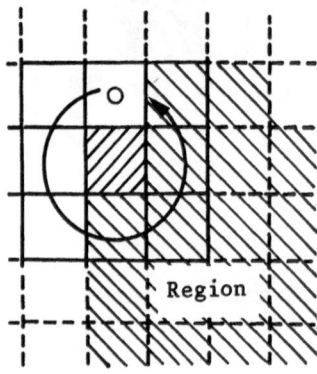

Fig. 6   Contour tracking

2.3   Connection Information

In general, the shape of the organ, particularly of the cerebral
ventricle, is complicated, and the number of regions may differ from
slice to slice.  For example, in the case as shown in Fig. 7, the
regions will be as shown below.  The example has four patterns to
connect between regions in two contiguous slices.

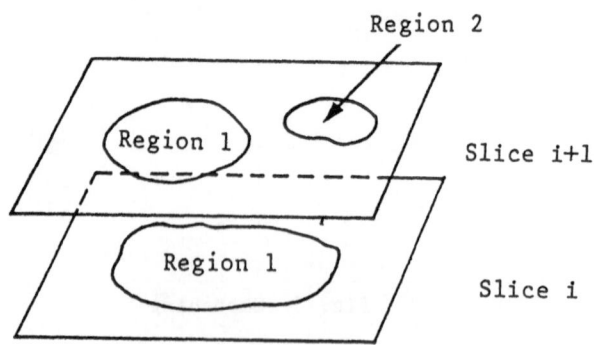

Fig. 7   Multi-regions

| Slice i | | Slice i+1 |
|---------|--|-----------|

Region 1 ——————————⟍ Region 1

Region 2

Region 1 ——————————— Region 1

Region 1 ——————————— Region 2

(Region 1)    No connection    (Region 1, 2)

It is difficult to recognize automatically connection of the regions when slice intervals change in various ways. In this algorithm, the information concerning connection between regions of slices must be specified by the operator.


2.4  Creation of Cerebral Ventricle Image

1)  Creation of patch

A triangular patch and a square patch are created by joining the contour point sequences of regions of two contiguous slices by use of the connection information. The algorithm is as shown below.

Step 1:  Contour points of the corresponding region are extracted by use of the connection information.

The contour point sequence of one slice is taken as $\{P_i\}$ i=1∿N, and that of the other slice is tanken as $\{Q_j\}$ j=1∿M.

Step 2:  As I = [1,N], $J_1$ = [1,M] at which $\overline{P_I Q_{J1}}$ is the minimum is calculated.

Step 3:  $J_2$ at which $\overline{P_{I+1} Q_{J2}}$ is the minimum is calculated.

Step 4:  A patch is created with $P_I$, $P_{I+1}$, $Q_{J1}$, and $Q_{J2}$. The normal line of the patch is decided on the basis of the normal line vector of $\Delta Q_{J1} P_I P_{I+1}$, $\Delta Q_{J1} P_I Q_{J2}$, etc. The patch is the triangular patch when $J_1 = J_2$.

Step 5:  Repeat step 2 to 4.

Step 6:  Perform steps 2 to 5 by interchanging $P_i$ and $Q_j$.

2) Calculation of the lightness of patches

In order to provide the three-dimensional image with shadow, various methods have been studied in computer graphics. However, in three-dimensional image display for medical purposes, it is adequate for three-dimensional characteristics to be expressed correctly. In this system, lightness is calculated by a function of the angle between the normal line of the patch and the light source direction.

3. PROCESSING RESULTS

The results appearing on a display device after three-dimensional image processing by this algorithm are shown in Figs. 8, 9, 10 and 11. In Figs. 8 and 9, surface display images of the cerebral ventricle are shown, and the point of view can be changed as desired. In Figs. 10 and 11, images obtained by combining the surface display images of the cerebral ventricle and the head surface wire frames are shown. By the combination display method, it is possible to grasp accurately the position of the cerebral ventricle.

Fig. 8  Cerebral ventricle image 1

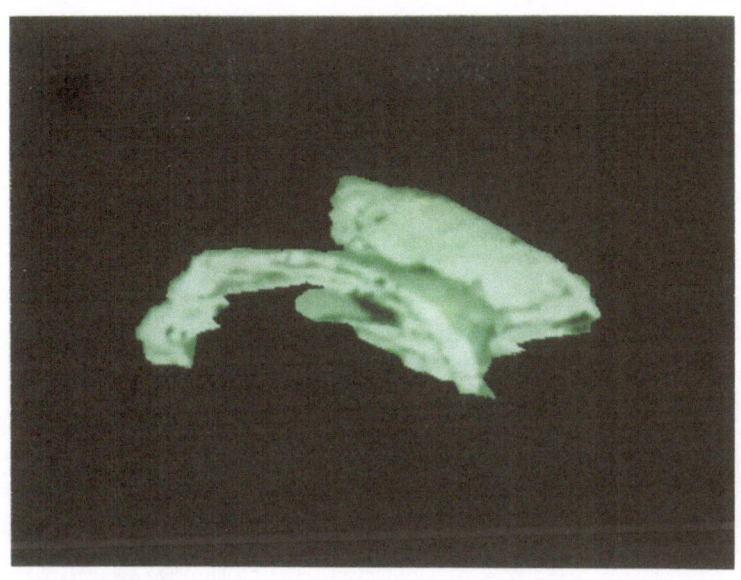

Fig. 9  Cerebral ventricle image 2

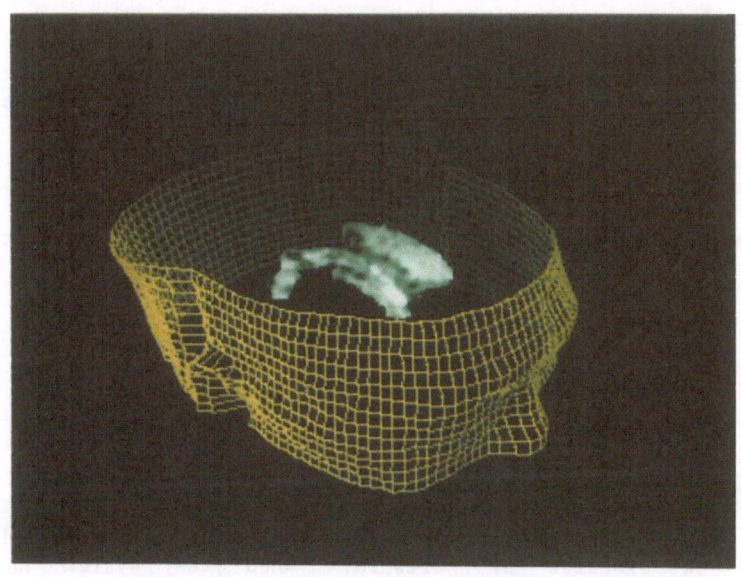

Fig. 10  Cerebral ventricle image 3

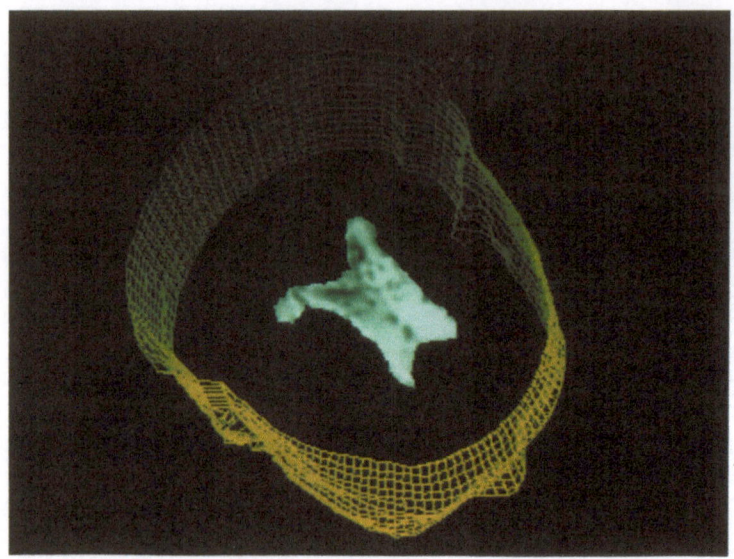

Fig. 11  Cerebral ventricle image 4

## 4.  CONCLUSIONS AND FUTURE RESEARCH

An effective three-dimensional display system for the cerebral ventricle has been developed by introduction of a conversational technique. This technique is considered to be directly applicable to surface display of organs the boundary regions of which are comparatively clear, such as bones.

For organs the boundary regions of which are not clear, pre-processing such as image enhancement will be necessary.

The following should further be studied:

(1)  High-speed processing of the algorithm

(2)  Clinical evaluation of the algorithm

(1)  High-speed processing of the algorithm

At present, the system is at the stage of algorithm evaluation, and is executed by software. When the system has been established, it will become possible to conduct high-speed processing of the algorithm by forming hardware and software of major items of the subroutine.

Additionally, a high-speed large-capacity memory which can store large amounts of information on three-dimensional images will become effective for high-speed execution of the algorithm.

Therefore, a hardware system suitable for high-speed three-dimensional image processing should be studied further.

(2) Clinical evaluation of the algorithm

The efficacy of the algorithm will be clinically evaluated by clinical field tests. The clinical evaluation should be conducted from both the standpoints of diagnosis and medical treatment.

The authors thank Dr. Yamakawa who of Toshiba Central Hospital for his valuable advice on this study.

Reference

1) Kaneda, Fujii, Matsuo
    : Pattern Extraction from Head Continuous CT Image and
      Three-dimensional Display, "Medical Electronics and
      Somatology", Vol. 19, No. 4, pp. 265-270 (August,
      1981) in Japanese.

2) Udupa, J.K.: Display of 3D Information in Discrete 3D Scenes
      Produced by Computerized Tomography, Proc. IEEE, Vol.
      71, No.3, pp. 420-431 (March 1983)

3) Frieder, G. et al
    : Back-to Front Display of Voxel-Based Objects, IEEE
      CG&A, pp. 52-60 (Jan. 1985)

4) Yorozu, Yokio, Tsuruoka, Miyake
    : Three-dimensional display of Head CT Image by
      Cylindrical Coordinate System Data Configuration,
      Treatise Magazine of Information Processing Society,
      Vol. 23, No. 5, pp. 516-521 (Sept., 1982) in Japanese.

5) Batnitzky, S., Price, H.I., Cook, P.N., Dwyer III, S.J.
    : Three-dimensional Computer Reconstruction in The
      Study of Brain Automedica, Vol. 4, pp. 37-50 (1981)

6) Totty, W.G. and Vannier, M.W.: Complex Musculoskeletal Anatomy
    : Analysis Using Three Dimensional Surface
      Reconstruction, Radiology, Vol. 150, No. 1,
      pp. 173-177 (Jan. 1984)

7) Brewster, L.J. et al
    : Interactive Surgical Planning, IEEE CG&A, pp. 31-40
      (March 1984)

# Color Blindness Tests by Color Graphic Display

Giichi Tomizawa, Yooichiro Ban, Kooichi Takahashi and Hiroshi Mieno

Department of Industrial Administration, Faculty of Science and Engineering, Science University of Tokyo, 2641 Higashikameyama, Yamazaki, Noda, Chiba, 278 Japan

ABSTRACT

This paper reports a basic research on color blindness tests[1] employing the microcomputer. The graphic display having 4096 colors and the tablet device are installed in the microcomputer. Ishihara's Color Blindness Test and Lanthony's Desaturated 15 Hue Test are employed in the research.

Figures may be generated by the tablet device at need. The examiner does not have to intervene in the test, as the examinee has the tests by himself watching the screens.[2] The resutls of the tests are processed automatically, and then they are printed out. The good operational and inexpensive system is described and a few experiments are indicated.

Keywords: microcomputer, color graphic display, Ishihara's Color Blindness Test, Lanthony's Desaturated 15 Hue Test

## 1. Introduction

The microcomputer has made remarkable progress in recent years. The color graphic display has become stable, high dense and multicolored. In this paper, we have tried the color blindness test using the popularized microcomputer. The Ishihara's Color Blindness Test and Lanthony's Desaturated 15 Hue Test are employed for our research.

Until now the former has been widely used for a group medical examination because it did not take a long time for the test. The weak point of this test is that a examinee can memorize the characters in the test papers easily as there are only a few pages. The latter has been used for rather an easier close investigation. But this test needs a considerable amount of time and effort to get the result.

To make up for these week points mentioned above, we made a quick and good system to operate by employing the microcomputer.

## 2. Configuration of the system
### 2.1 Hardware

This system comprises a microcomputer; APPLE II; the tablet device and the color display with R,G and B inputs as shown in Fig.1. This color display, DDY 8020B employed for this research is made in Anritsu Electric Company. We can change the colors on the screen by changing the levels of RGB. As

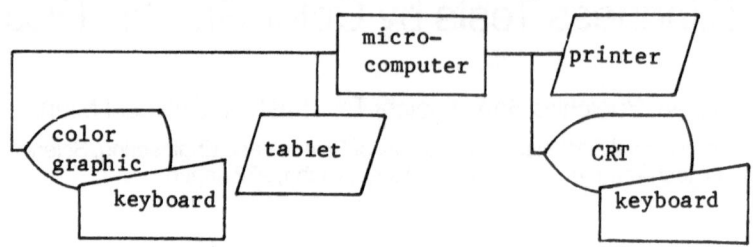

Fig.1  configulation of the system

each of RGB signals has 16 levels, colors can be changed continuously with R,G and B channels each receiving one out of 4096 possible values. But the graphic display permits display of only 16 different colors containing the background color at a time.

2.2 Ishihara's Color Blindness Test system
This system is developed based on Ishihara's Color Blindness Test Table. This tables are designed as follows to get the colors confused:
(1) Spotted colors are used without coloring all over.
(2) The difference of the colors is gradated by mixing the main color with some similar colors.
(3) Light and shade in the same color have to be clearer than two different colors for the abnormal.
(4) The effort of masking is made by spreading the color which has no connection with confused colors.
The test screen and the diagnostic system were made considering the things mentioned above.

2.2.1 The test figures on the screen
The color screen has seven kinds of FIGUREs which are called FIGURE 1 – FIGURE 7.  They are corresponding to the kinds of the color blindness. Each FIGURE has eight figures. Each figure has the patterns from character "2" to "8" and of a curved line. Therefore 7*8=56 kinds of test figures are provided as shown in Fig.2.  We can select them freely and display on the screen. The test figures are generated by using our tablet system. Picture, Hiragana, Katakana etc. in addition to the patterns mentioned above are also able to be made at will by using the system. The figure is

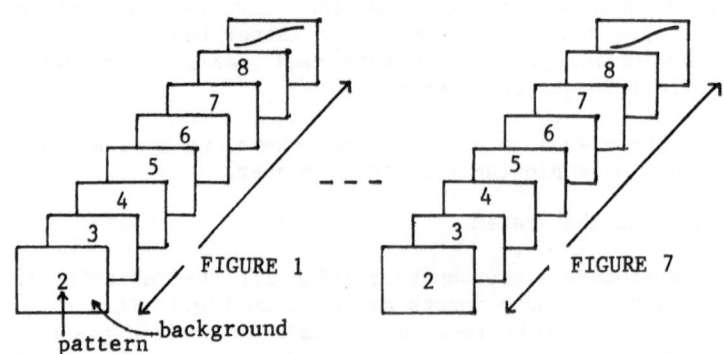

Fig.2  The kinds of the test figure

composed of a pattern and a background. The part that eliminate the pattern from the figure is called a background. Pattern and background are composed of the picells.

The figure in a circle with radius 115 dots are composed of five kinds of picells which have 7,5,4,3,2 dots as shown in Fig.3(a). The combination of colored picells is different in each FIGURE. The pattern on the background is composed of five kinds of picells like the combination of colored picells in background. Two patterns in one figure are made from the different combination of colored picells. One of them can be recognized by an abnormal examinee.

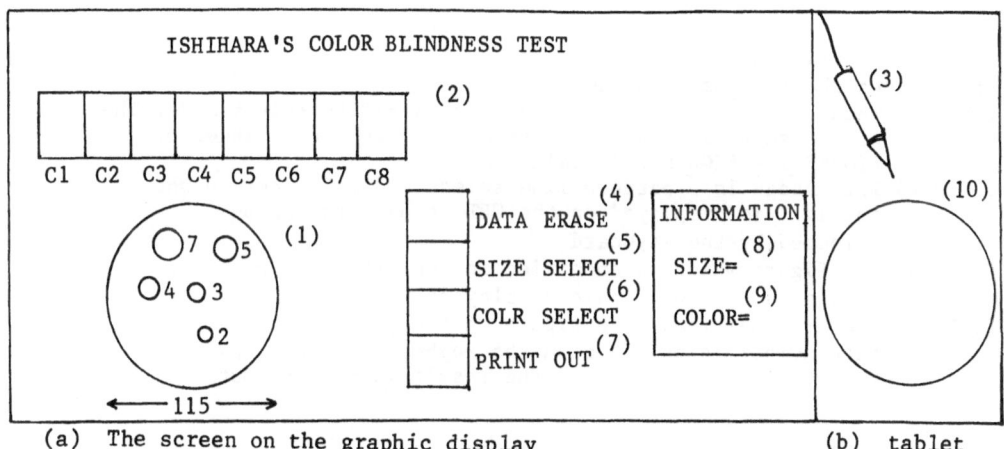

(a)  The screen on the graphic display            (b)   tablet

Fig.3   The tablet system

2.2.2 The tablet system to generate the figure

This system has the function of choosing a color, a size and filing the information about the test figures. The tablet plate corresponds to the screen on the graphic display, namely the pen position on the tablet plate is shown by the cursor position on the screen. The command to generate the test figure can be chosen by the pen position on the tablet. The screen in Fig.3(a),(b) is explained as follows:

(a) The test figure is made in the circle(1) whose radius has 115 dots.
(b) A color is chosen by one of eight boxes(2)C1-C8.
(c) The test figure composed of the colored picell is made by the light pen(3).
(d) The box(4) is used to erase a picell.
(e) The box(6) is used when we want to change the colors specified in the color boxes C1-C8.
(f) The box(7) is the command to print out and file the information about a test figure.
(g) The box(5) is the command to specify the radius of a colored picell. The picell size specified is display at the box(8)
(h) The box(9) is the command to specify a color.
(i) The test figure is made in the area(10) on the tablet plate.

Fig.4 shows the illustration of the figure made by the tablet system.

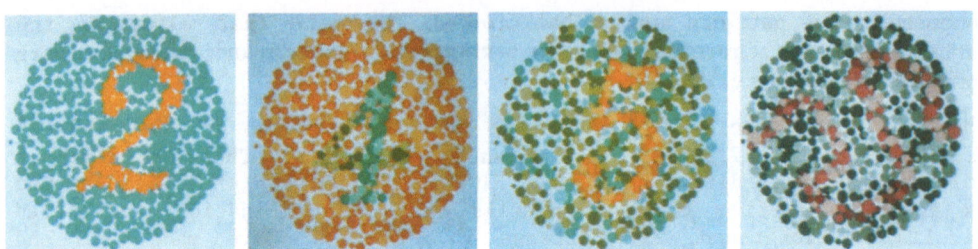

Fig.4  The figure by the tablet system

## 2.2.3 The operation

Fig.5 shows the flowchart to operate.

(STEP 1) When the system is run, it becomes a FIGURE select mode. The screen shown in Fig.6 is displayed on the CRT. Either of FIGURE 1 – FIGURE 7 is selected.

(STEP 2) This stage is a pattern line select mode. The screen shown in Fig.7 is displayed on the CRT. A pattern can be selected by the keyboard.

(STEP 3) The figure which is specified in the STEP 1,2 is displayed on the graphic display as shown in Fig.8.

(STEP 4) The examinee reads the figure on the screen. And then the pattern number is put in from the keyboard by the subject. When test is over, "E" is put in. The result is printed out.

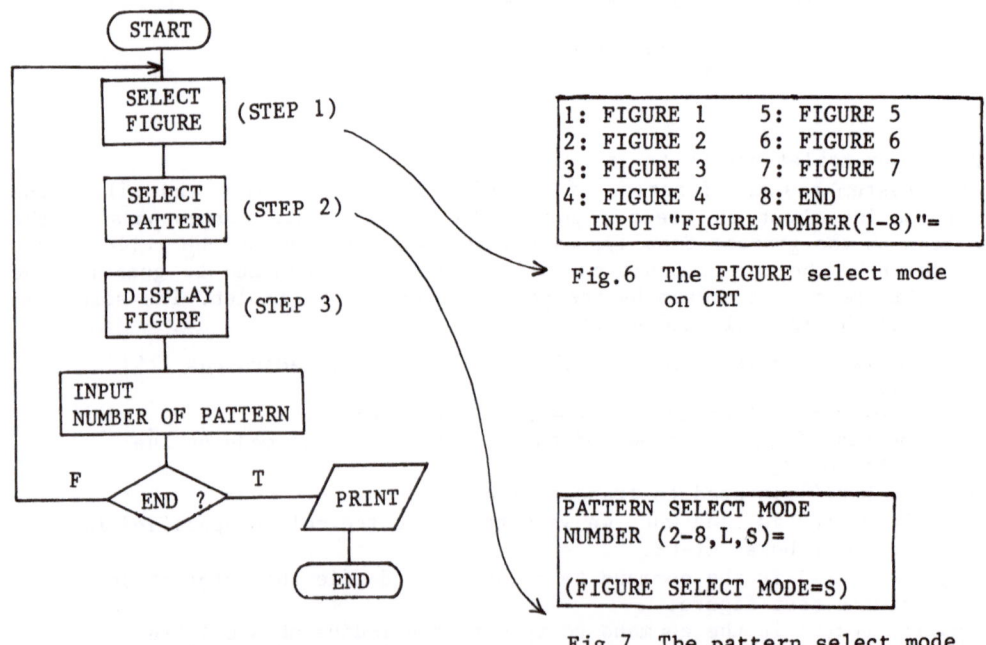

Fig.6  The FIGURE select mode on CRT

Fig.7  The pattern select mode on CRT

Fig.5  The flowchart to operate

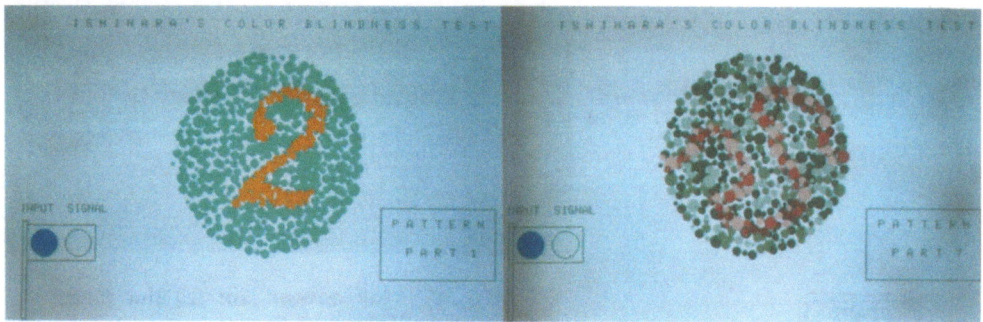

Fig.8  The figure on the graphic display


2.3  Lanthony's Desaturated 15 Hue Test system
The fifteen different color caps are used in this test. The order of the
colors is written with the backs of these color caps. The degree of
colors, munsell value and croma between the adjoining color caps are the
same. The examinee is requested to arrange the caps in order according to
the color.   The examiner writes the order on the uniform chromaticity
scale diagram and makes a diagnosis of the color blindness.

In this research, we realized the 15 Hue Test on the color display.
Fig.9 shows the initial screen before the test.  Fifteen color caps on the
upper row are arranged at random.   An examinee selects the color caps
similar to the refernce cap. And he puts in the number on the cap by the
keyboard.   The cap number put in is arranged on the right side of the
reference cap.  When fifteen caps are all arranged on the same row of the
reference cap, the test is over. And then the rsult on the uniform
chromaticity scale diagram is displayed on the graphic display as shown in
Fig.10. The flowchart to operate is shown in Fig.11.
(STEP 1) The color caps at random is display on the color graphic
         display as shown in Fig.9.
(STEP 2) Watching the reference cap on the screen, the examinee
         selects the cap similar to it and puts in the number on the
         cap.
(STEP 3) The result is displayed on the graphic display as shown in
         Fig.10(a),(b).  The examiner makes a diagnosis by the results.


3. Result and discussion
Three examinees who have already been known to defective color vision and
twenty normal examinees were tested by our system under the condition of
the standard illumination 500 lux. Table 1 shows the comparison of the
results of our system with the results of the traditional Ishihara's Test.
The table indicates that our experimental results agree approximately
with those.

Lanthony's Desaturated 15 Hue Test and Farnsworth Dichotomaous Test Panel
D-15 were employed in the traditional tests. As the former has a lower
degree of saturation than the latter. Therefor the former is more
difficult for the examinee with defective color vision to distinguish the
colors.   Table 2 shows the results of our system and the traditional
Lanthony's Desaturated 15 Hue Test.   The results of our system have a

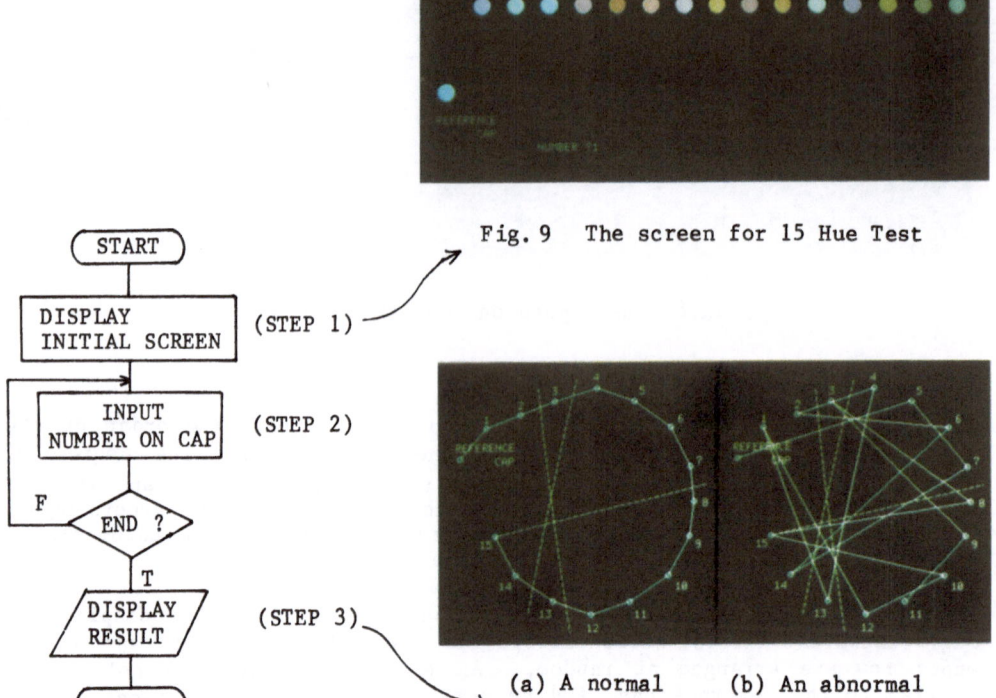

Fig. 9   The screen for 15 Hue Test

(STEP 1)

START

DISPLAY
INITIAL SCREEN

INPUT
NUMBER ON CAP   (STEP 2)

F

END ?

T

DISPLAY
RESULT   (STEP 3)

END

(a) A normal        (b) An abnormal

Fig. 10   The results of the test

Fig. 11   The flowchart
          to operate

tendency to indicate the examinees with defective color vision slight, compared with the traditional Lanthony's Desaturated 15 Hue Test. They agree with the results of Farnsworth Dichotomaous Test Panel D-15 (STANDARD). For the low degree of saturation we have to make an experiment about various R,G and B values. In the traditionl test, the color are distinguished by the reflected light, but in the graphic display by the transmitted light.  We will have to research the effect of the light having different properties each other.

The purpose of our research is to automate the color blindness test through the microcomputer.  We tried to make color blindness test system containing software, hereafter intend to try a clinical study of our system.

Table 1  The experiment of the Ishihara's Color Blindness Test

| examinee / test method | A(twenty normal) | defect | | |
|---|---|---|---|---|
| | | B | C | D |
| Ishihara | normal | red.green color-blindness | red.green color-blindness | total color-weekness |
| Our system | normal | red.green color-blindness | red.green color-blindness | total color-weekness |

Table 2  The experiment of the Lanthony's Desaturated 15 Hue Test

| examinee / test method | A(twenty normal) | defect | | |
|---|---|---|---|---|
| | | B | C | D |
| Lanthony | normal | slight color-weekness | protanopia | protanopia |
| Our system | normal | slight color-weekne | slight protanopia | slight protanopia |
| Standard | normal | slight color-weekness | slight protanopia | slight protanopia |

Reference
1) A.Majima, Farnsworth Dichotomous Test Panel D-15, Ganka Mook No.16, 1982
2) S.Hamazaki,H.Mieno,H.matsuo,Semi-Automatic Campimeter with Graphic Display, 3th International visual Field Simpo., 1978

# Author Index

The page numbers refer to the list of references provided by each contributor.

# Subject Index

The page numbers refer to the page on which term is defined.

# Computer Science Workbench

Editor: **T. L. Kunii**

**N. Magnenat-Thalmann, D. Thalmann**

## Computer Animation

**Theory and Practice**

1985. 156 figures, 54 of them in color. XIII, 240 pages.
ISBN-13: 978-4-431-68032-1

*Computer Animation: Theory and Practice* is the first presentation of all aspects of computer animation in a single volume.
It is conceived as an introduction for designers and animators,
a reference book for professionals in computer graphics, as
well as manual for university teachers in computer graphics
and computer animation.
Both theoretical and practical apsects are presented in detail.
Computer animations is treated using concepts familiar to
those working in traditional animation. Readers will find techniques involved in computer-assisted animation such as key-
frame interpolation and coloring and painting techniques, as
well as great deal of information on the state-of-the-art in
computer animation and a history of animation systems and
languages. The book also include a complete list of computer-
generated films produced between 1961 to 1984.

**B. A. Barsky**

## Computer Graphics and Computer Aided Geometric Design Using Beta-splines

(tentative)

1985. Approx. 78 figures
Approx. 200 pages. ISBN-13: 978-4-431-68032-1

This book describes the Beta-spline representation for curves
and surfaces. This technique enables objects delineated by
complex curved surfaces to be represented in the computer.
Such representations are necessary for the design and manufacture of three-dimensional parts, as well as for the generation of synthetic computer images. The Beta-spline technique
is sufficiently general and flexible to be capable of representing a wide class of complex objects, while at the same time
using input specification parameters which are natural and
intuitive.

Springer-Verlag
Berlin
Heidelberg
New York
Tokyo

# Frontiers in Computer Graphics

**Proceedings of Computer Graphics Tokyo '84**

**Editor: T. L. Kunii**

1985. 266 figures, 82 of them in color.
XI, 443 pages.  ISBN-13: 978-4-431-68032-1

**Contents:** Geometry Modelling. – Graphic Languages. – Visualization Techniques. – Human Factors. – Interactive Graphics Design. – CAD/ CAM. – Graphic Displays and Peripherals. – Graphics Standardization. – Author Index. – Subject Index.

Computer graphics, taken as a whole, is an area in which progress is very rapid. It is not easy for anyone, including the experts, to keep abreast of the various basic and applied fields. This book has been compiled to present you with the substance of progress in computer graphics. It also serves as the final version of the Proceedings of Computer Graphics Tokyo '84 held in Tokyo, Japan, in April. Eight major frontiers of computer graphics are covered: geometry modelling, graphic languages, visualization techniques, human factors, interactive graphics design, CAD/CAM, graphic displays and peripherals, and graphics standardization.

Springer-Verlag
Berlin
Heidelberg
New York
Tokyo